MORNINGS
with JESUS
2016

DAILY ENCOURAGEMENT *for your* SOUL

366 DEVOTIONS

SUSANNA FOTH AUGHTMON

GWEN FORD FAULKENBERRY

GRACE FOX

TRICIA GOYER

SHARON HINCK

REBECCA BARLOW JORDAN

ERIN KEELEY MARSHALL

DIANNE NEAL MATTHEWS

CYNTHIA RUCHTI

SUZANNE DAVENPORT TIETJEN

Guideposts

New York

Mornings with Jesus 2016

Published by Guideposts & Inspirational Media
110 William Street
New York, New York 10038
Guideposts.org

Acknowledgments

Every attempt has been made to credit the sources of copyrighted material used in this book. If any such acknowledgment has been inadvertently omitted or miscredited, receipt of such information would be appreciated.

"Joyfully" by Ed Cash, Mia Fieldes, and Kari Jobe Copyright © 2009 SHOUT! Music Publishing (APRA) Gateway Create Publishing (BMI) (Adm. at EMICMGPublishing.com)/ Wondrously Made Songs (BMI) All Rights Reserved. Used by permission. International Copyright Secured. All Rights Reserved. Used by Permission.

Scripture quotations marked (AMP) are taken from *The Amplified Bible*, © 1954, 1958, 1962, 1964, 1965, 1987 by The Lockman Foundation. Used by permission. www.Lockman.org

Scripture quotations marked (CEB) are taken from *Common English Bible*. Copyright © 2011 Common English Bible.

Scripture quotations marked (ESV) are taken from the Holy Bible, English Standard Version, copyright © 2001 by Crossway Bibles, a division of Good News Publishers. Used by permission. All rights reserved.

Scripture quotations marked (GNT) are taken from *Good News Translation*. Copyright © 1992 by American Bible Society.

Scripture quotations marked (GW) are taken from *God's Word Translation*. Copyright © 1995 by God's Word to the Nations. Used by permission of Baker Publishing Group.

Scripture quotations marked (HCS) are taken from the *Holman Christian Standard Bible*. Copyright © 1999, 2000, 2002, 2003 by Holman Bible Publishers, Nashville, Tennessee. All rights reserved.

Scripture quotations marked (KJV) are taken from *The King James Version of the Bible*.

Scripture quotations marked (MSG) are taken from *The Message*. Copyright © 1993, 1994, 1995, 1996, 2000, 2001, 2002 by Eugene H. Peterson.

Scripture quotations marked (NAS) are taken from the *New American Standard Bible*, copyright © 1960, 1962, 1963, 1968, 1971, 1972, 1973, 1975, 1977, 1995 by the Lockman Foundation. Used by permission. www.Lockman.org

Scripture quotations marked (NCV) are taken from the *New Century Version*. Copyright © 2005 by Thomas Nelson, Inc. Used by permission. All rights reserved.

Scripture quotations marked (NIV) are taken from two editions: *The Holy Bible, New International Version, NIV.* Copyright © 1973, 1978, 1984, 2011 by Biblica. All rights reserved worldwide. *The Holy Bible, New International Version.* Copyright © 1973, 1978, 1984 International Bible Society. Used by permission of Zondervan Bible Publishers.

Scripture quotations marked (NKJV) are taken from *The Holy Bible, New King James Version.* Copyright © 1997, 1990, 1985, 1983 by Thomas Nelson, Inc.

Scripture quotations marked (NLT) are taken from the *Holy Bible*, New Living Translation. Copyright © 1996. Used by permission of Tyndale House Publishers, Inc., Wheaton, Illinois 60189. All rights reserved.

Scripture quotations marked (NRSV) are taken from the *New Revised Standard Version Bible*. Copyright © 1989 by the Division of Christian Education of the National Council of the Churches of Christ in the U.S.A. Used by permission. All rights reserved.

Scripture quotations marked (RSV) are taken from the *Revised Standard Version of the Bible*, copyright © 1946, 1952, and 1971 the Division of Christian Education of the National Council of the Churches of Christ in the United States of America. Used by permission. All rights reserved.

Scripture quotations marked (VOICE) are taken from *The Voice Bible*. Copyright © 2012 Thomas Nelson, Inc. The Voice™ translation © 2012 Ecclesia Bible Society. All rights reserved.

Cover and interior design by Müllerhaus
Cover photo by Shutterstock
Indexed by Indexing Research
Typeset by Aptara

Printed and bound in the United States of America
10 9 8 7 6 5 4 3 2 1

Dear Friend,

As I've read and reread *Mornings with Jesus 2016* these last few weeks, I've been overwhelmed by the amazing message of Jesus's love for us. Woven into every devotion are the powerful promises that Jesus offers over and over again: "Peace I leave with you." "You are my beloved." "Take heart, I have overcome the world." These truths have taken on new meaning for me as I've watched my two young sons grow, become more independent, and even start school! Many times I've had to take comfort in releasing them to Jesus, knowing He loves them and watches over them every moment of the day, especially when I can't be present.

Begin each day with a brand-new reading and discover the blessings that come through daily reflection on Jesus. Our faithful writers' insights guide you to discover Jesus's kind instruction on how to live a godly life: how to be a good friend, how to courageously stand up for what you believe, how to love deeply, how to pray wisely, and how to forgive when it's hard. The daily bounty of Scripture, companionship, and prayer in *Mornings with Jesus* also nurtures new spiritual growth and a deeper understanding of Jesus's promise: "Peace I leave with you; my peace I give to you. Not as the world gives do I give to you. Let not your hearts be troubled, neither let them be afraid" (John 14:27, ESV).

Mornings with Jesus 2016 is an easy-to-use devotional. There is a one-page reading for every day of the year. A Bible verse opens each of the devotions, written by one of ten women, including best-selling authors Grace Fox, Tricia Goyer, and Cynthia Ruchti, who connect the Scripture to a moment in their lives, sharing their wisdom and insights with the deep desire to encourage and uplift you. "Faith Step" grounds each reflection and helps you realistically apply what you've read to your life and continue to think about the day's lesson by implementing its truth. It will challenge you to make a change in your life or to simply encourage you to praise and thank Jesus.

It is my hope that you'll find abundant inspiration and encouragement to lay aside your fears, doubts, and failures and, instead, seek the kingdom of God, revel in the simplicity of Jesus's love, and hold tight to Him as He works all things together for good.

Faithfully yours,
Keren Baltzer
Mornings with Jesus Editor

Mornings with Jesus in Your In-box

Now you can enjoy the daily encouragement of *Mornings with Jesus 2016* wherever you are! Receive each day's devotion on your computer, tablet, or smartphone. Visit MorningswithJesus.org/MWJ2016 and enter this code: MWJ2016.

Sign up for the online newsletter *Mornings with Jesus* through Guideposts .org. Each week you'll receive an encouraging devotion or personal thought from one of the authors about her own devotional time, prayer life, how focusing on Jesus impacted her relationship with Him, and more!

FRIDAY, JANUARY 1 done

---

*"All who want to come after me must say no to themselves,
take up their cross daily, and follow me." Luke 9:23 (CEB)*

"Lord, we'll follow where You lead." These are the first words I hear on New Year's Day, a moment after midnight. They flow from my husband as he bows his head over me, holding me close.

The previous year's challenges have been put out to pasture, no longer in the foreground of our thinking. My husband and I stand on the brink of a new year, highly unlikely to be a repeat of the one just past.

I mean, how crazy would it be to have two years in a row with five surgeries before May and another in December, with hitting our maximum out-of-pocket expenses on March 1, with having our pipes freeze next to the well house deep underground and not having safe drinking water in the house from mid-January to mid-July?

So, my husband and I face this new year bravely, fairly certain it can't be a duplicate of the one before.

But we've been around this new-year block enough times to know that the turn of a calendar page or a new date to write on checks doesn't guarantee the year will be uneventful. What better way to ring in the wonder of a fresh start with a should-be-traditional prayer: "Lord, we'll follow where You lead."

I've thought of my husband's prayer many times since that moment right after midnight. It said so much in so few words: "Jesus, we don't know where the path will lead, but we welcome another year to follow You." —CYNTHIA RUCHTI

FAITH STEP: *Whether you feel most comfortable singing in the shower, the car, or on your knees before Jesus in prayer, make it a point to worship Him today with the now almost two-hundred-year-old song: "Where He Leads Me I Will Follow." Or begin your morning with a simple "You lead. I'll follow."*

SATURDAY, JANUARY 2

Yet the Lord set his affection on your ancestors and loved them, and he chose you, their descendants, above all the nations—as it is today. Deuteronomy 10:15 (NIV)

MY SON ADDISON HAS a very deep affection for his cousins. My side of the family lives in three different states. We four siblings don't get to see each other enough. But every Christmas, all four of our families converge on my parents' home in Colorado. All eleven cousins are together for a week. I hardly see my kids the whole time. They have found their happy place. Cousinland. There is so much love and laughter there. And wrestling. Seven of the eleven cousins are boys. This year when we got home from Colorado, Addison came into my room, bereft. "Mom, I miss my cousins."

"I know, Addie! I miss my family too."

He let out a giant sigh. "I wish it could be Christmas all year long." Then he brightened a little. "At least we can text!"

Thank goodness that the cousin connection cannot be conquered. There is something so important, so beautiful, about family. I miss my family. I miss my sisters and my brother. I call my parents just so I can hear their voices. I grew up knowing I was loved by my family. Those family connections are powerful. Like Addison, there is no one I would rather be with.

Jesus chose us to be His family. His brothers and sisters. He wants us to get in on His inheritance. He chose at the beginning of time to set His affection on us and He still does today. He loves us like crazy. And we get the amazing pleasure of loving Him back. It just doesn't get any better than that. —SUSANNA FOTH AUGHTMON

FAITH STEP: *Map out your spiritual family tree. When did you become a part of Jesus's family? Thank Him for choosing you and for the great love and affection He has poured out on you.*

SUNDAY, JANUARY 3 *one*

Do you think their faithlessness cancels out his faithfulness? Not on your life! . . .
The God-setting-things-right that we read about has become Jesus-
setting-things-right for us. Romans 3:3-4, 22 (MSG)

A FEW YEARS AGO I was flipping through my journal pages, beginning with January of the new year. That last year had been a particularly trying time, and it seemed like my eyes focused only on myself. My personal needs and problems jumped off the page, not to mention my failures.

Sometimes the refusal to let "memories be forgotten" and the harsh focus on our own faithlessness cause us to forget the meaning of grace, and what Jesus has done in our lives.

Fortunately, in the middle of my memory journey, Jesus reminded me of His love for me, faults and all. So I started reading through the pages again. This time I saw answers to prayer, victories won, and praises recorded again and again: times of grace, mercy, and Jesus's faithfulness.

As believers, our faithlessness or self-criticism, be it true, false, or exaggerated, never cancels out Jesus's faithfulness. His forgiveness and grace always rise higher. We will fail often. But Jesus never intended for us to focus on our human weakness. He made a way. We don't have to earn enough good points to negate the bad. He set things right between us and God.

He faithfully carried out God's plan and died for us despite our faithlessness. At the start of each new year and all year long, Jesus makes all things new. —REBECCA BARLOW JORDAN

FAITH STEP: *If you haven't already done so, begin a journal this year. Start by thanking God for His faithfulness in the past year—and throughout your life.*

MONDAY, JANUARY 4

"Don't store up treasures here on earth, where moths eat them and rust destroys them, and where thieves break in and steal. Store your treasures in heaven. . . . Wherever your treasure is, there the desires of your heart will also be."
Matthew 6:19–21 (NLT)

LET THE NEW-YEAR PURGE BEGIN!

This week several *Today* show hosts are allowing cameras into their closets. Matt Lauer said one of his resolutions is to donate or discard half of what's in his closet, and Hoda Kotb is on a similar mission.

I love it! Something in me needs to be able to recall each item of clothing and accessory I own, otherwise I live with an underlying sense of chaos that's distracting. Looking through my closet, I see things I've kept (way) too long. For instance, I have several heavy wool sweaters from years living in Chicago. I may use them on a ski trip one day, but who needs six of them?

The undone sense I have when I start acquiring too much makes me wonder what other treasures I don't often consider that clog my spiritual clarity.

Irritability or jealousy or self-protection can become treasures I guard at the expense of spiritual, emotional, and relationship blessing. And then there's fear: If I allow that to take hold, in essence I'm choosing something lesser above my faith in Jesus. And how about free will? If I value that more than Jesus's truth, I'm treasuring something that will not last.

When I hold on to anything more than my connection with Jesus, my "treasures" are misplaced. Today is the perfect day to purge anything that allows moths to eat our joy and steals our connection with Jesus.

—ERIN KEELEY MARSHALL

FAITH STEP: *Commit to study one book of the Bible this month. Ask Jesus to help you know Him better through His Word. Talk to Jesus about misplaced treasures that might be lurking in the closets of your life.*

TUESDAY, JANUARY 5 done

"Therefore do not worry about tomorrow, for tomorrow will worry about itself. Each day has enough trouble of its own." Matthew 6:34 (NIV)

WHEN I'M ON A PLANE, I mentally inventory my backpack's contents in case we crash on a deserted island (never mind that we're flying over the Midwest). Back home, I muse about how well my vegetable garden could support us if society crumbled and all the stores closed.

My creative imagination is useful for writing novels, but it can be my enemy when it invents worst-case scenarios. Perhaps I believe a pre-planned response for every bad thing guarantees I'll have solutions ready to go and can control the fallout. But my "just in case" imaginings steal joy from my day.

If one of my children doesn't respond to a text, my imagination jumps to pictures of them in a hospital bed. When my husband is late coming home from work, I have to push away the mental picture of a car accident. I see a stack of mail and worry it holds an unexpected bill. Soon my emotions slip into a dismal place of expecting the worst.

That's why I love Jesus's words in Matthew. I catch a humorous tone here, as if He's saying, *Really? You don't have enough actual challenges to face? You have to waste energy mulling over imaginary ones?* He longs to free us from our need to control each possible eventuality. He invites us to turn our focus to Him. If the plane goes down, we are in His hands. If society crumbles, He is still our Savior. We don't have the power to avoid all of life's troubles, but as we face them, we can trust that He will be with us. By entrusting our lives fully to Him, we can stop living in fear. —SHARON HINCK

FAITH STEP: *Next time your mind jumps to worrying about something, tell Jesus you want to put all of your tomorrows in His hands. Allow Him to lift the burden of control from your shoulders.*

WEDNESDAY, JANUARY 6 *one*

Then Jesus said to his disciples, "Whoever wants to be my disciple must deny themselves and take up their cross and follow me." Matthew 16:24 (NIV)

YEARS AGO I STARTED PRAYING, "Lord, give me Your heart." Because of that, I was able to stop worrying about whether I would be ever good enough in my pursuits.

When did "being good enough" become the right pursuit for Christ-followers? Attending church, reading the Bible, praying with our kids, not yelling, volunteering at church, loving our neighbors? When I focus on being good, it's easy to get discouraged. I'm human. I'm never going to live up to the perfect standard in my mind.

There are many examples from God's Word—things Jesus urges us to do: "Go ye into all the world," respect your husbands, pray for your enemies, and care for the widows and the orphans. Being obedient to Christ is acting out His heart on this earth.

Obedience is not easy. It takes patience to drive my grandma around town on errands when I'd rather be working on my own projects. It's difficult trying to calm a newly adopted child who's lashing out. Following Christ in these ways invites suffering into my desire-for-comfort life. But isn't that what we're supposed to do?

First Peter 2:21 (NLT) says, "For God called you to do good, even if it means suffering, just as Christ suffered for you. He is your example, and you must follow in his steps." I wonder what would happen if more Christians obeyed these directives. Would the watching world be drawn to Christ-in-us in new ways? Would we stop worrying about being good and instead start working at being available? —TRICIA GOYER

FAITH STEP: *Write down three areas in which you've struggled with "being good enough." Below those areas write, "Jesus, give me Your heart." Then think of three ways you can be obedient to the tenets of Christ's heart, like praying for an enemy or helping a widow.*

THURSDAY, JANUARY 7

Jesus Christ is the same yesterday, today, and forever. Hebrews 13:8 (NLT)

THE PAST YEAR HAS HELD a lot of change for a friend of mine. For starters, she remarried after several years as a single mom. That meant adjusting not only to her new husband but also to being a stepmom. Shortly after her wedding, she lost the job she loved as a result of budget cuts. Then the women's singing group, of which she was a member, disbanded.

My friend finds change difficult. We've talked about her feelings and agree that sometimes it hurts or feels scary—like when her previous marriage ended and divorce thrust her into single parenthood. We've discussed how losing the familiar and stepping into the unknown can be unsettling.

On a positive note, however, change is often necessary to promote personal growth or to spur us on to new ventures. We might resist change initially, but in the end we realize it was a good thing.

So long as we're warm and breathing, we'll face change. We'll quit a job to start a different one, welcome new family members and say good-bye to others, move to a different house or city, adapt to life as empty nesters, deal with challenges that health issues bring, and more.

No doubt you—like most other people—have encountered change. Maybe you, like my friend, find it difficult. If so, be encouraged today in knowing one thing's for certain: Jesus remains the same. His presence offers stability when circumstances shift. His peace prevails when we focus on His promises. And His power undergirds and strengthens us to navigate our changes successfully. —GRACE FOX

FAITH STEP: *Think of someone in your life who's experienced a difficult change recently. Perhaps she's lost a loved one, has received a cancer diagnosis, or has moved far from friends. Phone that person or drop a card of encouragement in the mail.*

FRIDAY, JANUARY 8

Jesus said, "Let the little children come to me, and do not hinder them, for the kingdom of heaven belongs to such as these." Matthew 19:14 (NIV)

ARE YOU ENAMORED WITH creative photographs of newborns? World-renowned photographer Anne Geddes changed our way of thinking about the word *adorable*. She dressed newborns in ladybug costumes, planted them in flowerpots with sunflower hats surrounding their sweet faces, nested them together as peas in a pod.

Other photographers, inspired by her creativity, began changing the once-traditional "bare newborn on a white faux-bearskin rug" expectation to heart-tugging works of art for parents, grandparents, and friends.

I saw one today that touched me deeply. The newborn's feet are facing the camera, in clear focus. All but his feet is blurred for artistic effect. Draped on the tiny guy's little/big toe are his mom's and dad's wedding rings. The picture—worth more than a thousand words—said, "You, little one, are the product of our love, a symbol of a mom and dad who first loved Jesus, loved each other, and love you. May you thrive in the shade of our marriage commitment to each other, and our commitment to Christ."

Jesus has His arm around a single mom today with no rings to drape on her infant's toes, no money for an artistic photographer, but with a commitment to the One Who said, "Let the little children come to me. This little one can thrive in our shade."

Jesus invited the little children to Himself, as reported in the books of Matthew, Mark, and Luke. The couple whose infant wore his parents' wedding rings on his big toe as well as the single mom or single dad can rejoice in this follow-up verse. "Then," reads Mark 10:16 (CEB), "he hugged the children and blessed them." —CYNTHIA RUCHTI

FAITH STEP: *Consider gifting an unwed mom with a photography session as a symbol of the unconditional love of Jesus. Or donate Scripture-themed photo-memory albums to a local pregnancy home. Yes, Jesus loves them.*

SATURDAY, JANUARY 9

*While they were ministering to the Lord and fasting, the Holy Spirit said,
"Set apart for Me Barnabas and Saul for the work to which I have called them."*
Acts 13:2 (NAS)

WE USUALLY START OUT the new year with some type of fast at our church. It is a physical reminder of the fact that we want to make a new start in the year. Fasting is never easy. But I know that fasting is a way for me to humble myself, practice self-control, and let Jesus know I mean business. I am saying "no" to myself and "yes" to Him. My husband, Scott, has been sending out encouraging e-mails to keep our church on track. This morning he wrote, "Fasting is a time to set aside for ministering to the Lord. It's not about getting what we want from Him all the time. It should be a time when we can minister to Him, love Him, get to know Him more, and draw close to Him."

I know that fasting is something I do to show Jesus that I am serious about following Him, but I never realized that it ministers to Him. That changes everything. After all He has done for me and how He has ministered to me by loving me, giving me so much grace, and changing my life, I would love to be able to minister to Him! Sometimes I forget that Jesus longs for me to spend time with Him because He loves me and He wants me to love Him back.

My relationship is not all about what I can get from Him, although He overwhelms me with His blessings. My relationship is also about what I can give to Him. My love. My time. My service. My praise. Myself. He, of all, deserves it. —SUSANNA FOTH AUGHTMON

FAITH STEP: *Decide to minister to Jesus today. Sing Him a song of love. Praise Him. Tell Him, "Jesus, today I am going to focus on loving You back."*

SUNDAY, JANUARY 10

So we are Christ's ambassadors; God is making his appeal through us. We speak for Christ when we plead, "Come back to God!" 2 Corinthians 5:20 (NLT)

EVERY SUNDAY MORNING, Brother Nathan, my pastor, ends the service by reciting the priestly blessing from Numbers 6:24–25 (NIV): "The Lord bless you and keep you; the Lord make his face shine on you." Then he sends us off with this encouragement: "Remember, you may be the only Jesus someone sees this week. Make sure you give them the right story."

Every believer has been assigned the role of being an ambassador for Christ. We represent Jesus to a world of people suffering from the effects of sin, hungering for acceptance, longing for love. What a privilege to carry His invitation to find forgiveness of sins and unconditional love through a personal relationship with Him. We have words to share that will bring healing and peace to those who are hurting.

Despite their desperate need for Jesus, many won't be receptive to the message. It's crucial that we represent Christ not just with our words but through the way we live. Each of us is surrounded by people watching our attitudes and actions. They take note of how we respond to negative circumstances and how we treat others. Their opinion of Jesus will be influenced by what they see through us.

If I follow my natural instincts, I will often give a distorted view of Who Jesus is. To be His ambassador means treating others with respect. Responding in a spirit of forgiveness and love. Living a life of selfless service. That's why I need help from an active prayer life, study of the Word, and the Holy Spirit's guidance. I want to help people get the right version of Jesus.
—DIANNE NEAL MATTHEWS

FAITH STEP: *Do you have an attitude or behavior that needs changing? Do you need to make better use of the resources at your disposal? Choose one thing you can do to represent Jesus more accurately.*

*one*MONDAY, JANUARY 11

The steadfast love of the Lord never ceases; his mercies never come to an end; they are new every morning; great is your faithfulness. Lamentations 3:22–23 (ESV)

I LOVE DO-OVERS. Making a fresh start in the new year is the ultimate do-over. Last year, I vowed to get strong and fit in January and started a new eating and exercise plan. By February, I had thrown my back out and was eating whole bars of chocolate on the couch. But this is the thing, life…is…wild. Sometimes all your plans and hopes and dreams get turned on their ear and you are left remarking, *Well, this year sure didn't turn out like I thought it would.*

I have an idea for you. Don't pin your every hope and dream on this shiny new year. Pin them on the One Who set the stars in place and Who breathes life into everything He touches. If that new year feeling is slipping through your fingers and your pants are still tight and you still don't have a regular devotional time with Jesus, don't feel that this year is shot and your chance at bright and shiny is gone. Jesus loves do-overs more than we do. He is a do-over kind of God and He doesn't just wait until the new year. He wants to give you do-overs all year long. In January, mid-April, and late October. Jesus has new mercies for us every day, and His great faithfulness is at the ready to keep us lifted and full and sustained no matter what this year holds. He sees our great hopes and says, *Why don't you give Me this year and let's see what we can do together?*

Jesus is offering daily do-overs, steadfast love, never-ending mercy, and unwavering faithfulness throughout. I think we should take Him up on His offer, don't you? —SUSANNA FOTH AUGHTMON

FAITH STEP: *Set your clock for sunrise. Watch the beauty of the sun coming up and recognize it as a symbol of Jesus's new mercies for us each and every day, a symbol of His never-ending love.*

TUESDAY, JANUARY 12

In Him we live and move and have our being.... Acts 17:28 (NKJV)

I HAVE DELUSIONS OF GRANDEUR. I don't know why; perhaps it's because I'm an overachiever and people have expected me to do great things all my life. But I've always wanted to change the world—evangelize India, cure cancer, win the Pulitzer prize, end world poverty. You get the idea.

The good thing about this is that I'm driven. I work hard, have vision, and always try to keep growing. The downside is that I can be prone to a sense of dissatisfaction with the everyday things of life, missing out on the godliness with contentment Paul says is great gain. I tend to look for Jesus in big worship experiences or mission trips rather than seeing Him in my dirty dishwater. But this should not be.

Micha Boyett, in her book *Found*, writes about feeling like she lost her prayer time when her kids were little. She'd try to pray, but fall asleep or find herself breathing quick SOS-type prayers on the run. One night as she lay in bed feeling bad and unspiritual about this, the thought came to her that maybe her kids *were* her prayers.

Brother Lawrence wrote: "The time of business does not with me differ from the time of prayer, and in the noise and clatter of my kitchen, while several persons are at the same time calling for different things, I possess God in as great tranquility as if I were upon my knees at the blessed sacrament."

They both have learned a secret I need to practice—the secret of living, moving, and having my being in Jesus. The secret that there are no great things or small things. It's all just Him. —GWEN FORD FAULKENBERRY

FAITH STEP: *As you go through your day today, look for Jesus in the most mundane places. He can turn your laundry room into a cathedral, your work desk into an altar, your weedy flower bed into holy ground.*

mve WEDNESDAY, JANUARY 13

God saved you by his grace when you believed. And you can't take credit for this; it is a gift from God. Salvation is not a reward for the good things we have done, so none of us can boast about it. Ephesians 2:8–9 (NLT)

WHEN I WAS A YOUNG MOM I made many decisions concerning my parenting, and the truth is that deep down those decisions were not Christ-motivated. As a mom, I wanted the approval of others. I was trying to live up to unrealistic expectations I'd set up in my mind. And I was trying to earn Jesus's approval, instead of understanding what He'd already provided through His grace.

"If we take our meaning in life from our family, our work, a cause, or some achievement other than God, they enslave us," says Pastor Tim Keller. Too often I filled my schedule with activities that I thought were for my kids, but really they were to make me look good.

I don't need the approval of others to be worthy. I already have Jesus's approval because of what He has done *for* me and *in* me. God sees me as His child, and He loves me completely. "This is My daughter, and I am preparing for her a heavenly home." When I live my life out of those thoughts of approval, everything changes.

Now, after being a mom for twenty-five years, what do I want most? To seek Jesus's approval. To look at Him first. To lift my children up to Him in prayer. To encourage the unique gifts Jesus has given my children, and to look into His eyes and hear, "Well done."

When as a mom I focus on Jesus first, He will guide me on how to raise children who love Him first, who serve others, and who will be smart and successful (according to Jesus's wisdom and idea of success). This is truly what I've wanted all along. —TRICIA GOYER

FAITH STEP: *Find ten ways to tell someone your approval of them today. Also find ten ways to reaffirm Jesus's approval of them. Then, at the end of the day, look in the mirror and remind yourself of Jesus's approval of you.*

THURSDAY, JANUARY 14

Later, a great many people from the Gerasene countryside got together and asked Jesus to leave—too much change, too fast, and they were scared. Luke 8:37 (MSG)

CHANGE AFFECTS US ALL in different ways. I usually handle change well—until I hit something like a technical glitch that challenges my routine, releasing the fear of too much information and too fast a learning curve.

That's what happened to the people who witnessed Jesus's miraculous healing of a demon-possessed man who lived chained in the cemetery.

When Jesus confronted the demons who controlled the man, immediately things were set in motion that would upset the villagers' routine. First, the demons begged for a new home: a herd of pigs on a nearby hill. Jesus agreed. The pigs then stampeded down a cliff and drowned in the lake. Later, witnesses were amazed to see the formerly mad man, clothed, in his right mind, sitting at the feet of Jesus. "It was a holy moment" (Luke 8:35, MSG).

But the people, instead of being awed by the miracle, were instead uncomfortable with the sudden change in the possessed man. Things happened that they couldn't explain, or accept—and, in the case of the swine owners, the man's healing affected their very livelihood. They reacted in fear, begging Jesus to leave.

When Jesus asks us to follow Him, He challenges our normal routines. Some changes may make us or others uncomfortable. We—and those around us—may even react initially with fear: "too much change, too fast." But as we tell the good news of what Jesus has done for us, just like the healed man, we'll find the moment of change worthwhile—truly a "holy moment." A new life with Jesus is always better than the old. —REBECCA BARLOW JORDAN

FAITH STEP: *What changes has Jesus brought into your life lately? What changes would you like Him to make? Tell someone today about one positive change that Jesus has made in your life.*

FRIDAY, JANUARY 15

All the treasures of wisdom and knowledge are hidden in Him. Colossians 2:3 (HCS)

WHEN I'M WORKING AT MY DESK, I like to be surrounded by pretty things. Especially if those items remind me of fun trips or events. For example, hanging from a door pull in the hutch above me is a small plaque from a gift shop in Natchez, Mississippi. The artist carved a primitive-style flower with large leaves, then painted it with vibrant pinks and greens on a beige background. Since that side always faces out, I tend to forget what she etched on the back.

One day I sat down in my office, feeling overwhelmed and unable to concentrate on work. I'm not sure what problem I was struggling with, but I do remember that the situation had begun to look hopeless. How would I ever find a solution? Then my eyes fell on the answer. Apparently, the last time I'd opened the door in the hutch, the plaque had twisted around. Instead of a bright pink flower, I saw these words: "Ask God about it."

How many times have I suffered stress and sleepless nights, worrying over a problem without seeking divine help? The Bible describes Jesus as the ultimate source of wisdom and knowledge. I seem to forget how that translates into practical answers for everyday problems.

His Spirit within me reveals how to apply scriptural truth to difficult situations. Sometimes He connects me with people or resources needed to solve a problem. Other times He simply opens my eyes to see the circumstances from a new angle. But it all starts with asking Him about it. That's why I'm thinking about keeping that little plaque turned around backward all the time. —DIANNE NEAL MATTHEWS

FAITH STEP: *What problem is troubling you today? Each time you think about it, take a moment to ask Jesus to give you the wisdom and knowledge you need to deal with your circumstances in a godly manner.*

SATURDAY, JANUARY 16

My question: What are God-worshippers like? Your answer:
Arrows aimed at God's bull's-eye. Psalm 25:12 (MSG)

WHEN I WAS A TEENAGER, I competed on a junior rifle team. Although I'm left-handed, I scored higher when I shot right-handed. When I tried archery recently, the instructor figured it out. I'm left-handed but right-eyed. I'm more awkward wielding a longbow right-handed but that's the only way I can hit the target.

Whether I'm sending an arrow to the bull's-eye or flipping a crumpled-up wad of paper into the wastebasket, I take aim so often I don't give it any thought. If I want a glass of water, I head to the kitchen (first target), turn toward the cupboard by the sink (second target), reach for the handle (third target) to open it, choose the glass I want (fourth target). I reach for the faucet (fifth target) and finally line up the glass (sixth target) with the stream of water—you get the point. We take aim all day long.

The direction of our gaze reveals our objective.

Jesus looked up to heaven before He fed the five thousand and when He raised Lazarus from the dead. Far from hiding it, He made His connection with God obvious. Jesus always lived like an arrow aimed at the Father's heart. And He told us to follow Him. Jesus said, "Walk with me and work with me—watch how I do it. Learn the unforced rhythms of grace" (Matthew 11:29, MSG).

I want to look to Jesus. Not around me or behind me, but with my gaze firmly fixed on Him. By His grace, my aim will be straight and true.

—SUZANNE DAVENPORT TIETJEN

FAITH STEP: *You may be used to bowing your head when you pray. When you pray today, try looking up. Jesus did this when He prayed. Does the direction of your gaze make a difference for you?*

SUNDAY, JANUARY 17

There is neither Jew nor Gentile, neither slave nor free, nor is there male and female, for you are all one in Christ Jesus. Galatians 3:28 (NIV)

I ONCE ATTENDED A Christian conference where a great deal of teaching focused on roles in the church, and seemed to particularly emphasize things women should not do. Although I'm sure it wasn't the intent of the speakers, I left feeling very second class.

In the safety of my room, I poured out my heart in prayer. "Jesus, is that how You see me? Am I not as valuable to You because I'm a woman?"

Immediately, a picture came to my mind of a shepherd surrounded by little woolly lambs. In the mental image, differences were hard to discern. They were all fluffy and muddle-headed, and dearly loved by the shepherd. Comfort washed over me as I remembered that our Good Shepherd doesn't prioritize whom He loves the most. We certainly differ in many ways, and sometimes fill specific roles, but ultimately we are one in Christ Jesus. We share equally in His grace and acceptance.

None of us who follow Christ can feel superior to our siblings, and none of us need to believe we're inferior. Our ethnicity, our social or vocational standing, our gender fade in importance as we follow Jesus. We are all equally sinners, all equally saved by grace, all equally loved by the Shepherd of our souls. —SHARON HINCK

FAITH STEP: *Think of a time when you felt unvalued because of gender, race, or other unique qualities. Memorize Galatians 3:28 to carry in your heart.*

MONDAY, JANUARY 18

One of them took a swing at the Chief Priest's servant and cut off his right ear. Jesus said, "Let them be. Even in this." Then, touching the servant's ear, he healed him. Luke 22:50–51 (MSG)

ON THE NEWS ONE NIGHT I heard the hate-filled words of a parent whose son had been murdered, apparently in a burglary gone awry. The parent wanted revenge. An innocent young man caught in police crossfire, his son didn't deserve that kind of brutal killing.

Recently, I was listening to the same news channel, this time featuring another disaster. A woman's son had also died in a tragic accident when a bus full of prisoners veered off an icy road, careering into a moving train. Though not a violent offender, her son had broken the law and was serving only a short sentence. But the mother responded differently from the previous parent. Her response was one of love, not anger. Her son had found Jesus only months earlier. She knew he stood now in Jesus's heavenly presence.

On the night Jesus was arrested, He remained calm as always. Soldiers stormed through the Garden to take Jesus. Fear and panic struck the eleven disciples, and Peter moved quickly to defend His beloved Master and take revenge, slicing off the guard's ear. But Jesus would have none of that. Even in His deepest pain, He cared about others more than His own suffering. Reaching to the soldier, He healed the man's ear. Throughout His ugly trial, scourging, and Crucifixion, Jesus, the innocent Son of God, did not lash out in anger. On the Cross, He asked His Father to forgive His murderers. And when the criminal who hung with Him called out to Jesus, Jesus granted him eternal life.

Even in His darkest moments, Jesus's thought was for others. Fully human, yet fully divine, He could have chosen revenge. Instead, He chose love, showing us the better way. I'm so glad He did, aren't you?
—REBECCA BARLOW JORDAN

FAITH TEST: *When someone hurts you, what is your first reaction? Ask Jesus to make love your first—and last—response.*

~~DONE~~ TUESDAY, JANUARY 19

There is now no condemnation for those who are in Christ Jesus. Romans 8:1 (NAS)

I WAS RECENTLY ASKED HOW you can tell if you are being convicted. Is there a way to know if it's really the Holy Spirit, and not just your own feelings, or the judgment of someone else? That question got me thinking about Romans 8:1.

I believe there is a way to tell if something is true conviction, but first you have to recognize the distinct difference between conviction and condemnation. The Bible says there is no condemnation in Jesus. So what is it? Condemnation means there is no hope. For instance, if a building is condemned, it means it's going to be torn down. Its purpose has ended. Its time has passed. It's over. Condemnation leads to despair.

Conviction is always going to lead you to hope.

Condemnation says, "You're a loser. You'll never get it right." Conviction says, "This is wrong. But there's a better way. Let me help you find it." Condemnation says, "You should give up. The situation is hopeless." Conviction says, "Keep trying. Learn from your mistakes." Condemnation says, "No one will ever love/want/believe in you after what you've done." Conviction says, "I love/want/believe in you. Let's move forward together."

See the difference? Jesus's heart toward us is always love. While condemnation leads to death, conviction's aim is newness of life. True conviction brings with it the hope of something better, of growth, of coming to a place of peace and healing. —GWEN FORD FAULKENBERRY

FAITH STEP: *Do you sometimes struggle to recognize true conviction? "Test the spirits" by asking whether what you're experiencing leads you to darkness and despair, or to light and hope. Even if the situation seems grim, the conviction Jesus brings will provide a candle of hope to help you see the way through.*

WEDNESDAY, JANUARY 20

Rejoice always, pray continually, give thanks in all circumstances;
for this is God's will for you in Christ Jesus. 1 Thessalonians 5:16–18 (NIV)

YEARS AGO I READ this list of commands—rejoice always, pray continually, and give thanks in everything—and wondered how in the world anyone could fulfill them, especially the one about praying nonstop. Seriously? I grew up believing that God would hear me only if I assumed the prerequisite body posture—closed eyes and folded hands. Easier said than done when driving on the freeway or supervising kids at the playground.

Thankfully, Scripture's commands are always doable, and this one is no exception. So how can we pray continually when we're at work, watching our kids, engaged in a critical conversation, or suffering to the degree that we can scarcely string a sentence together? Here are six simple suggestions that work for me:

When I'm in a difficult situation, I pray, "Jesus—wisdom."

When circumstances cause anxiety, I pray, "Jesus—peace."

When finances fall short of monthly bills, I pray, "Jesus—provision."

When noise and activity surround me, I pray, "Jesus—rest."

When a difficult person offends me, I pray, "Jesus—love."

When I don't know what to pray, I pray, "Jesus—help!"

I find this prayer method helps me maintain a constant awareness of Jesus's presence and power. It prompts me to talk with Him as with a good friend not only when I need something, but at all times. It even helps me obey the other command in today's verse by saying many times each day, "Jesus—thank You."

Maybe you'll find these phrases helpful, or perhaps you already have a favorite method. The bottom line is pray continually. —GRACE FOX

FAITH STEP: *Read Luke 11:1–13. Ask Jesus to teach you to pray as He did. Thank Him for promising to hear and answer your prayers, and choose to trust Him when He doesn't answer your requests when and how you wish.*

mk THURSDAY, JANUARY 21

Be still and rest in the Lord; wait for Him and patiently lean yourself upon Him.
Psalm 37:7 (AMP)

STILLNESS CAN BE A BATTLE. It has been for me.

I was that kid who never sat still. I climbed trees—even the tetherball pole. I was enrolled in dance classes to burn up all that energy. I bounced through my childhood ("Can't you just settle down somewhere?"). When I did, I wiggled my sweaty self in under my parents' arms and wrapped myself around them for as long a hug as they could stand in those hot Florida days before air conditioners.

I was diagnosed recently with ADHD (attention deficit/hyperactivity disorder)—gray hair and all. The only medication safe for me caused side effects, so it's still a problem. My husband has been known to put his hand on my knee in church, not because he's feeling romantic, but to stop my jiggling. How can I "be still and know that He is God" when I haven't mastered being still? I asked Jesus to help me.

First, I looked at His example. Jesus often withdrew to lonely places and prayed (Luke 5:16, NIV). His public prayers were brief, but He prayed all night before choosing His disciples. Jesus had to be comfortable with stillness. Since He prayed in the early morning dark, I've made stillness my first appointment of the day. Then, I looked at His followers. Mary of Bethany sat at His feet listening when other demands (and voices) clamored for her attention. Jesus praised her because she had chosen the better part. Like her, I want to love Him so much that nothing can pull me away. Now, nearly every day, I sit silently in the presence of Jesus.

When I don't, I notice. —SUZANNE DAVENPORT TIETJEN

FAITH STEP: *Find a quiet spot and set a timer for five minutes. Tell Jesus you'd like to be with Him. Don't use any more words—just relax and be still in the silence. Did this affect you? How?*

onk FRIDAY, JANUARY 22

Blessed is the one who does not walk in step with the wicked or stand in the way that sinners take or sit in the company of mockers, but whose delight is in the law of the Lord, and who meditates on his law day and night. That person is like a tree planted by streams of water, which yields its fruit in season and whose leaf does not wither—whatever they do prospers. Psalm 1:1–3 (NIV)

WHEN I WAS A CHILD, my Sunday school teacher handed out bookmarks listing the books of the Bible. You marked off each chapter you read by filling in a little box. My goal was to fill in every box. I treated Bible reading like a race to be won. How fast could I read Genesis? Exodus was a piece of cake. Deuteronomy? I won't lie. I got bogged down in it. There are a lot of laws in there.

But I think the speed-reading mentality of barreling through the Scriptures has stuck with me throughout the years. I am mentally checking off each chapter like an item to check off my to-do list. The problem is that there is very little delighting that is going on while I read through these words of life.

Jesus didn't come so that I could check items off of my to-do list. He came to revolutionize my life. He came to turn my heart inside out and transform the way I think. He came so I could be free and so that His love and grace could pour out of me. These things happen when I spend time with Him. When I soak up His truth. When I talk to Him and listen to what He has to say to me through His Word. His words bring life and light. And I am ready for both. —SUSANNA FOTH AUGHTMON

FAITH STEP: *Pick a favorite chapter of Scripture and reread it every day for a week. Notice how Jesus reveals His truths to you as you meditate on His Word.*

SATURDAY, JANUARY 23

He lifted me out of the pit of despair, out of the mud and the mire. He set my feet
on solid ground and steadied me as I walked along. Psalm 40:2 (NLT)

OUR FAMILY ENJOYS PLAYING a domino game called Mexican Train. On
one occasion, my six-year-old granddaughter, Anna, missed several turns
because she lacked the dominoes she needed. She watched wistfully as
everyone else built their trains, then blurted, "I need to get out of my stuck."

That's an insightful comment, I thought. *No doubt many adults feel the*
same way about their life circumstances.

Several months ago I realized my "need to get out of my stuck" in the context of physical health. I increased my exercise routine, purged my cupboards
of unhealthy foods, began wearing a little gizmo that tracks my daily steps,
and found an accountability partner. I also asked Jesus to help me persevere.
Doing these things moved me from stuck to improved physical well-being.

How about you? Maybe Jesus has planted a dream in your heart but fear
of the unknown hinders you from pursuing it. As a result, you feel stuck.
Perhaps you struggle with an addiction—overeating, smoking, alcohol
or drug abuse, or even an addiction to social media. Maybe you harbor
unforgiveness, jealousy, or ingratitude. Beware—unconfessed sin works
like superglue and keeps us stuck in defeat until we decide that enough
is enough. Any of these can keep us stuck in a wilderness of the soul.

But there's hope! Being stuck in negative circumstances needn't be a
permanent position. Jesus promises to set us free, and to steady us as we
walk along. His power enables us to rise above our circumstances and
walk in victory. —GRACE FOX

FAITH STEP: *Are you stuck in a sinful or harmful habit? Admit this to Jesus, ask Him*
to show you specific actions necessary to overcome it, and then ask Him to help you.
Thank Him in advance for what He'll do.

SUNDAY, JANUARY 24

When she heard about Jesus, she came up behind him in the crowd and touched his cloak, because she thought, "If I just touch his clothes, I will be healed."
Mark 5:27-28 (NIV)

ONE NIGHT ON CHURCH VISITATION, I listened to a woman complain about unexplainable symptoms, chronic illness, and years of pain. A host of other emotional problems and relationship issues clung to her like relentless fleas, complicating her situation. I wanted to be empathetic, but even my greatest problems paled in comparison to hers.

I thought about the woman who had endured constant bleeding for twelve years. Rules of cleanliness and ritual purification conflicted with her dilemma, pushing her away from those she loved. She suffered not only physically and financially, but also socially and spiritually. Obviously she'd heard about Jesus, the Healer and Great Physician. He was her only hope, her last chance. So pushing through the crowd, she lunged in faith, knowing if she could just touch the hem of Jesus's garment, she would be free from her suffering.

As soon as her fingers touched the edge of His robe, healing shot through her like a bolt of lightning. Jesus turned and declared her healed—physically and spiritually, for her faith had freed her.

The woman I was visiting needed Jesus too. I wanted to introduce her to the One Who could meet all her needs, especially her spiritual ones. But the woman couldn't muster the courage to call out His name.

When others are too weak or fearful to try, we can be the hands that reach out to Jesus for them. While Jesus doesn't always grant complete physical healing to all in this lifetime, He does offer spiritual freedom to anyone who asks. Our prayers for these can help span the distance between fear and faith. —REBECCA BARLOW JORDAN

FAITH STEP: *Do you know someone whose problems seem to exceed his or her small or nonexistent faith? Reach out to touch Jesus's garment through prayer for her.*

MONDAY, JANUARY 25

"That times of refreshing may come from the presence of the Lord, and that he may send the Christ appointed for you, Jesus." Acts 3:20 (ESV)

I'VE BEEN A HOUSEGUEST in a friend's home for the last several days. It's been so good to catch up with each other's lives, to see her at work in both the professional and ministry opportunities in her path, and to be the blessed recipient of her warmhearted hospitality. The details of her hospitality included great pillows for the guest bed, a great mattress, a truly comforting comforter.

My friend knows how to make a guest feel comfortable, honored, and refreshed. When I told her that I felt rejuvenated in every way after being in her home, she said, "Good! That's just what I prayed would happen."

A favorite song says, "I come in empty, I leave filled." It's talking about entering the sanctuary of the presence of Jesus and being changed by having been with Him. This week, it has also touched me as one of His children—my friend—provided sanctuary for me. I came energy empty. I'm leaving energy filled.

So often, we assume that an overflowing to-do list or a crisis season in our lives means no time to luxuriate in His presence, unplug from the world, and spend time alone with Him, to pillow our heads on His listening heart. Must we need to give ourselves permission to do what our soul most needs?

Feeling empty? Come into His presence that way. He invited you to do so. Leave filled. —CYNTHIA RUCHTI

FAITH STEP: *When something needs updating on a computer, we're often told to "refresh" the page. If it's your soul that needs refreshing, pillow your head in restorative time alone with Jesus . . . longer than you think you'll need. Everything else will look brighter and conquerable when you emerge.*

TUESDAY, JANUARY 26

I have seen all the things that are done under the sun; all of them are meaningless, a chasing after the wind. Ecclesiastes 1:14 (NIV)

MY EIGHTY-FIVE-YEAR-OLD GRANDMOTHER lives with our family, which includes me, my husband, and four of our six children who still live at home. She watches the busyness, the craziness, and every so often she offers advice: "These are the best days of your life." I laughed the first time I heard it, but now I know it's true. These are days I'll always look back on with a smile. Kids grow. The days pass so quickly.

God's Word says the same thing, "You have made my days a mere hand-breadth; the span of my years is as nothing before you. Everyone is but a breath, even those who seem secure" (Psalm 39:5, NIV).

Knowing this truth changes my daily choices. I won't regret putting the mail pile or the dishes to the side, yet I someday may regret that I didn't slow down and enjoy my kids. I know it's okay to take a nap—a rested mama is a happy mama. I find time to smile, too, because a smile changes my attitude. I also try to find joy in every situation, and if I can't do that, I can find joy by looking into my little one's eyes.

Each of us has a choice about how we live our days. We can either follow meaningless pursuits or focus on what really matters. Once the mind believes that these *are* the best days of our lives, the heart follows. And once the heart follows, the days improve. And as we find joy in them, they truly do become the best days of our life. —TRICIA GOYER

FAITH STEP: *Write the words* These are the best days of my life *on sticky notes and post them around your house. Every time you see one, think of something that makes this a "best day" and thank Jesus for that!*

WEDNESDAY, JANUARY 27

And he said, "My presence will go with you, and I will give you rest."
Exodus 33:14 (ESV)

HAVE YOU EVER REMINDED YOURSELF that "with God all things are possible"? Those words have been used so widely, it's almost easy to forget they came straight from the Savior's mouth (Matthew 19:26, NIV).

With them He spoke a great truth that complements today's verse well. God had commanded Moses to lead the people out of Egyptian captivity, an assignment that seemed impossible.

The assignments that we know are from the Lord usually seem impossible to us; in fact, they are impossible on our own. They push us to trust Jesus more, and they reveal His glory instead of our own.

Moses understood the "God thing" the Lord was asking of him. The Lord called him to stand up to the powerful Pharaoh and to lead a stubborn throng of people. That's the short version of a whole lot of "impossibles," which Moses grasped so well that he asked not to be sent unless he'd have the Lord's presence with him.

When Jesus asks something of us that is impossible without Him, He's also inviting us to rely on Him, which is the only way we can rest in those circumstances. If we could see what He sees, all that He wants to do and show us, we would ask to partner with Him in otherwise impossible situations so that we can have a front-row view of His glory.
—ERIN KEELEY MARSHALL

FAITH STEP: *Ask Jesus to partner in His work that's impossible without Him. Praise Him for His presence and His rest.*

THURSDAY, JANUARY 28

Jesus declared, "I am the bread of life. Whoever comes to me will never go hungry, and whoever believes in me will never be thirsty." John 6:35 (NIV)

MIDAFTERNOON, I WAS WORKING at my desk and getting increasingly frustrated. Tension squeezed my skull, and I couldn't solve the simplest problems with the manuscript I was working on.

I walked out to the kitchen to get a cup of tea, hoping that a fresh perspective would help. While the water heated, I ran my hand over the clean countertop. No crumbs. No dishes in the sink. No signs of anyone having eaten a recent meal.

That's when it hit me. I'd forgotten to have lunch. No wonder I felt cranky.

My husband shakes his head, bewildered, whenever I tell him I've forgotten to eat. Apparently his stomach does a better job of reminding him when he needs to refuel. I've had to endure some good-natured teasing about being so absentminded that I forget to eat.

There are even more serious consequences if I forget to seek nourishment for my soul.

In the big eternal picture, Jesus is our Bread of Life. His body, broken for us, gives us everlasting life. But in our day-to-day activities, He also is our nourishment, our sustenance, our source of life. When I don't include Him in my thoughts throughout the day, it's like ignoring my body's need for food. Soon I'm grumpy, weak, and empty without realizing what's gone wrong. Time in His Word, a worship song, or a few minutes of prayer can restore my spiritual strength as my hungry heart feasts on love and truth. —SHARON HINCK

FAITH STEP: *Next time you eat, thank Jesus for nourishing your spirit with His presence. Along with the meal, take time to receive food for your soul.*

~~dnk~~ FRIDAY, JANUARY 29

Therefore if any man be in Christ, he is a new creature: old things are passed away; behold, all things are become new. 2 Corinthians 5:17 (KJV)

MAYBE IT'S JUST ME, but I believe there's a tendency for believers to think in terms of arrival. Often we interpret a verse like the one above as a one-time thing, as though we come to Christ, become a new creature, and that is it. We've arrived spiritually. And while I do believe salvation is the turning point, a radical transformation of our lives, I think it's inaccurate to see it as arrival. This limits us, limits God, and sets us up to feel like failures.

I realized I had a problem with this when I went through a really difficult season in my marriage. I kept wanting things to be fixed, all better, new. I don't think I did this consciously, but when we would get over one hurdle I would hope it was our "arrival." I had an idea of what I wanted the "new creature" of our life to look like, and I was desperate to feel we were finally there, only to find there was a new hurdle to cross.

One night, after a particularly hurtful setback, I felt like giving up. Even though I believed Jesus was helping us grow, it felt like we were never going to get there. I was exhausted, tired of taking one step forward and two steps back. In desperation, I picked up the first book I saw and read this quotation: "Always we begin again. —The Rule of St. Benedict"

Those four words soaked down into my soul, filling me with peace. I knew they were the words Jesus had for me in that moment. It was a time when I changed in my thinking, from striving to arrive at a destination to trusting Jesus every step along the journey and accepting that His vision is something better, something more. —GWEN FORD FAULKENBERRY

FAITH STEP: *Is there an area of your life where you need to be made new? Write down this quote from St. Benedict and put it where you can see it every day. Begin again with Jesus. Again and again He makes us new.*

SATURDAY, JANUARY 30

But what happens when we live God's way? He brings gifts into our lives, much the same way that fruit appears in an orchard.... We find ourselves ... not needing to force our way in life, able to marshal and direct our energies wisely.
Galatians 5:22–23 (MSG)

MY DAUGHTER CALLS THEM "RABBIT TRAILS" and the Internet is full of them. You check your e-mail, peek at social media, click one link, then another. You surface an hour later, holding a cup of cold coffee and wondering what happened to the time.

Or you decide to straighten the house and start off strong until you sort the magazines and riffle through the pages to be sure you read this one. Oops! No, you didn't, but now you are.

Temperance is an old word that all but lost its original meaning early in the last century when it came to be defined as abstaining from alcohol. It originally meant restraint. Today, we'd call it delayed gratification.

Researchers studied delayed gratification by giving children a marshmallow they could eat whenever they chose. If they waited until the researcher came back, they'd get another marshmallow. The test picked out high achievers in many categories. Generally, those who can delay gratification do better in life.

I don't know about you, but I need temperance. Temperance is a fruit of the Spirit. Peter maintains that everything we need to please God is a gift— it begins with the faith God gives us, which leads to good character and understanding; then restraint (temperance), steadfastness, and godliness; and, in godliness, kindness that develops into love (2 Peter 1:3–8). These qualities shine in us as we come to reflect Jesus's divine nature. He will help us direct our energies wisely. —SUZANNE DAVENPORT TIETJEN

FAITH STEP: *Ask Jesus to order your day and help you focus. Every so often, tell Jesus, "I trust You." Notice any difference?*

one SUNDAY, JANUARY 31

"Give us today our daily bread." Matthew 6:11 *(NIV)*

WHEN GOD CALLED MOSES to deliver His people from years of slavery in Egypt, He took them through the wilderness. After a few days in the desert, the people began to grumble. How would the huge multitude survive? What would they eat?

But God answered their need one day by dropping a sweet, sticky substance to earth called *manna*, something like honey. But what about tomorrow? And the next day after that? Instead of trusting God daily, some of the people ignored His instructions and saved up an extra supply just in case God didn't come through. But the extra food rotted. God wanted to teach them daily dependence.

They griped, longing for the food from their past enslavement. But past nourishment and empty longings wouldn't satisfy their appetites now. They needed fresh food daily (Exodus 16).

The same is true of our spiritual lives as it is with our physical. A spiritual meal now and then won't suffice. Nor can we depend on yesterday's moments with Jesus. We need His *daily bread*, His manna every day. That's one of the things included in Jesus's instructions to the disciples on how to pray: "Give us today our daily bread."

In John 6:35, Jesus even referred to Himself as the "Bread of Life." He wants day-by-day, moment-by-moment dependence and trust in Him, not in ourselves. And it's not about rules or traditions. Every day, spending time with Jesus, meditating on His Word, and communicating in real-time fellowship are all a part of our relationship with Him. It's acknowledging that without Him, we can't make it in life. I've fallen on my face so many times. I *know* I need Him every moment. —REBECCA BARLOW JORDAN

FAITH STEP: *How can you improve your spiritual meals this week? In what area of your life will you exercise more dependence on Jesus? Write down one way, and begin today!*

MONDAY, FEBRUARY 1

Speaking the truth in love, [we] may grow up in all things into Him who is the head—Christ. Ephesians 4:15 (NKJV)

AN AUTHOR I LIKE, James Baldwin, once said, "If I love you, I have to make you conscious of the things you don't see." Baldwin's stories deal with racial prejudice in such a way that he makes others see how ugly it is. When you encounter his writing you are moved to empathy, to social responsibility, to action.

As disciples of Jesus we are instructed to speak the truth in love, that we—the body of Christ—may mature in all things, becoming more like Him. But speaking the truth in love sometimes sounds easier than it is. Let's assume we know the truth. We've done our homework, researched the facts, studied the Bible, and allowed the Holy Spirit to lead us into it. The two words on either side of "truth" in that opening verse also can be problematic.

First, we're commanded to speak. For some, this is the most difficult thing. Maybe it means not keeping silent about an issue in church, or around the family dinner table. Speaking the truth, especially when it is unpopular, can be dangerous. We have to risk what others think of us, and that is hard. The other challenging word is *love*. Love moves us to share truth. But sometimes love isn't our motivation. Sometimes we want to win an argument or get our own way. In those times it's probably more loving to keep our mouths closed.

Whatever the situation, we can trust Jesus to give us what we need. He is the truth, and He gives us the courage to speak as well as the humility to be loving—and the wisdom to make the timing right.
—GWEN FORD FAULKENBERRY

FAITH STEP: *Before you speak today, think about the verse above. Let Jesus speak through you (or help you keep silent) and trust Him with the results.*

TUESDAY, FEBRUARY 2

They called Rebekah and said to her, "Will you go with this man?"
She replied, "I will go." Genesis 24:58 (HSC)

WHEN ABRAHAM LOOKED FOR A WIFE for his son, he prayed for God's guidance. His servant was led to Rebekah as Isaac's future spouse. Rebekah's brother gave his consent to the marriage and negotiated the contract, as was his right. But then he called Rebekah and asked if she was willing to "go with this man."

Every time I read that story, I think about the decision faced by busy fishermen when Jesus passed by and called out, "Come, follow Me!" I think about the believers who followed Jesus from village to village to learn from Him and help in His ministry. The crowds who followed Him by the thousands to hear Him speak. The faithful few who followed Him to the Cross. And I remember the choice I make every day to go with this Man.

There are times when I sense Jesus leading me in a direction that pulls me away from my comfort zone. I get uneasy if I don't have a clear idea of what lies ahead. But Jesus wants me to trust Him whether He's calling me to move to the other side of the world, or asking me to serve Him in some new way that seems frightening. When I think about the blessings of obedience versus the consequences of disobedience, there's only one logical answer.

I want to be like Rebekah when asked if she would leave her home behind to go with a stranger and marry a man she'd never met. I want to be like those fishermen who immediately left their nets to follow Jesus, no questions asked. Even if He's pushing me into uncharted territory, I want to say without hesitation, "Yes, Lord, I will go." —DIANNE NEAL MATTHEWS

FAITH STEP: *Think about a time when Jesus asked you to follow Him somewhere you didn't want to go. Now examine your response and how that shaped your life in positive or negative ways.*

WEDNESDAY, FEBRUARY 3

---

*I ask him to strengthen you by his Spirit—not a brute strength but
a glorious inner strength—that Christ will live in you as you open the door
and invite him in. Ephesians 3:16–17 (MSG)*

I'D COME TO A ROADBLOCK early in my Christian walk. I sensed something was wrong. I didn't even know what the problem was, but I felt as if the next step was mine to take.

I prayed. And God answered. In a dream or some kind of vision I saw Jesus sitting in my living room. We were comfortably visiting and I asked Him what my problem was. He told me that when we invite people into our homes they come into the living room, or if the relationship is more casual, they might gather in the kitchen while the hostess cooked the meal. Good guests don't, however, go through closed doors into the bedrooms or check out the medicine cabinet, much less go rummaging through the drawers. Jesus said, "I'll take part in as much of your life as you open to Me. I'll move in altogether if you want Me, but I'll wait for you to open every door. Take your time. Open them one by one and I'll walk through."

He has been faithful in doing that. I tried to tell Him to come into every room right then but, for me, anyway, that wasn't the way it worked. Instead, He points out through His Word a part of "my house" I may not have even known was there and asks, "How about that room? That drawer? That dark closet?"

By His grace, with the faith He provides, I turn the knob.

Let the Word of Christ—the Message—have the run of the house. Give it plenty of room in your lives (Colossians 3:16, MSG).
—SUZANNE DAVENPORT TIETJEN

FAITH STEP: *Our individuality is important to Jesus. Ask Him to show you what He wants to deal with in your life and always stay in the Word. Is there a door you need to open?*

THURSDAY, FEBRUARY 4

"He said to himself, 'What should I do? I don't have room for all my crops.'
Then he said, 'I know! I'll tear down my barns and build bigger ones.
Then I'll have room enough to store all my wheat and other goods.'"
Luke 12:17–18 (NLT)

A FEW YEARS AGO as home interest rates kept declining, we considered a change. Should we buy a larger home? Our nest had emptied, but unfortunately, lifelong accumulations lingered longer than the children.

We weighed our options. Closets and other storage areas were as modest in size as our brick home. And our current thirty-year-old house needed updates. We visited model homes and checked out other possibilities. As a woman, I had to keep my wants in check every time I viewed those high ceilings, open living areas, not to mention huge closets. But did we really need more space? Which would be better?

I remembered the rich farmer Jesus met one day who'd grown a bumper crop on his farm. He faced a decision: whether or not to tear down his old barns and build bigger barns. Actually, he thought of no other options. That was probably his first mistake. Of course, his real issue was not adding more storage, but satisfying his greed.

We didn't feel like greed was a factor in our decision, and we had always tried to spend wisely the money Jesus had entrusted to us. However, just because you can doesn't mean you should.

In the end, keeping our older, paid-for home and making the necessary and wanted updates worked better for us. As for the years' accumulations, we're gradually clearing out stuff. And I am learning to organize better.

Jesus is teaching us something about wisdom, the older we grow: keep it simple. —REBECCA BARLOW JORDAN

FAITH STEP: *Is there any area of your life that needs simplifying? Ask Jesus to give you wisdom for any decisions you may be facing.*

FRIDAY, FEBRUARY 5

"Whoever drinks from the water that I will give will never be thirsty again. . . ."
John 4:14 (CEB)

THE WATER FROM OUR KITCHEN FAUCET was the color of clay. I'm no plumber, but that didn't seem right to me. Bathroom faucets. Washing machine. Dishwasher. Clay-colored water came from each one. My husband checked the water filter in the basement. It was completely clogged with sand and clay. Somewhere underground, a pipe had broken or the well had failed, neither of which was an appealing prospect in the d-e-a-d of winter with the ground too frozen to dig and temps hovering in the double digits below zero.

We found every clean container we could and accepted our neighbor's invitation to fill them at their house, a quarter mile away. Twice a week, sometimes more often, we hauled water from the neighbor's house for drinking and cooking.

We lived that way from mid-January to the middle of July before conditions were right for the problem to be resolved.

The drama heightened my appreciation for one of the most powerful and life-altering scenes in Scripture—Jesus with the woman at the well.

We didn't have clean water, but, as the woman at the well pointed out, Jesus didn't even have a bucket (John 4:11). What He did have was Himself— the Living Water. The endless, never ceasing, never cloudy or contaminated Living Water. The woman's life had been contaminated, clouded with poor judgment and wrong choices. What Jesus offered her, He offers us. Living Water. Drink deep, often, and appreciatively! —CYNTHIA RUCHTI

FAITH STEP: *For a day or two, keep two clear glasses within sight. Fill one with clean water and the other with muddy. Let it be a reminder of what Jesus has offered you. Turn to His Word for a big, long drink before this day is through.*

SATURDAY, FEBRUARY 6

"Glory to God in the highest heaven, and on earth peace to those on whom his favor rests." Luke 2:14 (NIV)

FOR SOME REASON PUTTING UP Christmas decorations is invigorating and taking them down feels like the death of a holiday. I had all three boys offering to hang ornaments and candy canes on the tree, but trying to get them to help take them down is almost impossible. We just don't want to see the magical season of Christmas go.

Last year I purchased two different signs that light up. One says Joy and the other says Peace. The Joy sign I put on top of the bookcase in our living room. Every night I would plug in the Joy and it would radiate its loveliness all over the room. The Peace sign we hung out on our carport. While other houses on our streets boasted lit-up icicles and blow-up Santas, ours illuminated the night with a message. Last year, I left up our Joy sign all year long. This year I can't find it in myself to take down Peace.

I know we are supposed to leave Christmas behind and face the new year, but from what I can tell we all need a little more peace. Reading the news or talking with friends about struggles or facing a mountain of bills, we need the peace of Jesus to flood our hearts and lives. Experiencing His peace doesn't mean that we won't have craziness and heartache in life. But it does mean that in the chaos of real living, His love, His guidance, and His mercy will hold us steady. I think I will leave the sign up a little bit longer...just to remind myself of that. —SUSANNA FOTH AUGHTMON

FAITH STEP: *Print the word **Peace** from your computer. Color it in vibrant shades and hang it someplace where you'll see it every day to remind yourself of Jesus's peace.*

SUNDAY, FEBRUARY 7

Let your eyes look forward; fix your gaze straight ahead. Proverbs 4:25 (HSC)

IN FEBRUARY 2014, I FACED a daunting challenge. My husband and I had driven from Texas to Memphis to celebrate his mom's birthday. On Sunday afternoon, I drove an hour north for a quick visit with my parents. Overnight an unexpected major storm moved in, leaving my car covered with several inches of snow and ice. Since Richard had to be at work on Tuesday, I had to get to Memphis ASAP so that we could drive the final six hundred miles home.

One of my brothers spent an hour helping me pry open the door and chip off enough ice just to see through the windshield. I eased down the middle of a narrow country road, sliding even at five miles per hour. Once I reached the highway, I began a harrowing trip that took me over roads that had not been cleared and often were littered with tree branches. Cars decorated the ditches. Driving at a snail's pace, I kept my eyes straight ahead, sending up frequent prayers and calculating how much distance I had left to travel. The trip to my mother-in-law's house took twice as long as usual, but I was grateful to arrive at all.

Looking back at that trip, I wish I could say I always approach life with such a single-minded focus. But when I face a challenge, I often get distracted by my circumstances. Or I allow myself to get sidetracked by focusing on what can go wrong or the possibility of failure. How much better my life journey would be if I kept my eyes straight ahead on the One Who is leading me forward. Even if I feel like I'm moving at a snail's pace, Jesus has promised to safely get me to my destination. —DIANNE NEAL MATTHEWS

FAITH STEP: *Are you facing a daunting challenge or a frightening situation? Ask Jesus to keep your eyes focused on Him and His promises to help you finish your journey well.*

one ## MONDAY, FEBRUARY 8

Behold, as the eyes of servants look to the hand of their master, as the eyes of a maidservant to the hand of her mistress, so our eyes look to the Lord our God, till he has mercy upon us. Psalm 123:2 (ESV)

KHAKI WAS A ONCE-IN-A-LIFETIME DOG. She had the big ears, stubby legs, and herding instincts of a Cardigan Welsh Corgi. She brought order to our farm. Before Khaki came, we wasted hours chasing sheep. On one memorable occasion, I accidentally rode my most obstreperous ewe backward out of the barn when she dove through my legs!

Khaki was having none of that. Her calling was to move the sheep wherever we wanted. She lived to work her "woolies." Since I couldn't whistle and didn't like shouting, I taught Khaki to respond to hand signals. Outside, I used large motions she could see across the pasture. Inside, though, the tiniest hand motion told her to stand, wait, walk up, or lie down. Her eyes met mine first, to check that we were in working mode, then she watched my hands. She maintained that intent, hyperobedient state until she heard the working dog's equivalent of the soldier's "at ease"—the phrase "That'll do." She took obvious joy in her work. Remembering her intensity still gives me pleasure. Her desire to carry out my will is a picture of the wholehearted servant Jesus wants me to be.

I'm not always that willing worker. Sometimes I forget to check in with God at all. When I remember, I may still get distracted and go my own way. Maybe you do too.

We have the almost unbelievable privilege of being of service to Jesus. Let's look to and follow His leading, paying attention to His often subtle signs.

I want to be always ready—instantly, in a second. Jesus shouldn't have to shout before I obey. —SUZANNE DAVENPORT TIETJEN

FAITH STEP: _Today, ask Jesus to help you want whatever He wants. Now tell Him that's what you want to do._

TUESDAY, FEBRUARY 9

*He has made everything beautiful in its time. He has also set
eternity in the human heart; yet no one can fathom what God has done
from beginning to end. Ecclesiastes 3:11 (NIV)*

MY HUSBAND AND I HAVE a dream we'd like to chase someday. We want to flip houses. The dream has been born from his heritage as a builder, my love of home, and our inability to move into a house without redoing it.

When we met, Steve was building a house. Then we renovated nearly all of our next home and much of our current one. Just last weekend Steve replaced the faucet in our powder room, and this morning I saw a piece of base trim on our bathroom counter—not sure what his plans are yet with that. As for my part, I've learned nearly all I know about painting in the decade-plus that I've known him. I enjoy finding decorative treasures at flea markets, and I'd love a side career in design.

There's something satisfying about making the old new, and we love to re-create and refresh and dream about it together. Our template may be brick and mortar, but I'm pretty sure the heart of the dream comes from the Lord.

I might appear to be spiritualizing the ordinary, but I believe Jesus invades every part of the ordinary and makes it extraordinary. What better way to remind us that He makes all things new than by giving us a dream that echoes His eternal heart?

Ecclesiastes 3:11 says He puts the dream of eternity in the human heart, and just as we can look at an old home and see its potential before it's finished, we can only imagine the grandness of all Jesus plans for us.
—ERIN KEELEY MARSHALL

FAITH STEP: *What would you like Jesus to make new in your life? A character hang-up? A relationship? A financial or health problem? Memorize today's verse and trust Jesus's mission to make you new.*

ASH WEDNESDAY, FEBRUARY 10

To console those who mourn in Zion, to give them beauty for ashes,
the oil of joy for mourning, the garment of praise for the spirit of heaviness. . . .
Isaiah 61:3 (NKJV)

IN THE OLD TESTAMENT, people expressed sorrow and repentance by dressing in sackcloth and ashes. After Job lost almost everything he had, he was confused about the nature of God. He said, "I take back everything I said, and I sit in dust and ashes to show my repentance" (Job 42:6, NLT).

Upon hearing that the Jewish people were about to be eradicated, Mordecai—Esther's cousin—mourned with sackcloth and ashes (Esther 4:1). But it was Jesus who challenged all with His words: "Unless you repent you will all . . . perish" (Luke 13:5, NKJV).

The tradition of Ash Wednesday can symbolically remind us of Jesus's sacrifice at Easter. Some believers wear the symbol of the cross in ashes on their foreheads. Others simply begin a season of sacrificing something in their lives to show their repentance.

Repentance is a teaching I've embraced and understood ever since I first gave my heart to Jesus as a child. As I've grown older, I've come to understand an enlarged view of the symbolism of *ashes*. It takes my breath away, just thinking about it.

Isaiah prophesied Jesus would bring beauty for ashes, joy for mourning, and garments of praise through His death, Resurrection, and second coming. When we repent and believe in the promises of God, Jesus gives us the beauty of His complete forgiveness, now and forever. Our sins lie in ashes, with no more power to overcome us. Tears of sadness—for cheers of gladness. What a beautiful exchange!—REBECCA BARLOW JORDAN

FAITH STEP: *Confess any sinful habits that may have crept into your life. Then thank Jesus for taking the ashes of your sin in exchange for the beauty of His forgiveness.*

THURSDAY, FEBRUARY 11

Blessed are the meek: for they shall inherit the earth. Matthew 5:5 (KJV)

IN WHAT WE CALL "The Sermon on the Mount," Jesus outlines some of the traits He wants His followers to display. One of them, possibly the most difficult and most representative of His own character, is meekness.

I often hear people misunderstand the definition of meekness, describing it as shyness or quietness, not wanting to ruffle any feathers. It seems so many Christians embrace a definition like this, believing it's a sin to ever offend anyone else by speaking up or saying no to a request. Nothing could be further from the truth of Jesus's teaching.

What He meant by meekness, what He Himself embodied, was self-control in the face of adversity. Gentleness. It's the idea of wild horses that have been tamed. We see this time and time again in the New Testament, but never more than when He is on the Cross. Imagine the restraint Jesus had to show in order to fulfill His mission. He could have come down unscathed; He could have obliterated His enemies. But He chose obedience. He chose love.

Meekness does not seem to have much value in today's world. With credit cards, fast food, and social media, people seem more willing than ever to throw off any sense of self-restraint. If I want it I can buy it. If I'm hungry, I can eat within minutes. And on social media I can tell my story to an international audience. We often suffer from consequences we never took the time to consider because we aren't meek. But we need to be if we want to be blessed. —GWEN FORD FAULKENBERRY

FAITH STEP: *Consider the wild horses in your life that need taming. Don't make a purchase, send a text, or write a Facebook post today unless you can do it in the name of Jesus. See what blessing a little meekness brings!*

FRIDAY, FEBRUARY 12

---

*Delight yourself in the Lord, and he will give you the desires of your heart.
Commit your way to the Lord; trust in him, and he will act. Psalm 37:4–5 (ESV)*

SCOTT AND I HAVE BEEN MARRIED a little over eighteen years. We can hardly believe that we now have three children and that we are getting gray hair. It is possible that the children are the ones giving us gray hair but the years have flown by. When we got married, we were madly in love. We stood at the altar and gazed into each other's eyes and said, "I am in this for the long haul. No matter what!" For some reason we thought if we loved each other enough, honoring our commitment would be easy. Then life happened. We struggled with the stress of life in the ministry and becoming new parents. Our finances took a hit. We moved cross country twice. We were stretched and stretched some more. But we have stuck with it. Because our commitment to each other means something. We love each other differently from the way we used to. There is a depth to our relationship that came from walking through hard things and still choosing each other.

It is the same in your relationship with Jesus. When you choose to follow Him, you are committing your life to Him. For better or for worse. And He has committed Himself to loving you wholly and completely. Even when you are a mess. Even when you make mistakes. In each season of life, you can count on Him to stand with you. He will never leave you or forsake you. And when you commit to loving Him more with each passing year, no matter how glorious or how difficult your path is, He will hold you close and see you through. —SUSANNA FOTH AUGHTMON

FAITH STEP: *Write out your "vows" to Jesus, how you plan to love Him and commit your life to Him today.*

SATURDAY, FEBRUARY 13

For God saved us and called us to live a holy life. He did this, not because we deserved it, but because that was his plan from before the beginning of time— to show us his grace through Christ Jesus. 2 Timothy 1:9 *(NLT)*

FOR THE PAST YEAR John and I have been praying about opening our hearts to adoption once again. For the last five months we've had a sibling group in mind. It's taken time to get all the paperwork complete. There are income reports, home studies, and criminal background checks. We've had every part of our lives scrutinized, and the whole time we've been focused on one thing: those children. We pray for them by name. We are working to set up their rooms. We have their photos on our cellphones. In our minds it's not "if" they will be ours, but "when."

And the thing is, these children have no idea that they've been chosen. They are still praying for a forever family.

Someday we're going to be able to tell our future children the whole story of how we planned for, waited for, and prayed for them...until we could make them our own. And in God's Word we read the whole story about us. "Even before he made the world, God loved us and chose us in Christ to be holy and without fault in his eyes" (Ephesians 1:4, NLT).

Working through this adoption, I've come to understand God's love for His children even more. We are loved. We are chosen. And Jesus's gift of grace allows us to have a forever home. —TRICIA GOYER

FAITH STEP: *Write down a list of twenty important moments in history, starting with creation. After each one write, "I was on His mind." Thank Jesus for that fact.*

done ✓

SUNDAY, FEBRUARY 14

What do workers gain from their toil? I have seen the burden God has laid on the human race. He has made everything beautiful in its time. He has also set eternity in the human heart; yet no one can fathom what God has done from beginning to end. Ecclesiastes 3:9–11 (NIV)

THIS MORNING, SUNRISE PAINTS colored rays across the snow in perfect stillness. Soon squirrels will perform acrobatic acts through the treetops, birds will dart around looking for seeds, and wind will pick up and sculpt drifts against the shed. But for now, everything is still.

God created a universe with rhythms—night and day, work and rest, seasons of planting and harvest—and He created us to need those rhythms. He could have designed our bodies with no need for sleep, or food, or times of quiet, yet He put within our very cells the need for His rhythm.

I've had times in my life where I've pushed against those needs. I was so busy that the time it took to sleep or eat annoyed me. Sabbath rest? I'd take time to enjoy that in heaven.

"Busy" became a whip that beat my back when I slowed enough to breathe. "Busy" made me snap impatiently at my children. "Busy" became a competition with my friends as we complained about who had the most to do in the fewest hours.

Solomon wrote about life's rhythm as well as his struggle with a sense of futility. He caught a glimpse of the beauty of God's plan but yearned to understand more. Generations later, Jesus arrived and revealed a fuller picture. He demonstrated His love, the joyful eternity ahead, and the precious value of each day spent following Him. Because of Jesus, we can be free from the slavery of frantic busyness, and we can watch Him make everything beautiful in its time. —SHARON HINCK

FAITH STEP: *Thank Jesus for setting eternity in your heart. Ask Him to help you follow His rhythm today and to help you trust Him to make all things beautiful in the right time.*

MONDAY, FEBRUARY 15

Be cheerful no matter what . . . thank God no matter what happens. This is the way God wants you who belong to Christ Jesus to live. 1 Thessalonians 5:16, 18 (MSG)

RECENTLY, I ACCIDENTALLY LOCKED MYSELF out of the house without my phone or keys. It was a near freezing day and my husband was running some errands. I wasn't even sure when he'd be back.

Dressed in a thin blouse and "comfy" pants, I rubbed my arms for warmth and walked to one of my neighbors' homes. But no one answered the door. Shivering, I backtracked to try another neighbor. Same response. No one home.

"Lord, is anyone home today?" I prayed. "I could sure use some help." Almost twenty minutes had passed.

I decided to try one more home farther down the street. Within seconds, my cheerful neighbor opened her door, smiling. She handed me her cell phone to call my husband, then quickly heated a blanket in the dryer and wrapped it around me. The shivering stopped. I called my husband, but only a voice mail greeted me. So I chatted with my neighbor for half an hour longer as she told me about her experience several years ago when she'd fallen and broken her leg outside her front door in fifteen-degree weather. Only no one found her until an hour and a half later.

Jesus had not only answered my prayer, but He had prepared ahead for my blunder by providing a compassionate neighbor who understood exactly what I needed. My situation wasn't as dire as hers, but it opened the door to some sweet reconnection time with her.

It was also a reminder to be cheerful and give thanks—no matter what happens. —REBECCA BARLOW JORDAN

FAITH STEP: *Watch for ways to show cheerfulness and kindness to the ones in your neighborhood. Better yet, pray that Jesus will open that door of opportunity for you.*

~~one~~ TUESDAY, FEBRUARY 16

---

*You didn't choose me. I chose you. I appointed you to go and produce fruit
that will last, so that the Father will give you whatever
you ask for, using my name. John 15:16 (NLT)*

DO YOU BELIEVE YOUR LIFE MATTERS? It does! Jesus has handpicked you to
make an eternal difference in our world.

Unfortunately, life's day-to-day busyness can cause us to lose sight of
this exciting truth. Sometimes we feel as though we exist only to work,
pay bills, and juggle too many responsibilities. We rise in the morning, do
what needs to be done, fall into bed at night, and then repeat.

Perhaps our natural desire for security and comfort causes us to ignore
this truth. We love knowing that Jesus has chosen us, but the mandate to
produce fruit doesn't appeal because it might require personal cost.

Some folks want to live a fruitful life, but Satan's duped them into
believing lies. They mistakenly think youth or inexperience disqualifies
them. Others believe their sinful past renders them useless now. Nothing's
further from the truth because Jesus has redeemed our past. He turns our
broken places into our most effective ministry.

Jesus's mandate to go and produce fruit applies to all believers although
its specifics are unique to individuals and their life seasons. It may mean a
visible and far-reaching ministry, or it may mean faithfully serving where
no one's watching. Bottom line—Jesus's purpose for His followers is to
produce eternal fruit. The secret to doing this most effectively is this:
maintain a healthy and strong relationship with Him. If we do this, then
fruitfulness happens and His purpose is fulfilled. —GRACE FOX

FAITH STEP: *Savor a piece of your favorite fruit today. As you do so, ponder
John 15:5 (NLT)—"Yes, I am the vine; you are the branches. Those who remain in me,
and I in them, will produce much fruit. For apart from me you can do nothing."*

~~ONE~~ WEDNESDAY, FEBRUARY 17

I will praise the Lord at all times; His praise will always be on my lips.
Psalm 34:1 (HCS)

"THAT IS *YOUR* COLOR," I told my friend when we connected in a conference room for a meeting. "That lipstick is the perfect shade for you."

"Thanks. You'll never guess what it's called."

"What?"

"*Prayer*. Seriously. That's its color name."

I haven't been able to shake that short conversation since. Imagine wearing prayer on your lips every day... and having people comment about how beautiful it is. Praise and prayer are always a good look, always "becoming," as we read in Psalm 147:1.

Too often we let anger, bitterness, impatience, gossip, unkindness color our lips—all things Jesus abhors and teaches strenuously against. The overflow from our lips is anything but honoring to Him at those times.

Psalm 119:171 (CEB) has become the cry of my heart: "Let my lips overflow with praise." After seeing that subtle and beautiful color of lipstick on my friend, I've added *prayer* to that prayer. If prayer and praise were on my lips continuously, where would gossip or complaint or anger find room to roost?

Even after getting these thoughts on paper, the concept won't leave me alone. I'm on a mission now to track down other verses of Scripture that show what Jesus longs to see "on" my lips. Compassion, kindness, joy, encouragement, peace, patience, tenderness, truth...

I can't wait for the day when someone tells me, "You have a little something there on your lips," so I can truthfully answer, "I know. It's prayer."
—CYNTHIA RUCHTI

FAITH STEP: *Whether you wear lip balm, gloss, or lipstick, consider wrapping the tube or container with a sticker labeled "Prayer" as a reminder to let prayer and praise be continuously on your lips.*

THURSDAY, FEBRUARY 18

You keep track of all my sorrows. You have collected all my tears in your bottle. You have recorded each one in your book. Psalm 56:8 (NLT)

I CRIED TODAY. Alone in the cabin, when one too many things went wrong, I cried like a baby. And God cared.

I'm a crier. I was in the seventh grade before I went a whole day without shedding tears. As an adult, I went into nursing, fraught with joy and sorrow. I worked in the Neonatal ICU and cried with families whose dreams came true and others whose hopes died with their babies. When I became a neonatal nurse practitioner, tears became a luxury I couldn't afford, since I had to switch gears rapidly, moving from a dying baby to one who needed me to calculate an Isuprel drip. My tears distressed families with critically ill children.

It's unhealthy to bottle up your feelings, so I prayed, asking for help to grieve appropriately but later maybe, when it wouldn't affect my work or someone else's confidence in me as a caregiver. I cried in the call room, in the car, or when I got home, but I made sure I did it.

Fake tears, and those from laughter, pain, or peeling onions, differ microscopically from tears of sorrow. God knows when we're pushed past our limits, when we're beyond sorry and when our hearts break.

Jesus said those who weep are blessed and He promised they would laugh. He knows tears. He made some of His own. His Father cares enough about our tears to record them—even save them in a bottle.

Yes, we cry now, but someday we'll see Jesus—the Savior Who cried like us. On that day, the Lamb on the Throne will shepherd us and His Father will wipe every tear from our eyes. —SUZANNE DAVENPORT TIETJEN

FAITH STEP: *Many people are embarrassed by tears or refuse to cry at all—alone or with others. Do you hold back tears? Or weep with those who weep? Give your honest tears to Jesus.*

FRIDAY, FEBRUARY 19

The wisest of women builds her house, but folly with her own hands tears it down.
Proverbs 14:1 (ESV)

IN MY HUSBAND'S JOB as project manager for a commercial contractor, he oversees lots of building projects. Over the years he has managed the construction of schools, banks, churches, museums, medical offices, factories, warehouses, parking garages, dorms, you name it.

Right now he is working on a bank renovation that involves a reconfiguration of the customer space while the project is in process. Because of the issues associated with money and the vault, security is strict and space to move around is limited.

But Steve is earning a reputation among the employees as being a favorite contractor because he initiated a "Happy Hour" on Fridays when he passes around chocolate and other treats to the employees. It's a small but unexpected gesture that has proven to lift morale week after week. As he's building buildings, he is also building up people.

At the end of a long week his face lit up as he laughed and told me how one teller gets as excited as...well, as a kid in a candy store when he delivers the treats. It's only chocolate, but it says so much more.

His story has been a reminder to me of Proverbs 14:1 and my role in building up my family in our home. If I am wise, I will be a builder of their hearts instead of a demolisher. My attitudes, tone, expressions, body language, habits with time, and creative encouragement all build up or tear down.

If I am wise I will choose each moment well and look for special ways to encourage my husband and children. Small gestures that show I see them and care how they're doing may be just what they need today.
—ERIN KEELEY MARSHALL

FAITH STEP: *Find a creative way to build up someone today.*

SATURDAY, FEBRUARY 20

My heart has heard you say, "Come and talk with me." And my heart responds, "Lord, I am coming." Psalm 27:8 (NLT)

WHEN I NEEDED A NEW LAPTOP two years ago, I made the switch to a Mac. I've never regretted that decision, although there was a learning curve in the beginning. I attended training sessions in the store and watched online tutorials. Even so, I still occasionally discover some new feature I haven't made use of before.

I recently noticed the Reminders icon in the dock at the bottom of the screen and realized I'd never even checked it out. Clicking on the symbol that looks like a tiny to-do list, I was surprised to see that it already contained one item: "Call me, Lacey." What a sweet memento of my granddaughter's visit a month earlier. Not that I need a reminder to call her. I wish I could talk with her every single day, but with the distance between us and her family's busy lifestyle, that's not feasible.

I wish I could honestly say that I always have that much passion for talking with Jesus. I cringe to think of how many days I let slip by without making the time to talk with Him in prayer. How can I let a busy schedule keep me from praising the source of all the goodness and blessings in my life? How could I be so foolish as to not seek His guidance and supernatural strength for whatever the day will bring?

Since I like to-do lists, I decided to start topping mine with the reminder to talk to Jesus. What a difference this has made in my day. I've learned that I can live without crossing off every item on my list, but I certainly can't live very well if I don't complete the first item.
—DIANNE NEAL MATTHEWS

FAITH STEP: *Determine to make prayer your first priority. Add "Talk to Jesus" at the top of your to-do list, or use a sticky note on your mirror. After one week, examine how this has affected your life.*

SUNDAY, FEBRUARY 21

For I know that in me (that is, in my flesh,) dwelleth no good thing; for to will is present with me; but how to perform that which is good I find not. Romans 7:18 (KJV)

A YOUNG MAN SHOWED UP at our church after a long absence. My husband and I hadn't had any contact with him for years. What did it mean that when the worship service was over he didn't exit the sanctuary as others did, but sat, bent forward, weeping?

How easy it would have been to leave the sanctuary or ask one of the prayer team members or a pastor to go talk to him. But I couldn't escape the sense that God was tapping me on the shoulder to speak to him, sit with him, or pray for him.

The young man seemed both blessed and pained by what he'd heard in the service. "Why is it that the wrong thing is so irresistibly appealing?" he said pensively. "I know what I should do, what I want to do. But the pull of the wrong is so strong."

He cared what God thought. He longed to do what would please Jesus. His confession sounded so much like a great man of the faith—the Apostle Paul.

"The desire to do good is inside of me, but I can't do it. I don't do the good that I want to do, but I do the evil that I don't want to do" (Romans 7:18–19, CEB).

That Sunday, the young man went beyond that affirming passage to the one a few verses later: "Who will deliver me from this...? Thank God through Jesus Christ our Lord!" (Romans 7:24–25, CEB). Jesus reminded the young man that's exactly why He came.

The next week, the young man was not only back, but sitting in the front row, worshipping! —CYNTHIA RUCHTI

FAITH STEP: *Is your area of temptation related to what you watch, listen to, say, eat...? Put this victory verse on the television remote, refrigerator door, radio dial, phone: "Who will deliver me from this...? Thank God through Jesus Christ our Lord!"*

MONDAY, FEBRUARY 22

So neither the one who plants nor the one who waters is anything, but only God, who makes things grow. 1 Corinthians 3:7 (NIV)

I CURRENTLY HAVE THREE growing boys living in my house. They are eating. A. Lot. All. Day. Long. The cupboards are bare. The thirteen-year-old is inhaling food like it is air. In the past month he has grown an inch and leap-frogged a whole shoe size. Yesterday morning, the eleven-year-old was coming toward me down the hall and he looked taller. We had just measured their heights a week ago but I made him step up to the wall again. He had grown three-quarters of an inch in nine days. Nine days. The eight-year-old is taking them all down. He is about three inches taller than the other two were at his age.

Scott told me yesterday, "You have been spending a lot of money." I had made fifteen trips to the grocery store in a two-week period. Is it possible to eat a flat of nectarines in a day? Yes, it is. A box of cereal in one sitting? Yes. I am thinking of plowing up the lawn in the backyard and putting in corn for the coming winter.

But it has got me thinking about what it takes to keep us maturing in our faith. We are like growing boys. Every day is an opportunity to become more of the person that Jesus created us to be. Just like I can't neglect feeding my boys, we can't neglect feeding our spirits. Nourishing ourselves with His Word, stretching our faith with prayer, and encouraging that growth by surrounding ourselves with other Christ followers so we can grow and mature together. Let's keep growing into the people who look like the One Who loves us most of all. —SUSANNA FOTH AUGHTMON

FAITH STEP: *Ask yourself, "What am I doing to grow in my faith?" And pray, "Jesus, show me how to grow to be more like You today."*

oml TUESDAY, FEBRUARY 23

"When you're in rough waters, you will not go down. When you're between a rock and a hard place, it won't be a dead end. . . . That's how much you mean to me!"
Isaiah 43:2, 4 (MSG)

"EVERYTHING HAS GONE WRONG. I don't know what to do." The words from a stranger blinked from my e-mail box, begging for a reply, some kind of explanation that would soothe the heart's agony and confusion. The writer of the e-mail was suffering and wanted to know why.

The mercy in me wanted initially to soften the pain. But what could I say to encourage this person or to alleviate the suffering he or she faced? Trite words wouldn't suffice. I prayed for this stranger and asked God for wisdom.

Later, as I was reading my Bible, I ran across Jesus's words to Peter. This disciple wanted to short-cut suffering in his beloved Master's life. Reacting to Jesus's statement that He must suffer, Peter protested. But Jesus confronted Peter boldly: "Peter, get out of my way! . . . You have no idea how God works. . . . Don't run from suffering; embrace it" (Mark 8:33–34, MSG).

Jesus's words ripped at my heart. He was speaking to me too. I needed to get out of His way. No, I didn't understand suffering. No, I had no idea how God worked. But I did know that if we are to follow Jesus, we must let Him lead (Mark 8:34, MSG). When He's in the driver's seat, He'll show us what to do and how to trust Him. He'll make a way.

Suffering has its purposes. It can purify our lives. It can deepen our faith. It can even create a platform so others can know Him.

The promise in Isaiah still gives us hope. Jesus's own suffering secured that promise. We may not understand how God works. But we can bank on the truth that love is behind everything He does.

Because we mean the world to Him. —REBECCA BARLOW JORDAN

FAITH STEP: *Give thanks today for any painful circumstances. And thank Jesus that His pain was our gain.*

WEDNESDAY, FEBRUARY 24

Work hard so you can present yourself to God and receive his approval.
Be a good worker, one who does not need to be ashamed and who correctly
explains the word of truth. 2 Timothy 2:15 (NLT)

I'VE BEEN WORKING WITH teen moms for over a decade, but when I first started spending time with them I felt very intimidated. They often came to our support group meetings with their guard up. They answered my questions as briefly as possible. They had the Great Wall of China around their hearts. There were nights when I returned home from our meetings, and I wondered why they continued to come to the support group—they didn't seem to enjoy it at all. Slowly things began to change. First, I noticed a softened outward appearance, and then I noticed changed attitudes. Some of these young moms accepted Jesus Christ as their personal Savior. And soon our relationships began to grow.

What did this teach me? After the young moms trusted my heart, only then did they begin to trust my words. Once they trusted my advice about parenting and life, they started to also listen to me share my faith. In the end, the best tool to "win the hearts" of teen moms was to offer undivided love first. After they felt my love, then they were willing to hear of Jesus's love too.

People will believe what we say after they see how we love. I felt the call to serve Jesus, and He led me to loving these young women. As I continued to reach out and help them, they began to trust my heart, and soon they trusted Jesus's heart too. —TRICIA GOYER

FAITH STEP: *Is there someone whom you tried to help but who turned a cold shoulder to you? Did you give up trying to reach out again? Think of one way to keep trying. Your acts of love can penetrate a hard heart.*

THURSDAY, FEBRUARY 25

Then Abraham bowed down to the ground, but he laughed to himself in disbelief. "How could I become a father at the age of 100?" he wondered. "Besides, Sarah is ninety; how could she have a baby?" Genesis 17:17 (NLT)

JESUS SPECIALIZES IN DOING the impossible; humankind specializes in questioning how He's going to do it. This seems a common occurrence even in the lives of those we consider spiritual giants.

The angel of the Lord promised Abraham that senior Sarah would bear a son, and Abraham responded with amused unbelief.

Sarah laughed and questioned too. She said, "How could a worn-out woman like me have a baby?" (Genesis 18:12).

When an angel visited Mary and told her that she would conceive God's son, she said, "But how can I have a baby? I am a virgin" (Luke 1:34).

Impossibilities are nothing for Jesus. He heals the sick and gives sight to the blind. He calms the wild waves, feeds the masses with a few loaves and a couple of fish, and raises the dead. Why then do we doubt when He asks us to trust Him to provide for our needs, care for our kids, and equip us to do what He's calling us to do?

Abraham laughed in disbelief even as he bowed in worship. We do the same thing when we nod in agreement with Luke 1:37—"For nothing is impossible with God"—and then grow anxious and question, "How in the world is Jesus going to pull that off?" The odds may seem stacked against you, but don't lose heart. Jesus specializes in doing the impossible. Trust Him with the details. —GRACE FOX

FAITH STEP: *For what need are you trusting Jesus today? List your "how" questions on a sheet of paper. Write "nothing is impossible" across them, and then praise Jesus for His ability to do anything, especially to beat the odds.*

one # FRIDAY, FEBRUARY 26

I can do all things through Christ who strengthens me.
Philippians 4:13 (NKJV)

MY TWO-YEAR-OLD, STELLA, has gotten into the habit of saying, "This is too hard for me." And while I want to teach her to know her limitations when something truly is beyond her resources, she can't say that every time she encounters a difficulty in life. So, instead of encouraging this habit, I've been counteracting it with, "But you can do hard things!"

At first, she was skeptical of my tactics. She'd become frustrated with a puzzle, trying to cram a piece the shape of a chicken into the space for a pig. "This is too hard!"

I'd help her fit the piece into the correct place. "But you can do hard things."

Picking up messes is apparently also a fierce challenge. "Maybe just pick up one thing at a time. Remember, you can do hard things!"

The other day we were cracking peanuts. I wasn't thinking about our learning exercise when I said, "These peanuts are hard to crack open."

Stella looked at me with her big blue eyes. "Yes, Mommy. But I can do hard things."

I burst out laughing and hugged her. "That's right! You can do lots of hard things, can't you?"

She nodded in all seriousness. "I am awesome at doing hard things."

Sometimes a thing we face may seem so challenging we think there's no way we can do it. But, hard things are Jesus's specialty. The Bible says His strength is made perfect in our weakness. It's not that we need to go seeking hard things, but when challenges come our way we don't have to be afraid of them. We can be awesome at doing hard things through Christ Who gives us strength. —GWEN FORD FAULKENBERRY

FAITH STEP: *What's the most difficult thing you are facing today? Memorize Philippians 4:13 and remember you can do it, whatever it is, because Jesus lives in you.*

SATURDAY, FEBRUARY 27

Cast all your anxiety on him because he cares for you. 1 Peter 5:7 (NIV)

"DOES ANYONE REALLY CARE?" A woman's comment left on my blog grabbed my attention.

The woman who had found her way to my Web site was facing homelessness for the first time. Early in our marriage we experienced some lean times, and we lived on fifteen-cent hamburgers for a few weeks. But I'd never walked in this woman's shoes.

I did know Someone who could identify perfectly with her situation. Jesus, too, had no permanent place to call His own on earth (Matthew 8:20). At times, His only pillow was a rock. Yet in His lean times He showed us God is always there.

Jesus was teaching some life principles to a crowd one day. Comparing how much He cared for His creation, like the birds of the air, and how He met their needs, Jesus said, "Are you not much more valuable than they?" (Matthew 6:26, NIV). Later, Jesus taught, "Not one sparrow...can fall to the ground without your Father knowing it" (Matthew 10:29, TLB).

Those words always bring tears to my eyes, especially when I see a baby bird fallen to the ground from its nest. Jesus knows! And He cares for even the smallest creature.

But imagine how Jesus feels when we hurt: we, the crowning glory of His creation, who were created "a little lower than the angels" (Psalm 8:5, TLB). Any of us could experience homelessness one day. But one thing is for sure. Jesus, the One Who knows us, hurts with us, and died for us—this same Jesus cares about everything we go through, and He will provide what we need. That brings tears to my eyes—and a smile to my heart.
—REBECCA BARLOW JORDAN

FAITH STEP: *Thank Jesus today for the many ways He cares for you. Then pray for someone else who needs to know that too.*

SUNDAY, FEBRUARY 28

LAST WORDS OF CHRIST
ONE: MERCY

Jesus said, "Father, forgive them, for they do not know what they are doing."
And they divided up his clothes by casting lots. Luke 23:34 (NIV)

DURING THE LENTEN SEASON, followers of Jesus through the centuries have taken time to ponder the "Seven Last Words" of Christ on the Cross. In the moments where He was fulfilling His promise to bring salvation to all humankind, each sentence He spoke echoes with the music of love, grace, and compassion.

Because of the gift of Scripture, we can join those who stood beneath the Cross and hear His voice as He continues to speak to us today.

The first recorded words are a prayer, very fitting for the Son who spent so much time in communion with the Father. Yet the prayer is no longer "Remove this cup," or even, "Give me strength to endure." He intercedes for the very soldiers who pounded nails into Him, for the jeering crowd who had screamed, "Crucify Him," and even the men who scrabbled around in the shadow of the Cross ignoring His suffering and greedily grasping for His few possessions.

Suffering in our life comes in many forms. Sometimes others are intentionally cruel. We may face injustice, attacks, or betrayals that affect our work or our relationships. We may be harmed by crime, war, poverty. Other times the wounds are less deliberate. The deepest pain sometimes comes through a thoughtless statement from a child or spouse or a careless act by a dear friend. When others hurt us, let us fight through the pain and tears to grasp this prayer of mercy: "Father, forgive." —SHARON HINCK

FAITH STEP: *Who has hurt you recently? Ask Jesus to help you pray this prayer of mercy for them.*

MONDAY, FEBRUARY 29

LAST WORDS OF CHRIST
TWO: WITH ME

Jesus answered him, "Truly I tell you, today you will be with me in paradise."
Luke 23:43 (NIV)

I'M FASCINATED BY THE GLIMPSES that Scripture gives about heaven and the sequence of events after we die. But studying the theories of various theologians befuddles me. The uncertainties don't cause anxiety, though. Jesus hasn't revealed every detail about the joys ahead—probably because our puny brains can't fully grasp the heights of beauty and depths of fellowship around the corner. But the analogies He gave for heaven give us plenty to go on: joyous wedding banquets, a new home lovingly prepared for us, treasures stored up, new glorified bodies, a place where tears are wiped away.

I held my grandmother as she drew her last breath. I've prayed and cried with friends in the last stages of terminal illness. Life on earth is a precious gift, and we rightly fight for each minute. Yet my loved ones who were on the threshold of heaven also expressed peace because they knew their journey was about to take them into even truer life.

Perhaps my favorite peek into why heaven will be glorious is found in Jesus's words from the Cross. He promises a thief hanging beside Him, "Today you will be with me in paradise." While scholars debate the meaning in that statement, my heart is gripped by two words: "with me."

That's all I need to know about what will happen after I die. I will be with Jesus. Yes, He lives in my heart. Yes, prayer allows me to commune with Him. But I long for the day when I'll see Him face to face. I'm so grateful that even while He suffered on the Cross, Jesus took time to reassure the man about to die—and through those words He reassures us all.
—SHARON HINCK

FAITH STEP: *Using a concordance, find Bible verses that describe heaven. Thank Jesus for His promise that He is with you now, and will be with you later.*

TUESDAY, MARCH 1

LAST WORDS OF CHRIST
THREE: PRACTICAL COMPASSION

*When Jesus saw his mother there, and the disciple whom he loved standing nearby,
he said to her, "Woman, here is your son," and to the disciple, "Here is your mother."
From that time on, this disciple took her into his home. John 19:26–27 (NIV)*

OF ALL THE VERSES that depict Jesus's deep, profound, and tender
love for us, this one has always felt the most poignant to me. He was in
excruciating pain, beaten, bleeding, hanging on a Cross, bearing the sins
of the entire world. Yet as He struggled for breath, He took time to assure
the future care of His mother.

When I'm in pain, I rarely muster much interest in those around me.
It doesn't take hanging on a cross. To be honest, even a simple headache
can make me cranky toward everyone in my path. I don't spare any extra
energy to think about their needs. It's all about me.

So the way that Jesus showed care for His mother in this moment when He
was fulfilling His purpose on earth seems particularly comforting. His words
show me His love, but something else as well. His compassion was eminently
practical. He made sure she had a home, someone to provide for her.

There are times when I hesitate to bring my day-to-day concerns to
Jesus. Surely with all the huge problems in the world, and in the lives of
those I know, He has bigger needs to answer than a broken car, a remodeling project gone awry, or a decision about where to live. But then I
remember that at the most painful and crucial moments of His mission
on earth, He cared about His mother's welfare and tangible needs. He
cares for us as well. —SHARON HINCK

FAITH STEP: *Have you ever held back from talking to Jesus about some down-to-
earth concerns? Pick three today and ask for His help, knowing He cares.*

WEDNESDAY, MARCH 2

LAST WORDS OF CHRIST
FOUR: FORSAKEN

And at three in the afternoon Jesus cried out in a loud voice, "Eloi, Eloi, lema sabachthani?" (which means "My God, my God, why have you forsaken me?")
Mark 15:34 (NIV)

IN THE SOUTH DAKOTA BADLANDS, the sun beat down without mercy. Stark red cliffs rose toward the dizzying sky. Our family vacation hike had reached a new level of adventure. The trail led to a rough rope ladder that snaked several stories up the side of a cliff. Climbing up didn't worry me, but the return route required climbing down the same ladder, grappling for footholds. "I'll wait here."

"Are you sure?" my husband asked. "It'll take about an hour for us to get to the end and come back."

I convinced them all I'd like nothing better than to find a patch of shade and wait for them. I watched them disappear over the ridge. I paced the barren ground. No people, no animals, no plants. No company but the relentless sun as I realized my husband had our canteens, cell phone, snacks. The isolation hit me hard. I felt forsaken.

Forsaken. We've all had moments of that vast, empty, painful feeling. A teen hears that all her friends were at a party—and she wasn't invited. Or a son stands at his father's graveside, bereft. Or a woman hears her spouse say, "I'm leaving you." In our times of feeling utterly alone, we can cling to the knowledge that Jesus understands. He bore the deepest and most complete forsakenness as He carried the sins of the world and accepted His Father's rejection for our sakes. And because He endured desolation and suffering, we are now never forsaken. Jesus's love is as close and present as our next heartbeat. —SHARON HINCK

FAITH STEP: *Inspired by today's verse, pray this out loud: "My God, my God, thank You that because of Jesus I am never forsaken."*

THURSDAY, MARCH 3

LAST WORDS OF CHRIST
FIVE: "I THIRST"

After this, Jesus, knowing that all was now finished, said (to fulfill the Scripture),
"I thirst." John 19:28 (ESV)

THE FIRST FEW HOURS AFTER my friend's surgery, she was clearly in pain but wasn't coherent enough to talk. Sitting by her bed, I longed to do something to help. The only thing I could think of was to rub ice chips on her chapped lips. Later she told me that in the fogginess of her memories, she vividly recalled how much she craved a trickle of water, and how much those ice chips helped.

Of all the words of Jesus from the Cross, "I thirst" brings home His human nature. Two simple words, and such a basic longing.

I also hear the undercurrent of the deeper longings of Jesus's heart. He thirsts for us to receive the salvation bought for us with His own blood. He hungers for humanity to stop hiding from the Father. He longs for the day when all will be restored.

The Gospel of John tells us that Jesus spoke these words to fulfill Scripture. The Old Testament overflows with prophesies about the Messiah, and Jesus completes them all. His place of birth, the timing of His birth, the miracles of healing He brought during His earthly ministry, the manner of His death, and even this fulfillment of Psalm 69, "for my thirst they gave me sour wine to drink."

In this painful and poignant moment, it's a joy to remember that in a few days, Jesus would fulfill yet another prophesy: His promise that He would rise again. —SHARON HINCK

FAITH STEP: *Today, each time you take a drink of water, remember the thirst—both physical and emotional—that Jesus endured for your sake.*

FRIDAY, MARCH 4

LAST WORDS OF CHRIST
SIX AND SEVEN: "IT IS FINISHED"

When he had received the drink, Jesus said, "It is finished." With that, he bowed his head and gave up his spirit. . . . John 19:30 (NIV)

YEARS AGO, BUT STILL VIVID in my memory, I labored to deliver my baby. The hours were intense, the pain was real, the effort grueling. With a final push, she burst into the world. The hard work was finished. Except, of course, it wasn't. The adventure of parenting was only beginning.

Last year my daughter graduated from college. Years of hard work, struggle, growth, and sacrifice were finished. Except then the job search began. Turns out her journey is not over.

For years I worked on a novel, page by page, word by word. Joy filled me as I hit "send" and turned it in to my editor. A few weeks later I received editorial notes with suggested improvements. Rolling up my sleeves, I dove back into the story to tackle revisions. My work wasn't finished.

When Jesus commits His life into the hands of the Father and proclaims, "It is finished," it truly is. He lived a sinless life, and then carried the penalty of all the sins of the world and sacrificed Himself to save us. Yet sometimes I live as though His work isn't enough. As if I still have to please God in my own power, to earn forgiveness somehow.

We can hear the last words of Jesus from the Cross thunder across the ages. No more sacrifices, no more hiding in fear from our righteous God, no more doubt about whether we are loved. The debt is paid. It is finished! Rejoice! —SHARON HINCK

FAITH STEP: *Are there sins of attitude, word, or action that burden you today? Jot them on a piece of paper and then in bold letters write, "It is finished!" across them all.*

SATURDAY, MARCH 5

Jesus said . . . "I am the resurrection and the life.
Whoever believes in me will live, even though they die." John 11:25 (CEB)

SOMEONE I DON'T KNOW IS DYING, affecting me profoundly. She's let me and her thousands of blog followers behind the scenes in the emotional and spiritual process of saying a Jesus-enriched good-bye.

The medical community exhausted its resources for her. Jesus hasn't exhausted His, but at this moment is being most lavish with His remarkable resource of peace-when-death-is-imminent.

She's surrounded by friends and family, a caring husband, little ones who understand way too much about what's happening to Mommy. I am acutely aware that as I write these words, she may be drawing her last breath of earth-air, that poor substitute for all that lies ahead for her.

I wrote to her on a day when her blog reported her as *fading*. I'd hoped she—and I—could take comfort in the scene in my kitchen.

My husband had just brought me a bright bouquet of fuchsia daisy mums. They brought a stunning pop of joy to a string of gray days. The fuchsia dye leached into the water in the clear glass vase, turning the liquid a startling pink. The mums faded, but they faded exquisitely, leaving petals of white with fuchsia streaks and others with delicate pink. Beautiful when vibrant. Beautiful when being drained of color.

That's the wonder of the life Christ came to give us. The Jesus life—beautiful when in its prime, and expressing an even more delicate beauty when that life is about to transition to the eternal one Jesus died to offer us. Beauty upon beauty. Grace upon grace. —CYNTHIA RUCHTI

FAITH STEP: *During the process of living, it's easy to forget to thank Jesus for what He did to change the face of dying. Become part of the groundswell of gratitude. He offers life beyond this life.*

SUNDAY, MARCH 6

And while he was still a long way off, his father saw him coming.
Filled with love and compassion, he ran to his son, embraced him, and kissed him.
Luke 15:20 (NLT)

IN OUR YEARS OF CHURCH MINISTRY, my husband and I have empathized with the stories tumbling from parents' lips: tales of rebellion, disappointment, and angst resulting from the poor choices their children made as teens or young adults. Many of these parents were overcome with sorrow and heartache.

Each time I listened to their pain, I thought of the story Jesus told in Luke about the prodigal son. A young adult, headstrong and determined, demanded his early inheritance from his godly parents and set out on a path to self-destruction. Acting on prideful dreams and foolish lifestyles, he ended up slopping pigs. A famine left him penniless and destitute. He longed for home again. But how could he return?

His father, always watching and waiting, kept on working. One day in the distance, he spotted his long-lost son. To prevent the neighbors from shaming his rebellious son as he approached, by noisily smashing their jars filled with corn and grain—a common practice of that time—the father was "filled with love and compassion." He *ran* to embrace his son and gave him not the kiss of death, but the kiss of life.

Jesus's parable is not just about parents and children. It's about me—and you. We, who've made our share of bad choices and selfish indulgences; we have gone our own way, sometimes away from Him. Yet we are the ones Jesus embraces, erasing the shame of our errant past before others can drive it deeper into our souls. He offers the kiss of life, and like the father for his prodigal son, Jesus plans a feast for us in heaven. Why? Because His love will always trump our weakness. —REBECCA BARLOW JORDAN

FAITH STEP: *Review the entire story of the prodigal son in Luke 15:11–32. Thank Jesus today for His unconditional love.*

MONDAY, MARCH 7

This day I call the heavens and the earth as witnesses against you that I have set before you life and death, blessings and curses. Now choose life, so that you and your children may live and that you may love the Lord your God, listen to his voice, and hold fast to him. For the Lord is your life, and he will give you many years in the land he swore to give to your fathers, Abraham, Isaac and Jacob.
Deuteronomy 30:19–20 (NIV)

THIS MORNING AS I WAS TRYING to get the boys out the door for school, they made an exciting discovery on the fireplace mantel. In a lacy pocket of spider web between a starfish and a candlestick, a mother spider had hatched about fifty tiny spiders, each the size of a straight pinhead. They were crawling all over the web, testing out their tiny legs. My boys were ecstatic. "That is so cool!" "*Awwww*! They are so cute." Jack breathed a sigh of happiness. "This is life."

"No...," I said, reaching for a nearby magazine. "This is death."

There was a communal outcry. "No! Mom! Don't kill them." "You can't! They are babies!" Jack started singing the song... "Speak life! Speak life!"

I couldn't begin the morning with an arachnid massacre. I slid the magazine under the starfish and deposited the magazine on the floor of our outdoor patio, which, I am sure, is full of spiders already. I chose life for those little spiders...but we have a personal choice every day between life and death. We forget that every time we choose to follow Jesus, we choose life. Every time we choose to follow our own selfish desires, we choose death. Jesus has chosen to set us free... now all we have to do is choose to listen for His voice and hold fast to Him. I don't think it is a very hard decision to make. —SUSANNA FOTH AUGHTMON

FAITH STEP: *Make your own reminder sign that reads "I choose life" and put it on the front of your fridge.*

one TUESDAY, MARCH 8

For God gave us not a spirit of fearfulness; but of power and love and discipline.
2 Timothy 1:7 (ASV)

THERE ARE TIMES WHEN I've had to step out with courage. Like during a mission trip when I handed out Bibles on the street. Or when I walked through the slums of Nairobi, Kenya, behind an armed guard (because the place we were going to was dangerous). I discovered that sometimes it's easier being courageous during big events than it is during daily ones. It takes courage to approach a new visitor at church. It takes courage to incorporate family devotions into your schedule.

Sometimes being courageous is simply stepping outside of your comfort zone. It's setting up a chore chart for your children even when you worry it'll take a lot of work to maintain. It takes courage to ask your husband to pray for you, especially when you don't want him to know how weak you really are. It's courageous to sign up for that Bible study when you don't know the other women well. Thankfully there is some place we can go when we need courage—straight to the heart of Jesus. He wants us to have peace even when peace seems far away.

As John 14:27 (NIV) says, "Peace I leave with you; my peace I give you. I do not give to you as the world gives. Do not let your hearts be troubled and do not be afraid."

Fear isn't only found when you walk into physical danger or walk onto a busy street with a Bible in your hand. It's about the little things, too, and Jesus will give you peace for whatever you need courage. Turn to Him. If it's worth worrying about, it's worth talking to Jesus about. —TRICIA GOYER

FAITH STEP: *What's one thing that you need courage for in your daily life? Turn to Jesus. Ask Him to give you strength. Ask Him to give you peace.*

~~one~~ WEDNESDAY, MARCH 9

I prayed to the Lord, and he answered me. He freed me from all my fears. . . .
In my desperation I prayed, and the Lord listened; he saved me
from all my troubles. Psalm 34:4, 6 (NLT)

TWO THINGS USED TO MAKE ME SQUIRM: snakes, and driving on dangerous mountain roads. Living in Nepal in the eighties meant facing both.

One day a six-foot rat snake slithered into my house, and I nearly died of fright. Seriously, I wanted to catch the first bus to Kathmandu and return to North America forever. Trouble was, making that trip meant riding on dangerous mountain roads, and I didn't fancy that, especially with my three-week-old baby. Besides, running from my God-given task would have been disobedience, and I didn't consider that an option.

Fear of snakes and dangerous mountain roads could have paralyzed me. Instead, I asked Jesus for help. He didn't free me from snakes and mountain roads, but He freed me from my fear of them. That freedom remains to this day. My husband and I have returned to Nepal several times. Doing so revives memories of snake encounters. It also means driving for twenty hours on narrow mountain roads. But I refuse to succumb to my fears because Jesus has set me free.

With what fears do you struggle? Perhaps the fear of financial insecurity haunts you. Or the fear of failure or of your kids falling into harm's way. How intense is that fear's grip on you? Does it hinder you from experiencing the abundant life Jesus promises to His followers?

Fear needn't paralyze us. Let's view it as the catalyst to knowing Jesus better. In His presence we find freedom from all our fears for all time.
—GRACE FOX

FAITH STEP: *FEAR stands for "False Expectations Appearing Real." How does this acronym apply to you today? Hold a conversation on this topic with a friend. Ask what his or her fears are, and pray together.*

~~one~~ THURSDAY, MARCH 10

He keeps us in step with each other. His very breath and blood flow through us,
nourishing us so that we will grow up healthy in God, robust in love.
Ephesians 4:16 (MSG)

I REMEMBER STRUGGLING to stay awake during a lecture in nurse practitio-ner school, when my professor surprised me into sitting up straight. I glanced to see if my colleagues had been struck by his amazing statement, but they looked as bored as I'd been. He said: "Wellness or illness is a cellular phe-nomenon." Maybe he noticed he'd caught my attention because he looked my way and said it again. When we're ill, we may feel bad all over, but ill-ness starts with the cell—invaded, destroyed, or malfunctioning. These tiny units (roughly one-hundred trillion of them) constantly absorb nutrients, process them, make energy, and reproduce. They're interdependent; one cell's problem affects many other cells. When cells get sick or broken, so do we. Wellness is the same. Each cell performs vital functions so life goes on. Our bloodstream moves what's needed and what isn't wherever it needs to go.

That lecture changed the way I saw the human body. And the church. Even the Lord's Supper. We are the church—the Body of Christ—indeed, each one of us a part "of his resurrection body, refreshed and sustained at one fountain—his Spirit—where we all come to drink" (1 Corinthians 12:13, MSG). When I eat the bread and wine Jesus called His body and blood, I picture the elements moving in a very real way to my cells. Some of their molecules become part of me. We are indwelt in ways we can't fully understand.

For the body of Christ to be healthy, we each play a part with Jesus as our source, careful of those around us. Part of something beautiful, bigger than we can imagine. —SUZANNE DAVENPORT TIETJEN

FAITH STEP: *Think small today. Small, but crucial, like your trillions of cells. Ask Jesus to show you what to do; then serve in secret. Start over if someone finds out.*

FRIDAY, MARCH 11

Look, today I am giving you the choice between a blessing and a curse! You will be blessed if you obey the commands of the Lord your God that I am giving you today. But you will be cursed if you reject the commands of the Lord your God and turn away from him and worship gods you have not known before.
Deuteronomy 11:26–28 (NLT)

WE'VE HAD A LOT OF GRAY DAYS LATELY. The leaves are still gone from the trees, and the branches reach up to the sky like skeleton hands grasping for a bit of life. It is early spring and soon their time will come. But for now they appear desperate.

Gray is like that—desperate for light to add color and vitality. Gray commitment to Jesus looks much the same, as if it needs a fresh reminder of the redness of His blood that pulsed out of Him to give us life.

Every day we face choices between living Jesus's way or doing our own thing, which often strips us of life, like a curse. Yet when we choose to live His way, we are choosing to be blessed by Him. *Obedience always brings blessing. Disobedience always brings pain.* These truths are spoken frequently at my church, and they come right out of Deuteronomy 11:26–28.

We humans can be smart. We can earn degrees and study to fill our heads with knowledge. But intelligence and knowledge are not synonymous with wisdom and holy living. The God who gave the commands in the Old Testament is the One Who sent His Son, Jesus, to teach us more about living His way. And Jesus sent His Spirit to empower believers to understand and choose the blessing of walking in His truth.

The leaves on the trees outside my window will soon bud and grow. They do not choose whether to do so. They simply act as they've been commanded. But we have options to either live the default but detrimental way of our own nature or to pursue Jesus's blessing. —ERIN KEELEY MARSHALL

FAITH STEP: *Consider an area where you struggle to live by Jesus's standard. Ask Him to reveal any idols that work to pull you away from Him.*

SATURDAY, MARCH 12

"Here on earth you will have many trials and sorrows. But take heart, because I have overcome the world." John 16:33 (NLT)

LAST MARCH DURING A WEEKLONG TRIP through several states, my friend Kathryn surprised me with a potted shamrock. Although I love the shape of the leaves and the delicate white blooms, I'd always thought the shamrock might be a finicky plant to care for. And my thumbs aren't exactly green. Now I wondered if the shamrock (which I'd named "Lucky") would survive the nine-hundred-mile trip from Illinois back to Texas.

At my daughter's house in Tennessee, I accidentally left Lucky on the front porch overnight while the temperature dipped to an unusual low. Two days later we set out for my parents' house a few hours away. I gave Lucky a good soaking and set it in the sunny rear window of the car. Then I read online that shamrocks don't like direct sun or being wet.

That evening my mom saw the leaves folded up for the night and assumed it indicated a need for water, so she doused Lucky. Two nights later, my mother-in-law did the same thing. Amazingly, a few days after I got home with my drowned shamrock, Lucky produced a stem of tiny white blooms. At that point I changed its name to "Blessed."

We may talk about good luck, but the truth is, anything good in my life comes from the blessings I have in Christ. And if I'm able to thrive in the midst of trials and troubles, it's only because of Jesus. He overcame persecution, humiliation, and a horrible death. Now He wants to give me the power to bloom even in the worst of conditions. I see a reminder of that every time I look at the plant formerly known as Lucky.

—DIANNE NEAL MATTHEWS

FAITH STEP: *The next time you face a trial, or simply feel unlucky, write a note that says "I am Blessed." Keep it in a conspicuous place and ask Jesus to help you overcome your circumstances.*

SUNDAY, MARCH 13

But if we hope for what we do not yet have, we wait for it patiently.
Romans 8:25 (NIV)

A LOT IS SAID ABOUT living the Christian life—joy, love, patience, prayer, worship...the stuff of faithfulness. But there's a lesser-acknowledged display of spiritual maturity that deserves a moment in the limelight. It's the practice of waiting well.

For the past several months my family has been waiting for an answer to a prayer on behalf of a loved one. We feel discouraged by our inability to fix the situation. Every week or so my husband and I remind each other that God seems to be saying, *It's your time to wait. It's my time to act.* Understanding that He is often working most during the waiting times boosts our faith once again.

To wait well and live with character as Jesus did shows some of the greatest spiritual muscle we ever could develop.

Although Job lived long before Romans 8:25 was written, he understood its truth. He waited for healing, but it did not come soon. As he writhed in pain, he grieved the deaths of his children, the losses of livelihood and reputation, and his wife's grief and pressure to turn on the Lord.

Imagine not having real hope in the wait. I'm not sure we can wait well without real hope. First Corinthians 15:19 (NIV) says, "If only for this life we have hope in Christ, we are of all people most to be pitied." Hope has no meat unless it's rooted in a power that guarantees it. And hope doesn't carry much weight if it only gets us through our mortal life. We wait with hope for *more*.

Jesus ushered in a hope that lives forever; it is our life-breath, and it will not fail (1 Peter 1:3). It was born out of God's mercy and guaranteed through Jesus's sacrifice. This mercy-filled hope carries us through the wait into eternity. Embracing it helps us wait well. —ERIN KEELEY MARSHALL

FAITH STEP: *Write out one of the three Scriptures from today's devotion. Keep it nearby to remind you to wait well.*

ᴅᴍᴋ MONDAY, MARCH 14

"As I was with Moses, so I will be with you; I will never leave you nor forsake you . . . Do not be afraid; do not be discouraged, for the Lord your God will be with you wherever you go." Joshua 1:5, 9 (NIV)

THERE'S NO DOUBT WE LIVE in a transient society. I once met a military family who had moved twenty-three times during twenty-four years of marriage. Three moves to different states in forty years have been more than enough for me. Our last move brought us somewhat closer to family, but separated us from dear friends on the other side of the country.

Even though moving can have advantages, I hate the feeling of being a stranger. It makes me lonely knowing that when I go to the mall or the movies, I won't see a single familiar face. It's times like that when I appreciate more than ever having a Savior Who will never leave me.

As Joshua prepared to lead the Israelites into the Promised Land, he knew they would face fierce opposition. God assured him he would not be alone. He promised to be with Joshua wherever he went, to never leave or forsake him. Wonderful, comforting promises.

But we have something even better. When Jesus returned to heaven, He sent the Holy Spirit to live inside those who believe in Him. That meant He was no longer limited to being in one place at one time as when He lived on earth. Now Jesus is with us every moment, every day, wherever we go. I love the beautiful words of God's promise to never leave me, but I'm so grateful I have the reality of the promise in Christ's presence, especially when I move. —DIANNE NEAL MATTHEWS

FAITH STEP: *The next time you struggle with loneliness, read the promises in Joshua 1. Thank Jesus for always being with you, no matter where you go.*

TUESDAY, MARCH 15

But if you do not forgive others their trespasses, neither will your Father forgive your trespasses. Matthew 6:15 (ESV)

"I'LL NEVER FORGIVE HIM FOR THAT." "I can't forgive her for that." "Some things can't be forgiven."

An unforgiving spirit is like rancid air. It's like trying to carry on normal living in a home with spoiled, six-day-old raw chicken sitting on the counter. Eventually, you have to move or die. And if you move, how are you going to put the house on the market with a smell like that?

One of Jesus's oft-revisited themes was forgiveness. And He was a master at it, at BIG forgiveness. He forgave His earthly parents for not understanding His God-given call. He forgave His disciples, repeatedly, for their ignorance. He continually ministered to people who were bent on His destruction. He forgave His murderers, and forgave His closest friends who deserted Him when He needed them most. Betrayal. False accusation. Abandonment. False imprisonment. False conviction. Fraudulent sentencing. Bullied. Misunderstood.

We could argue, "Yes, but it was easy for *Him* to forgive. He's God the Son." But His Spirit lives within those of us who've committed our lives to Him and received His forgiveness of all the wrongs we've done. That Spirit—the one that forgives betrayal, false accusation, abandonment, bullying, misunderstanding…

The men who pounded the spikes into His wrists and feet, who crammed a crown of thorns on His head, who stabbed at His bare side with spears heard Jesus pray, "Father, forgive them; for they know not what they do."

What grudge could I ever hold that Jesus would say to me, "Oh, well, yes. You hang onto your lack of forgiveness for that. Some things just can't be forgiven"? —CYNTHIA RUCHTI

FAITH STEP: *Will you bravely pray this prayer? "Jesus, I think I can't forgive _____ for _____. I ask You to do the forgiving for me, by the power of Your Spirit living within me. You forgive BIG. That's what I need."*

WEDNESDAY, MARCH 16

Brothers and sisters, I do not consider myself yet to have taken hold of it. But one thing I do: Forgetting what is behind and straining toward what is ahead, I press on toward the goal to win the prize for which God has called me heavenward in Christ Jesus. Philippians 3:13–14 (NIV)

I LOVE LOOKING AT PHOTOGRAPHS of my boys when they were little. Mostly, because I can't remember that time period. I had three babies in five years. It did something to my brain. There are whole sections of time that I've lost. I chalk it up to seven years of sleep deprivation. But when I see those sweet babies, my heart aches to go back in time. I miss their small chubby arms around my neck. Now they are so big, I will soon be the one hanging onto their necks. It's easy to lose myself in the glorious baby days. Or maybe I should call them the horrible baby days...did I mention the seven years of sleep deprivation?

Either way, when I am focused on the past, I am missing out on the present. My boys are changing right now before my eyes. If I am stuck in the past, I am losing out on what's going on today.

It is the same with our relationship with Jesus. Jesus calls us to live in the here and now. He doesn't want us stuck in the past. What's done is done. It can't be changed. Good or bad. But if we are embracing today and inviting Him to be a part of our day, He can move in our hearts. He can change us. He can move us in the direction that He wants us to go in. So forgetting what is behind, good or bad, let's press forward into the life that Jesus has for us today. —SUSANNA FOTH AUGHTMON

FAITH STEP: *Make a "today" pledge. Say to Jesus, "I am letting go of the good and bad of the past and I am embracing today. Do what You want to do in my life right now!"*

THURSDAY, MARCH 17

*For the appeal we make does not spring from error or impure motives,
nor are we trying to trick you. On the contrary, we speak as those approved by God
to be entrusted with the gospel. We are not trying to please people but God,
who tests our hearts. 1 Thessalonians 2:3–4 (NIV)*

THE WORDS IN MY BIBLE seemed to glow with a sharp light. I'd planned an uplifting, mellow quiet time with Jesus before finishing my preparations for a speaking engagement. Instead, reading about people-pleasing motives pulled me up short. I examined my heart and didn't like what I saw.

I enjoy meeting new people, sharing my love for Jesus, and offering encouragement to fellow pilgrims on difficult roads. But I had to acknowledge that my excitement for the speaking engagement was also colored by how much fun it was to feel respected and important.

I tried to fix my attitudes, which left me only more frustrated with myself...until I caught on that the deep motives of my heart were something only Jesus could change. What a relief to confess the muddle of desires, and ask Him to forgive, to cleanse, and to give me His heart for others. He even reminded me that if I waited to serve Him until all my motives were perfect, I wouldn't be serving Him at all on this side of eternity.

The talk that evening was a blessing. I was inspired by those I met, and shared from my heart. On the drive home, I weighed how well the presentation had gone and began to slip into a fretful people-pleasing mindset again. Why did that one woman never smile? Why did one of the men leave early? I caught myself and prayed, "Jesus, accomplish the work that You desire from this evening. I surrender the results—including how people view me—to You." —SHARON HINCK

FAITH STEP: *Do you ever struggle with needing to please people? Today, ask Jesus to free you from that burden, and to fill your heart with a longing to please God above all else.*

FRIDAY, MARCH 18

So now there is no condemnation for those who belong to Christ Jesus.
And because you belong to him, the power of the life-giving Spirit has freed you
from the power of sin that leads to death. Romans 8:1-2 (NLT)

AS A FIFTEEN-YEAR-OLD YOUNG WOMAN, I found myself pregnant, and I opted for an abortion. I believed it was the best choice. But the pain of that decision overwhelmed me.

I found myself pregnant again at age seventeen, and this time I chose to carry my baby. Later I accepted Christ, and God brought me an amazing Christian husband and a father for my son.

A few years after John and I were married, I became pregnant. I was so excited to have a baby with my husband. Yet a couple of months later I woke up in a pool of blood, and I knew two things: First, I'd lost our baby. And second, Jesus was punishing me for my abortion.

Looking back, my heart aches for the young me, a woman who still didn't understand Jesus's complete forgiveness. I saw Jesus as a stern judge who was weighing all my deeds and found me wanting.

For years I felt my abortion was too much for Jesus to forgive. I also had a hard time forgiving myself. It was only when I worked through the book *Forgiven and Set Free* that I realized Jesus's death covered all my sins. Who was I to say my sin was greater than His sacrifice?

The freedom I'm walking in today comes from understanding Who Jesus is. My sin was horrible, yes, but I'm thankful for the eternity to come. I'm thankful that in Jesus's eyes I stand clean before Him, as white as snow. —TRICIA GOYER

FAITH STEP: *Do you have a sin that you feel is too big for Jesus to forgive? Pray and ask Jesus to remind you that His sacrifice covered all your sins.*

SATURDAY, MARCH 19

I was hungry and you gave Me something to eat; I was thirsty and you gave Me something to drink; I was a stranger and you took Me in; I was naked and you clothed Me; I was sick and you took care of Me; I was in prison and you visited Me.
Matthew 25:35–36 (HCS)

I ONCE HEARD LAUREN WINNER speak about her faith. She said that during her biggest crises in life and faith—her divorce and her mother's death—she was sustained by community, specifically, the habits of going to church and teaching in a prison.

I thought that was so interesting. She's a professor at Duke and a great writer. Even though I don't have that kind of pedigree, I would expect people like her to be like me, and seek the remedy for a spiritual crisis in more introspection, like Bible reading, prayer, etc. Instead, she said she thinks that tends to be isolating. She believes that sometimes, in crisis, God invites us to participate in bringing about His kingdom on earth. In other words, we meet Jesus in prison or when we're helping the poor. We meet Him in the faces of fellow sojourners at church. And when we meet Him, He brings us out of ourselves.

It's tempting to keep ourselves isolated when we're hurting. But as long as we stay inside ourselves, we won't find what we're looking for, and we'll stay miserable. In isolation, we are also of no help to anyone else.

Jesus's way is better. The above verses basically say, "Go find someone who needs help and you will find Me." We need look no further than the next hungry person we see. —GWEN FORD FAULKENBERRY

FAITH STEP: *Set up a meeting with Jesus. Write it on your calendar today and keep the appointment—volunteer at a homeless shelter, visit someone in a nursing home, invite the new people in your neighborhood to dinner.*

PALM SUNDAY, MARCH 20

Always be prepared to give an answer to everyone who asks you to give the reason for the hope that you have. But do this with gentleness and respect.
1 Peter 3:15 *(NIV)*

EVERY PALM SUNDAY my kids bring home palm branches from church to represent hope and welcome for the Savior of the world.

That first Palm Sunday was quite a day. First Jesus entered Jerusalem on a colt while people laid out palm branches and shouted "Hosanna!" (Matthew 21). It was such a scene that "the whole city was stirred and asked, 'Who is this?'" Hope rang out. Genuine hope.

From the gates of the city Jesus went to the temple courts, where He drove out those who defiled it and overturned the money changers' tables, but He showed compassion and healed the blind and lame (Matthew 21:14). To some He was an enigma, to others a pariah. To many, including some of the smallest ones, He was hope—the Savior to be praised.

Have you ever wondered what bystanders thought when Jesus's followers, children in particular, praised Him with "Hosanna to the Son of David" (Matthew 21:15)? Do you think some of them wondered at the reason for such hope-filled rejoicing, or were kids just being kids?

I picture His enemies seething. "'Do you hear what these children are saying?'" (Matthew 21:16). I can see their faces twist in disdain at the young ones' faith. Can you picture the word *hope* dripping from their bitter mouths?

One thing is sure, though. The hope that danced from the children's mouths in praise was unmistakable and unmissable. And Jesus was prepared with the answer.

Is your hope in Christ evident? Will others see Jesus in your countenance and words today? —ERIN KEELEY MARSHALL

FAITH STEP: *Ask Jesus to enlighten and lighten your heart with His hope. Ask Him for an opportunity to share His hope with someone.*

MONDAY, MARCH 21

So he sent other servants to tell them, "The feast has been prepared. The bulls and fattened cattle have been killed, and everything is ready. Come to the banquet!"
Matthew 22:4 (NLT)

A FEW YEARS AGO I got hooked on TV singing competition shows. I enjoy hearing the background stories of the contestants and seeing them step out in courage to pursue their dreams. Some of them are so talented and poised, they already seem like professionals, but I like seeing the ones who blossom before the viewers' eyes, thanks to their growing self-confidence and the expert coaching they receive.

The negative thing about these shows is the audition phase. It's tough to see some hopeful contestant sing her heart out and get no positive response. On one show, the judges' chairs are turned around with their backs to the singers. If judges like what they hear, they push a button. Then their chair turns around as a sign lights up saying "I Want You."

I'm so glad we don't have to approach God like that. He has already done all that's needed for me to become His adopted child. I don't have to audition for His love. I don't need to work as hard as I can to become good enough for His approval. Through His life, death, and Resurrection, Jesus made it possible for me to enter into a personal relationship with Him. He wants me just as I am.

Unlike television judges, Jesus doesn't have His back turned to us until we do something worthy of His attention. He pursues us with outstretched hands and love in His eyes, saying, "Come!" Once we answer His call and submit to His coaching, we will blossom before His eyes. And our life, while not perfect, will indeed be a banquet. —DIANNE NEAL MATTHEWS

FAITH STEP: *Do you sometimes feel like you don't measure up, that you need to earn God's favor? Read Jeremiah 31:3, John 3:16, and Ephesians 2:8–9. Meditate on the unconditional love that Jesus demonstrated for you on the Cross.*

TUESDAY, MARCH 22

Finally, be strong in the Lord and in his mighty power. Ephesians 6:10 (NIV)

I'M GUILTY OF SOMETIMES SKIMMING over Scripture, especially if I'm running late in the morning. As a result, I miss little gems hidden in plain view. One such gem is in today's key verse. It's a three-word phrase: "in the Lord."

I'd read that phrase countless times and never really stopped to consider what it meant until I heard a message about it. The pastor explained that, in this context, "in the Lord" means "to be locked up inside Jesus."

The pastor said, "Followers of Jesus are locked up inside Him. For believers, He is our address, our dwelling place. When we place our faith in His sacrificial death and Resurrection, we take up our position in Him with no need to worry about whether or not we're good enough to live there."

The thought of being locked up inside Jesus ought to flood us with courage, a sense of security, and an attitude of restfulness. But there's more. Consider this: God's power is also locked up in Jesus. That means we who dwell there have full access to it at all times.

Why, then, do we often feel or act as though we're powerless? Because sin gets in the way. We think we know better than Jesus about how to live so we disregard His commands. We doubt His wisdom, and we question His love. We end up acting like wimpy warriors rather than bold soldiers of the Cross.

Be strong, my friend. Not in the world's strategies for strength but in knowing your position. You're locked up in Jesus with full access to God's power. Do I hear an amen? —GRACE FOX

FAITH STEP: *Do you have access to a wee plastic soldier or a Lego-type warrior? If so, great. If not, find an object of similar size. Place it in the palm of your hand and squeeze your fingers around it. Thank Jesus for locking you up inside of Himself.*

one WEDNESDAY, MARCH 23

All our praise is focused through Jesus on this incomparably wise God! Yes!
Romans 16:27 (MSG)

HAVE YOU EVER WATCHED the Academy Awards presentations on TV? Speeches follow as winners in the film industry receive their Oscars. The awards often continue for three hours or more.

Even though the awards differ, one thing is common in every speech: a roll call of gratitude to those who played a part in the winner's success. Most quickly realize the impossible task of thanking everyone responsible.

In the Apostle Paul's letters to believers in Rome, he took almost an entire chapter to list the people he encountered. The names included women, men, and even those considered as unimportant in society at that time. One couple had risked their lives for Paul and had opened their home as a church. Another was gifted in hospitality, giving herself tirelessly to others.

He also included former jail cellmates, veteran believers, and even the first Christian convert in Asia. Paul was both greeting them and thanking Jesus for their work as believers and for their help and support for him. Ultimately, he focused his thanks on Jesus Himself, Who makes all things possible. He ended his honor roll of friends with a generalized "thank you": "Holy embraces all around!" (Romans 16:16, MSG).

I love Paul's example. What if I wrote letters to all the friends through the years who have shared both the load and the joys of ministry? Impossible! The list would never end. But I could thank Jesus for them as their names come to mind. As I end each one of those prayers with "hugs to all," I realize the one common denominator for all of us is our abiding focus on Jesus.
—REBECCA BARLOW JORDAN

FAITH STEP: *Thank Jesus for all the people who have made an impact in your life. Pick out a few special ones and send them a note of thanks as well.*

MAUNDY THURSDAY, MARCH 24

"The blood on the doorposts will serve as a sign, marking the houses where you are staying. When I see the blood, I will pass over you. . . ."
Exodus 12:13 (NLT)

WHEN WE WERE SHEPHERDS, we supplied a lamb every year for a Seder supper. We chose our finest firstborn lamb for the honor and, although our Passover meals wouldn't have met Orthodox standards, the images of the feast worked in our hearts in a way words could not.

The Haggadah or narration of the meal is key. Participants drink four cups of wine, each with a different meaning; they wash their hands, and eat foods symbolic of elements of the Exodus: a hardboiled egg in salt water for Pharaoh's hard heart and the tears of slavery; parsley dipped in salt water for new life after passing through the Red Sea; the shank bone (unbroken) for the sacrifice. The middle loaf of three loaves of unleavened bread is broken in two, wrapped in linen napkins, then half is hidden (burial).

After the meal, the children search for the broken bread and bring it back to the table (resurrection), where it is shared as the last food eaten (it's called the Afikomen, meaning "dessert"). No food can follow it—its taste must linger. This last bread is broken for everyone. It was the Afikomen that Jesus gave to His friends at His last Passover, saying, "This is my body, which is given for you" (Luke 22:19, NLT).

As it is for each of us. —SUZANNE DAVENPORT TIETJEN

FAITH STEP: *Jesus not only spoke, He also used drama and images: a basin and towel, real blood, roasted meat. Be in awe at His sacrifice. Now, look for His lessons all around you.*

GOOD FRIDAY, MARCH 25

A man named Joseph ... asked for Jesus' body. Then he took it down, wrapped it in linen cloth and placed it in a tomb... It was Preparation Day, and the Sabbath was about to begin. Luke 23:50, 52–54 (NIV)

CAN YOU IMAGINE A DAY WITHOUT JESUS? I've grown so accustomed to the belief that He lives in me and is always with me that it is hard to think of Him as ever being dead. But He was. He was laid in a tomb and buried. Dead. I can't even wrap my mind around it.

Probably the closest thing we can relate to when we're thinking about Holy Saturday is the death of a loved one and how that feels. The night my Granny died I was shocked and saddened. But the day of the burial— that day I was numb. Even though I knew she was in heaven, the burial made it all seem so final. I would never hear her laugh, feel her hug me, smell her homemade rolls cooking. I would never see her in this life again.

N. T. Wright said, "We cannot be an Easter people if we are not first Good Friday people and then Holy Saturday people. Don't expect even a still, small voice. Stay still yourself, and let the quietness and darkness of the day be your companions." Thank goodness Holy Saturday only lasts a day, but it's right and proper to ponder the meaning of Jesus's death. There is nothing more terrible or terrifying. Nothing darker we could face. And yet, there He is in the midst of it. He went there for us, even death on a Cross. That has to be real to us if we are ever going to begin to grasp the hope of His Resurrection. —GWEN FORD FAULKENBERRY

FAITH STEP: *Go into a dark room and light a candle to read this devotion. Then blow it out as you meditate on the death of Jesus. (Don't worry—Sunday's coming!)*

Please join us for Guideposts Good Friday Day of Prayer.
Find out more at guideposts.org/ourprayer.

SATURDAY, MARCH 26

If you try to hang on to your life, you will lose it. But if you give up your life for my sake, you will save it. Matthew 16:25 (NLT)

YOU MAY HAVE SEEN A COMMERCIAL that shows a panel of kids who are offered lollipops. Once they have those, they're offered something different if they'll give up their lollipops.

No takers. Not one would give up that treat for the unknown, despite the promise that it would be worth it.

This verse strikes at our selfishness, our desire for self-protection, and our greed, and it asks us to trade our lives for Jesus's sake.

Is it worth it?

No other question matters as much. But the only way to answer that question with an honest "yes" is to know Him well enough. We don't give our lives if we don't learn to love more than we love ourselves.

We face an uphill battle learning to love. "The human heart is the most deceitful of all things, and desperately wicked. Who really knows how bad it is?" (Jeremiah 17:9, NLT). Our hearts deceive us constantly. They convince us that secondary things are primary priorities, and they fool us into thinking we're less self-seeking than we really are. Just when we understand that we ought to give up everything, our deceptive hearts tell us we're giving up more than we'll be receiving from the Lord in return.

In truth, we give up what is less so that Jesus can fill us with what we really need. We cannot experience His fullness until we let go of our agenda. But we're a hard sell on this because some of our desires go deep.

We want what's good. But Jesus wants what is best for us. When we can't trust our own hearts, we can trust His.

That is a deal we cannot afford to refuse. —ERIN KEELEY MARSHALL

FAITH STEP: *How has your heart led you astray in the past? Ask Jesus to help you see what it means for you to give up your life for His sake.*

EASTER SUNDAY, MARCH 27

"Even though you planned evil against me, God planned good to come out of it. This was to keep many people alive, as he is doing now." Genesis 50:20 (GW)

JOSEPH'S BROTHERS HAD ABUSED HIM and sold him to slave traders years earlier. Now they found themselves at his mercy, the second most powerful man in Egypt. No wonder they quaked with the fear that Joseph might take revenge. But Joseph assured them of his care and protection. He explained that although they had meant to harm him, God brought great good out of their evil intentions. The brothers' actions had brought Joseph to his present position, where his leadership saved many lives during the long famine.

The Old Testament includes other instances of God bringing good out of evil. The supreme example, however, is found in the New Testament's Easter story. The anger, hatred, and brutality that led men to crucify Jesus. The pain and suffering He endured that day. The confusion and horror His followers felt after His death. All of these things paved the way for His Resurrection a few days later when God's plan was fully revealed. The very actions used by Christ's enemies to stop His ministry and destroy Him actually fulfilled His mission: to sacrifice His life as payment for the sin of anyone who chooses to believe in Him.

If God brought the greatest good for the human race out of the worst evil ever committed, surely I can trust Him to do the same in my personal life. Romans 8:28 promises that God is working everything out for the good of those who love Him. I find comfort knowing He can overrule every wrong committed against me and turn it for His own purposes. And every year the Easter story reminds me that God's goodness can overcome any evil. —DIANNE NEAL MATTHEWS

FAITH STEP: *Think about the most hurtful thing you've recently experienced. Ask Jesus to use this situation to accomplish His good purposes in the lives of everyone involved.*

MONDAY, MARCH 28

Jesus said to her, "I am the resurrection and the life. The one who believes in me will live, even though they die; and whoever lives by believing in me will never die. Do you believe this?" John 11:25–26 (NIV)

A YEAR AGO MY MOM experienced sudden cardiac arrest. One moment she was sitting on the couch next to my dad and the next she was gone. She was airlifted to the hospital and placed in a medicated coma. And seventy-two hours later, Jesus in his mercy, brought our mom back to us. And we are standing in a place of joy. Mom is fully recovered, working in her garden, laughing with her grandkids, loving Dad and us with everything she has. She says it is the diligence of man and the hand of God that saved her. And we will never be the same. We see life through a different lens now.

The other night we were having dinner with Scott's sister, Cheri, and her family. Jack and his cousin, Brian, were talking about the phrase YOLO, You Only Live Once. That is, unless you are a cat. Then you get nine lives. Will piped up from across the table, "You only live once. Unless you are Jesus, Lazarus, or Grandma." We couldn't be more thankful.

The Jesus Whom we know and love is the One Who resurrects the dead, who breathes life into us, and makes all things new. In impossible situations, in fearful moments, in life-altering circumstances, He is the God of incredible power, unfathomable strength and insurmountable hope. We can trust in Him to do and be more in our lives than we could ever hope or imagine. —SUSANNA FOTH AUGHTMON

FAITH STEP: *Think back on a moment in your life where Jesus has brought life and hope to you. Praise Him for what He has done and thank Him in advance for what He is going to do in the future.*

TUESDAY, MARCH 29

These are all warning markers—DANGER!—in our history books, written down so that we don't repeat their mistakes. 1 Corinthians 10:11 (MSG)

HAVE YOU EVER WONDERED WHY so many "R" rated stories are included in the Bible? Accounts of murder and rebellion, lust and promiscuity, you name it: people rebelling against God's way. Couldn't God have inspired and instructed the writers to omit those gory scenes? But Paul's letter to the Corinthians helps shed light on that question. He compares the story of the Exodus to our salvation from enslavement. His sad statement gives us a heads up when he says of our ancestors: "Most of them were defeated by temptation during the hard times" (1 Corinthians 10:1–5, MSG).

These and other failures in the Bible serve as "warning markers— DANGER!—in our history books." God included these so we wouldn't "repeat their mistakes" and "fall flat on your face" (1 Corinthians 10:11–12).

We see the same things happening today. Every day we experience temptation that could either lead us away or draw us closer to Jesus. If we think we're exempt from temptation, Paul reminds us of our naiveté. But Paul also encourages believers: Jesus always makes a way of escape (1 Corinthians10:13). He knows our tendencies; yet He is always there to help us get through any temptation. With that sober reminder, we find another reason for the inclusion of those stories and biblical warnings. Jesus offers grace. Someone once defined grace as "the power to do what's right."

Jesus's promise is a great reason to both learn from, and heed warnings of, disaster, but also a powerful motivator to trust Him—and accept His overcoming grace to make the right choices. —REBECCA BARLOW JORDAN

FAITH STEP: *Think about the kind of temptations you've experienced in the past. Memorize 1 Corinthians 10:13, and thank Jesus for His overcoming grace.*

WEDNESDAY, MARCH 30

Jesus looked at them carefully and said, "It's impossible for human beings.
But all things are possible for God." Matthew 19:26 (CEB)

WHILE DOING RESEARCH for a book, I learned the ASL (American Sign Language) sign for *impossible*. As a friend of mine with several deaf family members told me, the sign is often used with force. Body language and facial expressions contribute much to ASL comprehension.

It's a sign that resembles applause, but with the three middle fingers of one hand closed.

I know so little of the background of ASL. Experts would explain things much differently and know the rationale behind every movement. But as a novice—or even less skilled than that—I'm fascinated by all the nuances. *Impossible* intrigues me.

With the intervention of Jesus—we could look at those three fingers as representing God the Father, Jesus the Son, and the Holy Spirit—it's applause.

Without? Impossible.

In the Matthew passage mentioned above, Jesus explained to His disciples about the difficulty they'd just witnessed—a young man wealthy financially but spiritually impoverished. The young man was offered hope through Jesus, but turned it down in favor of the wealth to which he clung.

"Then who can be saved?" the disciples asked, stunned.

That's what Jesus referred to when He said that it was impossible without God—closed fingered slap—but nothing is impossible with God. Applause! —CYNTHIA RUCHTI

FAITH STEP: *If the symbolism resonates with you, too, see how much applause you can work into your day today. Nothing is impossible when Jesus is involved!*

THURSDAY, MARCH 31

The Lord is good, a strong refuge when trouble comes. He is close to those who trust in him. Nahum 1:7 (NLT)

As I WRITE THIS, one of my cousins—a forty-eight-year-old mother of two—sits in the local hospital's emergency room. Doctors recently diagnosed her with an aggressive cancer, and she began chemotherapy last week. Unfortunately, she's all-too-familiar with what's involved; this is her second diagnosis in three years.

There's no easy cure for my cousin's cancer, and there's no easy answer for why God has allowed the disease to strike twice. I wish I could snap my fingers and make this situation go away, but that's a pipe dream. Thankfully, amidst the uncertainties lies a promise to which our family clings, and it brings hope: "God is our refuge and strength, an ever-present help in trouble" (Psalm 46:1, NIV).

Sometimes we question Jesus's sovereignty or goodness or wisdom when we land in hard places. Our faith falters, our finite minds fail to grasp His infinite ways, and we wonder, *Where is He in the midst of this mess?* Fatigue, fear, and stress take their toll, and we may soon feel as though He has abandoned us. Nothing's further from the truth.

Jesus was present with the disciples when waves threatened to drown them in the darkness at sea. "Don't be afraid," He said. "Take courage. I am here!" (Matthew 14:27, NLT). The same reassurance holds true for us today, no matter what circumstances we face.

Jesus is our ever-present help. He's close to those who trust in Him. May these words bring hope and strength to all who need them today.
—GRACE FOX

FAITH STEP: *Pray Nahum 1:7 for a loved one who's experiencing a difficult time: "Jesus, please show Your goodness to _____ at this time. Be her strong refuge. Reveal Your closeness to her in a tangible way as she trusts in You. In Your name, amen."*

FRIDAY, APRIL 1

Jesus responded to them, "Have faith in God!" Mark 11:22 (CEB)

IT'S THE EXCLAMATION POINT that gets me. Jesus didn't pat His followers on the hand and say, "Come on, guys. Have a little faith." He put an exclamation point behind it.

Jesus didn't often raise His voice or stir crowds to frenzy with His impassioned rhetoric, but instead He used calm authority and insights.

Here, though, when talking to the people closest to Him, He added an exclamation point. As if to say—"You've been following me *how long* and still don't get it! As if you've never seen Me act with God's power before?"

Psalm 78 relates a similar story, revealing human tendencies toward "forgetfulness of former mercies" (Spurgeon). The psalmist reports the Israelites "spoke against God! 'Can God set a dinner table in the wilderness?' they asked. 'True, God struck the rock and water gushed and streams flowed, but can he give bread too?' When the Lord heard this, he became furious... because they had no faith in God, because they didn't trust his saving power" (Psalm 78:19–21, CEB).

Jesus dealt with the same attitude among the people with whom He walked. He answered with a reminder of an old truth, punctuated with an exclamation point: "*Have faith in God!*"

I wonder if Jesus doesn't use exclamation points in my life when I look at our need for new tires and wonder how He's going to provide. *True, He's bailed us out of far more difficult predicaments in the past, but...*

Imagine what it would be like to have Jesus say, "Huh. I haven't had to use an exclamation point with you in a long time." I expect He'd punctuate that statement with... an exclamation point! —CYNTHIA RUCHTI

FAITH STEP: *What concern on your heart today could be construed as a forgetfulness of former mercies? By faith, remove Jesus's need to use an exclamation point when He assures you that He hears, understands, and is working it out.*

SATURDAY, APRIL 2

Sow for yourselves righteousness; reap steadfast love; break up your fallow ground, for it is the time to seek the Lord, that he may come and rain righteousness upon you. Hosea 10:12 (ESV)

ON THE FIRST WARM DAY OF SPRING, I gathered my gardening supplies and headed to the backyard. After a long cold winter, I couldn't wait to begin digging in the dirt. We have several raised beds for vegetables and now that the snow had melted (mostly), I was ready to plant my spinach and peas.

We rotate crops so none of the beds gets depleted from growing the same thing year after year. Looking at my diagram from the past year, I started with a bed that hadn't been used the year before. My trowel dug in, and I tried to turn the dirt. The earth barely budged. I nearly bent my hand tool. I switched to a full-size spade, but even jumping on the shovel, I struggled to break up the stubborn earth.

If I skipped this step, and just poked a few holes and dropped seeds in, their little roots would struggle to find air and moisture in the hard-packed ground. So I persisted in loosening all the dirt and stirring in compost, even though it was hard work.

When Jesus asks us to break up our fallow ground, it's because He wants to grow good fruit in our lives. My garden gave me a clue about what causes my heart to become hard and inhospitable for His seeds: disuse. When I regularly spend time in worship, hear Bible teaching, read the Word, enjoy the communion of fellowship, and serve in whatever ways Jesus guides me, my soil is being turned, fed, aerated. It's ready for whatever Jesus wants to plant next. Instead of a one-time crop, He can bring an ongoing harvest of steadfast love. —SHARON HINCK

FAITH STEP: *Find ways to loosen the soil of your heart today. Sing a hymn, talk with a friend about how Jesus is at work in your life, or seek out a community of worship.*

SUNDAY, APRIL 3

He erased the certificate of debt, with its obligations, that was against us and opposed to us, and has taken it out of the way by nailing it to the cross.
Colossians 2:14 (HCS)

AS THE SERMON BEGAN, I reached inside my purse for a pen. My fingers brushed against something I'd forgotten lay in the bottom of the zippered pocket. Leaning down toward my granddaughter, I whispered, "I'm holding the key to the meaning of life in my hand right now." Lacey's back stiffened, her eyes widened, and she pulled my fingers away. One look at the tiny wooden cross in my hand and she relaxed, nodded, and gave me a knowing look.

A very talented and kind man at my former church crafts pocket crosses out of exotic woods and then gives them away. Jim cut my one-inch high cross from rich dark rosewood; my husband's is made out of African Blackwood. I accepted this surprise gift gratefully, but wondered how I would use it. I've met people who carry a religious symbol or object like a talisman. I certainly didn't want to give the impression of treating a cross like a good-luck object.

Crosses have become standard decorative objects for clothing, jewelry, and the home. So much so, that many overlook the precious truth they represent for Christ's followers. It was on the Cross that Jesus paid our sin debt in full so we would be free to live for Him. Because of the Cross, we no longer need to fear death; we can look forward to eternal life.

That tiny cross has been more of a blessing than I ever imagined it could be. Each time I unexpectedly come across it, it reminds me of Jesus's greatest demonstration of His love. I may sometimes forget that I have a little wooden cross in my purse, but I'll never forget what it stands for. —DIANNE NEAL MATTHEWS

FAITH STEP: *Do you have a visual reminder of your faith? If not, consider getting a plaque, a Scripture bookmark, or a decorative object that is meaningful to you.*

MONDAY, APRIL 4

After sending them home, he went up into the hills by himself to pray.
Night fell while he was there alone. Matthew 14:23 (NLT)

CELL PHONES AND WI-FI ACCESS make it easy for many of us to stay in touch with what's happening locally and globally. We can plug in almost anywhere to read the news, watch movies, transmit e-mails, and communicate via social media.

Back in the eighties, my husband and I lived in a remote Nepalese village. Electricity didn't exist there at the time, so we learned to survive without phones.

We visited our former village in 2014. Imagine our surprise to see a television in one hut and to watch villagers use cell phones to spread the news of our arrival. We were delighted to learn that at least one woman has a Facebook and a Skype account. Now we can maintain contact a half-world away, and we anticipate future ministry opportunities there.

Modern technology brings both benefits and drawbacks. Staying connected worldwide is fun and informative, but it can easily distract us from the things that matter most. Ultimately, we need to guard our hearts and our time lest our connection with God suffers.

Jesus placed high priority on communicating with His Father. He often withdrew from the crowds and His responsibilities in order to pray. He sought silence to hear God's voice. Doing so enabled Him to know His Father's will regarding His life's purpose and strengthened Him to accomplish it.

If Jesus intentionally sought time in God's presence, how much more ought we to do the same? —GRACE FOX

FAITH STEP: *Unplug your electronics for one day. Spend your usual plugged-in time reading a good inspirational book, studying the Word, or praying. Ask God to help you place as much priority on your relationship with Him as Jesus did.*

TUESDAY, APRIL 5

Flowers appear on the earth; the season of singing has come....
Song of Songs 2:12 (NIV)

I SAT INSIDE THE HOUSE, looking out the window one morning early in April. Some purple flowers were blooming, standing at attention as if they were shouting, "It's time for spring!" But all the other flowering plants remained dormant and silent around them. Meanwhile, the enemies of beauty—weeds—crowded in, trying to take over and screaming, "We plan to rule!"

I watched, nursing my two-week case of bronchitis, eager to defend my garden. But it was not the season of singing for me, but a season of sickness. So I waited. And waited. And watched. When healing came, I gratefully embraced springtime and enjoyed working in my garden again.

The Master Gardener, Jesus, has not abandoned His garden. He didn't plan for weeds in the beginning. Seeds were sown by our enemy, and they spread throughout time, emptying our hopes, dashing our dreams, making the "growing" season appear shorter at times in our lives.

I remember a few of those seasons—times when no flowers bloomed, when waiting seemed like forever. Weeds, whether defined as an unpleasant sickness, an unplanned loss, or an unproductive period, will come and try to rule. But, eventually, hope will arise—full-blown, majestic, and beautiful, as Jesus sends us His promise of restoration. In the middle of the weeds, He'll shout to us, like a soldier commanding our attention: "It's time for spring!"

And if, by His Sovereign hand, delays continue beyond our desires on this earth, it's okay. Jesus's promise of heaven, our eternal springtime home, still waits for us: a season for singing, in full bloom.
—REBECCA BARLOW JORDAN

FAITH STEP: *What season of life are you in right now? Memorize Psalm 33:22 today, and remind yourself that your hope lies in Jesus.*

WEDNESDAY, APRIL 6

"Give your entire attention to what God is doing right now, and don't get worked up about what may or may not happen tomorrow. God will help you deal with whatever hard things come up when the time comes." Matthew 6:34 (MSG)

I WAKE UP NEVER KNOWING what's going to happen. Even on days I'm not scheduled to work, I can find myself pulling on scrubs, speeding to the gas station at the end of the forest highway and hopping into an ambulance to go stabilize a sick baby and transport her to the Neonatal ICU hundreds of miles in the opposite direction. I'll figure out how to get back to my car *afterward*. If I knew what the day would be like ahead of time, I'd be afraid to get out of bed in the morning.

Life is scary. We may think we're in control but ultimately, we aren't. We keep calendars and make plans, but we can't really know what the next month, week, day, or minute holds. Surely, we do our best, put survival kits in our cars and smoke alarms in our houses, but preparedness isn't a guarantee.

Look at the disciples, freaking out when a storm sent waves sweeping over their boat. Jesus? He was sleeping calmly. When they woke Him, He commented on their lack of faith and asked why they were afraid before He told the wind and sea to quiet down.

We need to look to Jesus. Paul said, "Keep your eyes on Jesus, who both began and finished this race we're in. Study how he did it" (Hebrews 12:2, MSG).

When I lead a resuscitation I pray, *Jesus, help me*. And He does—I'm unnaturally calm and speak in a normal voice during what should be a scary time. I might shake later but while there's a baby to save, Jesus calms me.

Jesus trusted His Father. We can too. —SUZANNE DAVENPORT TIETJEN

FAITH STEP: *You're preparing to play the role of Jesus. How does He carry himself? Speak? What expressions are on His face as He talks with people? When He looks at you?*

THURSDAY, APRIL 7

When the cares of my heart are many, your consolations cheer my soul.
Psalm 94:19 (ESV)

THROUGH THE YEARS I've learned the value of sharing my worries and concerns with someone I trust. It can be difficult, but opening up to a close friend paves the way for encouragement, counsel, and emotional and prayer support. More important, I'm learning what it means to cast my anxieties on the One Who cares most about me. For some reason, it's not an easy lesson for me to learn. I tend to hold on to problems and worries that seem rather trivial when compared to more serious issues. It's as though I can't expect Jesus to be bothered with the small stuff. It's also hard for me to let go of burdens caused by my disobedience or wrong choices.

That's why I love that Peter quotes from Psalm 55:22: "Cast your cares on the Lord and he will sustain you." Jesus worked in Peter's life in miraculous ways: letting him walk on water, restoring a servant's ear that Peter had impetuously sliced off. Jesus also dealt with the more mundane: He helped Peter haul in a huge catch of fish. Later, after Peter denied knowing Jesus three times, Jesus helped him get rid of that heavy burden.

We were not meant to carry our burdens alone, but to entrust them into the hands of a loving Lord. If I know Jesus as my Savior, that means I have trusted Him with the destiny of my soul. Why should I hesitate to share any of my everyday concerns or worries with Him? We never know when those "little" problems will morph into major troubles. But even if they don't, we can be confident that Jesus cares about every facet of our well-being. —DIANNE NEAL MATTHEWS

FAITH STEP: *Examine your life to see what unresolved issues and problems are causing you anxiety. Tell Jesus you are handing those over to Him. Thank Him for taking on your burdens.*

FRIDAY, APRIL 8

Let us hold fast the confession of our hope without wavering,
for he who promised is faithful. Hebrews 10:23 (ESV)

LIFE IS BUSY. CRAZY. WILD. And flying by at the speed of light. I know this because I have a teenager. It seems like just moments ago when I had a preschooler, a toddler, and an infant. Yesterday, I toured a high school campus with my oldest son, Jack. He is shadowing at different schools over the next few weeks as we try to find the best fit for him. And I remember when "finding the right fit for him" meant going up the next size in Thomas the Train slippers. How did we end up here? How can it seem like yesterday I was changing diapers and chasing little ones and today I am surrounded by three boys on the brink of manhood? As Jack and I walked the campus, I turned to look at him and realized we were eye to eye. Soon he will surpass me in height. I am trying my best to enjoy this process of seeing my son grow and mature, but I can't help thinking that the only constant we have in life is change.

We change. Kids change. Jobs change. Life changes. And with that change comes uncertainty. So much about life is unknown. We can be smart and try to determine how life is going to go but, in an instant, everything can be upended. Every day brings change that we can't foresee or control.

But there is one thing we can count on. One person. That is the person of Jesus Christ. He is faithful. No matter what life brings, Jesus stays the same. He alone brings consistency to our lives. His mercy? His forgiveness? His joy? His grace? His faithfulness? They will stay the same until that day when we see Him face-to-face. And that is the wonderful truth we can lean on in the days ahead. —SUSANNA FOTH AUGHTMON

FAITH STEP: *What is your favorite quality about Jesus that never changes? Focus on it throughout the day, thanking Him for His constancy in your life.*

SATURDAY, APRIL 9

For the word of God is alive and active. It is sharper than the sharpest two-edged sword, cutting between soul and spirit, between joints and marrow. It exposes our innermost thoughts and desires. Hebrews 4:12 (NLT)

SOMETIMES AS A MOM, I get overwhelmed with all I should be doing for my kids' spiritual development. I should be reading the Bible with my kids, teaching them Scripture, training them on character qualities, helping them understand prayer. The list is endless.

Equally important are my prayers for my kids...but when I started considering all I should be praying for, I got so overwhelmed that I didn't do anything. That's when I came upon this beautiful simple Scripture. This makes a perfect prayer that we can pray for our children:

"I pray that your love will overflow more and more, and that you will keep on growing in knowledge and understanding. For I want you to understand what really matters, so that you may live pure and blameless lives until the day of Christ's return. May you always be filled with the fruit of your salvation—the righteous character produced in your life by Jesus Christ—for this will bring much glory and praise to God" (Philippians 1:9–11, NLT).

When we don't know how to pray, the Bible provides perfect examples.

There is a lot that goes into training up godly children, and our prayers will prepare us for the task and they will go to work in the Spiritual realm too. Our prayers take us to where we can't go ourselves—to the throne of God. And our prayers will do more for our children than we can hope or imagine. —TRICIA GOYER

FAITH STEP: *Write out Philippians 1:9–11 on a few three-by-five index cards. Post them in places you see often, like the dashboard of your car or your mirror. Read it as a prayer for your family members.*

SUNDAY, APRIL 10

I praise you because I am fearfully and wonderfully made;
your works are wonderful, I know that full well. Psalm 139:14 (NIV)

THIS MORNING I WAS PICKING up around the house and found Will's craft from his class last Sunday. The lesson was about Jesus dying on the Cross and what Jesus did for us. The kids made a cross to illustrate what He did on our behalf. On one side of Will's construction-paper cross he had small pieces of black paper that listed the bad things Jesus saved us from: fear, sin, and sickness. And on the other side, it listed all the things that Will was thankful to Jesus for. On colorful pieces of paper the following were listed: life, faith, peace, hope...and hair. I laughed out loud when I saw that. And then I choked up a little.

Will has naturally curly blond hair that he is fond of. It makes him unique. No one else in our family has hair like that. From the depths of his heart, Will is thankful that Jesus gave him curls. I love that about him.

We could learn a little something from Will. We were created with great care and forethought, from our unique personalities to our gifts and talents to the roots of our curly or straw-straight hair. Jesus crafted us in our mom's bellies with great delight. There may be things we would like to change about who we are but how can we not look at ourselves and see the detail and love that went into the making of who we are? How can we not praise Jesus for how wonderfully He has made us? The One Who created the stars also created us. And He likes what He created. He wants us to like it too. I think it is only fitting to thank Jesus for the good work He has done, don't you? —SUSANNA FOTH AUGHTMON

FAITH STEP: *Look in the mirror and tell Jesus, "I will praise you for I am fearfully and wonderfully made." And mean it.*

MONDAY, APRIL 11

Silver and gold have I none, but such as I have give I thee.... Acts 3:6 (KJV)

WHEN MY FRIEND CHERYL was in the hospital fighting for her life with complications from chemotherapy, I got into a little cyberwar with someone on her Facebook page. Granted, I was nutty. I needed to unplug, rather than reading all of the posts. "Everything happens for a reason." "God's got this!" "*Like* if you love Jesus and hate cancer." People were writing the most annoying stuff, even though most of it was harmless. Then one person posted something about how this experience was all designed to make her stronger, an even better Christian than she ever was before. I couldn't take it anymore. I typed in just how inappropriate and heartless I thought that was to say. And I meant it.

It took me about a second after hitting "Post" to realize I was being petty by responding to someone I didn't even know who surely meant well. But, really, why do we say things like that to people who are hurting? In light of the thoughtless things that were posted in Cheryl's situation, one has to wonder whether it would be better to say nothing at all.

When people suffer we really have one thing of value to offer them, and one thing only. Thankfully, it's something we all have: Jesus. We may not have money, or magic words that make it better, or even something to say that sounds good. But we have Jesus. We can reach out just by being there. By saying how sorry we are and offering our prayers. By giving hugs or holding someone's hand. His love is what everyone, and especially someone who's hurting, needs. —GWEN FORD FAULKENBERRY

FAITH STEP: *Make a call to someone who is sick today. Ask her how she's feeling and let her know you are praying for Jesus to be near to her.*

TUESDAY, APRIL 12

Do you not know that your bodies are temples of the Holy Spirit, who is in you, whom you have received from God? You are not your own; you were bought at a price. Therefore honor God with your bodies. 1 Corinthians 6:19–20 (NIV)

MY HUSBAND AND I WERE THRILLED to buy our first house. It was the cheapest property in the area listings. Fleas infested every corner, windows wore amber stains from years of cigarette smoke, and mold bloomed across the bathroom walls. But with love and effort, we created a home. How strange would it have been if the previous owners said, "Yes, you bought the house. You own it now. But you aren't allowed to change anything."

Jesus bought me with a price too. In fact, it cost Him everything—His suffering, death, and Resurrection. He showed tremendous love to leave the glories of heaven and come into our world, a place far from inviting. And that love became personal when He took up residency in my heart, another place every bit as decrepit and damaged as that old first house we bought. He comes to live among the mess of my life. In the same way my husband and I worked to clean up and remodel our house, Jesus is eager to transform my life.

Even though I'm now the former owner of my life, I sometimes try to dictate what Jesus is allowed to do with the new place. Perhaps we've invited Jesus to live in our hearts, but fear His transformation in our lives.

Instead, let's celebrate the new ownership. Let's invite Him to rip out the rancid carpets of selfishness and add a new room of service, to tear down suffocating walls of fear and build a skylight of faith. Because of His presence within us, we can become the beautiful temples He intended us to be. —SHARON HINCK

FAITH STEP: *Write a deed to your life and tuck it in your Bible as a reminder that you are under new ownership.*

WEDNESDAY, APRIL 13

"You yourselves know how plainly I told you, 'I am not the Messiah. I am only here to prepare the way for him.' It is the bridegroom who marries the bride, and the best man is simply glad to stand with him and hear his vows." John 3:28–29 (NLT)

I LOVE THAT JESUS is described as a bridegroom in Scripture. As a preteen I loved daydreaming about who my Prince Charming would be. I looked forward to being loved and cherished. Then the high school years came, and I spent way too much time watching soap operas and movies like *Pretty in Pink.* Drama, drama, drama. When I started dating there were nervous glances, stilted conversations, and the excitement of first kisses. There were also fights and breakups. It was like a roller coaster of emotion!

Then, after high school, I met and married a wonderful man. John was generous, kind, and forgiving. We could talk easily, and I felt secure in our relationship. Maybe love was simpler than Hollywood dramas. True love was finding someone you could talk to with ease, whose heart cared for the same things, and whose dreams could meld with your own.

The same is true with Jesus. So many times we want the "emotional" experiences that come with falling in love, but Jesus is a bridegroom who is caught up in our hearts—not in the drama. This definition of love is a definition of Jesus: "Love is patient, love is kind and is not jealous; love does not brag and is not arrogant, does not act unbecomingly; it does not seek its own, is not provoked, does not take into account a wrong suffered, does not rejoice in unrighteousness, but rejoices with the truth; bears all things, believes all things, hopes all things, endures all things" (1 Corinthians 13:4–7, NAS).

Now that is a successful relationship! —TRICIA GOYER

FAITH STEP: *Write out 1 Corinthians 13:4–7 on a piece of paper, and then write down all the ways Jesus has shown you patience, kindness, and love. Consider it a love note from Him to you.*

THURSDAY, APRIL 14

God our savior and . . . Christ Jesus our hope. 1 Timothy 1:1 (CEB)

A HOME-PARTY JEWELRY COMPANY had a major sale, which I could have ignored if it hadn't been for the delicate silver bracelet engraved with the word *Hope*. The font used for the engraving made the word seem as elegant as the concept so often is in my life.

Hope. Only a wish and longing until Jesus arrived on the scene. Jesus—the embodiment of Hope for those who trust Him.

I wear the bracelet often, glancing at it as frequently as some would look at a wristwatch. *Hope, Cynthia. Remember?* it seems to say.

Today, I noticed that it is sporting a scratch on one side. I wear it a lot. I'm not going to stop wearing the hope bracelet because it's scratched. In fact, it may make a stronger statement this way. Because hope isn't always tidy. Life isn't always smooth. Only hope that stays tucked away and unused avoids signs of wear.

I chose to wear the bracelet again today—not a fashion statement, but a faith statement. As I rubbed my finger over the surface, I was reminded that the engraving is deeper than the scratch. Much deeper. We have been "born anew into a living hope through the resurrection of Jesus Christ from the dead" (1 Peter 1:3, CEB). It's a hope that bears the nicks and scratches of life with grace, because Jesus carved *Hope* deep when He conquered death.

Hebrews 6:19 tells us that Jesus is a hope "which is a safe and secure anchor for our whole being." Solid. Sure. Deeply engraved. Unfazed by the scratches and dents of life. —CYNTHIA RUCHTI

FAITH STEP: *What's your favorite Bible verse about the hope we find in Jesus? Watch for someone to cross your path today who might need those very words of hope. Inscribe your own bracelet with the word* hope. *As you wear it, remember where you find your hope.*

omy FRIDAY, APRIL 15

When they arrived at the Jordan, they began cutting down trees.
But as one of them was cutting a tree, his ax head fell into the river.
"Oh, sir!" he cried. "It was a borrowed ax!" 2 Kings 6:4–5 (NLT)

HAVE YOUR WELL-MEANING PLANS ever ground to a sudden and scary halt? If so, you can understand the prophet's dismay when his borrowed ax head flew off its handle and sank beneath the Jordan's murky water.

Ax heads were a costly tool. It's likely this prophet couldn't afford one, hence he borrowed it. Losing it meant he could no longer cut trees for his building project. Worse, he'd have to replace it. Imagine his relief when Elisha came to the rescue and retrieved it.

Years ago our family's house-building plans stopped suddenly when a neighbor changed his mind about selling us a necessary property easement. This happened forty-eight hours after we'd sold our home and bought a camping trailer in which to live temporarily as we built our new place.

The neighbor's decision meant we couldn't secure the necessary building permits. Having just sold our home meant living in the camping trailer indefinitely, with three children. Like the prophet, I panicked. Then I prayed. And Jesus came to our family's rescue. He reminded me that this detour was no surprise to Him and asked me to trust Him.

Two months later, we bought a lovely home. A few months after that, the county changed its permit requirements so we didn't need the neighbor's easement after all. We sold our recently purchased house for an unexpected profit, which made building more affordable than originally thought.

Life presents countless opportunities to trust Jesus, for Whom nothing is a surprise. Even when we think circumstances are hopeless or out of control, He's able to redeem them—not always as we expect, but always good nonetheless. —GRACE FOX

FAITH STEP: *The next time you stop at a red traffic light, take a moment to thank Jesus for watching over every detail of your life and praise Him for His wisdom.*

DML SATURDAY, APRIL 16

Relax, everything's going to be all right; rest, everything's coming together; open your hearts, love is on the way! Jude 2 (MSG)

I DIDN'T WATCH THE NEWS on TV in December. It's not that I'm uninterested. I'm probably *too* interested. I'd been watching maybe three hours a day. Some terrible things had been happening, and I didn't realize how listening to so much bad news was weighing me down until I stopped. But I didn't quit the news because of that—it was because I was way too busy. Whenever I took a breather, I found I just couldn't handle the urgent tone of the newscasters. After a week or two away from the twenty-four-hour news cycle, I was still just as busy but much more calm.

I'm not going to slip into the ranks of the uninformed—I've started watching again. The busy time passed, but I'm now limiting my exposure to one or two well-chosen shows. And thanks to the little book of Jude, my attitude has improved.

Jude wrote to a group of believers in a time when some people inside the church used grace as a license for open sin. They behaved badly and acted as if there was nothing wrong with their behavior. People mocked believers and followed their own selfish passions. Kind of like now.

In his letter, Jude didn't launch right into what was going wrong. First, he told the community they were chosen and dearly loved. They needed to build themselves up in the Spirit, fight for the faith, and, yes, speak truth to the troublemakers, with the approach tailored to their various needs.

Finally, Jude set their minds (and mine) at rest by reminding them to stay surrounded by God's love, in a posture of openness, always ready to receive the mercy of Jesus Christ. —SUZANNE DAVENPORT TIETJEN

FAITH STEP: *Do you need to step away from an area of your life? Try eliminating or cutting back on stressful activities. Add a walk or hot bath for balance. Pray. Rest some every day in His presence.*

SUNDAY, APRIL 17

But Caleb tried to quiet the people as they stood before Moses. "Let's go at once to take the land," he said. "We can certainly conquer it!" Numbers 13:30 (NLT)

TEN OF THE TRIBAL LEADERS sent to explore Canaan brought back a discouraging report. The fortified cities boasted high walls impossible to breach. The people were huge and powerful, making the Israelites feel like grasshoppers. These spies convinced the people that they would never overcome such formidable adversaries. Even though God had miraculously delivered, protected, and provided for them.

Caleb and Joshua refused to let fear intimidate them. Caleb urged the people to move out at once and take what God had promised them. After that unbelieving generation died wandering in the wilderness, we see Caleb once again ready to fight, forty-five years later. Hebron was still home to Anakites, the same people who had terrified the spies. But the eighty-five-year-old declared that he was just as strong and ready to fight as when Moses first sent him to explore Canaan. With the Lord's help, he would drive the enemies from his inherited land.

I can certainly identify with feeling puny and inadequate. That's how I felt the first time God called me to teach a Bible study, to write a book, and to speak at a conference. I almost let fear and doubt make me miss out on these blessings. Now I try to remember that these destructive attitudes are enemies that need to be driven out of my life.

If Caleb had lived in later times, one of his favorite verses might be Philippians 4:13: "I can do everything through Christ, who gives me strength." Whenever fear threatens to weaken my faith, I have a choice to make: I can look at the odds I'm facing, or concentrate on the One Who promises to give me the strength to succeed. —DIANNE NEAL MATTHEWS

FAITH STEP: *Are you facing something that makes you feel small and inadequate? Tell Jesus what you need from Him to help you overcome the obstacle. Then be ready to move.*

one MONDAY, APRIL 18

When the servant of the man of God got up early the next morning and
went outside, there were troops, horses, and chariots everywhere.
"Oh, sir, what will we do now?" the young man cried to Elisha.
"Don't be afraid!" Elisha told him. "For there are more on our side than on theirs!"
Then Elisha prayed, "O Lord, open his eyes and let him see! . . ."
2 Kings 6:15–17 (NLT)

WHEN ELISHA'S SERVANT AWOKE one morning and saw the overwhelming odds against the two of them, he panicked: "What will we do now?"

But Elisha viewed what his servant couldn't see: "the whole mountainside full of horses and chariots of fire" (2 Kings 6:17, MSG). Heaven had them covered. When the Lord opened the servant's eyes, he could see the same thing.

Most of us have felt like we've been backed into a corner at one time or another. We wake up one morning to a multitude of unplanned events: weather disasters, illness, even costly mistakes. Things can look hopeless. But it's what we do next that counts. John reminded us of Jesus's teaching when he wrote to encourage other believers who felt boxed in by persecution: "Greater is he that is in you, than he that is in the world" (1 John 4:4, KJV). And when two of Jesus's disciples felt their world had caved in after Jesus's death, the same question probably tore at their emotions: "What will we do?" But then they saw the truth: "Then their eyes were opened and they recognized him, and he disappeared from their sight" (Luke 24:31, NIV).

The familiar phrase, "It's what you do next that counts," challenges us. Will we focus on our problems? Or will we allow Jesus to open our spiritual eyes and trust Him, believing He is greater than our circumstances? The choice is ours. —REBECCA BARLOW JORDAN

FAITH STEP: *Is there a difficulty you are facing? Today, ask Jesus to open your eyes, to help you see the truth, and to trust Him for the outcome.*

TUESDAY, APRIL 19

Now may our God and Father himself and our Lord Jesus clear the way for us to come to you. 1 Thessalonians 3:11 (NIV)

BARRIERS. JUST WHEN I THINK I have a good plan in place—for my relationships, for my career, even for my list of chores for the day—something interferes. A family member doesn't respond to a text, or a friend pulls away without explanation. A project is rejected or someone else gets the job I longed for. Sometimes we face small interruptions that cause tiny detours. Other times we confront barriers that bruise our fists as we pound against them. I love the apostle Paul's response to barriers in this verse. He asked Jesus to clear the way.

I confess that my first response to an obstacle is to complain about it, then roll up my sleeves and attack it, and perhaps to ask friends or family to help me surmount it. How much easier would it be if, when I confronted a problem, I immediately asked Jesus to clear the way? Perhaps He'll call me to dig in and fight to conquer it, but I'll be handling the situation with His direction and not my own wisdom. Perhaps He'll prompt me to ask others for help, but in His timing and way that will foster kinship rather than feelings of neediness or guilt. Sometimes, Jesus may even clear away the barrier Himself, giving me an opportunity for deeper faith as I watch Him accomplish what I never could.

When we pray for Jesus to clear the way, and a barrier remains, we can trust that He knows, He cares, and He is working a good purpose in our lives. —SHARON HINCK

FAITH STEP: *Face a closed door in your home while picturing a barrier in your life. As you ask Jesus to clear the way, open the door as a reminder that He can work in our circumstances.*

WEDNESDAY, APRIL 20

*The Lord observed the extent of human wickedness on the earth,
and he saw that everything they thought or imagined were consistently and totally
evil. So the Lord was sorry he had ever made them and put them on the earth.
It broke his heart. Genesis 6:5–6 (NLT)*

ONE OF MY PASSIONS is to help people move from where they are to where they want to be in their personal and professional lives. Their progress frequently requires a shift in their thinking patterns. That's because often, without even realizing it, people habitually linger on thoughts contrary to God's truth, and those thoughts determine the direction their lives take.

Wrong thinking is an age-old problem identified in Noah's day. Not much has changed. Our thoughts are often self-centered, proud, critical, and conniving. No wonder our relationships break apart and hope falters.

As Christ's followers, we're called to live differently, and that includes the way we think about life. "Since you have heard all about Jesus and have learned the truth that comes from Him, throw off your old sinful nature and your former way of life, which is corrupted by lust and deception. Instead, let the spirit renew your thoughts and attitudes" (Ephesians 4:21–23, NLT). Aligning our thoughts with biblical truth ultimately reshapes our behavior. We display a new nature that reveals Jesus to a watching world. We become the salt of the earth, creating a thirst in others to know this Jesus we profess. We become lights, shining rays of hope into the darkness.

Humankind's consistently evil thoughts break God's heart because they result in sin, and sin cost Jesus His life. Let's determine not to contribute to God's sorrow. Let's apply the truths found in Jesus's teaching and please Him instead. —GRACE FOX

FAITH STEP: *Write a brief description of where you'd like to be in your physical, emotinal, or spiritual state. Specifically, write out which wrong thought patterns might hinder change. What biblical truths can you begin implementing today?*

THURSDAY, APRIL 21

Then Jesus said, "Come to me, all of you who are weary and carry heavy burdens, and I will give you rest." Matthew 11:28 (NLT)

I CHOSE THE WRONG SUITCASE for my cross-country trip. I had a regulation rollaway but, since I wasn't taking much, I chose a smaller bag. With a shoulder strap. And no wheels. I hefted it and decided it would even fit under the seat if space was limited.

So I set off for San Francisco, checked my big bag and kept my purse and carry-on, feeling confident. I noticed many women carried nothing, throwing their purses onto their wheeled bags.

During a day of delays and widely spaced gates, that bag I'd lifted easily at home grew heavier with every step. It clunked against doors and sat on questionable restroom floors. When I arrived, I unpacked that little carry-on and stuffed it in my checked bag. No way would I use it again! What originally seemed light became more of a burden the longer I carried it.

Sometimes I let my cares wear me out in the same way. An issue arises and I'm sure I can manage it on my own. I don't take it to Jesus in prayer—it's such a little thing. So I go on about my day without realizing how much it's taking out of me. The moment I do become aware, my fatigue offers another chance to take it to Jesus. I may—but I don't always do it. Maybe it's pride—I want to take care of myself. I forget my humanness and imagine I'm more than I am. I could cast my cares on the Lord, but why bother Him? Pretty soon, though, I find myself carrying an unexpectedly heavy load.

Jesus always relieves our burdens when we come to Him. He offers rest.
—SUZANNE DAVENPORT TIETJEN

FAITH STEP: *Jesus invites you to come. He wants your company. Today, imagine yourself walking beside Him. Share your heart and problems with the One Who knows the way.*

FRIDAY, APRIL 22

See what great love the Father has lavished on us, that we should be called children of God! And that is what we are! The reason the world does not know us is that it did not know him. 1 John 3:1 (NIV)

I AM NEW TO the parenting/sports dynamic. Our oldest son, Jack, likes outrigger paddling. That's a sport that does not require much interaction. But our second son, Will, is just getting into basketball. We have been going to his games and I have to be honest, I find that I completely lose myself in the game, yelling out things like, "Oh no!" and "Get the ball!" and "Help him!" Clearly, the things that I yell out with great emotion are spurring the entire team on to victory.

Last night's game was a nail-biter. It was tied up at the end of the game and went into overtime. My friend Jenn and I were screaming and clapping. Her son, Josh, is also on the team. We won the game with four seconds on the clock and I thought we would lose our minds with the joy of it.

Jenn gets it. She is a mom. We were cheering our kids on not because of their great skills but because we love them. It didn't matter if they missed shots or made mistakes, we were on their side. We were fully engaged, rooting them on. We wanted them to keep going, trying their best. We wanted them to win.

Sometimes we forget that Jesus is on our side. He loves us more than we could ever imagine. He sees us at our best and worst. He is on our side, fully engaged, cheering us on, wanting the absolute best for us. He is yelling at the top of His lungs, "I love you! I am proud of you! Keep going! Keep trying! Keep trusting me! I've got you!" What lavish love He's waiting to offer us! —SUSANNA FOTH AUGHTMON

FAITH STEP: *How has Jesus lavished His love on you? Make a list of ways. Then read 1 Corinthians 13 as a reminder.*

SATURDAY, APRIL 23

Let the message of Christ dwell among you richly as you teach and admonish one another with all wisdom through psalms, hymns, and songs from the Spirit, singing to God with gratitude in your hearts. Colossians 3:16 (NIV)

MANY MORNINGS AS I LOOK AHEAD to the day, I imagine how I want to create an atmosphere in our home that welcomes my husband and kids after school and work. I have an image of windows open to soft breezes on mild days with music playing throughout the house. And I'd welcome them, calm and unhurried, because I've crossed off everything on my to-do list and have the satisfied feeling of a day well done.

More often than not life doesn't look like that. I'm typically scrambling to eke out all I can from the last minutes of quiet before the family gets home. Most days, several "should'ves" nag at my peace and pound on my gratitude.

But Colossians 3:16 talks about an atmosphere of richness and singing and gratitude. The verse makes it clear that I have a choice about my frame of mind, which has a rich life separate from circumstances. Perhaps Paul meant gratitude to predetermine our attitude, not to come in after the stresses overwhelm. Might it be that gratitude must come first, before we succumb to busyness?

Psalm 100:4 seems to agree with that idea: "Enter his gates with thanksgiving and his courts with praise." Not after busyness sets in, but as we *enter* His gates. Thanksgiving is key as we begin the day He gives us.

There is no better time to be thankful than right now; an attitude of gratitude makes for an atmosphere of welcome. —ERIN KEELEY MARSHALL

FAITH STEP: *Make a list of the top twenty blessings you're thankful for. Praise God for each one in prayer, then thank Him for each one first thing tomorrow morning.*

one SUNDAY, APRIL 24

"Live as people worthy of the call you received from God. Conduct yourselves
with all humility, gentleness, and patience. Accept each other with love."
Ephesians 4:1–2 (CEB)

MY FAVORITE CHINESE RESTAURANT is often a place I settle in to write, reflect, organize my thoughts. It's a refueling station before I run errands. It's also a place ripe with conversation I can't avoid overhearing.

One day, the people in the booth behind me were discussing the people seated at the table to my right. The booth people gave clues they were not Jesus followers. The table people were leaders from a local church. The church people spent their mealtime cutting down members of their congregation. It was a conversation that should have happened in private, behind closed doors, if at all. The talk was graceless, condemnatory, and judgmental. And the world was listening. It was unavoidable. The conversation was loud enough for anyone nearby to hear.

"See?" one of the booth people said. "That's the problem with Christianity. People who talk like that."

What if the overheard conversation from the church leaders had been grace-filled, hope-hemmed, overflowing with forgiveness, and a clear representation of the love of Jesus? Might I have then heard the booth people respond, "See? That's one of the reasons I'm considering Christianity. Because of a love like that."

The world is always listening and watching. Jesus longs for us to behave in a way worthy of the Gospel, so those overhearing find a reason to believe. —CYNTHIA RUCHTI

FAITH STEP: *Today—or for a lifetime—keep a journal of any word or action that comes from you that might push someone away from Christ rather than draw the person to Him. Work toward a journal of blank pages.*

MONDAY, APRIL 25

Don't be concerned about the outward beauty of fancy hairstyles, expensive jewelry, or beautiful clothes. You should clothe yourselves instead with the beauty that comes from within, the unfading beauty of a gentle and quiet spirit, which is so precious to God. 1 Peter 3:3–4 (NLT)

"DO I LOOK BEAUTIFUL, MOMMY?" My four-year-old daughter gazed up at me with big brown eyes. She looks beautiful to me. But is that what really matters to her? To her heart?

"You do look beautiful today, honey." I pulled her into a squeeze. "But your joy *on the inside* is especially sparkly this morning—and what's in your heart is the most beautiful part."

It's easy to tell my daughter that beauty comes from the inside. It's easy to teach Scripture verses about godly character, but my girls pay the most attention to what they see. They notice if I groan when I get on the scale. They watch me applying my makeup, trying to get it just right. They see me trying on three dresses right before church and finding none of them works.

When I'm overly concerned about *my* outside, I have a hard time convincing my daughters that it's what's on the inside that counts. That's why it's so important to live what I want them to believe. To do this I need to see myself as beautiful in Jesus's eyes. I need to trust what I read about in God's Word, even more than what I see in ads or on runways. And as I believe it, my daughters will too.

My daughters are beautiful; I can see that in their big eyes looking up at me. And as I reflect that I feel beautiful in God's eyes, my daughters will learn to lift their heads and look to God too. —TRICIA GOYER

FAITH STEP: *Every time you look in the mirror over the next week, take time to appreciate something about yourself.*

TUESDAY, APRIL 26

There is no Jew or Greek, slave or free, male or female; for you are all one in Christ Jesus. Galatians 3:28 (HSC)

IN ONE OF MY CLASSES we do a lot of gender studies, mapping the construction of gender roles through the influence of such things as family, education, social class, and media. We read literature from lots of different perspectives, trying to understand varying experiences in order to better come to terms with our own. We discuss why and how people are typically divided into categories, with rules and expectations for the different roles we have to play.

While I am fascinated by my students' responses to this kind of study, I usually feel sad at the same time. It becomes apparent how divided we are and how much pressure people are under to perform according to the way society defines us. As it turns out, this kind of division and pressure represents exactly the opposite of who we are in Jesus.

Paul writes that we are all one in Him. The above verse is not a homogenation; no one is denying our uniqueness as individuals and trying to say we are all the same. What Paul is saying is that in the eyes of Jesus we are equal. He doesn't favor one gender, social class, or race. He made and loves us all. He laid down His life for all people because He values all people, and so should we. —GWEN FORD FAULKENBERRY

FAITH STEP: *Take a look around you. Where do you see an example of "the least of these" in your community? Decide on an action you can take to show that you value who Jesus values.*

WEDNESDAY, APRIL 27

Trust in the Lord with all your heart and lean not on your own understanding;
in all your ways submit to him, and he will make your paths straight.
Proverbs 3:5–6 *(NIV)*

"OH, AND THAT TOOTH needs a filling." The pediatric dentist's tone was friendly and confident as she pointed to one of my daughter's molars.

My surprise surely showed. "Really?"

"Yep. See there—" she gently tugged the tooth with her instrument. "See how it catches? That means a cavity. You can schedule a filling before you leave." I thanked her, paid the receptionist, and ushered my kids out the door without making a filling appointment. Something wasn't sitting right.

Two days later we heard a different story at my dentist's office. "I wouldn't treat this. One dentist says fill it, but just because it catches doesn't necessarily mean decay. Since she hasn't complained of pain and the films don't show a cavity, I wouldn't do anything." We thanked her for the advice, and even more for not charging us, and left the office.

Oh, the difference perception makes! The first dentist's perception would have cost me several hundred dollars, reminding me of the cost of our perceptions in the bigger issues of life. Most of the relationship disagreements I've had have been due to a difference of perception. One person sees a situation or a comment one way, which may not be how another person intended it. For that matter, most of my faith questions boil down to how I perceive Jesus and His Word.

Because our perceptions can guide so much in life, we're wise to count the costs of them. Our Source of truth is Jesus. He can straighten out misconceptions and give us clear direction and peace in His leading.

—ERIN KEELEY MARSHALL

FAITH STEP: *Memorize John 16:13 (ESV): "When the Spirit of truth comes, he will guide you into all the truth, for he will not speak on his own authority, but whatever he hears he will speak, and he will declare to you the things that are to come."*

THURSDAY, APRIL 28

The Lord will guide you continually, giving you water when you are dry and restoring your strength. You will be like a well-watered garden, like an ever-flowing spring. Isaiah 58:11 (NLT)

FOR YEARS I HAD DREAMED about lush flower gardens, and even filled a notebook with pictures of beautiful flowers and various styles of gardens. Each time I found a new idea online or in a garden magazine, I'd show my husband. I knew gardening was my passion, not his, so I tried to be careful not to pressure him. I never thought my dreams would become reality.

But a few years ago he actually suggested we draw up some ideas for a perennial garden. I was in garden heaven, creating, planning, choosing—and then planting several garden areas. They were not as exquisite as the ones in my idea notebook, but they were beautiful to me.

I soon discovered, however, that what I enjoyed was not gardening, but gardens. Gardening requires maintenance: watering, fertilizing, mulching, and yes, pulling weeds. At times, the work is overwhelming just to keep the garden growing and beautiful. Maintenance was low on my "enjoyable" list. But, oh, the joy of sitting in my garden among the fragrant flowers! It is well worth the work.

The Christian life is sometimes like that. We fall in love with Jesus, with His Word, with becoming more Christlike. Everything looks beautiful. Until the maintenance comes. The discipline of faithfulness challenges us; temptation distracts us; and difficulties threaten to overwhelm us. Growth requires intentionality. To keep the garden of our heart beautiful and well-watered, we must cooperate with Jesus, the Master Gardener. Sometimes, that work costs us time, comfort, pain. But a well-watered, maintained garden—whether a physical one or a spiritual one—will proclaim His beauty. Jesus makes all the work worthwhile. —REBECCA BARLOW JORDAN

FAITH STEP: *Do you enjoy gardens or gardening? Ask Jesus to make you like a beautiful "well-watered garden." Cooperate with Him today by including a spiritual discipline such as time in His Word, prayer, or Bible study.*

FRIDAY, APRIL 29

"So I say to you, keep asking, and it will be given to you. Keep searching, and you will find. Keep knocking, and the door will be opened to you." Luke 11:9 (HCSB)

ONE FRIDAY AFTERNOON LAST YEAR my nine-year-old granddaughter's bicycle went missing. Lacey always rode the pink and white bike (named "Rosie") to the school just a few blocks from her house. The bike riders had their own entrance to the school by the bike rack; they didn't bother with locks. To make matters worse, Lacey's bike went missing on the day her family left town for the weekend.

The next Monday Lacey walked to school hoping to find her bike back in its usual place. She was disappointed. I started praying that whoever took the bicycle would feel bad and bring it back. About a month passed by and Lacey began to make plans to purchase a new bike with her savings.

I woke up around four o'clock one morning and felt prompted to pray about the bike. *That would be silly,* I thought. *After all this time?* When the nudging continued, I prayed. That afternoon my daughter texted me that Lacey had her bike back. A friend had seen it in the park close to school.

I struggle with a tendency to give up too easily. Sometimes that spills over into my prayer life. It's hard to keep on praying and waiting for an answer when nothing seems to be happening. That's why I appreciate Jesus's encouragement to be persistent in prayer. He urges us to demonstrate our faith by keeping on asking, searching, knocking. His timing might be different from ours, and the answer may not be what we expect, but Jesus promises that our persistence will pay off.
—DIANNE NEAL MATTHEWS

FAITH STEP: *Do you have a prayer request that you feel like giving up on? Write it down and keep the paper in your Bible. Tell Jesus you commit to ask and seek until the answer comes.*

SATURDAY, APRIL 30

"Love your neighbor as yourself. . . ." Mark 12:31 (NLT)

STELLA HAD BEEN HAVING a particularly bad week by a two-year-old's standards. It seemed every time she turned around she was knocking something over or dropping something breakable. One evening during a tea party she dropped the little porcelain teapot she and her sister shared. It shattered into a thousand pieces. As I helped her pick it up and throw it away, Stella sighed. "I break things," she said. "I tear up things." A tear escaped from the edge of one of her big blue eyes and rolled down her cheek.

I scooped her up in my arms and held her tight. "It's okay. We all break things sometimes." Her look said she didn't believe me, though. She whispered, "But I break lots of things." In the conversation that followed, I tried to remind her of all of the good things she does: the block houses she builds, the puzzles she puts together, the train tracks she constructs. But it was clear she felt defined by the things she had broken that week.

As I tried to move Stella toward a new perspective, I thought about how we adults do the same thing. We may be good people who do lots of good things, but we can get stuck on the things we've messed up and then allow those mistakes to define us. "My house is a mess...My relationship failed...I never finished my degree...I lost my job..."

The truth is that we do mess up. And I hope we are always learning and growing and doing better. But self-loathing was never part of God's plan for us. After all, Jesus loved us enough to die for us. With all of our flaws, we were worth it to Him. And before we can show anyone else His love, we really need to love ourselves. —GWEN FORD FAULKENBERRY

FAITH STEP: *Have you been allowing your shortcomings to define you? Write down: "I won't be defined by _____." And focus on Jesus's commandment today: Love... yourself.*

SUNDAY, MAY 1

Casting the whole of your care [all your anxieties, all your worries, all your concerns, once and for all] on Him, for He cares for you . . . 1 Peter 5:7 (AMP)

"WE ARE ASKED to care about too much." When I first heard the statement, it was in the context of social media coupled with pleas for financial support coupled with a nationwide exhaustion and heart-wrenching news reports.

Thought-provoking, if nothing else. So I did. Think.

Even without leaving my home, I can hear reports about friends with serious health issues, the death of an acquaintance's loved one, another friend whose husband lost his job. I read stories about youth who age out of the foster system with no good options awaiting them. TV spots will ask me to care about starving children and abandoned animals.

On some level, I care about them all. But are we truly asked to care about too much? Where would Jesus draw the line for our compassion? How much caring is too much?

Matthew 9:36 (NKJV) says, "But when He saw the multitudes, He was moved with compassion for them, because they were weary and scattered, like sheep having no shepherd." The NIV version describes the multitudes as "harassed and helpless." The *Voice* expresses their condition as "deeply distraught, malaised, and heart-broken."

How much should we care? As much as He did. But with a caveat. He can bear caring about all of our needs at once. We can bear it only as long as it takes us to carry the needs to Him. —CYNTHIA RUCHTI

FAITH STEP: *Do you habitually say, "I'll pray for you," automatically taking on all the concerns that cross your path? Keep a list of what you believe Jesus wants you to make ongoing prayer concerns. For the rest, pray immediately and then roll the concern onto Him.*

MONDAY, MAY 2

"Here I am! I stand at the door and knock. If anyone hears my voice and opens the door, I will come in and eat with that person, and they with me."
Revelation 3:20 (NIV)

As a teen, I was passionate about sharing my faith, but often clumsy. When someone told me they weren't interested, my zeal burned hotter and I kept talking, longing to convince. Or when I wasn't being pushy, I was playing past conversations in my mind, trying to think of a brilliant response that would have smashed their arguments. Not the most loving of approaches.

When I face a closed door, my impulse is to kick it down like an aggressive SWAT-team member, or maybe pick the lock like a master thief. Yet Jesus, who has all the power in the universe at His command, describes His approach so differently. He chooses to grant us the gift of free will. He doesn't force, doesn't barge in, doesn't trick or manipulate. He simply knocks and allows us to either continue to shut Him out, or open the door.

Jesus's patient and gentle description here is a good reminder for me when I'm sharing the Good News with others. It's so tempting for me to insist on a positive response, try to force faith onto another, or find sneaky ways to pry that door open from the outside. I've especially noticed that tendency with family members. My heart is so desperate for them to follow Jesus, I can overwhelm them with my constant preaching, demanding, or finagling.

I'm trying to learn to follow Jesus's example: to knock, invite, call, and allow. To give Him time and room to work.

I'm also seeking to be more sensitive to hearing when Jesus is tapping on the door of my life, offering to interact in a new place, or to visit a new part of my heart that I've barricaded. —Sharon Hinck

---

Faith Step: *Think of one truth you know about Jesus. Share that with a friend or family member today, with no pressure or demand for a response.*

TUESDAY, MAY 3

"The Lord your God is with you, he is mighty to save. He will take great delight in you, he will quiet you with his love, he will rejoice over you with singing."
Zephaniah 3:17 (NIV)

RECENTLY I WAS ASKED by a teenage girl what I write. "I write many things, like devotions, historical novels, and romance novels." The young girl's eyes widened, and she looked up at me with a smile. "I like romance," she said. I like romance, too, although my books are extremely chaste, and even more important than my characters' relationship with each other is their growing relationship with Jesus.

The Bible is filled with romantic stories—look at Ruth and Boaz or Mary and Joseph. (And I won't even mention Song of Solomon!) Romance isn't just about butterflies in our stomachs and heart-pounding attraction. It's about choosing another and expressing love in considerate ways.

I know that not every person gets to experience the type of sweet romances I write about in my books, but *every* reader can have a loving relationship with Jesus.

One of my favorite moments with my husband is when I lay my head on his chest and he strokes my head and kisses my forehead. When I read Zephaniah 3:17, that's how I picture Jesus, quieting me with His love. The Bible says Jesus cares for us, even rejoices over us. Isaiah 62:5 (NIV) says, "As a young man marries a young woman, so will your Builder marry you; as a bridegroom rejoices over his bride, so will your God rejoice over you."

Just like my young friend, I love romance. Mainly I take delight in Jesus rejoicing over me with singing because His love for me is so great.
—TRICIA GOYER

FAITH STEP: *Write out a list of some of your favorite romances in the Bible. How do these romances give you insight into Jesus's love for you? Picture Jesus singing over you.*

WEDNESDAY, MAY 4

Noah was a righteous man, the only blameless man living on earth at the time.
He consistently followed God's will and enjoyed a close relationship with him.
Genesis 6:9 (NLT)

OCCASIONALLY WE SEE OLD TESTAMENT characters whose reputation for godliness sets them apart from their peers. Noah is one of these guys. He lived an exemplary life amid a culture that made God regret He'd created humankind. Enoch did the same: "He enjoyed a close relationship with God throughout his life. Then suddenly, he disappeared because God took him" (Genesis 5:24, NLT). And then there's Caleb: "But my servant Caleb is different from the others. He has remained loyal to me, and I will bring him into the land he explored" (Numbers 14:24, NLT).

These fellows lived in an age when righteousness wasn't the norm. The majority around them worshipped idols and chose a lifestyle contrary to God's commands, but these men remained loyal to their God.

We, too, live in an age when righteousness isn't the norm. The world around us drifts further and further from biblical principles, but we mustn't settle for "status quo spirituality." Doing so guarantees losing the opportunity to influence those struggling to survive without Jesus, Who is the Giver of life.

Walking in close fellowship with Jesus makes us different from the norm. Let's pray for Him to give us a burning passion to know and obey Him. Let's strive to honor Him with every thought, word, and deed.

Jesus needs men and women who make friendship with Him an utmost priority. Let's invite Him to invade every cell of our being with His holy presence so that we can commune with Him and make a difference in this world. —GRACE FOX

FAITH STEP: *Collect three identical items. Now add one different item to the mix. Notice how that item stands out from the others. Ask Jesus to make you stand out from the crowd in a positive way.*

THURSDAY, MAY 5

"Blessed are the poor in spirit, for theirs is the kingdom of heaven."
Matthew 5:3 *(NAS)*

ONE SEMESTER DURING FINAL EXAMS—literally right after I passed them out in a particular class—a student said she needed to talk to me. "I don't see why I need this class! I don't need to know about writing and literature to be in the medical profession!" She proceeded to critique my teaching, blaming me for her poor performance. I calmly tried to explain that even if I agreed with her, which I didn't, it was not within my power to change the requirements of her program, and that, in any case, the day of the final exam was not a day to debate such matters.

Granted, she was extremely stressed out, but the student's attitude annoyed me. The low grade she had going into finals was the result of her choices. She continually turned in shoddy work, despite my suggestions for change and my offers to help. Now, on the last day of class, she was in a panic, and behaving as if it was my fault she might fail.

Later that day I got an e-mail from her: "I am sorry for how I acted this morning. I have not done what I should in your class. I admit I am somewhat lazy. You are a good teacher. Please forgive me for the things I said."

I suppose a cynic might say she was covering her tracks, but I believe she was truly sorry. Just like any normal person, she made mistakes and hadn't wanted to take responsibility for her actions. When she did, however, my heart softened toward her. I thought about the above verse and what a difference humility makes. We all sin and fall short of the glory of God. But when we are humble—owning our mistakes and trying to make amends—Jesus says the kingdom of heaven is ours. —GWEN FORD FAULKENBERRY

FAITH STEP: *Is there something you need to take responsibility for—a mistake you need to own? Say you're sorry and mean it, doing everything you can to make it right.*

✦ FRIDAY, MAY 6

I pray that you may be active in sharing your faith, so that you will have a full understanding of every good thing we have in Christ. Philemon 1:6 (NIV)

WHEN WE MOVED INTO our new home, the backyard had nothing to attract birds. So I was surprised one day when a hummingbird flew up close to the glass wall of our living room. I'd never seen a hummingbird stay in one place for more than a few seconds, but this one lingered on our patio. Over the next week, I periodically saw it streak across the yard, sometimes coming in close, as though checking to see if we'd hung a feeder. I finally hung a beautiful glass feeder with copper accents.

I was excited to see the little bird quickly accept our offering. The next day, a second hummingbird swooped in, but instead of drinking, it chased the other one away. This happened frequently for several days. Then one day, I noticed three hummingbirds chasing each other around the backyard. I felt like thumping their tiny heads together for fighting over the nectar instead of sharing it. I had purposely bought a feeder with four separate perches and sipping holes.

Sometimes people have a hard time sharing too. It doesn't come naturally to us, but as followers of Christ we're expected to do a lot of sharing. We are to share our material resources with the needy. We are to share the burdens of others and use our spiritual gifts for the good of fellow believers. And we are to share the wonderful news of forgiveness and eternal life through Jesus Christ.

When I share my faith, it always benefits me as well as others. As I adopt a sharing way of living, I will develop a greater awareness of all the blessings I have through Christ. And I will drink more deeply of Him.
—DIANNE NEAL MATTHEWS

FAITH STEP: *Each time you interact with someone today, ask Jesus what He wants you to share with that person. Is it compassion? Material resources? A listening ear? The news about His love and forgiveness? Share joyfully.*

SATURDAY, MAY 7

In your strength I can crush an army; with my God I can scale any wall.
Psalm 18:29 (NLT)

A TV PROGRAM SHOWED police cadets in physical training. One of the exercises required them to scale a wall that towered above them.

One by one, the cadets ran toward the obstacle and, with a flying leap, grabbed the top edge to hoist themselves up and over. Then came two jokesters. They looked at the wall and, without skipping a beat, ran around it.

Given my lack of athleticism, I would do the same thing in those circumstances. But I've chosen a different attitude when it comes to real-life challenges that tower over me. I've chosen to believe that I can overcome whatever obstacles I encounter—not in the power of positive thinking or with my own abilities, but in the strength Jesus gives.

Still, there are times I think, *This situation is too hard. There's no way you can move past this pain. Give up—you deserve to sulk in self-pity.* But the moment I recognize these thoughts, I can refute them with truth.

The truth says that Jesus arms me with strength and makes my way safe (Psalm 18:32, 39). He prepares me for battle and strengthens me to draw a bow of bronze (Psalm 18:34). His right hand supports me (Psalm 18:35).

Focusing on these promises replaces cowardice with courage and inspires me to trust Jesus to accomplish through me what I could never do on my own.

What wall do you face today? Find confidence in focusing on the truth and trusting Jesus. He will strengthen you, and you will overcome.
—GRACE FOX

FAITH STEP: *Memorize today's key verse. Personalize it: "In your strength I can _____; with my God I can _____." Find confidence in the truth of these words.*

SUNDAY, MAY 8

I lift up my eyes to the mountains—where does my help come from? My help comes from the Lord, the Maker of heaven and earth. Psalm 121:1–2 (NIV)

EVER SINCE I HURT MY BACK three years ago, my ice pack and I have spent a lot of quality time together. When Addison was filling in a Mother's Day questionnaire last year about my favorite things to do, he wrote, "My mom likes to lie on the couch with her ice pack." The other day, my oldest, Jack, passed by me on the couch and said, "Look, everybody, it's Mom in her natural habitat." So sad.

I tried out a new walking regimen the other day and my back rebelled. It laid me out flat. So, today as I curl up with my ice pack, I am left with two options: (1) feel sorry for myself or (2) focus on what I can do. I reserve the right to do both. But I have noticed when I am laid out, my face is pointing heavenward.

It seems that I have a third option. Focusing on the One Who is my healer. In my moments of deep despair at being immobilized, I have a physical reminder that my help comes from the One Who spoke stars and planets into existence. My grandma Blakeley ended every birthday card with the saying, *Keep looking up.* She had her fair share of wildness, joy, heartache, and adventure in her lifetime but she knew the living truth that her help came from keeping her eyes on Jesus. I have resigned myself to the couch today. But I am also lifting my eyes to the One Who saves, delivers, heals, and brings more relief than an ice pack. I'm going to do what Grandma says. Keep Looking Up. —SUSANNA FOTH AUGHTMON

FAITH STEP: *Go find a patch of grass to lie on. Look into the great expanse of the sky and repeat the verse, "Where does my help come from? My help comes from the Lord, Maker of heaven and earth."*

MONDAY, MAY 9

And we, who with unveiled faces all reflect the Lord's glory, are being transformed into his likeness with ever-increasing glory, which comes from the Lord, who is the Spirit. 2 Corinthians 3:18 (NIV)

I KEPT PICKING UP the picture frame and then setting it down again. The last thing my mom needed for Mother's Day was another frame. With four children and nine grandchildren, along with spouses, plus thirteen great-grandchildren, almost every wall and shelf in my parents' home is partially covered by framed photos. But this glossy ceramic frame was special—by the opening for the photo were the words: "Mother, I hope others see a little bit of you in me."

Although I didn't inherit my mother's beautiful brown eyes or thick dark hair, I would be pleased to know that people thought I resembled her in terms of character. To imitate her hardworking, generous, and self-less nature and devout faith is a worthy goal. But even more important, I want people to see the character of Jesus in me.

How can I ever come close to reflecting the character traits of the sinless Son of God? Thankfully, I have the Holy Spirit living inside me, changing me from the inside out. The more time I spend with Jesus in prayer and in the Word, the more I will grow to be like Him. My attitudes and character will gradually be transformed so that I can respond in a more Christlike manner in every life circumstance and in each interaction with others.

That white ceramic frame with gold lettering now contains a photo of my mother and me, displayed proudly on her nightstand. Each time I see it, it reminds me of my ultimate goal: to have others see a lot of Jesus in me. —DIANNE NEAL MATTHEWS

FAITH STEP: *Focus on one of Jesus's character traits, such as gentleness, compassion, or forgiveness. Ask Him to help you display that trait today as you interact with others, then look for the opportunities He provides.*

TUESDAY, MAY 10

"You shall know the truth, and the truth shall make you free." John 8:32 *(NKJV)*

JESUS, FREEDOM, AND THE TRUTH are inextricably joined. Jesus promises in the above verse that the truth frees us, and in John 14:6 He states that He, Himself, *is* the truth when He says, "I am the way, the truth, and the life. No one comes to the Father except through Me."

Many people think of truth as binding. We are "bound" by our oath or by the law to do certain things. In this kind of thinking freedom would be considered something outside of our duty to the truth. I love how Jesus turns that idea on its head. In His way of thinking, the truth is Who He is—and Who He is brings us freedom.

Consider this example. A person evades the law of God (and possibly the law of the land) by covering up some addiction—maybe to illegal drugs, sex, alcohol, whatever. He or she thinks they have to continue lying in order to be free to keep the addiction. Jesus comes into that situation and shines the light of truth. For the first time the person no longer hides, but owns the problem and seeks help. By exposing the truth—and walking in it—the person is able to be truly free from the addiction that has held him/her enslaved, truly freed by the Truth Who sets us free.
—GWEN FORD FAULKENBERRY

FAITH STEP: *Surrender your hold on anything false—and let Him Who is the Truth take hold of your life today.*

WEDNESDAY, MAY 11

*If another believer sins against you, go privately and point out the offense.
If the other person listens and confesses it, you have won that person back.*
Matthew 18:15 (NLT)

A NEW NURSE JUST OFF ORIENTATION, I was caring for a preemie with an ostomy, an opening in his abdomen that allowed his intestines to empty into a tiny bag. He was able to kick the bag off, so the first order of the day would be replacing it. The off-going nurse asked if I knew how or if she'd have to stay and do it.

I'd done it once and I thought I remembered how. I certainly didn't want to make her stay over. I should've asked Cheryl, the charge nurse, to listen to me run though my plan and give me her feedback. Instead, I proceeded. I cleansed his fragile skin but left out the crucial step of surrounding the opening with a skin barrier before attaching the bag to his tiny tummy. An hour later Cheryl pulled me aside. "Don't feel bad," she whispered, "but we're going to have to redo that ostomy."

Thankfully, she'd caught my mistake. She helped me carefully soak the bag off and talked me through reapplying it. When another nurse cruised by to see what was up, Cheryl just said I was applying an ostomy bag without mentioning my mistake. As far as I know, she never told anyone, even though it would've made for juicy break-room gossip.

If only we Christians were as compassionate to other believers. Jesus said when we have a problem with someone we should go to that person and work it out. That crucial step is often left out. It may be tempting to share someone else's failings, but Jesus always wants us to make the loving choice. I'll never forget that Cheryl did. —SUZANNE DAVENPORT TIETJEN

FAITH STEP: *Has someone in the church hurt you? Have you hurt someone else? How did you address it? Or did you? Prayerfully consider how you might handle this or a similar situation in the future.*

one THURSDAY, MAY 12

I myself in my mind am a slave to God's law, but in my sinful nature a slave to the law of sin. . . . Therefore, there is now no condemnation for those who are in Christ Jesus. Romans 7:25—8:1 (NIV)

MY FRIEND AND I VISITED while our kids enjoyed an after-school play date. We're both introspective types, and our conversations often turn toward how we want to grow as mothers, wives, and friends. All of that means we admit ways we have made mistakes or felt inadequate for those we love.

I think it's safe to say we understand the hammer sound of condemning voices in our heads, and I'm guessing you've heard them too. They're nasty and heavy; they press us until we cannot breathe under them. They tell us, *You fail too much. You've never been good enough. Your mistakes set back others.* Those voices are definitely not from Jesus. In Him there's no condemnation.

My friend and I both know Jesus as Savior, which means the freedom from condemnation that He gave us through the Cross also applies to the continuing ways we fail.

The Holy Spirit does not condemn. Instead, He lovingly convicts. Condemnation and conviction are not synonymous; the difference is a crucial one to understand if we're to live free from those accusing voices. When we're convicted, it is to address the action or character quality that needs repentance, whereas condemnation strikes at our identity. Jesus doesn't tear us down but saves and empowers us.

My friend and I can help each other listen for the Spirit's voice instead of listening to enslaving thoughts. A slave of something bad feels pressed by a negative control. A slave of Christ (Ephesians 6:6) is free to live empowered by Him. In Christ we're free to choose whom to listen to.

Listen well and be free today. —ERIN KEELEY MARSHALL

FAITH STEP: *Next time you feel beaten down, check the source. If you know Jesus as Savior, you're free to be convicted and grow, not condemned and burdened.*

FRIDAY, MAY 13

Pray like this: Our Father in heaven, may your name be kept holy.
May your Kingdom come soon. May your will be done on earth, as it is in heaven.
Matthew 6:9–10 (NLT)

FOR MANY YEARS I TRIED to figure out how to pray effectively. I wouldn't admit it out loud, but I believed deep down that if I said the right things, at the right moment, and in the right way, that Jesus could be swayed. I didn't realize my prayers shouldn't be about my will, but about His. Even Jesus prayed, "Father, if you are willing, take this cup from me; yet not my will, but yours be done" (Luke 22:42, NIV).

What I've since discovered is that I don't need to figure out a formula to get what I want. Jesus has good plans for my life. He has hopes for me and a future. It's not my job to get Jesus to answer my requests in the way I desire, but instead to seek what He's doing in the world around me and to become a part of that.

After years of praying I've learned that things do change. The number one thing that changes when I pray...is me. Prayer softens my heart to the will of Jesus and fosters a connection between Him and me.

My prayers change the future as I connect with Him. It's then I become willing to submit my will to His. I take different paths than I would have taken myself. As I go down different paths the future is changed. Instead of seeing my desires fulfilled, I see Jesus's desires fulfilled.

You'd think I'd be disappointed when I don't get my way. Instead, I rejoice because Jesus's ways are better than mine. It's His will being done on earth, as it is in heaven...through me. —TRICIA GOYER

FAITH STEP: *Sit down to pray and start with the words: "Change me, first." Then read through the Lord's Prayer found in Matthew 6:7–15. How does this prayer inspire you to change?*

SATURDAY, MAY 14

When we were children, we thought and reasoned as children do.
But when we grew up, we quit our childish ways. 1 Corinthians 13:11 (CEV)

THE LURE OF RELIVING a childhood experience influenced me to talk my husband into a Disney World vacation last year. I had visited Disneyland as a child, and we had taken our own kids as well. But a few decades had passed since then, and I had been nurturing those memories.

Of the four parks available, I anticipated Fantasyland the most: spinning teacups, the Mad Hatter, the fairy-tale princesses of my storybook days, and yes, even the repetitive chorus of "It's a Small World." I expected to re-create that same childhood wonder I remembered.

But things don't always work out like you imagine. Even though it was springtime, a heat wave hit Disney World on the day we picked the park at Fantasyland. We arrived at my favorite park around one o'clock just as the temperature topped ninety degrees. From the moment we stepped into the park, crowds of people poured into every attraction. By the time we elbowed our way to my favorite section, strollers and lines were so thick we could barely see any of the sites. The heat and crowds prevented us from doing more. Childish grumblings replaced my wonder. In only one hour, we were done.

Jesus reminded me of something that day—and later on the trip. Trying to recreate our childhood is probably impossible. There's nothing wrong with enjoying childlike things, but Jesus didn't encourage unrealistic expectations or childish behavior. True wonder comes from knowing the One Who is Wonder-full (Isaiah 9:6). —REBECCA BARLOW JORDAN

FAITH STEP: *In what ways do you still act like a child? List at least one way you can exercise more childlike faith and wonder.*

SUNDAY, MAY 15

By this everyone will know you are my disciples, if you have love for one another.
John 13:35 (NRSV)

WE HAD AN ANNIVERSARY CELEBRATION at our church this year. The theme was "I love my church," complete with T-shirts. It was fun but also a time for me to reflect on the years I've spent as part of that local body of believers. I remembered a lot of good times and some that were not-so-great. In that reflection I realized I could wear my shirt in complete honesty.

For some of us, church is a complicated aspect of life as a Christian. In our imagination, the church should be some kind of Christian utopia. But the reality, in my experience, is far from that. This used to upset me. However, as I've grown, I've come to believe the ideal I imagined was never what church is intended to be. What is intended all gets back to that pesky, messy word: love.

Love is easy in theory. It looks good on cards, sounds good in songs, works well on a T-shirt. In practice...not so much. And yet it's the one thing Jesus said would identify us to the world. What that means in practical terms is that I love the ultraconservatives in my church family, though they think I'm a liberal. I love the people who can't carry a tune as much as the ones who sing with me on the praise team. And they love me. When my kids misbehave or I'm a stubborn ox or I burn what I was bringing for potluck—they love me. Mostly the way we show our love is by sticking together in good times and bad.

I think this is what Jesus meant when He admonished the disciples to love one another. Stick together, even if you disagree. Let your common ground be Me. —GWEN FORD FAULKENBERRY

FAITH STEP: *Say a prayer today for that person who is difficult for you to love. Keep at it every day until loving becomes easier.*

MONDAY, MAY 16

He leads the humble in what is right, and teaches the humble his way.
Psalm 25:9 (ESV)

ALTHOUGH IT DOESN'T CALL attention to itself, humility can't help but be intriguing. In its genuine form it's a beautiful and rare thing, but often it's only partly real.

Have you ever given someone a compliment, only to receive a nod in return, as if the person agrees completely with your grand assessment of her? *Ah yes, I know I'm good.* On the flip side, I had a friend years ago who never accepted a compliment. She disagreed with me to the point where I felt as if I had to argue with her just to say something kind. A lack of humility is obvious, but too much humility smacks of a different kind of self-absorption, of self-deprecation that denies our worth as our Creator's masterpiece. If we don't value ourselves as Jesus does, created in His Father's image and loved enough to die for, we're missing something critical. False humility can show up as choosing chronic victimhood or refusing to stand up for ourselves because we don't value our God-given worth.

True humility causes us to carry ourselves with the dignity Jesus showed. He did not try to draw attention to Himself, but He lived with complete confidence in His identity as His Father's Son. Belonging to the heavenly Father meant everything to Him.

Fortunately, real humility is teachable, but we must release ourselves, our preconceived ideas, and our patterns to Jesus. When we relinquish ourselves to Jesus's leading, He shows us His way. He even recreates our spirit with His own.

When we embrace our need for Him, He scatters unhealthy pride and replaces it with humility that reveals His glory. —ERIN KEELEY MARSHALL

FAITH STEP: *Remind yourself of the beauty of Jesus's real humility by keeping this verse somewhere visible.*

TUESDAY, MAY 17

In that day the deaf will hear the words of the scroll, and out of gloom and darkness the eyes of the blind will see. Isaiah 29:18 (NIV)

I WAS BLESSED TO LEAD a young mom to Christ a few months ago. Elizabeth has been in my life for a few years as part of a teen-mother support group. After struggling with bad choices, she approached me ready to turn everything over to Jesus. The transformation has been amazing!

Previously the Bible was hard for her to understand, but with Jesus's Spirit in Elizabeth it's becoming alive to her. The world also looks different. She's been appalled by the unwholesome lyrics of secular music. The television shows that she used to watch are now unappealing. It's almost as if she was given new eyes and new ears!

As Galatians 5:1 (AMP) says, "In [this] freedom Christ has made us free [and completely liberated us]; stand fast then, and do not be hampered and held ensnared and submit again to a yoke of slavery [which you have once put off]."

So many times I feel that I have to "talk" people into making good choices. Instead, I simply have to share about the freedom that Christ brings. Once people accept Jesus, He begins the work. It's not my words that make the difference but Christ's light of truth.

Elizabeth won't completely change overnight—none of us do—but the changes are real. Once eyes are opened and ears are unstuck, then it's hard to keep that type of transformation to yourself. Elizabeth is already sharing with others, inviting them to join her on her freedom journey. She may not be able to talk them into change, but she can share with them the changes that are possible in Christ. —TRICIA GOYER

FAITH STEP: *Kneel before God and surrender your efforts of trying to convince someone to make positive changes. Spend time praying for them instead. Trust that Jesus can do good work—more than you'd ever expect.*

WEDNESDAY, MAY 18

"My days are past; my plans are broken off, the desires of my heart." . . .
*"For I know that my Redeemer lives, and at the last he will
stand upon the earth." Job 17:11, 19:25* (ESV)

THERE IS A WHOLE INDUSTRY to encourage people to dream big, to chase their vision, to make their five-year plans happen. Although setting goals can be useful, what happens when our desires don't play out like our dreams?

The business that took a lifetime to build crumbles under a bad economy. In spite of prayers and the best medical intervention, the cancer returns. Even after counseling and every effort at reconciliation, a spouse leaves, grinding marriage vows under his heel. All the cheerful calendars and upbeat posters don't help when our plans are broken off. We can understand Job's painful cry.

Yet only a few chapters later, from the midst of a type of suffering we can barely comprehend, Job utters the words of faith that have inspired Easter hymns. "I know that my Redeemer lives." Many generations passed from Job's time until the birth of Jesus. Many more generations have lived while we wait for Him to come again to stand on the earth. Even so, Job put his hope in the coming Redeemer, and so can we.

When our plans are destroyed—by unjust actions of others, by our own mistakes, by illness or accident or disaster—we can join Job's bold declaration. We have a Redeemer. Jesus can bring blessing out of the worst circumstances, and ultimately He will bring the complete fulfillment we long for. Like Job, we may feel "my days are past," and there is no more hope. But the story isn't finished yet. Our life has triumphant pages ahead. —SHARON HINCK

FAITH STEP: *Which of Job's contrasting statements do you most identify with today? Ask Jesus to kindle your faith in His unfolding plan.*

THURSDAY, MAY 19

"Love the Lord your God with all your heart, with all your soul, with all your mind, and with all your strength. This is the first commandment. And the second, like it, is this: 'You shall love your neighbor as yourself.' There is no other commandment greater than these." Mark 12:30–31 (NKJV)

I AM OFTEN ASKED questions about my faith that I can't answer, either by my kids, students at school, or churches where I speak. There are so many things in the Bible I don't understand. And there are things not in the Bible I don't understand either, much less reconcile with my experience as a Christian human being. This is a difficult aspect of being a follower of Jesus. Just like I don't believe love is blind, for me, faith isn't either. It requires rigorous intellectual seeking in order to be authentic. But the fact remains that faith goes far beyond where my intellect can take me. Like the Bible says, it's the evidence of things not seen.

So how is one to live? What I tell myself, as well as anyone who comes to me with an honest question that I have no idea how to answer, is that I do a lot of seeking, but when I come to the end of my search without a satisfying answer, I go back to Mark 12:30–31. That is the most simplified version of Christianity I have ever found.

The famous astrophysicist Neil deGrasse Tyson once said he is "driven by two main philosophies: know more today about the world than I knew yesterday and lessen the suffering of others. You'd be surprised at how far that gets you." That's how I feel about the above verse. I find that if I focus all of my energy on loving God and loving others, that gives me plenty to do. There is so much contained in those two commandments that I could spend my lifetime trying to understand and perfect the art of following them. Really, everything else is a distraction. —GWEN FORD FAULKENBERRY

FAITH STEP: *Commit Mark 12:30–31 to memory, and use it as your guidepost through the questions and quandaries of the Christian life.*

FRIDAY, MAY 20

Come near to God and he will come near to you. Wash your hands, you sinners, and purify your hearts, you double-minded. James 4:8 (NIV)

MY THREE BOYS HAVE all gone through different phases of how affectionate they are with me. They seem to hit a wall right around fifth grade when it is no longer cool for me to grab them and smother them with kisses. They definitely don't allow me to kiss them when I drop them off at school. And, just recently, my youngest son, Addison, decided he didn't want to kiss me goodnight anymore. Sometimes it is hard to be a mom. I love that little boy. I want all the kisses that I can get. But I am not going to give him kisses that he doesn't want. The funny thing is, even though Addie doesn't want to kiss me goodnight, every morning around five o'clock he finds his way into our bed and snuggles as close as he can. He snuggles into my side and puts his cold feet on my shins and his breathing settles into a relaxed rhythm. It is in these early-morning moments that I can't help but kiss his warm little face. And Addie smiles. I love being close to my boys.

I think Jesus feels the same way about us. He is not going to force His attentions on us. He is not going to charge in where He is not wanted. But in those moments, when we draw near to Him, when we make time and space for Him in our lives, He is able to draw near to us, showing His great affection for us. He speaks truth and wisdom into our minds and hearts. And He reminds us, one more time, just how much He loves us.
—SUSANNA FOTH AUGHTMON

FAITH STEP: *Set aside a moment in your favorite chair or hangout place in your house. Bring your Bible and your journal. Tell Jesus, "This morning I am drawing near to You. Will You remind me how much You love me?"*

SATURDAY, MAY 21

He said, "Cast your net on the right side of the boat and you will find some."
So they did. . . . John 21:6 (CEB)

MANY CURIOSITIES LACE the life Jesus lived on earth. One of the incidents happened the day several disciples turned their uncertainty into a fishing trip. Their Master, Jesus, had suffered a cruel death on a Cross, had been buried for three days, rose to life again, and had appeared to them with the announcement that He was soon to leave them again.

What were they to do with that information? They went fishing.

They'd fished all night with their nets on the port side of the boat. All night. Nothing. Although they didn't recognize Who He was, in the morning a man on the shore called out to them, asking if they'd caught anything. The Man said, "Cast your net on the right side of the boat, and you will find some."

The distance between the port and starboard sides of the boat couldn't have been more than a few feet. For reasons unknown to us, the expert fishermen obeyed the stranger's advice and cast their nets on the opposite side. The haul of fish was so great, they struggled to drag them all to shore.

Was the story told to log yet another miracle in the journal of the life of Jesus? Or is there an application for us?

"Cast your net on the other side," speaks to my heart. Sometimes I miss the right thing, but not by much. What I perceive as failure could be a misjudgment by a few feet. Solution? Listen carefully to the direction Jesus gives me, whether it seems to make sense or not. —CYNTHIA RUCHTI

FAITH STEP: *In what arena of life have you felt just a few feet off from where you need to be—in your career, your relationship, your emotions, your spiritual health? Where is Jesus asking you to cast your net instead? Spend a moment right now aligning your response with those of whom it was said, "So they did."*

SUNDAY, MAY 22

"Whenever someone has a ready heart for this, the insights and understandings flow freely. But if there is no readiness, any trace of receptivity soon disappears. That's why I tell stories: to create readiness, to nudge the people to receptive insight."
Matthew 13:12–13 (MSG)

I LOVE STORIES. Around a campfire, in a book or a theater, anywhere and just about anytime, I love a story. Almost everyone does. They fill us like a good meal. Each of us is one person before hearing a story and a different person afterward. Imagine a roomful of people being told a story and compare them to people listening to a lecture. Was your story-time group leaning forward, shiny-eyed, and focused in their chairs? Were your students slumped or leaning back half-asleep?

Jesus knew how to tell a good story. He taught in parables so people could grasp His teachings. People were drawn in to Jesus's stories. They started to imagine the scene and, if they were like most listeners, to place themselves into the story. As a result, they opened up and the lessons started to sink in. Since the meanings of His stories were anything but obvious, people pondered them.

We still ponder them today. And when we do, we too can learn something—about ourselves and about God. Brilliant truths may be too much for us to handle when they come straight at us head-on. We stand a better chance of coming away with new knowledge if the storyteller would, as American poet Emily Dickinson recommended, "Tell it slant."

We, too, can find creative ways to talk with people about our faith, using words anyone can understand. —SUZANNE DAVENPORT TIETJEN

FAITH STEP: *Get out your pencil and paper and write a modern-day parable. Think of a biblical truth and make up a story that paints a picture of it. Read it out loud and test it with your ears.*

MONDAY, MAY 23

The Lord of heavenly forces proclaims: Pay attention! Summon the women who mourn, let them come; send for those best trained, let them come. Jeremiah 9:17 (CEB)

A WOMAN WHO HAS BEEN MY FRIEND for almost four decades lost track of how many surgeries she's logged. Multiple corneal transplants, appendectomy, gall bladder surgery, bypass surgery, hip surgery, knee replacement, back surgeries, shoulder replacement, hand surgeries...Now in her mideighties, she's facing another corneal transplant.

Jackie is a woman of strong faith. She leans on Jesus. But, years ago, the doctor's pronouncement of yet another surgery rocked her for a time. I didn't know what to say. It was just rotten. No getting around that.

No one could call me a mourner "best trained." Both of us knew Jesus would sustain her as He always had through this unwanted and unexpected surgery. He would hold her through it all. And so only two words came out of my mouth: "Oh, Jackie!"

Everything else, she knew. What she longed for, she told me, was that simple acknowledgement that someone understood it was miserably hard news to hear. It became a tradition for us through the years. She'd report another surgery scheduled, and I'd respond with a heartfelt, "Oh, Jackie!" Other words passed between us later, but that initial heart-to-heart communion of caring drew us even closer. And when it was her turn to say, "Oh, Cynthia!" I knew exactly how much it meant to have a mourner in my corner.

When Lazarus died, Jesus mourned. Knowing what lay ahead, knowing God's power, knowing Lazarus would live again, Jesus mourned. Might He have said, "Oh, Mary! Oh, Martha!"? When Jesus speaks to you that way in a difficult time, it makes a difference, doesn't it? —CYNTHIA RUCHTI

FAITH STEP: *Send yourself a text to refer to when needed, or write on a card you keep in your Bible: "From His heart, Jesus is saying to you, "Oh, [INSERT YOUR NAME HERE]. He cares!*

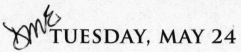

TUESDAY, MAY 24

But he said to me, "My grace is sufficient for you, for my power is made perfect in weakness." Therefore I will boast all the more gladly about my weaknesses, so that Christ's power may rest on me. 2 Corinthians 12:9 (NIV)

I LIKE TO ASK PEOPLE, "If you could do anything and know it would succeed, what would it be?" When I first asked this question I expected answers like, "Win *American Idol*," but the answers were far different: start a Bible study, become a foster parent, write a book. All of these answers came from dreams that Jesus put on their hearts. They are also things that people feel inadequate to do…otherwise they would have already started them.

It's easy to see dreams as things we need to accomplish in our own strength, but that's like going to the ocean of Jesus' availability with a teaspoon and hoping He'll be willing to help us out. When we truly focus on what Jesus can accomplish we can dip into His vast resources, and never finding an end to the supply.

We like to look at our weakness, but Jesus looks at His own strength. We focus on our limits, but Jesus knows He's limitless. Because we can't achieve our dreams on our own, we get to see Jesus-at-work in us.

"No eye has seen, no ear has heard, no mind has conceived what God has prepared for those who love him" (1 Corinthians 2:9).

Jesus has a plan and He's looking for men and women who are willing to put their meager dreams aside and enter into a dream world of His making.

If there is something in your heart that you wish to succeed at, you need to ask why it's there. Then you need to step out in all the ways that you feel inadequate and let Jesus lead you. —TRICIA GOYER

FAITH STEP: *Answer this question, "If you could do anything and know it would succeed, what would it be?" Then make two lists: "What I can do to make this happen," and "What Jesus can do to make this happen." Finally, turn to Him for His supply.*

WEDNESDAY, MAY 25

Pray continually. 1 Thessalonians 5:17 *(NIV)*

A FEW YEARS AGO I bought a notebook for my grandchildren's prayer requests, keeping an updated picture of them beside each petition. I included their favorite Bible verses at the time, then listed their requests, allowing several pages for ongoing needs.

Even though distance separates us, each time I see them, we check off the answered prayers, and they give me new ones. It's been exciting to experience those answers to prayers as well as to see three of our four grandchildren come to know Jesus personally.

Soon after beginning that prayer notebook, another special thing happened. We were watching our grandchildren. One of our granddaughters, who had already started asking us for our prayer requests, surprised us by spontaneously praying out loud in the car on the way to school. She began asking God to bless each family member and classmate, and she mentioned other things on her heart. She quietly finished with her sweet "Amen" and continued any normal conversation with whoever was in the car. Now every time we are together, before her bedtime, she asks for our prayer requests, as well as everyone in her household.

Jesus set the example for us in prayer. He prayed for others everywhere He went. He gave thanks and offered a model prayer for those who followed Him (Matthew 6:9). He even prayed intensively for His disciples—and for us—with His own death approaching. Understanding the need to intercede and draw strength from His heavenly Father, He prayed continually (Luke 5:16).

Following the examples of both Jesus and my granddaughter motivates me to pray, not just when it's convenient—at all times.
—REBECCA BARLOW JORDAN

FAITH STEP: *Besides keeping a written prayer list, try breaking into spontaneous prayers often. Who can you pray for today?*

THURSDAY, MAY 26

Pure and lasting religion in the sight of God our Father means that we must care for orphans and widows in their troubles, and refuse to let the world corrupt us.
James 1:27 (NLT)

THE MINISTRY IN WHICH my husband and I are involved serves orphans in the Ukraine. Russia's invasion in 2014 opened an amazing door to expand our ministry there. As the conflict escalated, a government representative contacted one of our missionaries who works year-round with orphans there. "We typically provide one week of camp for eight hundred orphans every summer," he said. "Unfortunately, the war has affected our funding, and we have no money. Will you provide camp for them this year? We know you'll tell them about Jesus, but we don't care so long as these kids get camp."

Our staff member joined forces with another orphan ministry, and they crunched numbers. They concluded that transportation, sleeping bags, tents, food, and other supplies would cost about fifty thousand dollars. They put out a plea, and they prayed. So did many others.

Jesus answered. Donations exceeded fifty thousand dollars, and eight hundred orphans learned about Him at summer camp.

Working among these kids is emotionally draining and often discouraging. Some folks might wonder if the expense and toll are worth it. One glimpse at Christ's teaching puts that question to rest.

The world might say the efforts are futile, but let's not let that voice influence us. Caring for widows and orphans matters to Jesus. Orphans need hope. They need to know someone cares. And we need to give without expecting anything in return. When we show love in practical ways to "the least of these," we're doing it as unto our Lord. —GRACE FOX

FAITH STEP: *Do some research online for credible ministries that serve orphans, or find a North American ministry that helps to arrange adoptions. Make a financial donation to that ministry.*

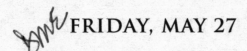

FRIDAY, MAY 27

*A week later his disciples were in the house again, and Thomas was with them.
Though the doors were locked, Jesus came and stood among them and said,
"Peace be with you!" Then he said to Thomas, "Put your finger here; see my hands.
Reach out your hand and put it into my side. Stop doubting and believe."*
John 20:26–27 (NIV)

EARLY ON A DARK MORNING, unanswered prayers weighed down my heart. My words rose to the ceiling and then crashed around my feet. Day after day, month after month, I brought my secret longings to Jesus. I knew He heard me. Or did He? Was He there? Did He care? The doubt slid in, and I hurried away from my quiet time, embarrassed by my uncertainty.

Thomas knew doubt too. In fact, he boldly stated his demands for proof. When the other disciples marveled at seeing the risen Lord, Thomas said he wouldn't believe until he not only saw and spoke with Jesus, but also touched him. Did Jesus banish him, condemning him for his doubts? No, of course not. Jesus invited Thomas to touch His wounds, then called him back to trust.

I long to be strong and full of faith, so when doubts sneak in, I feel ashamed and want to hide my fears and questions. Yet throughout Scriptures, many of God's children grappled with doubt. They found that Jesus didn't reject them in their times of questioning. He engaged with them.

We can bargain like Abraham, argue like Moses, wrestle like Jacob, question like Job, and doubt like Thomas. Jesus can handle it. He rejoices in our faith, even when it's the size of a mustard seed. And He helps us in our struggle to believe more fully. When doubt assails us, we can pray like the father in Mark 9:24, who brought his son to Jesus, "I do believe; help me overcome my unbelief!" —SHARON HINCK

FAITH STEP: *What truth from Scripture is difficult for you to believe? Bring your doubts to Jesus and ask Him to overcome unbelief.*

SATURDAY, MAY 28

*You can help those in need by working hard. You should remember the words of
the Lord Jesus: "It is more blessed to give than to receive." Acts 20:35 (NLT)*

"WHOEVER BRINGS BLESSING will be enriched, and one who waters will
himself be watered" (Proverbs 11:25, ESV). That's another way of looking
at today's verse. Jesus understands our innate bent toward looking out for
ourselves. At our most human level, we want to know what's in it for us.
This isn't a trait Jesus blesses. He isn't a "gimme giver" who promises to
grant us stuff and other nonsense if we'll be his lackeys.

To understand the heart of these verses, we need to get to the heart of
our Savior. When we spend time with Him, He changes us. As He changes
us, He develops His heart in us. When we love what He values, we desire
eternal blessings that far outweigh blessings of this temporary life. So, yes,
we can and should expect Him to bless us for serving others. But what
types of blessings we want will mature as we grow to be like Him.

I struggle with this one. Maybe it's because sometimes I feel I give a
lot and I get tired. Maybe by helping me to recognize this struggle, Jesus
offers me yet another route to grow deeper in Him. Sometimes even when
I want nonfrivolous blessings such as a family member's healing, Jesus
leads me further for something greater that requires more giving beyond
weariness and, most assuredly, requires additional growth.

We've all heard the mantra "Give until it hurts." Giving and serving
require sacrifice, but I believe Jesus's blessings in return will one day feel
as though we've given until it doesn't hurt. In fact, we'd give and serve far
more if we could see the blessings to come. —ERIN KEELEY MARSHALL

FAITH STEP: *How can you serve someone today? Ask for Jesus's blessing, then release
your expectations and watch Him work in His way.*

SUNDAY, MAY 29

Yours, Lord, is the greatness and the power and the glory and the majesty and the splendor, for everything in heaven and earth is yours. Yours, Lord, is the kingdom; you are exalted as head over all. 1 Chronicles 29:11 (NIV)

IT'S FUNNY TO ME how I can see Jesus move in my life and still want to give Him my spiel about how He should carry out my plans. The truth is, I want to bend His power to my will. I want Him to move where and how I want Him to. And isn't that what we all really want? For Jesus to do what we want Him to do? We stand on His grace and His grace alone. But we still think, *Great! Now I will take it from here.*

Well, I am finding that doesn't work. When you ask Jesus to be Lord of your life...He actually wants to be Lord of your life. He calls the shots. He clears the path. He makes a way. He heals your heart. He gives you peace.

And you? You are not in charge. You are the recipient of His glory and goodness and strength. You get to experience a huge way of living only because of Who He is and what He does.

Lately I have been trying to be the lord of my life. And I have this picture in my mind of Jesus sitting back on His heels taking in my chaos and my sorry attempts at controlling my circumstances and my astounding lack of resources and saying, "So how is that working for you?" Of course, He knows it is absolutely not working for me and mostly, I am a wreck. So today I am trying something different. I am going to let Him be Lord. Because...He is. I know it will make a difference. —SUSANNA FOTH AUGHTMON

FAITH STEP: *Before you start your day, take a moment to recognize Jesus as Lord of your life. Each time you have to make a decision today, invite Him to be Lord over that decision.*

MONDAY, MAY 30

He took bread, and when he had given thanks, he broke it and gave it to them, saying,
"This is my body, which is given for you. Do this in remembrance of me."
Luke 22:19 (ESV)

MY FOCUS ON MEMORIAL DAY used to be planning family gatherings. But once my husband and I moved too far away to host the day for loved ones, I looked for ways for us to spend the day together.

As I flipped through sales flyers, I stumbled upon an article that made me rethink the way we typically spend the day. The essay argued that Memorial Day has morphed from a somber reflection on those who died to gain our freedom to a day for parades, parties, and cookouts. It called for an end to such "frivolous celebrations" and the return to a day of mourning and prayer.

While the piece reminded me of the holiday's real meaning, I also thought about the need for balance. In the Old Testament, God instituted observances to remind the Israelites of major events in their history. These included days of fasting and feasting, times for mourning and merry-making. Even Jesus, at His last Passover meal, introduced a new observance—communion taken "in remembrance" of Him—to memorialize His upcoming death and what it would accomplish for the world.

Memorial Day now reminds me of Jesus at His last Passover meal because it is also celebrated "in remembrance" of those who died to gain our freedom. As I reflect on the meaning of this day and maybe even take in the parade, I bow my head in thanks, not only for the men and women who've given their lives for this country but also for Jesus, Who gave His life for us all. —DIANNE NEAL MATTHEWS

FAITH STEP: *Take time to meditate on the costs of our national and spiritual freedoms. Thank Jesus for His sacrifice and for the sacrifices of brave men and women who died for us. Then celebrate this day!*

TUESDAY, MAY 31

Be imitators of God, therefore, as dearly loved children. Ephesians 5:1 (NIV)

I HAVE A PHOTOGRAPH of my oldest son, when he was not yet two, trying to walk in his father's Army boots. He didn't get very far. But oh, how he loved to try!

Those boots *were* cool! His daddy spit-shined them into mirrors. But as enticing as they were, it wasn't the boots themselves, but the man who wore them that drew my son in.

This isn't unusual. Anyone who has children probably has a picture like mine. Fathers loom large in a young child's eyes. Little ones know they can't do everything they'd like. They lack abilities they'll gain with time. To them, Daddy is their own personal superhero—he can do anything. They want to be like him, instead of always hearing, "You're not big enough."

Imitating God can prove to be difficult. His chosen people tried and often failed, like so many of us do today. We can't see God (and live). How could we know Him? He wasn't like *our* fathers. So people either tried their best or didn't try at all.

But God found another way to show us who He was and what He was like. He sent Jesus to live a life of love in front of us. He called God "Daddy" and said, "Anyone who has seen me has seen the Father!" (John 14:9).

Jesus makes His home in our hearts when we trust Him, but we still need to grow up in our faith. God's Spirit gives us the power we need to throw away our old way of life and put on a new nature.

Jesus showed us the Father and He showed us the Way.
—SUZANNE DAVENPORT TIETJEN

FAITH STEP: *Jesus lived a life of love that pleased His father. Ask Him to renew your mind and change you from the inside out. Let His influence show in something you do today.*

WEDNESDAY, JUNE 1

"I am with you always...." Matthew 28:20 (NKJV)

A COLLEAGUE SHARED WITH ME that he is battling depression and extreme doubts in his Christian faith. It seems the crux of the matter is an age-old question, and the same one I struggle with from time to time: *Where is God?* He recently lost his mother; a friend and fellow believer is plagued with schizophrenia; and, in general, he looks around and sees so much suffering in the world he just wonders, *Where is God in all of this?*

The human condition is one to make any thinking person wonder if God even exists. I told my friend that sometimes I wake up a Christian and, after pondering questions like his, go to bed an atheist. The thing is, when I wake up I'm always a Christian again.

I think that's because, in my heart, I believe the answer to the question of where God is can be found in Matthew 28:20: Jesus is with me always. I can't get away from Him. He doesn't always give me what I want, like world peace or a cure for schizophrenia or cancer.

John Green wrote in *The Fault in Our Stars* that "the world is not a wish-granting factory." Jesus isn't either. I don't pretend to understand why He allows what He allows, although I imagine all suffering has something do with free will and the fact that we live in a fallen world. But in all of this— the good, the bad, and the ugly—He is with us. He sees us. He loves us. He redeems us. Always. —GWEN FORD FAULKENBERRY

FAITH STEP: *Write it on your heart that Jesus is with you no matter what. In your pain, your loneliness, your confusion and questions and doubts, He is with you. He will never leave you nor forsake you.*

THURSDAY, JUNE 2

Do not conform to the pattern of this world, but be transformed by the renewing of your mind. Then you will be able to test and approve what God's will is— his good, pleasing and perfect will. Romans 12:2 (NIV)

MY GRANDMA HAD A TALENT for sewing and crafts of all kinds. When I was a girl, she taught me to crochet, beginning with simple potholders and progressing to more elaborate blankets.

I recently bought some yarn and a new crochet hook and revisited the old hobby. The feel of yarn in my hand and the rhythmic movement of chaining was calming. The beautiful multicolored fiber made me smile. I remembered how to do a single and double crochet stitch so I soon had the beginning of a warm throw.

There was a problem, though. I like to crochet while chatting or listening to music or watching a movie. I don't like counting stitches or following a pattern.

After a few days, when I spread out my work, the edges wove drunkenly in and out. Instead of a rectangle, the blanket had a weird trapezoid shape.

Some projects work better when we read the instructions. Jesus invites us to follow the pattern He has designed for us. We aren't doomed to meander, looking back on our life to see a tangled mess. And we don't have to conform to the world's idea of a meaningful life. Instead we can let Him renew our minds as we read about His life in the pages of Scripture, as we talk to Him, as we let His Holy Spirit counsel us, as we worship and fellowship with other followers of Jesus. He can weave the events of our day into a purposeful work of art. —SHARON HINCK

FAITH STEP: *Ask Jesus to renew your mind and follow His example for life today with each choice. Thank Him for freeing you from the world's pattern.*

FRIDAY, JUNE 3

*Therefore encourage one another and build each other up,
just as in fact you are doing. 1 Thessalonians 5:11 (NIV)*

I MET WITH A PHYSICAL THERAPIST recently who gave me some exercises to help strengthen my back. When I got home, I retried the exercises on my bedroom floor. My youngest, Addison, came in and perched on the edge of the bed to watch me. As I concentrated on pulling my belly button toward my spine per the instructions, Addie said, "Mom, can I be your personal trainer?"

As I exhaled and inhaled and tried to concentrate I said, "I don't think I need a personal trainer. I just have to do these exercises to help my back."

He ignored me. "I'm going to be your trainer. You can do this, Mom! You can do it."

"Addie…" I tried to hold my back in the correct position.

"One more time. Just one more time." He was hanging over the footboard of the bed, his face coming close to mine.

"Buddy, you are distracting me…"

"You are doing great!" As I struggled once more to suck in my stomach, stretch out my leg and breathe, Addison smiled at me and yelled, "You got this, Mom! You got this."

I had to smile back at him.

Maybe I do need a personal trainer. Maybe we all need someone like Addie to encourage and exhort us when we are struggling. And maybe we need to be like Addie to those around us. It is one of the ways Jesus moves and works in our lives, when we encourage our brothers and sisters. We are like Jesus when we become His mouthpiece and His arms of love when we encourage those He has put in our lives. Isn't that exactly the kind of person we want to be?

I think Addie is right. We've got this. —SUSANNA FOTH AUGHTMON

FAITH STEP: *Encourage someone you love with a hug, a note, a call, or a text.*

SATURDAY, JUNE 4

Dear brothers and sisters, one final thing. Fix your thoughts on what is true, and honorable, and right, and pure, and lovely, and admirable. Think about things that are excellent and worthy of praise. Philippians 4:8 (NLT)

IF YOU WERE TO COME into our laundry room, most days you would find one or more toys on the counter, waiting to be fixed. Some just need recharged batteries, while others need superglue or duct tape. Once they are fixed, they're good to go for another round of play.

The idea of fixing something applies to the Christian life as well. The state of being fixed suggests that something is in good working order, stable, functional, useful for its purpose, free of faults that keep it from doing its job.

Many times it's much easier to fix my kids' toys than to fix my mind. My thoughts wander a lot. Most times when I let them go, they take me to areas of criticism of myself or others, to fears that detract my focus on Jesus's sovereign power, or to the priorities He wants me to align myself with so I can function most effectively as a follower of His.

Fixed thoughts mean that I'm solid. I'm not derailed, and I'm living in His strength that holds me together. Just as a motor or batteries empower toys, our thoughts have a way of empowering us or limiting our usefulness. One way to fix our weak areas is to fix our thoughts—on what is true, honorable, right, pure, lovely, admirable, excellent, and worthy of praise. When our thoughts are aligned with those pursuits, Jesus's character shows through in grace, mercy, truth, love, patience, kindness, and all the qualities of spiritual fruit.

What we think about reveals itself in how we live, whether by Jesus's Spirit or by our failings. Jesus can fix what's wrong when we fix our minds on Him. —ERIN KEELEY MARSHALL

FAITH STEP: *Memorize Philippians 4:8 and keep it written down somewhere you will see it frequently.*

one SUNDAY, JUNE 5

"Jesus is the only One who can save people. His name is the only power in the world that has been given to save people. We must be saved through him." Acts 4:12 (NCV)

DURING A GATHERING of my son-in-law's family, my three-year-old grandson fell in the pond. Heather, his other grandma, immediately jumped in. She came up under Roman and pushed him up; Great-uncle Shane plucked him out. Later, wrapped in a towel, Roman told the story of how Shane had saved him. When someone asked him why Grandma was also wet, he simply said, "Oh, she fell in the pond too."

Roman was oblivious to the fact that Heather had deliberately jumped in the water to save him from drowning. And most of the people present at Jesus's Crucifixion were clueless as to what He was doing for them. As Jesus hung, suffering on the Cross, onlookers jeered, mocked, and hurled insults. Roman soldiers gambled for His clothes. They had no idea that this condemned man willingly gave up His life to pay for their sins and save them from condemnation.

Many people mock the idea of the gospel message while casually tossing around the word "savior" or "salvation." I've heard the terms applied to a politician, a prescription medication, a romantic partner, a new job, even a cruise vacation. With a strong emphasis on self-help and self-improvement, our culture seems to promote the idea that we can become our own saviors.

Even after we begin a personal relationship with Jesus, it's important to remember that we still need Him every moment, every day. I need His help to face physical, emotional, and spiritual problems. And sometimes, I need Him to save me from myself. I never want to forget Who it is that lifts me up and plucks me out of deep waters. —DIANNE NEAL MATTHEWS

FAITH STEP: *Tell Jesus what you need Him to save you from. Is it a destructive habit? An unhealthy relationship? A frightening situation? A troubling physical problem? Thank Him for being your Savior each and every day.*

MONDAY, JUNE 6

In the Messiah, in Christ, God leads us from place to place in one perpetual victory parade. Through us, he brings knowledge of Christ. Everywhere we go, people breathe in the exquisite fragrance. 2 Corinthians 2:14 (MSG)

WE SPENT A WEEK WITH one of our daughters and her family, nestled in a beautiful, mountainous river valley. Our family rented a two-story home with a wraparound porch along the river.

The rolling acreage offered the ideal spot for s'mores, eagle watching, games, or just nature gazing. The first year we stayed there, two of our grandchildren—having decided to follow Jesus a short time earlier—asked their dad and their grandfather (my minister husband) to baptize them in the nearby river. It was a precious time as we all waded out prayerfully, our cameras held high in our hands, capturing the sacred moment.

When we returned two years later, all those memories flooded back as I walked onto the porch of that same home on our first cool, crisp morning. With steaming coffee in hand and a jacket draped over my shoulders, I leaned over the back porch overlooking the river. Sniffing the air, I said to my husband, "You can inhale the fragrance of Jesus's presence here!" I didn't want to leave that sweet perfume behind.

The week passed much too fast, and we waved good-bye as we headed to the airport. Back home in ninety-degree weather later that week, I was spending a few quiet moments reading my Bible, missing, of course, the cool river valley, my loved ones, and Jesus's refreshing presence there.

But precious moments with Jesus reminded me of a familiar truth: We can inhale the fragrance of His presence anywhere. And not only that, He also fills us with that same fragrance, so that others can enjoy His presence too. —REBECCA BARLOW JORDAN

FAITH STEP: *What special places have you been to, where you particularly enjoyed Jesus's presence? How can you be His perfume to someone today?*

TUESDAY, JUNE 7

It's in Christ that we find out who we are and what we are living for.
Long before we first heard of Christ and got our hopes up, he had his eye on us,
had designs on us for glorious living, part of the overall purpose he is working out
in everything and everyone. Ephesians 1:11 (MSG)

I SPENT MY TEENS AND TWENTIES seeking God's will. I hoped to dance professionally but wasn't sure what God wanted. I found I couldn't perform at the highest levels, so I taught ballet, but we moved too often for me to establish a studio. Had I heard wrong? No. At church (and in my forties), I was the Dancer in Walt Wangerin's *Cry of the Whole Congregation*. I found much meaning there. Dance as worship is still part of my life.

I was blessed to have eleven years at home with my children when they were small. I fondly remember them helping with the geese, chickens, and garden. That sweet time echoes on into my empty nest, with grandchildren. Marriage and mothering are a most holy calling.

When my babies went to school, I did too. I had the privilege of caring for the sickest of newborns as a nurse, then neonatal nurse practitioner in a career that lasted for decades.

An abandoned 4-H project led to twenty years as a shepherd, where I learned more about Jesus and our mutual Father than I did in years of Sunday school and Bible studies. Shepherding and nursing led to writing and speaking, my current focus.

Did I really expect at twenty that God would lay all this out before me? I guess I did—but I'm glad He didn't. It's been far too beautiful and wonderful to be believed! Believe it, though. For yourself. Christ's eye is on you. He's at work in you. Just follow. —SUZANNE DAVENPORT TIETJEN

FAITH STEP: *Are you in an in-between time? Pray. Think about what draws you. Let Jesus show the way.*

WEDNESDAY, JUNE 8

The Lord has anointed me to bring good news to the poor. . . . to give them a crown of beauty instead of ashes. . . . Isaiah 61:1, 3 (HSC)

DURING THE DARKEST TIME of my life, a therapist told me it might get worse first, but after going through the worst, things would be better. "In fact," she said, "it can be better than it ever has been."

At the time, a part of me wanted to slap her. But after digging in deep, working hard, and holding on to my faith as if my life depended on it—which it did—I began to see that she was right. Because that's what Jesus does if we let Him. It's Redemption 101. He gives us a crown of beauty for ashes.

Ashes are no fun. They mean something has been demolished, destroyed, burned. Most of the time if you look at a pile of ashes, you can't even tell what was there before—fire reduces everything to dust. It's hard to imagine any life stirring from a pile of ashes.

In ancient times ashes symbolized mourning, death, and repentance. If someone wore sackcloth and ashes, they were making themselves as uncomfortable and ugly as possible on the outside to show how they felt on the inside. It was an outward sign of an inward condition.

So when Jesus said he was anointed to preach good news, and give us a "crown of beauty instead of ashes" he meant something amazing. He meant He can change our inward condition from one of death to life. Like the legend of the Phoenix, we rise out of the ashes. Re-created. Vibrant. Beautiful. —GWEN FORD FAULKENBERRY

FAITH STEP: *What's your inward condition today? Are you mourning a loss? Finding it hard to forgive yourself for a mistake? Give your ashes to Jesus. He'll exchange them for a crown of beauty if you let Him.*

THURSDAY, JUNE 9

In a loud voice they sang: "Worthy is the Lamb, who was slain, to receive power and wealth and wisdom and strength and honor and glory and praise!"
Revelation 5:12 (NIV)

YEARS AGO A FRIEND READ a book about the power of praising God regardless of our circumstances. She and her husband taught this principle to their children, including their younger daughter who had been born with part of her right foot missing. I was at their home one afternoon as the kids scrambled around looking for their shoes. The younger daughter raced through the room, saying, "I can't find my foot—but praise the Lord anyway!"

We've been created with a built-in need to praise and worship, but sadly, that often goes missing. We may let that part of our spiritual life be overshadowed if we focus solely on serving Christ and others. Or we may neglect to make time for praise because of our busy schedules. I think many people, including me, have an unconscious attitude that our circumstances and our mood have to be just right before we can legitimately offer praise to our Savior.

Recently I began to intentionally incorporate more personal praise into my weekdays. I developed the habit of beginning my day with worship as soon as I opened my eyes. I listened to praise music while getting dressed. Most important, I determined to choose praise whenever I least felt like it. Even when I don't like what's happening, I can choose to praise Jesus for Who He is, what He's done, and what He has promised to do. I discovered that while praise didn't change my circumstances, it transformed my attitude. —DIANNE NEAL MATTHEWS

FAITH STEP: *Make a plan to incorporate "praise breaks" throughout your day. Whenever a negative thought or circumstance pops up, tell Jesus that you will praise Him anyway. Afterward, note how this response changed your attitude.*

FRIDAY, JUNE 10

Though he brings grief, he also shows compassion according to the greatness of his unfailing love. For he does not enjoy hurting people or causing them sorrow.
Lamentations 3:32–33 (NLT)

MY ONE-YEAR-OLD GRANDSON, MICAH, recently developed a fever. He fussed and cried and obviously felt miserable, so his mom decided to give him a dose of liquid medication. His dad, who was cradling him, offered to administer it.

Daddy placed the syringe's tip in Micah's mouth. As though on cue, the tyke jerked his head backward, pinched his lips shut, and slapped at the syringe. But Dad persisted. "I know you don't like what I'm doing, Micah," he said, "but I'm doing it because I love you. I know you'll feel better in a few minutes."

I watched the scene unfold and marveled at its spiritual parallelism: How many times has Jesus acted in my best interest while I—not understanding His wisdom and ways—have fussed and kicked and wrestled against Him? How many times have I doubted His goodness while He lovingly cared for me? How many times has my spiritual immaturity caused me to misinterpret His intentions?

Perhaps you're reading this and thinking, *I know exactly what she's talking about because I've done the same thing.* If so, I'm glad I'm not the only one who occasionally mimics a one-year-old.

Let's ask Jesus to make us more sensitive to His wisdom and ways. Let's choose to trust Him even when we don't understand what He's doing. And let's choose to be willing participants in whatever He does in our lives, believing that His actions are rooted in love. —GRACE FOX

FAITH STEP: *Recall an experience that left you wondering whether Jesus had your best interest in mind. What truths about His character did that situation teach you? How did it help you grow spiritually? Thank Him for His never-ending love for you.*

SATURDAY, JUNE 11

He... didn't open his mouth. Like a lamb being brought to slaughter, like a ewe silent before her shearers, he didn't open his mouth. Isaiah 53:7 (CEB)

IMPRINTED ON MY MEMORY is the striking scene of hot-air balloons rising into the sky over Albuquerque, New Mexico. My travels had taken me to the city the week following their annual balloon festival, when the sky is filled with the magnificent spectacle of color and wonder. I loved gazing at the balloons against that supersaturated backdrop of blue. The hot-air balloons in that unique topography seemed to hover unmoving—as if painted on the sky. A perfectly captured calendar page from an expert photographer. Yet real, live, happening right before me.

I described it to a friend as "still, yet moving."

A dichotomy of thought. How can any object be still, yet moving?

When Jesus was still, silent as a lamb to the slaughter, or a ewe before shearers, as the Bible expresses it, He was in the process of moving forward in the Father's plan for His future. And ours. He was still, yet moving.

So often we assume the still times in our lives are "dead air." Nothing happening. We're hospitalized. Our job seems stagnant. A broken ankle or virus sidelines us temporarily. Our prayers seem to be tabled in heaven—no response. We apply for a position or college or grant and hear nothing. Our longings for our children seem to net no positive results.

The next time one of those "dead air" scenes happens to me, I pray that I remember the sight of a hot-air balloon painted on the sky—still, yet moving. And I pray my soul recalls that even when Jesus was silent, He remained on track in the Father's plan to bring about redemption. —CYNTHIA RUCHTI

FAITH STEP: *Consider adding a hot-air balloon calendar to your wall or finding an image online for the wallpaper of your phone or your computer as inspiration for the times you need the reminder that still doesn't always mean "not moving."*

Done

SUNDAY, JUNE 12

But let all who take refuge in you be glad; let them ever sing for joy.
Spread your protection over them, that those who love your name
may rejoice in you. Psalm 5:11 (NIV)

I LIKE BEING HAPPY. I would like to be happy every moment of every day of my life. But happy is a changeable kind of word. It seems to come and go and it is usually tied to my circumstances. If everything in my life is going well, I am superhappy. If things are not going so well? I tend to be unhappy. This kind of high/low living is crazy. It lacks the steadiness that can hold me in a peaceful place when chaos tends to break loose. If you have lived for any length of time, you know that chaos is bound to show up in your day one way or another.

I used to think that joy was just another word for happiness. But lately, I have been realizing it is something completely different. Joy isn't dependent on my circumstances. It is dependent on my inviting Jesus into my circumstances. Joy isn't simply an emotion. It is a by-product of Jesus's presence in my life. Joy is linked to the person of Jesus Christ, Someone Who is unchanging, faithful and rock solid, regardless of how wild life is becoming.

Leaning into Who He is, trusting in His word, asking for His guidance in the midst of life's craziness, is how we can have joy even when it feels like life is completely at odds with us. "The joy of the Lord is our strength" is a statement of deep and abiding truth. When we decide to believe that Jesus is Who He says He is, no matter what is happening in our lives, our perspective begins to change. And true joy floods in.
—SUSANNA FOTH AUGHTMON

FAITH STEP: *Think of the attributes of Jesus: merciful, forgiving, grace-filled, strong, and so on. How does knowing that He is in control of your life make you feel?*

MONDAY, JUNE 13

"Blessed are those who mourn, for they will be comforted." Matthew 5:4 (NRSV)

WHEN SOMETHING SAD HAPPENS, we mourn. Or at least we should—it's normal and healthy to do so. Some people don't allow themselves to mourn properly and this causes problems. But others of us may have trouble knowing when and how to stop mourning. We are so crushed by the death—whether it's the loss of a loved one or the loss of a relationship or a dream—that we can get stuck in the middle of it, never moving on through the process and into the Resurrection that is central to faith in Jesus.

Contemporary novelist Elizabeth Berg writes, "Don't spend so much time mourning that you forget to live your life." That is a good reminder for me. While mourning is important to our journey, we must not let it become a destination. The reason for this is that we have hope in Jesus. He brings purpose to our lives and even our losses. He promised we are blessed in our mourning, because He comforts us.

Like so many of His promises, comfort is not based on our feelings, but on the reality—the truth—of His Word. He says we will be comforted. So, whether we feel good or not, we can trust that we are comforted. Sometimes it is up to us to act on that promise, to move forward into Resurrection life, regardless of our feelings. And I have found that many times when I obey His Word as an act of my will rather than relying on my emotions to lead me, the good feelings follow. Even if it takes a while. —GWEN FORD FAULKENBERRY

FAITH STEP: *Are you stuck in a moment of mourning? No matter how deep the loss, Jesus meets you there. Write down one goal for this day—one choice you can make that leans into life. Maybe it's as simple as getting out of bed. Maybe it's taking a walk. Maybe it's calling a friend and going to lunch. Whatever it is, just do it. Jesus promises you will be comforted.*

one

TUESDAY, JUNE 14

I pondered the direction of my life, and I turned to follow your laws. I will hurry, without delay, to obey your commands. Psalm 119:59–60 (NLT)

A FRIEND OF MINE recently complained about her husband's using a GPS but ignoring its directions. On a recent trip, he programmed their destination into the car's built-in system. But when it advised him to turn off the highway, he was convinced that he knew a better way. The device kept recalculating the route to get him back on track, but it took the man a half hour to admit he had made a mistake. By this time, they were running so late that he almost hit another car while trying to merge onto the interstate too quickly.

I've lately seen online parenting articles about obedience being "overrated." These articles make some good points about raising children in an understanding and compassionate manner. But we all have to learn to obey rules; some of us learn the hard way. Even though we may inwardly rebel against the very word, obedience is at the core of the Christian life.

Jesus is not satisfied with mere lip service or outward expressions of faith. "Why do you keep calling me 'Lord, Lord!'" he asked, "when you don't do what I say?" (Luke 6:46). I can't claim to follow Him and then ignore His directions and commands.

We may think we know better than a GPS device, an instruction manual, or an expert on a particular topic. And sometimes that might be true. But the commands and principles laid down in the Bible are for our good, to help us have the most meaningful life possible. There are times when I don't like the direction in which my life seems to be going. That's when I need to recalculate my route and make sure I'm obeying Jesus's teachings.
—DIANNE NEAL MATTHEWS

FAITH STEP: *Is there an area of your life where you might be headed in the wrong direction? Ask Jesus to guide you to any Scriptures that reveal commands and teachings to help you get back on track.*

one

WEDNESDAY, JUNE 15

Happy are those servants whom the master finds fulfilling their responsibilities when he comes. Matthew 24:46 (CEB)

EXCEPT FOR THOSE IN REMOTE, unplugged areas of wilderness, none of us remembers when it took weeks or months for news of a battle, a discovery, or even a death in the family to cross our threshold. The telegraph improved on that time frame. Radio and television then brought us periodic news and occasionally a "This just in!" break in the regular broadcast schedule... as long as the news didn't happen in the middle of the night, since television broadcasting stopped at midnight or before.

Now, it's not just television, radio, telephone, or newspaper news that sends shivers or makes our stomachs clench. We hear bad news as it happens. It pops up on smartphone notifications. We find out about the death of a world leader or celebrity through social media, sometimes before their own family members know. We watch hostage situations unfold in real time. The constancy and immediacy of earthshaking news can keep us in a perpetual state of hand-wringing worry.

Wars, rumors of wars, pestilence, violence, plague, atrocities against humanity....Things that would make our hearts faint or make Jesus followers abandon their posts and wait for rescue. But Jesus said, "Keep doing what I've called you to do. Keep loving, serving, and telling others about Me."

End of the world? Maybe. "Happy," Jesus said, "are those servants whom the master finds fulfilling their responsibilities when he comes."

His counsel in tough times? His instruction during the worst of times? "Carry on." —CYNTHIA RUCHTI

FAITH STEP: *You may hear a piece—or multiple pieces—of worrisome news today. Practice this three-pronged approach: Breathe. Pray. Carry on.*

THURSDAY, JUNE 16

So here I am in the place of worship, eyes open, drinking in your strength and your glory. Psalm 63:2 (MSG)

THE OTHER DAY I forgot to check on my chickens. The next morning I found their fountain had run dry. I got some scolding clucks and sideways stares from the girls. I know from my shepherding days that water is the most important livestock nutrient. Before I even backed away from the now-full fountain, they were drinking. Dipping their beaks, tipping their heads back over and over, they were wholeheartedly drinking.

In the Bible, thirst is a metaphor for spiritual desire or love. David wrote Psalm 63 when he was in the wilderness of Judah, a dry and weary land. Instead of his physical thirst, he sang about his thirst for God.

Where was that love, that thirst, satisfied? In the place of worship, where he drew deeply from God's strength and His glory. David worshipped often, writing many love songs to God. He danced before the Ark with no concern for how he looked. Maybe God called him a man after His own heart because God loves wholeheartedly too.

We know Jesus loves us but we don't often think about Jesus wanting *our* love. He does, though. He longs for it.

Jesus said the greatest commandment is to love the Lord with all your heart, soul, and mind (Matthew 22:37). He wept over Jerusalem because He couldn't shelter the people like a mother hen because they weren't willing.

When we worship, we offer Jesus our love. It's not perfect, but He wants it anyway. With our eyes on our beautiful Savior, He touches us, filling us with His strength and glory. With His perfect love.

—SUZANNE DAVENPORT TIETJEN

FAITH STEP: *Every time you drink a glass of water today, ask Jesus to make you thirsty for Him. Spend some time in worship, telling Him you love Him. Then sit quietly, drinking in His love.*

DONE FRIDAY, JUNE 17

Teach us to number our days and recognize how few they are; help us to spend them as we should. Psalm 90:12 (TLB)

I'VE HEARD THE QUESTION OFTEN, even asked it myself: "What would you do if you had only a day, a week, or a year to live? The thought definitely challenges us.

But one day recently, I looked at that question from another angle. What did Jesus do, knowing He had exactly thirty-three years to live on earth? How did He live, when He knew he only had three years to accomplish His ministry? Did He worry about how He could make the most impact?

No, He simply spent His days honoring His Father, being faithful, teaching and loving others, and leading us to salvation.

Jesus knew death was coming. So do we. Only we don't know when, as Jesus did. But is there a reason to panic: What should I do? What should I change? Am I doing enough? Certainly if a believer is living a life of disobedience and has forgotten what he is here for, then a wake-up call is needed. Change has to happen.

In reality, every day is a wake-up call. Our prayer is that Jesus will change our hearts daily to reflect more of Him. But regardless of whether God gives us three days, three decades, or eighty-three years to live, we can answer the "what-if" question like this: "I will spend every day showing up, being faithful, sharing Jesus's love, enduring difficulties, and living life victoriously because of the One Who paved the way for me."

It's a great way to live. —REBECCA BARLOW JORDAN

FAITH STEP: *How would you answer that "what if" question? Write down your answer, and place it where you'll see it often.*

SATURDAY, JUNE 18

But their idols are silver and gold, made by human hands. . . . Those who make them will be like them, and so will all who trust in them. Psalm 115:4, 8 (NIV)

WHEN I TAUGHT BALLET, I'd sometimes use a simple mirroring technique. Students would face me and as I slowly moved through arm positions, they would follow, copying exactly. Facing the class I'd occasionally see droopy hands or awkward elbows. When I checked my position, I'd realize they were copying my sloppy habits.

The models that we choose to follow will affect us. The idols that capture our devotion will begin to shape us into their image. I don't have a statue of a golden calf in my living room, but that doesn't mean this psalm doesn't apply.

There's nothing wrong with having mentors that we admire, but all human role models are imperfect. Some of the people I've admired and followed have turned out to be gilded images with feet of clay. Since I'd much rather be shaped into the image of Christ, I want to keep my primary focus on Him.

Idols come in other shapes too. The longing to please people can become a false god. A desire for security or comfort can steal my devotion and effort. At times I've sacrificed at the altar of achievement. When the fruit of these false gods show up in my life, it's a clue that I've turned from my true Savior and am becoming like my self-made idols.

When we've put our trust in the wrong places, Jesus graciously forgives and invites us back to following Him. We can trace His movements in Scripture and seek to mirror His heart, His thoughts, and His actions.
—SHARON HINCK

FAITH STEP: *Is there an idol "made by human hands" that has captured your priorities? Ask Jesus to free you and help you focus on Him.*

SUNDAY, JUNE 19

A word fitly spoken is like apples of gold in settings of silver.
Proverbs 25:11 (NKJV)

IN MY OFFICE DESK DRAWER, I keep a few letters written in shaky handwriting. My father penned those almost two decades ago, as most of us did in the pre-e-mail and texting days. But I especially treasure the ones he wrote in the last years of his life.

Daddy was a pastor with a true shepherd's heart. A gentle man, he loved to encourage and build up others in their faith. Threaded throughout his rare, short notes and always before he signed them, "Love, Daddy," my father always included a word of encouragement to me. Sometimes he wrote a simple phrase like "Keep looking up" or a biblical admonition, "Patience will have its perfect work." Another time he told me to "remember what I have always told you: 'Don't be afraid to ask anything of God in His will.'"

In the last year of his life he included a story, reminding me that we (his children) were his jewels—his treasures. I only hope Daddy realized how much I treasured his words—and his life—like "apples of gold in settings of silver."

I was excited when I discovered that this verse in Proverbs was used to describe a beautiful piece of jewelry. It made my father's words even more valuable.

Psalm 12:6 (NKJV) says, "The words of the Lord are pure words, like silver tried in a furnace of earth, purified seven times." Jesus's words to His disciples and to us were also like precious jewels: "Don't be afraid"; "My peace I give to you"; "Love others as I have loved you"; "I am with you always."

Jesus's words have brought comfort to me in times of loss; hope to me in seasons of despair; and strength to me in moments of weakness. They are like rare, silver jewels that never tarnish with age. —REBECCA BARLOW JORDAN

FAITH STEP: *Write a letter today to someone who needs a good word. Tuck a "jewel" of encouragement inside, and seal it with prayer.*

MONDAY, JUNE 20

We now have this light shining in our hearts, but we ourselves are like fragile clay jars containing this great treasure. This makes it clear that our great power is from God, not from ourselves. 2 Corinthians 4:7 (NLT)

MY HAIR IS DUE FOR HIGHLIGHTS. If you ever get fake color to boost your look, you may understand why I feel drab these days. I find myself reaching for bigger, more colorful earrings, and all week I've been tempted to spend my lunch break in the jewelry section at a department store to find something sparkly for my neck as compensation for the lack of glow on my head.

A first-world problem if there ever was one, but I'm feeling it.

While distracted by such things, I came across 2 Corinthians 4:7. I have been reading a novel about the last days and the Second Temple treasures some scholars suspect are hidden throughout the Holy lands. Gold, silver, the Ark of the Covenant—true sparkly stuff of incalculable worth. Some scholars believe the discovery of those treasures, which were secreted away before Jerusalem fell to Rome in AD 70, will prompt the rebuilding of the Temple on the Dome of the Rock.

I am fascinated by biblical history, even more so by the fact that Jesus's sacrifice on the Cross and the sending of the Holy Spirit mean that the treasures of eternity now reside within believers. The Temple treasures, especially the Ark, will be something to behold whenever they are unearthed. But the same glory that filled it fills all who believe in Jesus as Savior.

This truth is enormous any day, but especially on a plain-Jane one when I'm missing my glow. No physical improvements can touch the radiance of the Lord living within. —ERIN KEELEY MARSHALL

FAITH STEP: *Decorate a blank note card and write the lines of 2 Corinthians 4:7 on it. Put it on the mirror where you get ready for the day. Pray over the verse and thank Jesus for creating you as His treasure house.*

TUESDAY, JUNE 21

This was now the third time Jesus appeared to his disciples after he was raised from the dead. John 21:14 (CEB)

IRON CHEF, BEAT BOBBY FLAY, Chopped, The Great Food Truck Race... I learned to cook when I was still a child and did most of the cooking for our family by the time I was in middle school. But I'm also one who is a better and more adventurous cook because of what I've learned from shows like the ones above. I discovered better techniques, expanded my knowledge of seasonings, learned about culturally rich foods, and the nutritional benefits—or not—of foods unfamiliar to me.

I watched the movies *Julie & Julia* and *The Hundred-Foot Journey*, fully immersed in the stories with cooking as their centerpiece. But no moment of cooking means as much to me as one small scene in the Bible.

Shortly after the death and Resurrection of Jesus, His disciples pulled a large haul of fish into the boat and brought it to shore. When they landed, they found a fire on the beach and breakfast waiting for them—cooked by Chef Jesus. He'd dealt with food miracles before, and food memories, as on the night He was betrayed. But this may be the only reference in the Bible to Jesus as cook. He didn't find it at all out of character to humble Himself to scrape scales from fish, gut and fillet them, mix ingredients for bread, tend the fire, and all the other duties related to making this meal.

We don't know every detail about why Jesus chose to make breakfast for His disciples that day. But isn't it intriguing that He did? That He not only fed them but *cooked* for them? The Complete Need-Meeter.
—CYNTHIA RUCHTI

FAITH STEP: *How has Jesus fed your soul lately? Have you kept that divine "meal" to yourself? Or did you share it with someone else? Before the day is over, find a way to tell someone about how He satisfied your soul's appetite.*

one WEDNESDAY, JUNE 22

"Look at the lilies and how they grow. They don't work or make their clothing, yet Solomon in all his glory was not dressed as beautifully as they are." Luke 12:27 (NLT)

MY FRIEND MICHELLE brought me a bouquet of flowers one night when she came to dinner. I was so excited! The bouquet was filled with a variety of flowers. Their unique colors and scents brightened my dining room. I was also excited because I'm a homeschooling mom, and we just so happened to be studying flowers in our curriculum.

The next morning I placed the vase in front of my children, and for the next hour we studied every tiny part. We looked at the petals and stems. We compared the colors and scents. I pointed out pistils, stigmas, stamens, and all the other parts.

As I took in the looks of wonder on my children's faces, I was awed again too. The details of a dozen different kinds of flowers overwhelmed me. It also reminded me again that Jesus cares about our lives, too, down to the smallest detail. Matthew 6:28 (ESV) says, "And why are you anxious about clothing? Consider the lilies of the field, how they grow: they neither toil nor spin."

Flowers feed our souls. They show us another side of our Creator who designs beautiful things and takes notice of the tiniest detail. Flowers can also feed our spirits. They can remind us that we don't have anything to worry about, because Jesus cares for us even more than the amazing flowers that fill the earth. My friend's gift was a beautiful reminder of that.

—TRICIA GOYER

FAITH STEP: *Pick up a bouquet of flowers for a friend. But before you give them away, spend time enjoying their tiniest details and thanking Jesus that He cares for every tiny detail in your life too.*

THURSDAY, JUNE 23

Blessed is a man who perseveres under trial; for once he has been approved, he will receive the crown of life which the Lord has promised to those who love Him.
James 1:12 (NAS)

A RECENT TV PROGRAM WARNED tourists about a mosquito outbreak in tropical climates. "Those bitten suffer from headaches and joint pain for several days," said the broadcaster. "So, how can you prevent becoming ill on your holiday? Avoid being bitten by a mosquito." Right.

I grew up in Brooks, Alberta. A small town developed on swampland, it was an ideal breeding ground for mosquitoes. Escaping the pesky insects was impossible. Countless itchy red welts left me with no appreciation for them. Mosquitoes—who needs 'em anyway?

Sometimes I wonder the same thing about life's trials. They're inconvenient, they cause pain, and they're never welcome. Trouble is, avoiding them for a lifetime is impossible. What purpose do they serve? Sir Isaac Newton shared a thought-provoking perspective: "Trials are medicines which our gracious and wise Physician prescribes because we need them, and He proportions the frequency and weight of them to what the case requires. Let us trust His skill and thank Him for His prescription."

Trials may be inconvenient, painful, and unwelcome, but they're a cure for our sin sickness. Through them we learn patience and perseverance. They teach us how to face our fears and develop thankful hearts. They awaken us to the reality of Jesus's presence and faithfulness. They deepen our relationship with Christ as we admit our dependency upon Him.

Trials—who needs 'em, anyway? We do. They serve an invaluable purpose in making us more like Jesus, and someday He'll reward us for persevering through them. —GRACE FOX

FAITH STEP: *Think of someone who's modeled a God-honoring response to a significant trial. Ask her to share her story. Ask, "How did this experience grow your faith in Jesus?" and "What Scripture promise became alive to you?"*

FRIDAY, JUNE 24

But thanks be to God! He gives us the victory through our Lord Jesus Christ.
1 Corinthians 15:57 (NIV)

WHEN I WAS A TEENAGER, I developed an eating disorder. It didn't threaten my life. But instead of food staying in its proper place in my life it became a psychological force, something I relied on for a sense of control as well as a stress release. As years passed, it became more and more of a bondage.

I looked to Jesus for help overcoming this problem. I prayed, journaled, tried all kinds of healthy eating plans, diets, medicine, and even hypnotism. Although I had periods of success, nothing worked long-term. At age forty, after having four kids, I was worried about developing health problems. I did a lot of research, consulted several doctor friends, and decided to have gastric bypass surgery. After transforming my eating habits and exercising regularly, my life truly changed and I am healthy today. Finally, I got a victory over something that had been the bane of my existence for twenty-five years!

Sometimes we can't understand why we aren't delivered from a difficult situation when we feel we are doing everything we can. It's easy to become discouraged and think God has abandoned us or isn't answering our prayers. But I believe Jesus was with me the whole time. He was working in my life, and in His time, He brought me through to victory. Although we don't all walk the same path, have the same hang-ups, or need the same solutions, Jesus is the same yesterday, today, and forever. He is with us. He is working in us all of the time. And He will bring us through to victory. We can count on Him! —GWEN FORD FAULKENBERRY

FAITH STEP: *Is there something you're struggling with? Don't give up. Keep seeking; keep trying; keep trusting. Victory is yours in Jesus.*

one SATURDAY, JUNE 25

Let the fields and their crops burst out with joy! Let the trees of the forest sing with praise. Psalm 96:12 (NLT)

I LIVE IN THE FOREST in a little cabin surrounded by very tall trees. The building site was cleared long after old-growth forest was logged out and densely packed seedlings raced each other up to the light. Unshaded and evenly matched, they all reached dizzying heights. If the clearing had been here first, the trees near its edges would have branched out instead of up. But the clearing came second, so my cabin window looks out on tall maple, birch, beech, balsam, hemlock, and white pine. The trees whisper before you even notice the breeze, sway when the wind comes up, and put on a spectacular show in a storm. I have the best seat in the house.

They seem to know a secret. They dance. Worship. The Bible tells us the earth can rejoice (Psalm 97:1) and that all God's works will praise Him (Psalm 145:10). Stars, planets, and moons; mountains and seas—indeed, every kind of creature—praises the Lord (Psalm 148). Before the written Word, Job declared the animals, birds, and plants would teach those who asked about God's character.

But we all too often don't ask or even notice. We, as a culture, spend more time in front of our various screens than outside.

Creation speaks—even preaches. When Jesus told listeners not to be anxious, He pointed to the birds and the lilies around them as examples. He made the world and holds it together. Nature will sing His name to those who pay attention. —SUZANNE DAVENPORT TIETJEN

FAITH STEP: *Spend time outside today. Hold still and listen. Watch any creature until you figure out what it's doing. Like my trees, look up and offer praise.*

SUNDAY, JUNE 26

I want to know Christ—yes to know the power of his resurrection and participation in his sufferings, becoming like him in his death, and so, somehow, attaining the resurrection from the dead. Philippians 3:10–11 (NIV)

POLITICAL SATIRIST STEPHEN COLBERT lost his father and two brothers in a plane crash when he was ten years old. His mother's faith helped him through the tragedy. Colbert said, "She taught me to be grateful for my life regardless of what that entailed, and that's directly related to the image of Christ on the Cross and the example of sacrifice that He gave us. What she taught is that the deliverance God offers you from pain is not no pain—it's that the pain is actually a gift."

How can pain be a gift? This is one of the great mysteries of the Cross, and one I find as challenging as it is alluring as a believer. Paul provides insight in the above verse when He says, "I want to know Christ." When I think about the people who know me best, and vice versa, they are not only the people I have things in common with, or have fun with, or even (necessarily) whom I've known the longest. They are the people who know my pain. The ones on the short list, the inner circle, the ones who have entered into the hardest times of my life with me so much that it has hurt them too.

In that way pain is a gift. Because if we want to know Jesus, and live out the Resurrection, meaning that our suffering can be redeemed through His Cross, the only way is pain. In the words of Paul, "I count all things to be loss in view of the surpassing value of knowing Christ Jesus my Lord" (Philippians 3:8, NAS). —GWEN FORD FAULKENBERRY

FAITH STEP: *What is causing you the most pain today? Thank the Lord that that very thing is also what will lead you into deeper intimacy with Jesus.*

MONDAY, JUNE 27

Taking the five loaves and the two fish and looking up to heaven, he gave thanks and broke the loaves. Then he gave them to his disciples to distribute to the people. He also divided the two fish among them all. Mark 6:41 (NIV)

THE DAY THAT I DO MY BILLS each month is always one of those days that invites faith. I can economize and save but there always seems to be something that comes up to throw off my carefully calculated budget. This month it was a two-hundred-dollar ER bill for a contused elbow. With three active boys, we are on a first-name basis with many of the doctors at the ER.

These unexpected bills make me want to throw out my careful calculations and say, "Forget it." I do the math and I think, *This is impossible. How in the world are we going to be able to pay for everything that we need to pay for?* And that is when I usually start asking Jesus for help.

The thing about Jesus is that He does a different kind of math. When Jesus starts answering prayers, things don't add up the way we think they will. Take the feeding of the five thousand. When I add up five loaves and two fish, it equals five loaves and two fish. When Jesus adds up five loaves and two fish, it equals a full-blown meal for a hillside of people, with twelve baskets left over. How do you start out with a bag lunch and end up with a fish fry for five thousand? I don't know. But Jesus does.

That is why we should trust Him with the dailiness of our lives. With our worries, our concerns, our bills, our grocery lists, and our visits to the ER. He does "divine math." And when He works in our lives, miracles can become everyday occurrences. —SUSANNA FOTH AUGHTMON

FAITH STEP: *Thank Jesus for what He has already done in your life and invite Him to use His "divine math" with any problems you are facing today.*

TUESDAY, JUNE 28

For right now, until that completeness, we have three things to do to lead us to that consummation: Trust steadily in God, hope unswervingly, love extravagantly. And the best of these is love. 1 Corinthians 13:13 (MSG)

WE'VE HEARD IT at any number of weddings, listened to it from the pulpit, and read it in our Bibles. I cross-stitched it once and hung it on the wall. As with many familiar passages, I sometimes go into I've-heard-this-before mode when I hear the opening verse of 1 Corinthians 13.

It wasn't written as wedding prose—it's more like an instruction manual for monitoring our motives. All the things we do, everything we've learned, even if they are excellent to the point of being miraculous, they're nothing without love. Giving away everything we have, even our very lives, counts for nothing without love. Not our own imperfect knock-off of the real thing, but *God's* love in us. God's love, it turns out, is entirely different from ours. His doesn't insist on its own way. God's love pays no attention when it is wronged. *Pays no attention!* I try to love others; I may forgive, but I always at least pay attention when someone hurts me.

Who can love like that? What human, anyway?

One human did. Jesus. And He wants us to love like that too.

The ability to love like this just isn't in us, but it must be possible or God wouldn't ask us to do it. We aren't being told to produce a feeling by exerting our wills; we are being asked to permit a renovation of our lives. The same Holy Spirit that empowered Jesus produces fruit in us. We just have to get out of the way and let Him love through us. He even supplies the hope. —SUZANNE DAVENPORT TIETJEN

FAITH STEP: *Thank Jesus that you don't have to come up with this kind of love on your own. Ask Him today to show you some evidence of God's love flowing through your life.*

one

WEDNESDAY, JUNE 29

Imitate me, as I also imitate Christ. 1 Corinthians 11:1 (HSC)

WE LIVE IN A WORLD with plenty of fakes, phonies, and imitations. What looks like wood furniture is often made out of—something else. Jewelers come up with fancy names for artificial diamonds and gemstones. Fake hair, nails, and eyelashes are getting to be the norm. The news sometimes carries stories of authorities arresting merchants selling knock-offs of designer name-brand clothing and accessories.

Although I do own a padfolio stamped with "Genuine Italian Leatherette," I generally prefer the real thing. I'd rather pay a bit more for pure vanilla extract than buy imitation. I prefer to own a couple of real leather handbags rather than a shelf full of purses in synthetic materials.

I'm sure all of us want to be someone who is perceived as genuine and real, not as a person who puts on a false front. As a writer, I'm often told, "Find your own voice." Singers are advised to "make the song your own." We're urged to discover our own niche, forge our own path, to "be yourself." And yet, one of the guiding principles of the Christian life is to imitate Somebody else.

As a believer in Jesus, my basic assignment is to imitate Him as much as I can. His godly character. His attitudes of humility, compassion, and forgiveness. His life of selfless service and devotion to worship and prayer. When I practice imitating Him, something amazing happens. The more I grow to be like Jesus, the more I develop into the person I was meant to be all along. The real me instead of the sin-marred version.

It's a paradox of our faith: Only when we imitate Christ can we become the real thing. —DIANNE NEAL MATTHEWS

FAITH STEP: *Choose one aspect of Christ's character or way of living to focus on this week. Put a reminder where you'll see it each morning and ask yourself, "How can I imitate Jesus's _____ today?"*

THURSDAY, JUNE 30

"Behold, I am the Lord, the God of all flesh: is there any thing too hard for me?"
Jeremiah 32:27 (KJV)

I LOVE TO DO RESEARCH for the novels that I write, but sometimes the research can be frustrating. A few years ago I was working on a novel, *Arms of Deliverance,* about Lebensborn Homes, run by the Nazi party. These homes, where young women would go to have their babies, was the setting for this novel. I had a specific home that I wanted to use in Belgium, but it was nearly impossible to find information about it. Since this was part of history, I didn't just want to make it all up. I kneeled before Jesus and prayed, "Lord, it may seem silly but I'd love help with this research. You were there. You are as close to Belgium as You are to me. I know You know the answers, please show me."

After praying I went to do the dishes, and I'd barely filled the sink when I remembered that I knew someone from Belgium. I rushed to my computer as the man's name filtered into my mind. Roger was a historian whom I'd met at a World War II reunion. I sent Roger an e-mail, requesting the information I needed. He e-mailed back quickly, and it turns out that he not only had access to the information, but he lived in the town where the Lebensborn Home was located! Roger even knew the museum curator who now was overseeing the home.

After wracking my brain, I'd come up empty, but after turning to Jesus, He provided me with everything I needed. Nothing is too hard for Him, not even bringing me a friend on the other side of the world who'd be able to offer the right kind of help just when I needed it. —TRICIA GOYER

FAITH STEP: *Do you have a need that seems too hard for you to handle? Turn it over to Jesus. Nothing is too hard for Him.*

FRIDAY, JULY 1

For God so loved the world that he gave his one and only Son, that whoever believes in him shall not perish but have eternal life. For God did not send his Son into the world to condemn the world, but to save the world through him.
John 3:16–17 (NIV)

THE STORY OF JOSEPH in the Old Testament has always fascinated me. But one day recently as I was rereading that Bible story, I saw something fresh.

When Joseph's brothers finally stood before him at Potiphar's palace in Egypt, Joseph—filled with love—drew close and revealed who he was to them. After so many years had passed, they did not recognize him. He identified not only himself, but what they did: sold him into slavery in Egypt. But before they could respond to him or act on the guilt overwhelming them, Joseph did something strange. "Don't blame yourselves for selling me," he said. "God was behind it. God sent me here ahead of you to save lives" (Genesis 45:4–5, MSG).

Joseph chose not to attack or shame his brothers, but to comfort them. They needed him, literally, for survival.

In the same way, Jesus didn't come into the world to condemn or to shame us, but to comfort us and draw us to Him. He wants us to see the greater purpose behind His coming. Yes, our sin led to His dying on the Cross. But Jesus wants us to know that God sent Him to save us.

He doesn't excuse us or our selfishness. He points out our sin—but not to turn us away, only to comfort us with His love and forgiveness—and to show us our desperate need for Him, for our eternal survival.

What a beautiful picture of love! —REBECCA BARLOW JORDAN

FAITH STEP: *Take time today to thank Jesus for His comforting love, and for coming into the world to save lives—especially yours.*

one SATURDAY, JULY 2

I am sure of this, that He who started a good work in you will carry it on to completion until the day of Christ Jesus. Philippians 1:6 (HCS)

ISN'T IT FRUSTRATING to take off with your family on a special road trip and then find yourself in a construction zone with stop-and-go traffic that stretches as far as you can see? When I see a sign warning of a work zone ahead, I often think of the inscription on Ruth Bell Graham's tombstone: "End of Construction—Thank you for your patience."

Apparently, Ruth had seen these words on a highway sign and expressed a desire to have them engraved on her headstone. What a great reminder that we are all still growing; as a matter of fact, we might as well consider ourselves and everyone we meet as works-in-progress. No matter how diligently we practice spiritual disciplines, there will always be more for us to learn and apply to our lives.

Conflict often erupts when one believer feels as though someone has let him or her down or hasn't behaved as a Christian should. But I find it even easier to get frustrated with my own shortcomings. There are times when I feel as though I'm slipping backward instead of maturing. Thankfully, I have God's promise that He will finish what He started in me on the day I accepted His gift of salvation through Christ.

Construction zones serve the purpose of improving our highways and making them safer. The messy construction zones of our lives serve to transform us into the image of Jesus Christ. We can be more patient with each other and ourselves if we remember that God considers our lives a "good work." —DIANNE NEAL MATTHEWS

FAITH STEP: *Is there someone in your life who frequently frustrates you? The next time you start to feel impatient, remind yourself that, just like you, he or she is a work-in-progress in God's hands.*

SUNDAY, JULY 3

But they did not understand what he meant and were afraid to ask him about it.
Mark 9:32 (NIV)

JESUS SHARED THE STORY of the persistent widow pestering a judge until he ruled in her favor, but His disciples (and we) have a hard time asking—much less asking boldly—for what we want.

God rewards those who bring their requests boldly to Him. When a widow's creditors threatened to take her sons as slaves because of an unpaid debt, she asked Elisha for help. He said to borrow jugs and bowls from all her neighbors—not just a few—all the containers she could get. He told her to pour her little bit of oil into the borrowed vessels, and the oil only stopped flowing when there was nowhere else for it to go.

Joash, king of Israel, came to a dying Elisha, fearing a Syrian invasion. Elisha had him take some arrows and shoot one out the window. Then he told him to strike the rest of the arrows on the ground and Joash did...three times before stopping. A furious Elisha said, "Why didn't you strike the ground five or six times? Then you would have beaten them entirely. Now you'll only defeat the Syrians three times."

Jesus said, "Ask." I do, and it's like I'm trying to fill my thimble from His waterfall.

He said, "If you make yourselves at home with me and my words are at home in you, you can be sure that whatever you ask will be listened to and acted upon" (John 15:7, MSG).

So ask boldly. —SUZANNE DAVENPORT TIETJEN

FAITH STEP: *We are to ask boldly, believingly, without a second thought (James 1:6, MSG). What have you been afraid to ask Jesus? Go ahead and ask Him today. You don't have to be afraid.*

MONDAY, JULY 4

Even youths grow tired and weary, and young men stumble and fall; but those who hope in the Lord will renew their strength. They will soar on wings like eagles; they will run and not grow weary, they will walk and not be faint. Isaiah 40:30—31 (NIV)

I HAVE BEEN THINKING a lot about Jesus lately. That and the fact that no hope or dream is too big or too small for the One who loves us the most.

He loves surprising His kids with His goodness and mercy in ways greater than they could ever imagine. He is unlimited in His greatness. His power is unmatched. His resources are endless. His love covers this earth and pins it among the stars. His compassion has no boundaries and it echoes down through the ages, shouting with each rising of the sun, "I am here!" His mercy floods the whole of the earth. His grace cannot be contained...not within nations or planets or galaxies.

We cannot fathom the depth or width or breadth of His majesty. And this great One holds us in the very center of His palm. He will withhold no good thing from us. This is the promise He has given us. He is the God of miracles and healing and deliverance and unspeakable joy.

All He asks is that we give Him the whole of our lives. The struggles and victories, the successes and failures, the wants and needs, the great joys and deep sorrows. And our silent hidden hopes? Those He would like us to place in Him. And then He asks one more thing...that we remember Who He is and that we not make Him small. Because He is anything but that.

I'm hoping big today. And do you know what the most remarkable thing is? Once you start putting your hopes in Jesus...it is hard to stop. So what are you waiting for? —SUSANNA FOTH AUGHTMON

FAITH STEP: *Draw an outline of the word Jesus in giant bubble letters. Inside, write down your struggles, needs, joys, sorrows, and great hopes.*

TUESDAY, JULY 5

one

And let us consider how to stir up one another to love and good works, not neglecting to meet together, as is the habit of some, but encouraging one another, and all the more as you see the Day drawing near. Hebrews 10:24–25 (ESV)

I WALKED TIMIDLY into the fellowship hall for Tuesday morning Bible study at a new church. Would I fit in here? Were relationships already firmly established with no room for a newcomer? My stomach tightened as if I were facing a high school lunchroom.

Immediately an older woman introduced herself. Another gal invited me to sit by her. Soon I was surrounded with interested questions and warm inclusion from women of all ages. Young moms passed babies around while seniors leaned on their canes to stand and share how Jesus had provided for them. Stories of faith in the face of challenge lifted my spirits. I felt warmed to my bones.

The experience reminded me of a trip my husband and I had taken to the mountains. Our hotel had a hot tub on the roof, and after a long day of hiking, we soaked in the soothing water while snowflakes fell. We could still see the harsh rocks and icy weather, but the cold was a distant memory as hot water bubbled around us.

Now a regular at Bible study, I appreciate how we talk about the harsh realities of life, but the warmth of fellowship coaxes away our pain. Being with other women who love Jesus is like easing into the healing water of a hot tub. While we wait for Jesus's return and seek to serve the world in His name, we need to "stir up one another to love and good works." Otherwise we can stiffen up or grow cold and discouraged. I'm so grateful that Jesus understands our need and gives us the precious gift of fellowship. —SHARON HINCK

FAITH STEP: *Do you have a small group community where you feel safe and cherished? If so, thank Jesus. If not, ask Him to guide you to a place where you can be stirred up and encouraged.*

WEDNESDAY, JULY 6

I'm sure now I'll see God's goodness in the exuberant earth. Stay with God!
Take heart. Don't quit. I'll say it again: Stay with God. Psalm 27:13–14 (MSG)

HAVE YOU EVER KNOWN ANYONE who viewed waiting as a beautiful thing? Me neither. It seems that most times when we ask for something in prayer, God's answers come later than our time frame. Rarely does it seem that He answers on the early side of things.

Why is that? Jesus is Lord, all powerful, all knowing, with kindness in His very being. Even when we understand that He will finish delivering any blessings in our lives that He starts, still the experience can be so hard we wonder if it will be worth it.

His reasons may be varied, but one particular reason lies in today's Scripture verses. It is easy to imagine having courage, but it is only through the practice of placing our courage in Christ that we grow. Outside of a difficult time, we can forget how much we need Him.

His waiting periods can be precious seasons of intimacy and deeper journeying with the One Who ordered the universe into motion, the same One Who sees each tear we shed as we learn to look to Him for the answer, to trust Him one more time.

As we wait close to Him, we are near enough to see Him more clearly, to hear His heartbeat that once was quieted into silence but overcame death to beat again forever.

Forever is the time frame He deals in. These earthly days and struggles are subject to His forever sovereignty. Someone who sticks close to the Lord through the struggle is truly a beautiful example of faith. Don't quit. Stay with Him and wait well. When you do, you will see profound realities of Who He is. —ERIN KEELEY MARSHALL

FAITH STEP: *Talk to Jesus about a longing you or someone you care about is waiting for. Pour out your heart to Jesus, and end your prayer with words of faith.*

THURSDAY, JULY 7

Yet when I surveyed all that my hands had done and what I had toiled to achieve, everything was meaningless, a chasing after the wind; nothing was gained under the sun. Ecclesiastes 2:11 (NIV)

IF ANYONE KNEW ABOUT living "the good life," it was King Solomon. Possessing more fame, wealth, and power than anyone on earth, he had unlimited resources at his disposal. After Solomon's heart strayed from God, he undertook magnificent building projects, amassed servants and wives, and experimented with every earthly pleasure he desired. Late in his reign, he looked back over the wasted years he'd spent searching for fulfillment. Although Solomon had found temporary pleasure in his pursuits, he concluded that all his endeavors lacked real meaning and lasting satisfaction. He might as well have been chasing the wind.

A depressing view of life—and quite a contrast to what Jesus offers in John 10:10: "I have come that they may have life, and have it to the full." Jesus lived and died so that we can have a life of meaning and purpose, enjoying fellowship with Him and each other. We can chase after material wealth, popularity, or earthly achievements, but we will end up feeling empty. Or we can follow Jesus, striving to know, love, and serve Him better each day, and have an abundant life.

The satisfaction that comes from earthly pleasures doesn't last. The deep, abiding joy that springs from walking with Jesus every day is permanent. Compared with the rich spiritual blessings our Savior generously pours out, the best the world has to offer amounts to nothing. Why would I want to chase after the wind when I can follow the only One Who gives life true meaning? —DIANNE NEAL MATTHEWS

FAITH STEP: *Think about where you've been focusing your time and efforts lately. If you've been chasing after worldly pleasures, make a commitment to turn in the other direction and follow Jesus instead.*

FRIDAY, JULY 8

Be kind to one another, tenderhearted, forgiving one another, as God in Christ forgave you. Ephesians 4:32 (ESV)

IT WAS TIME TO LEAVE THE RETREAT. I felt like a young person reluctant to say good-bye to summer camp. Home sounded great, but leaving the retreat and its idyllic setting prompted some serious foot-dragging.

I had one last meal in the restaurant on the water, a simple dinner to save money and calories. The sweet-tempered young server went out of her way to make my meal a pleasant experience, ensuring my iced tea never dropped below two-thirds full, pointing out how the cook could accommodate my particular food-allergy needs. At the end of the meal, she asked, "Would you like to see our dessert menu?"

I mentally fingered the last few dollars in my wallet and the shrinking waistband on my jeans. "No, thank you. The check, please."

She disappeared to calculate the bill and returned with a beautiful handmade pottery plate and two elegantly decorated chocolate-covered strawberries. "But I didn't order...," I began.

Her heartwarming smile started speaking before she did. "I know," she said. "They're 'just because.'"

How often does Jesus do that for us—offer us a "just because" moment in our mundane days? How often does He give us a breath of something we don't really need and didn't really ask for just to bless us?

Today, it was hearing a new birdsong. Yesterday it was a flat stretch of road after walking uphill too long. Tomorrow it may be a note from a friend, prompted by the One Who knew I'd need that chocolate-covered strawberry-like encouragement. Just because. —CYNTHIA RUCHTI

FAITH STEP: *Jesus is gracious, giving, merciful, kind. Whether it's chocolate-covered strawberries or some other "just because" generosity, surprise someone today with a nonverbal demonstration of the extravagant love of Jesus.*

SATURDAY, JULY 9

By grace you have been saved. . . . Ephesians 2:8 (NRSV)

IN A PARTICULARLY FIENDISH MOMENT after swimming, Harper popped his little sister, Adelaide, with a towel. I'm sure that the "pop" was much louder and harder than he intended, and it made a red welt on her leg. It hurt. She started crying, running into my arms for comfort. Then, to my surprise, Harper started crying because he realized what he had done. As he stood outside our circle of love holding a limp, wet towel, all of our conversations about not being wild, not bullying, having self-control, and so on, came crashing down on his head.

I was pretty mad at him. *When will he ever learn?* As I stroked Adelaide's white angel hair, I felt her loosen her grip and then slide out of my arms. Walking over to Harper, she reached out and enfolded him in a hug. His sobs grew louder as she patted him, saying, "It's okay. It's okay."

This move was vintage Adelaide, whose sweetness is like a drug that soothes all of our souls. But it was also the perfect picture of grace. We are the reason Jesus went to the Cross. We caused the wounds on His hands and feet, the thorns on His brow, the stripes on His back. And yet, because of His great love, He reaches out to us every day to remove our guilt, lift up our heads, and save us. —GWEN FORD FAULKENBERRY

FAITH STEP: *Who needs this kind of grace from you today? Send a card, letting them know Jesus loves them and you do too.*

SUNDAY, JULY 10

May you experience the love of Christ, though it is so great you will never fully understand it. Then you will be made complete with all the fullness of life and power that comes from God. Ephesians 3:19 (NLT)

I ATTENDED SUNDAY SCHOOL regularly as a kid. One of my favorite choruses described Christ's love as being wide as the ocean, high as the heavens, and deep as the deepest sea. Its lyrics remind me of Ephesians 3:18: "And may you have the power to understand, as all God's people should, how wide, how long, how high, and how deep his love really is."

The apostle Paul was right when he wrote of our needing power to understand Christ's love. It's far easier to sing or read about than to truly comprehend. Perhaps you can relate. Think about this: If we fully understood Jesus's love, we would never doubt His willingness to forgive us when we sin. We wouldn't question His wisdom or kindness for allowing trials or tragedies. We wouldn't fear saying yes when given a God-size task. We'd know contentment with His provision. And we'd live the joy-filled life promised to those who obey His commands. Obedience, in fact, would come quickly and easily, knowing His commands flow out of a loving heart rather than from a need to control.

Jesus left heaven's glory yielding His rights as God and assuming the form of a servant for our sake. He accepted criticism, mockings, beatings, scourgings, and, ultimately, Crucifixion on our behalf. That's true love.

May Jesus give us the power to understand His love for us. That's the key to living the power-filled lives He intends for us. —GRACE FOX

FAITH STEP: *Place a coffee mug under the tap in your kitchen sink. Turn on the water and let it fill the mug to overflowing for several seconds. That's the picture of Christ's overflowing love for you. Thank Him for this precious gift.*

MONDAY, JULY 11

If we confess our sins, he is faithful and just and will forgive us our sins and purify us from all unrighteousness. 1 John 1:9 (NIV)

THIS MORNING I WOKE UP EARLY to write and went into the kitchen to get a pot of coffee going. Because, let's be honest, coffee is the best way to greet any morning, writing or not. I was greeted by a sink full of dinner dishes. I always hope that sometime during the night the magical dishes fairy will show up and clean up the kitchen. It never seems to happen. So instead of writing, I spent the first twenty minutes of my morning washing dishes. For some reason, I can't write in a dirty environment. Everything around me has to be clean. I can't do the creative work I need to do when everything around me is cluttered and dirty and gross.

I think Jesus is the same. We want Him to do amazing work in our hearts and lives but there is a lot of clean up that has to take place before that can happen. The state of our hearts is messy with sin and weakness. Our minds are sullied with selfish thoughts and pride and ambition. On our own, there is nothing we can do to change. But Jesus says to us, *How about I take all that mess and ugliness and clean you up so I can do in you all that I long to do?*

He has much creative work to do in our lives if we let Him. When we ask Him to forgive us for our sins and allow Him to flood our lives with His righteousness, He gives us what we can never achieve in our own striving. A clean heart. A blank canvas for Him to do His good and beautiful work. I think we should do it. —SUSANNA FOTH AUGHTMON

FAITH STEP: *Make this psalm your prayer today, "Create in me a clean heart, O God. And renew a right spirit within me."*

TUESDAY, JULY 12

May the God who gives endurance and encouragement give you the same attitude of mind toward each other that Christ Jesus had. Romans 15:5 (NIV)

I ONCE HEARD A STORY about the behavior of crabs that has stuck with me and makes me think humans have more in common with those crustaceans than perhaps previously thought. The story goes that if you have a bucket full of crabs, you don't have to put a lid on it. Because even though they could obviously work together and escape by forming a ladder and pulling up one another, they don't do this. In fact, if one crab somehow manages to climb above the others and tries to escape, the others will reach up with their claws and pull that one back down into the bucket.

I have not tried this experiment with crabs. But I've seen it happen often enough with people. It's like that old saying, "Misery loves company." It seems we are more prone to drag each other down than to build one another up. And, certainly, if one person in a group does well, instead of celebrating that victory, people seem more likely to want to reach up and pull the successful person back down. We are uncomfortable with the success of others because we feel it makes us look bad. Or we're jealous. Or it challenges us and we'd rather not be challenged. Or whatever.

Christians should not be crabs. Instead, as imitators of Jesus, we should be the very opposite. We should be building ladders, propping up people on our shoulders, helping them escape hell, whether it be in the hereafter or the here and now. That means celebrating when someone else gets the raise you wanted. Being proud instead of jealous when a family member succeeds in school. Someone else's child won the music award? Good for them! Tell them congratulations. Your friend lost fifty pounds or gained a new grandson? Be happy and show your support. Every time you build another person up, you are building the kingdom of heaven. —GWEN FORD FAULKENBERRY

FAITH STEP: *Think of someone who needs encouragement today. Send a card or make a phone call to let them know you're in their corner!*

WEDNESDAY, JULY 13

*I'm convinced that nothing can separate us from God's love in
Christ Jesus our Lord.... Romans 8:38 (CEB)*

I KNOW ENOUGH NOW to keep a notebook handy when my grandkids are around. The wisdom or humor or combination of both that comes from their mouths is too rich to trust to memory alone.

Yesterday, three of them gathered in my too-small-for-one kitchen to watch me bake brownies and offer their help and advice. Disconnected from anything we were talking about at the time, my nine-year-old grandson said, "You know, Grammie, almost every show on television is either about love or problems."

I had to agree with him, and added that most books are like that too. They're either about love or problems or the problems love can cause.

The longer I thought about it, the clearer it became that Jesus taught the same principle. The whole of the Bible is related to love and problems. God's love. Our problems. God's love expressed through Jesus. Our problems when we ignore what Jesus taught.

In 1 John 2:15–17, the biblical writer explained how we get into the problem part of that equation. "Don't love the world," it reads, "or the things in the world. If anyone loves the world, the love of the Father is not in them. Everything that is in the world—the craving for whatever the body feels, the craving for whatever the eyes see and the arrogant pride in one's possessions—is not of the Father but is of the world. And the world and its cravings are passing away, but the person who does the will of God remains forever."

How many stressors or problems in my life would disappear if I focused more intently on the love of Jesus? —CYNTHIA RUCHTI

FAITH STEP: *Problems is a longer word, but love is the stronger word when referring to the love of Jesus. Today, find someone in your circle of family or friends or coworkers who needs to hear that truth and share it with him or her.*

THURSDAY, JULY 14

My child, don't reject the Lord's discipline, and don't be upset when he corrects you. For the Lord corrects those he loves, just as a father corrects a child in whom he delights. Proverbs 3:11–12 (NLT)

MANY YEARS AGO, I DREAMED of dancing for the American Ballet Theater, so I spent my nineteenth summer in New York to see if I could dance on that level. At the surprisingly nondescript Ballet Theater School, I climbed ill-lit stairs to a dressing room scented with sweat and baby powder.

Though not a scholarship student, I took the scholarship class. When we moved to floor work after warming up at the barre, I chose a position one row back and well wide of the middle. Like folks in church who own certain pews, better dancers claimed those center positions. Feeling like I didn't belong, I tried to create the shape of the combination we were working on. I forgot myself and breathed a little life into it when the instructor came over and touched my hip, gently nudging it into correct alignment. She nodded as I held the realigned position, then placed her hand at the flare of my rib cage and motioned up. "Lift," she said, already turning away toward the girls in the front row. I caught a glimpse of her looking at me in the mirror as I inhaled and arched my upper body toward the ceiling.

Now I was dancing.

So often, we want applause. Affirmation. But those don't change us for the better.

I knew the instructors didn't waste time on dancers who showed no promise. We all did, so we didn't shrink from correction—we *craved* it.

Jesus wants to bring out the best in us. We tie His hands if we refuse correction. Yield. You'll be dancing if you do. —SUZANNE DAVENPORT TIETJEN

FAITH STEP: *Ask Jesus to shine a light on anything in your life that displeases Him. Don't worry, He's been waiting for this, gentle as with a beloved child. Watch for His answer.*

FRIDAY, JULY 15

Stay alert! Watch out for your great enemy, the devil. He prowls around like a roaring lion, looking for someone to devour. Stand firm against him, and be strong in your faith. Remember that your family of believers all over the world is going through the same kind of suffering you are. 1 Peter 5:8—9 (NLT)

LAST SUMMER I WENT TO AFRICA to write about a Christian organization, and while we were there we went on a safari. It was something from my bucket list, and I wasn't disappointed. We saw zebras, water buffalo, giraffes, elephants, and all types of other animals, but nothing was as impressive to me as the lions.

Our jeep came across the lions right around dusk, and the lionesses were heading out for the hunt. The beautiful cats walked hunched over, just as I saw on *Mutual of Omaha's Wild Kingdom* as a child. They moved stealthily toward a herd of zebras just down the hill. I held my breath, waiting for the chase. It never happened. While their eyes were on the zebras, they made no sudden moves. Each one took the smallest steps, waited, and watched. We finally had to leave the reserve when dusk fell, but the next day we saw them again. We also saw evidence of their kill.

Our great enemy, the devil, acts in the same way. He has his eyes on us. As the dusk—the fatigue and troubles of the day—sets in, he's ready for the hunt. And when he gets close enough to roar, it's often too late—we become victims.

Yet in God's Word we are told to stand firm. While zebras might not have a chance against lions, we have Jesus standing up for us. And even when our enemy roars, our Lord stands stronger. No one is immune from the attack, but all believers have a shield of protection in Jesus Christ. —TRICIA GOYER

FAITH STEP: *Write out a prayer to Jesus thanking him for all the ways He's protected you. Ask Him to help you stand firm against the devil and to be strong in your faith. Also pray for the strength of other believers too.*

one SATURDAY, JULY 16

"I tell you the truth, anyone who believes in me will do the same works I have done and even greater works, because I am going to be with the Father."
John 14:12 (NLT)

MY GRANDKIDS LOVE TO CELEBRATE their birthdays at that place that has mediocre pizza and a giant mechanical mouse. (You parents know the one I'm talking about.) During the last party, I tried a new game to earn tickets for the birthday boy. As lights flashed around the outer edge of a giant wheel, I hit the button. Whichever spot the light stopped on determined how many tickets I won.

I tried my best to get the light to stop on the twenty-five-ticket spot on the right side. But each time it stopped either one spot before or after, netting three or four tickets. As the party ended, we all pitched in to use up leftover tokens. I decided to go for the one-hundred-ticket spot at the bottom of the wheel. I slammed the button and lights flashed as the machine spit out a very long strip of tickets.

I couldn't help wondering what would have happened if I'd set my sights higher in the first place instead of waiting until my last token. Then I began to wonder how many times in life I set my sights too low. Sometimes I have an idea or a dream that seems so big, it scares me. *You have to be realistic,* I scold myself. So I settle for something lesser, something more "reasonable."

Jesus wants His followers to do great things—what's more, He *expects* us to do great things. Guided by His wisdom and fueled by His power and strength, what once seemed out of reach begins to look like a reasonable goal. And when we set our sights high, we get a better look at Him.
—DIANNE NEAL MATTHEWS

FAITH STEP: *Do you have a dream that seems too big, a goal that looks impossible? Talk to Jesus about it. Ask for enough faith to pursue any dream that comes from Him.*

SUNDAY, JULY 17

Jesus cried again with a loud voice and breathed his last. At that moment the curtain of the temple was torn in two. . . . Matthew 27:50–51 (NRSV)

IT WAS A BAWL FEST at my house the other day. First, my niece Sophia took a joke too far and hurt her sister's feelings. When I fussed at her and made her apologize, big tears welled up in her eyes. I had to spend the next five minutes convincing her what a good sister she usually is and that we all make mistakes. Then that evening, Stella was too rough with our new kitty, and her dad reprimanded her. She burst into sobs, and we had to console her and help her not feel like a criminal. Finally, after talking "smarty" to me and getting a swat on her bottom, Adelaide hid in the powder room under the sink until I dragged her out and made her rejoin society.

All of these situations are examples of hyperconscience, or the shame we feel sometimes when we know we have done something wrong. Like in the case of Adelaide, sometimes we don't want to face others or ourselves—and certainly not God—when we've messed up. But Jesus made the way for us to do that.

I love the concept of the torn curtain. What a beautiful metaphor for our relationship with God through Jesus. Where there once was a barrier between us and His holiness, Jesus made the way by breaking it down. We don't have to be perfect. We don't have to be ritually clean. We just have to have Jesus, the one mediator between God and man.
—GWEN FORD FAULKENBERRY

FAITH STEP: *Share the story of the torn curtain today, inviting someone who is standing outside to come into a relationship with God through Jesus.*

MONDAY, JULY 18

Distress that drives us to God does that. It turns us around.
It gets us back in the way of salvation. We never regret that kind of pain.
But those who let distress drive them away from God are full of regrets.
2 Corinthians 7:10 (MSG)

I ENJOY READING ABOUT Jesus's encounters with people on earth, and how their lives were drastically changed because of Him. When I look at their sordid backgrounds and activities, I realize most were lost and without hope. But Jesus came "to seek and to save the lost" (Luke 19:10).

For the most part, those individuals made a 180-degree turn because Jesus's forgiveness and love spun them around and spurred them to a new way of living.

Zacchaeus, a short, hated tax collector was pursued by Jesus. After he encountered Jesus, he wanted to give away half of his possessions to the poor and return over four times what he'd acquired through his cheating habits (Luke 19:8). Jesus also shared His grace and mercy with the woman at the well. The first thing she did was to leave her water jar at the well and run to tell others about Jesus and what He had done for her (John 4:28–29).

In the past, I've wasted both time and energy looking over my shoulder. Regrets can paralyze us. But I noticed in each of Jesus's encounters, the people didn't focus time on regrets. They focused on Jesus, the great Life-Changer.

Years ago, I got tired of craning my neck to look backward. So I adopted a new slogan for my life with Jesus's help: "No guilt, no regrets; only grace and gratitude—and joy." Each time the temptation arises to linger on regrets, I remember to rest in Jesus and repeat those words.

What a difference that's made in my life! —REBECCA BARLOW JORDAN

FAITH STEP: *Do you waste time thinking about past regrets? Today, rest in Jesus and write your own life motto.*

one

TUESDAY, JULY 19

"For the bread of God is the bread that comes down from heaven and gives life to the world." John 6:33 (NIV)

MY CATS ARE EARLY RISERS. My husband and I aren't, preferring to sleep a little later than 4:30 AM. We tried feeding them late at night, hoping to avoid being prodded and yowled at before sunrise, but they woke us up no matter how late they ate.

Next I tried an automatic feeder loaded with four pounds of their favorite food. The cats get breakfast as soon as they want, and I get to sleep in on my days off.

Except it didn't work. One cat put on weight from the unlimited munchies, but most mornings they still sounded their feline reveille. Turns out it was our presence they wanted as much as the kitty kibble.

When God provided manna for the Israelites in the Sinai Desert, He didn't just drop a pile of it on the ground for them to scoop up whenever they chose. He provided it daily and each family was to take what they needed for that day and not save any for the next day. Of course some of them did it anyway and the manna became maggot-ridden. God wanted His people to come to Him daily, expectantly, out into the morning to gather His provision (except before the Sabbath when He gave them double and it stayed fresh). When they begged for meat instead, God dumped quail in a heap—practically buried the camp in meat. Why? Because they rejected Him, not just the manna, when they spurned His chosen sustenance.

God became physically present to us in Jesus, the Bread of Heaven, Who gave His life for the world.

Will we accept that precious gift or go after something else?

—SUZANNE DAVENPORT TIETJEN

FAITH STEP: *I imagine I sustain myself when, truly, I don't control whether I get another breath in this world. Write down three ways Jesus sustains you. Look at your list several times today.*

WEDNESDAY, JULY 20

Rejoice in the Lord your God! For the rain he sends demonstrates his faithfulness. . . . Joel 2:23 (NLT)

SWIM LESSONS FOR PAX AND Cali began today! But even before we left the house, it started to rain. In the past, that would have caused tears and meltdowns. But this morning they cheered, "Hooray for the rain!" They knew from experience that their fun was about to be doubled.

You see, lessons go on despite rain. The swim instructor cancels class only when lightning or thunder threatens their safety. Today's rain was a friendly one, so my children danced in the water while drops pebbled the surface of the pool.

From my spot on the uncovered patio, I felt the drops. It wasn't how I would have ordered the morning, but the rain brought relief here in Arkansas from an otherwise scorching sky.

As I observed Pax's and Cali's pure delight, I wondered, *What unique joys might Jesus have for me within storms?*

Right now my husband and I see one swirling overhead. We've had a couple of significant career disappointments in recent months, as well as some heartaches with extended family. At times it's hard to see through the clouds that darken our skies. Yet, those clouds are pregnant with the lesson of the rain. When they hover, I must remember the Keeper of the blessings within them: Jesus.

When I am stuck carrying on through the downpour, I can expect Jesus—the Keeper of the rains—to send surprising blessings in the storm. And, like my kids, I may even dance in the water!

—ERIN KEELEY MARSHALL

FAITH STEP: *Read Jeremiah 14:22. Thank Jesus for the blessings in your life's rains, and ask for help in focusing on Him as the source of those joys today.*

 THURSDAY, JULY 21

*The Son radiates God's own glory and
expresses the very character of God. . . . Hebrews 1:3 (NLT)*

MY SON AND HIS SIX-YEAR-OLD BOY bear a striking family resemblance. Besides sharing similar facial characteristics, they have similar personalities. Both are laid back, speak only when they feel words are necessary, and are gifted with similar interests and intellectual skills. Every time I see my grandson, I feel as though I'm looking at a miniversion of his dad.

I travel a lot for ministry purposes, and I often enjoy conversations of a spiritual nature with fellow travelers. Sometimes they ask, "What is God like?" I answer their question by pointing them to His Son, Jesus, Who is an exact representation of His Father. Here are a few examples:

Jesus touched the lepers; therefore we know God cares about outcasts.

Jesus cooked breakfast for His disciples; therefore we know God cares about our physical needs.

Jesus raised the dead; therefore we know God can do the impossible.

Jesus took our sin's punishment when He died on the Cross; therefore we know God loves us more than words can express.

If we doubt God's love for us, we need only look at the life and death of His Son. Jesus's willingness to die on our behalf confirms that He cherishes us deeply. And because He bears an exact representation of His Father, we know God loves us deeply too.

What is God like? Look at His Son. The family resemblance says it all.
—GRACE FOX

FAITH STEP: *Look at a family picture. Who bears a resemblance to whom? Think about how people share similar characteristics, but Jesus bears an exact representation of His Father. Which of His characteristics means the most to you?*

FRIDAY, JULY 22

I spread out my hands to you; my soul thirsts for you like a parched land. Selah.
Psalm 143:6 (NIV)

I KEEP A TRAVEL MUG OF WATER with me to sip throughout the day while working at my desk, doing household chores, or driving to errands and appointments. But when I read David's analogy in Psalm 143, I think back to times when I've been thirsty—really, really thirsty. Like those blistering summer days from childhood spent chopping down weeds on a cotton row that seemed to stretch for miles.

It's times like that when we truly appreciate water. While that might be an extreme situation, health experts tell us that in everyday life we can be dehydrated without knowing it. We may not realize that our headaches, fatigue, dizziness, or other symptoms stem from a lack of water. It's startling to think that we can be oblivious while our body is crying out for a basic need to be met.

Yet I believe the same thing can happen in our spiritual life. When we face trouble or hard times, we know we need to run to Jesus for help. On ordinary days, we may forget to draw from the well of His goodness, grace, mercy, and strength. We may be unaware that our discontentment, irritability, conflict with others, inability to make decisions, and other symptoms stem from a lack of time spent with Jesus.

We can guard against spiritual dehydration by developing the habit to drink of Jesus every day, throughout the day. And once we realize how much we need Him, we won't be satisfied with a little sip. —DIANNE NEAL MATTHEWS

FAITH STEP: *To avoid spiritual dehydration, take breaks throughout your day to drink deeply of Jesus through praise, prayer, Scripture reading, or meditation on His character and His presence in your life.*

ONE

SATURDAY, JULY 23

Submit yourselves, then, to God. Resist the devil, and he will flee from you.
James 4:7 (NIV)

I ONCE CUT MY FOOT with a piece of glass and had to have it scrubbed out with an iodine sponge by a very unloving ER nurse. I called on the name of Jesus as tears seeped from the corners of my eyes. I gripped the sides of the gurney and felt like I was going to be sick. And then it was done. I was cleaned up. No infection. No glass. I was ready to heal.

Sometimes reading Scripture feels like going through triage. Jesus wants to go to town with an iodine sponge of truth on the wounds of my soul. Those dark patches that are inclined to fester and turn ugly. Those parts that think, *I should have whatever I want, whenever I want it, and I don't really care what Jesus or anyone else thinks about it.* He knows that left to my own self-centered ways, I will destroy myself. It is just what we humans do. So He is working on my heart, poking at it, making me look at it and do something about it. I don't enjoy the process, and sometimes there are tears, but I do enjoy knowing that it is with great love that Jesus is working on my heart and soul and mind.

So I'm turning my face toward the One Who has the power to do something about the state of my soul and I'm saying, "Okay, Jesus, all this mess, the part of me that doesn't want to listen to You or to care about others, I am giving it to You. You are the only One Who can turn a hard selfish heart into a heart that beats with a strong love for You and You alone."

And the best part is? He will. —SUSANNA FOTH AUGHTMON

FAITH STEP: *Write the word* **Submit** *on a piece of paper. Underneath it, make a list of the different things you have submitted to Jesus in the past and how He has healed you in the process.*

one SUNDAY, JULY 24

May he produce in you, through the power of Jesus Christ, every good thing that is pleasing to him. All glory to him forever and ever! Amen. Hebrews 13:21 (NLT)

THINGS DON'T ALWAYS GO as we plan. The apostle Paul learned that lesson when he prepared to travel to Asia. "Now when they had gone through Phrygia and the region of Galatia, they were forbidden by the Holy Spirit to preach the word in Asia" (Acts 16:6, NKJV). Paul tried another route, but the spirit of Jesus prevented that trip as well. But Jesus spoke to him, leading him to a place He'd already prepared. The writer, Luke, reported it this way: "All the pieces had come together" (Acts 16:9–10, MSG).

I tracked Paul's pattern of obedience, seeing how the pieces had indeed come together. Atheists turned to Jesus; false spirits left; but Paul was also imprisoned. And Jesus had deterred Him for this? But when an earthquake miraculously freed Paul and his companion, Silas, the jailer's entire family accepted Jesus (Acts 16:34). Divine power continued in Paul's life, resulting in greater glory for Jesus.

I thought about my own dreams and plans in the past: write this; accomplish that; go there; turn here. But sometimes Jesus laid out other paths. Through His Word and His Spirit's impressions on my heart, confirmed by others, He assured me that His roadblocks held an important purpose.

Following Him is not trying to figure out which door to open. Nor is it trying to batter down the entrance, only to discover Jesus is not behind that door.

His new path for us may include unexpected or unwelcome events. But as His plan unfolds, and as we follow in obedience, we'll understand at least one of His reasons: greater glory for Jesus. —REBECCA BARLOW JORDAN

FAITH STEP: *Think about a time when one of Jesus's roadblocks led you in a more positive direction. Thank Him today for His infinite wisdom and direction in your life.*

one MONDAY, JULY 25

"A generation whose heart wasn't set firm and whose spirit wasn't faithful. . . ."
Psalm 78:8 (CEB)

ICE. JELL-O. Epoxy. Cement. Paint. Broken bones. Faith. What do they share in common? They're messy, useless and, in some cases, dangerous if they're not set. Most of us have stories about paw prints in the new sidewalk cement or soupy Jell-O. Maybe you have a photograph like one of my favorites—eighteen-month-old Luke, who decided to "help" by finger painting with the drywall mud that hadn't yet set on the walls of the addition we were building.

In Galatians, we're reminded, "Christ has set us free for freedom. Therefore stand firm" (Galatians 5:1, CEB). Standing firm in faith makes all the more sense when we think about how messy, useless, and dangerous our lives can get without that commitment to faithfulness, obedience, and assurance. During college days, I had a circle of friends whose faith was like underdone Jell-O. One week, they cried tears of joy as they worshipped Jesus and sang about His love. The next week, one or another in the group wept tears of grief, wondering if Jesus cared at all for their souls. Many of those people would now be in their sixties. I wonder if they ever "set."

Psalm 78:6–8 (CEB) says, "This [the Word] is so that the next generation and children not yet born will know these things, and . . . tell their children to put their hope in God, never forgetting [His] deeds, but keeping [His] commandments—and so that they won't become like their ancestors . . . a generation whose heart wasn't set firm. . . ."

From the moment Jesus breathed His first breath of earth's air, He was firmly set in Who He was and what He was sent to do. May that ever be true of us too. —CYNTHIA RUCHTI

FAITH STEP: *Did you catch the connection that a heart set firm is directly related to knowing and obeying the Bible? It's not a new concept. Today, when you open the Bible, tell Jesus how grateful you are for the way it "firms up" your faith.*

TUESDAY, JULY 26

"Be made new in the attitude of your minds; and . . . put on the new self. . . . "
Ephesians 4:23–24 (NIV)

OUR TWO-YEAR-OLD, STELLA, has gotten into the habit of being very grumpy in the mornings. She sleeps with my husband, Stone, and me, so when we get out of bed early to wake the school-age kids and start getting everybody ready for the day, we leave her in the bed asleep. On a normal morning, Grace is putting on her clothes, Adelaide is checking the weather, Harper is feeding the animals, I am in the kitchen cooking breakfast while Stone is packing lunches, and we hear, "Mommy! Daddy!" This repeats amid wails and gnashing of teeth till Stella finally gets out of bed and runs into the kitchen, crying all of the way. She wants to be held, she wants warm milk, and her feelings are hurt that we have to do anything else.

Needless to say, this is not acceptable. So after all kinds of patient, gentle exercises that haven't worked, we've started putting her back into the bed with instructions to stay there "till she can get up and act nicely."

This morning the scenario started out the same, except halfway to the kitchen she must have remembered what we told her. So, instead of whining, she said in a growly voice, "Good morning!" I had to stifle a laugh when I saw her little brows furrowed into a frown.

The training of a two-year-old is not unlike the training that a believer in Jesus must undergo daily. We are new in Jesus but must contend with the old self, old attitudes, old ways. Like Stella, we want what we want. But as we mature, we can see that His way is best and we begin to want what He wants more. —GWEN FORD FAULKENBERRY

FAITH STEP: *As you put on your clothes, think about inwardly putting on the new self you are in Jesus—with His attitude, His mind, His heart.*

ONE

WEDNESDAY, JULY 27

Perfect love drives out fear. . . . The one who fears is not made perfect in love.
1 John 4:18 (NIV)

A LOT IS WRITTEN ABOUT FEAR. How it cripples us and twists truth and causes destruction.

I'm coming to terms with a fear of mine I've only recently been able to name. It's the fear of not doing enough. Its relatives are perfectionism and impatience and humanism.

This fear focuses on what I think I need to be doing and fools me into fighting for the wrong priorities. It clogs the space in my heart reserved for Jesus, the perfect Love who can drive it out.

This fear strikes hard when I feel hurried and blinds me to my God-given life of offering grace and compassion. But instead of presenting itself honestly as the fear of not doing enough, it points the finger at people, the more important "interrupters." This fear is the real interrupter, and it pushes me to wound people.

Jesus does not give me the thumbs-up if I snap for more time to put holy insights on the page. He is not filled with pride if I smile close-lipped, to send someone the message that I have more valuable work to do.

The fear of not doing enough does not fix its eyes on Jesus. It is focused on me and my perceived strengths and shortcomings, as if the Lord's life in me depends on what I bring to the table.

When I feel the rush of ambition, I must realize that trait can be a greatest strength/greatest weakness thing. If my fear of not accomplishing the task supersedes Jesus's desire for me to care for people, then I am destructive and trying to make myself bigger.

That fact is sobering, humbling, convicting. But I can thank Jesus daily for being perfect Love, Who is more than enough. —ERIN KEELEY MARSHALL

FAITH STEP: *Ask Jesus to banish your fears and bathe you with His priority to love.*

THURSDAY, JULY 28

Therefore, rid yourselves of all malice and all deceit, hypocrisy, envy, and slander of every kind. Like newborn babies, crave pure spiritual milk, so that by it you may grow up in your salvation, now that you have tasted that the Lord is good.
1 Peter 2:1–3 (NIV)

SITTING IN THE AIRPORT with my family, I noticed a mom rocking her newborn baby. I was struck by the difference between us. My boys are thirteen, eleven, and eight. They were all chatting with each other and playing a word game on an electronic tablet. I was reading a new book I got for the trip. This young mom, on the other hand, was feeding, burping, changing, and comforting her little one. The baby needed her for everything.

I felt a little pang. The sweetness of holding a little one in my arms and the joy of knowing that you are all that they need is so amazing. But now I feel a different kind of joy. My boys are growing up. They are becoming strong young men with the ability to take care of themselves. I love that I can sit and read a book and not fear for their safety the way I did in their toddler years. It is a pleasure to watch them mature and become the young men they were created to be.

Maturing is a natural process both in our physical and spiritual lives. We are designed to grow up. Jesus offers His salvation to us, giving us a chance at a new life. So begins the process of us growing into the person He created us to be. He rejoices with each change in our heart, each milestone we pass and each step we take to become more like Him. And as we mature in Him, we bring Him joy. —SUSANNA FOTH AUGHTMON

FAITH STEP: *Take stock of how you have grown in this past year. What are some of the ways that you have matured in your faith? Thank Jesus for the growth that He has brought about in you.*

FRIDAY, JULY 29

There are many who say, "Who will show us some good? Lift up the light of your face upon us, O Lord!" You have put more joy in my heart than they have when their grain and wine abound. Psalm 4:6–7 (ESV)

YESTERDAY AS I SORTED through junk mail, I opened a flyer from a Realtor. Along with tips on fixing up a house, the letter was full of pop psychology and self-empowerment lingo. "Attract abundance to yourself by focusing on it. Affirm yourself. You deserve it. Make your dreams happen."

The philosophies are enticing, in part, because they have elements of truth woven into them. But the focus is relentlessly on human effort. Where do I look for answers? Myself. Who should I focus on pleasing? Me. Who creates good? I do.

Yet anyone who is honest can look into her own heart and see the mess that resides there apart from Christ. Looking around gives us more evidence that human answers are inadequate for spiritual problems. Today as wars rage, crime horrifies us, and ethics seem to have fled many of the powerful, people continue to ask the question recorded by the Psalmist: "Who will show us some good?"

When our friends, neighbors, and coworkers share that question, let's offer a better answer than mere human potential. Let's point them to Jesus. When the light of His face shines on us, we will know true good news and joy. —SHARON HINCK

FAITH STEP: *Leaf through magazines and junk mail and look for phrases pointing to self-reliance and self-worship. Thank Jesus that He offers us something better.*

SATURDAY, JULY 30

"I'm a mere stagehand... He's going to clean house—make a clean sweep of your lives. He'll place everything true in its proper place before God; everything false he'll put out with the trash to be burned."
Luke 3:17 (MSG)

AFTER USING THE SAME garage-sale dresser and nightstand for over four decades, we recently decided to buy new furniture, opting for a larger bed in our master bedroom. Careful research led us to just the right set that would fit both our tastes and our budget. But I never dreamed what that decision would entail.

I had to remove the contents of the old furniture so we could sell that set. And that meant sorting through the stacks before replacing them into the new drawers.

Moving our current bed to another bedroom shrunk that room, so more shuffling was needed. I eliminated sheets for a double bed, pulling out linen I hadn't used in years. I cleaned, sorted, and rearranged other neglected closets to make room for what was both important and useable. The rest would go to the garbage, giveaway, or a garage sale.

When John the Baptist preached to the people listening in the wilderness, He told them what Jesus's coming would do. John was only the "stagehand." But the "main character," Jesus, would literally "clean house," putting everything in His followers' lives in its proper place.

As I looked over the mounds of stuff still piled in each room, I saw a picture of my own heart. When Jesus came into my life, He made a clean sweep. But neglect in any area of my life opens up the constant need to both eliminate things He cannot use for His purpose and to hold on to the things that are most useful. —REBECCA BARLOW JORDAN

FAITH STEP: *Are there any closets or corners in your life that need another clean sweep? Invite Jesus today to "spring clean" your heart and put everything in its proper place.*

SUNDAY, JULY 31

Whatever you do, work at it with all your heart, as working for the Lord, not for human masters. Colossians 3:23 (NIV)

FOR MANY YEARS I couldn't say no when people asked me to serve.

Them: "Can you lead a woman's Bible study?" Me: "I'd be honored."

Them: "We need helpers in VBS." Me: "Uh, okay."

I didn't want to say no because I didn't want to disappoint others. It wasn't until later that I realized that maybe I was disappointing Jesus. Deep down I knew there were things that Jesus called me to do: mentoring teens, writing, and serving my children and husband. Yet these things took second place to all the other things I was doing because I didn't want to let anyone down. I didn't have time to serve Jesus in the way He asked because I was so busy trying to please people.

It wasn't until I was completely overwhelmed that I learned an important question to ask myself: "Am I doing what I'm doing because it's what Jesus desires, or because I'm afraid people will be disappointed if I don't?" That one question turned my schedule upside down. I took things off my schedule that were purely people-pleasing. I added things that were Jesus-pleasing. Once I focused on pleasing Jesus, I found peace.

Serving others is wonderful, but knowing our motivations behind the tasks on our schedule and to-do list makes all the difference, especially when pleasing Jesus comes first. —TRICIA GOYER

FAITH STEP: *Ask yourself, "What is one thing that I'm doing because I didn't want to say no?" Resign from that task. Then ask, "What is one thing that Jesus is asking me to do that I haven't made time for?" Make time for that.*

~~ONE~~ MONDAY, AUGUST 1

He who has an ear, let him hear what the Spirit says to the churches. To the one who conquers I will give some of the hidden manna, and I will give him a white stone, with a new name written on the stone that no one knows except the one who receives it. Revelation 2:17 (ESV)

A COMBINATION OF LACK OF SLEEP, hormonal fluctuations, and a big dose of stress all combined to make me cranky. My husband asked me a question and I snapped at him. Remorse hit me later and I apologized. "I'm not myself today."

Then who was I? I don't have an evil twin. Aliens hadn't taken over my vocal chords. There wasn't another irritable woman in the room who had stolen my identity.

Thankfully, my husband knew what I meant. That day I wasn't behaving as the self I was created to be. I wasn't the truest Sharon that I long to become.

The book of Revelation is packed with symbolism, and this promise of a stone with a secret name intrigues me. It reminds me that Jesus knows our true self. He died so that one day we will be fully the person He created us to be—free of our old sinful nature. As He sends His Holy Spirit to sanctify us, He calls us to our identity in Him.

Hosea was told to give his child the poignant name, "Not my people." Then in Romans 9:25 (NIV) we find the power of a new name: "I will call them 'my people' who are not my people; and I will call her 'my loved one' who is not my loved one."

We were once separated from God, with the same desolate name as Hosea's son. Then through the suffering, death, and Resurrection of Christ Jesus, we were named "loved." He has given us a new name. —SHARON HINCK

FAITH STEP: *List a few of the names you would call yourself apart from Jesus. Throw that list away and write the new names Jesus imparts to you.*

TUESDAY, AUGUST 2

"For I tell you, unless your righteousness surpasses that of the scribes and Pharisees, you will never enter the kingdom of heaven." Matthew 5:20 (HCS)

JESUS OFTEN SHOCKED PEOPLE with His teachings—and for good reason. Do good to our enemies? If someone tries to take our tunic, give him our cloak too? I can't imagine the crowd's reaction when Jesus told them they would never get into heaven unless their righteousness exceeded that of their religious leaders. The Pharisees and scribes were the most holy people in their society. What could be wrong with their righteousness?

The Pharisees did all the right things; they were diligent to obey each law to the letter, including the hundreds they added to the original Mosaic code. But they were so concerned about how they looked from the outside, they refused to believe in Jesus and be changed on the inside. Their righteousness was external and man-made.

Sometimes I'm ashamed to sense my own tendency to be like a Pharisee. When I focus solely on "correct" behavior, it makes me prideful, not godly. Jesus taught that true righteousness is a matter of character. Righteousness begins with a heart of love and gratitude for a Savior who died so that we can have a new life.

I can't rely on external signs of religion to please God. Attending every church service, studying the Bible for hours, writing big checks, using our free time to serve the needy—they all mean nothing if they don't spring from the right motives. If I belong to Jesus, I will love Him above all else, and I will love and serve those around me. Once my heart is in the right place, then my behavior will follow after. —DIANNE NEAL MATTHEWS

FAITH STEP: *List every spiritual discipline and church–related activity you participate in. Ask Jesus to examine your heart; then write down by each item your motivation for doing that activity.*

one WEDNESDAY, AUGUST 3

The Lord God is my strength; He will make my feet like deer's feet,
And He will make me walk on my high hills. Habakkuk 3:19 (NKJV)

MY MOM, WHO STOOD AT FIVE FEET SIX, wore spindly high heels, even into her nineties—without falling. Standing at almost five feet ten and being self-conscious about my height, I've usually chosen to stay grounded, thank you very much, with low-heel shoes.

Growing up I remember wearing white, brown, or black shoes, so in my adult years, I've enjoyed a variety of stylish, colored shoes. Up until a couple of years ago, my shoe rack was home to a dozen inexpensive but colorful shoes: pink, turquoise, gold, silver, red. I didn't feel too guilty, since most shoes cost me under twenty dollars, and I kept them until they—or my feet—wore out.

But all that changed a couple of years ago. I developed foot problems requiring orthopedic inserts. No more cheap shoes. Although reduced to two or three pairs (mostly brown and black), I've not missed the colors, only the comfort. Some days, even those shoes hurt my feet. Walking up high inclines? Forget it. I remain grounded.

But Jesus reminded me one day of His faithful provision to us all. I didn't need high heels like my mother to view the mountaintop. Age— or shoes—have nothing to do with it. When my strength is low, when troubles try to trip me up like uneven, rocky roads, and when testing feels like high, rugged terrain, no matter what shoes I wear, Jesus gives me supernatural strength. He helps me to "walk on my high hills." Without falling, I might add. —REBECCA BARLOW JORDAN

FAITH STEP: *Today when you slip on a pair of shoes, thank Jesus that He will allow you to walk on the "high hills" of your life and to face each problem with confidence—in His strength.*

THURSDAY, AUGUST 4

"Suppose one of you had a hundred sheep and lost one. Wouldn't you leave the ninety-nine in the wilderness and go after the lost one until you found it?"
Luke 15:4 (MSG)

I NEVER HAD A HUNDRED SHEEP, but I kept a flock of thirty to fifty for years, so I know sheep.

And the other shepherds I knew were good ones who put the welfare of their sheep ahead of their own. They knew that sheep don't have a whole lot going for them—being defenseless, distractible, and extremely self-centered (the last characteristic can be mistaken for stupidity).

Sheep don't mean to leave the shepherd. They don't wake up one morning and decide to run away. They're usually pulled away gradually by their appetites. Heads down, grazing, they spot a particularly juicy-looking patch of grass and they go to it; then they see another and another. The ninety-nine look around for the others at some point and head back to the safety of the group. The straggler doesn't. Maybe she's greedy or something scares her (lots of things scare sheep), and she takes off without getting her bearings. She can easily be unaware of her predicament. Finding the sheep is a picture of salvation by grace. The sheep's part is getting lost. The finding, the saving, are all done by the shepherd. The sheep's part is acquiescing—recognizing she needs her shepherd and letting herself be carried home.

Sometimes we have a hard time admitting we need a Savior. Thankfully He never stops pursuing us. —SUZANNE DAVENPORT TIETJEN

FAITH STEP: *Are you chasing after something other than Jesus? Or are you working hard to prove you love Him? It's you, He wants. You, He loves. Sit with that thought today.*

FRIDAY, AUGUST 5

*They weep as they go to plant their seed, but they sing as they return
with the harvest. Psalm 126:6 (NLT)*

MY TWO YOUNGEST DAUGHTERS are seven and four, and they love to help in the kitchen. From the time they were just toddlers, they've enjoyed standing on kitchen chairs and watching me slice, stir, and sauté. And ever since they could talk, they've asked me if they could help. For a long time I put them off. "Why don't you just watch?" After all, it's easier to do it myself.

Recently, I bought my girls two cookbooks and some kitchen tools, and that made them really want to cook. There were many days when I needed to get something whipped up in a hurry, and I regretted encouraging them. Cooking with my kids takes twice as long, requires twice the patience, and it sometimes means shells in the scrambled eggs. Yet I've started to plant seeds in my little cooks because I know they will take root. Someday my "harvest" will be daughters who know how to cook a great meal for their families. These seeds of learning will lead to a harvest of service in the future!

Jesus was diligent about planting seeds. He taught his disciples how to pray (Luke 11:1), how to have compassion (Mark 1:40–41), and how to forgive (Matthew 16:14–15). He knew that every seed planted would be harvested later. And he was right. Mark 6:30 (NIV) says, "The apostles gathered around Jesus and reported to him all they had done and taught."

Sometimes we want to weep when we have to spend time teaching someone else, whether it be a physical skill or a spiritual truth. Yet rejoicing comes when the harvest comes! And sometimes that harvest is as simple as chocolate chip cookies made by determined and happy little chefs. —TRICIA GOYER

FAITH STEP: *Has someone been asking you to teach them a skill or a spiritual lesson? Make time in your calendar to reach out to that person.*

SATURDAY, AUGUST 6

Then . . . he said to them, "Come with me by yourselves to a quiet place and get some rest." Mark 6:31 (NIV)

THE LITTLE GIRL WAS HESITANT to step up to the window of the ice-cream shop and place her order, even though her mother stood not more than four feet away. "You can do it, Emily. Tell the ice-cream lady what it is you want, then give her the money in your hand."

"By myself?"

"By yourself."

"I can't," the little girl whined. "By myself?"

"By yourself," the wise mother said.

Emily thought for a moment. "Okay. But will you go with me?"

That's how it struck me when I recently read the words of Jesus to His disciples following their rigorous traveling and speaking schedule. In Mark 6, we read that Jesus said, "Come with me by yourselves." With Him . . . by themselves. Alone, but not alone.

Isn't that always what He asks of us? With Him . . . and by ourselves. Simultaneously. Mysterious dichotomy.

It may just be the way the verse translates into English, yet it's beautifully true that we're nudged into new challenges or a rerun of an old challenge seemingly alone. But we're not alone. Every adventure into which we are called, we're accompanied by Jesus Who calls us to it.

Like the mother standing a step behind, nodding to the ice-cream lady, a reassuring hand on her daughter's shoulder, Jesus urges us forward for our growth's sake and remains with us through it all. —CYNTHIA RUCHTI

FAITH STEP: *"Come with Me by yourself" is both a comfort and an invitation to deeper intimacy with Jesus. Using a wedding or party invitation as a template, create a Bible bookmark "invitation" from Jesus to you: "Come with Me by yourself."*

SUNDAY, AUGUST 7

one

May all my thoughts be pleasing to him, for I rejoice in the Lord.
Psalm 104:34 (NLT)

EVERY THOUGHT? That sounds like a surefire way to remain defeated about consistently pleasing Jesus. But this verse claims "all my thoughts." Even that eye-rolling one this morning because I needed to repeat myself several times before my kids got their coats on and got in the car. Even the judgmental ones that plague me about some people who make life difficult.

I've read about controlling my tongue, how my words are indicators of my heart. If I can't control my words, then I'm really not in control of my character. Just when I feel like I'm zipping my lip well, I read this verse that feels even more demanding—my thoughts are an issue too!

Jesus knows the depths of our humanness. He isn't surprised by our struggle with ungodliness in our minds. In fact, He understands that's our default without the Holy Spirit's power.

Recently I read a pastor's insight that will stay with me forever. He said that we shouldn't be shocked or defeated by every thought passing through our head. Many of those are temptations; all are evidence of our need for the Savior. But what we do with them matters. A part of us wants the object of temptation; otherwise it wouldn't be tempting. Jesus was tempted by Satan in the wilderness (Matthew 4:1–11). That means that the human part of Jesus was tempted by power and riches and worshipping other gods. Those thoughts crossed His mind as He was tempted. But He did not sin.

Every word that crosses my mind may not be pleasing to the Lord, but I have a choice to feed it and let it reign or commit my character to Jesus. When I claim His pure thought, He is pleased. —ERIN KEELEY MARSHALL

FAITH STEP: *Instead of berating yourself for a negative thought, offer it to the Lord and ask Him to change your mind with His character.*

MONDAY, AUGUST 8

Let us hold unswervingly to the hope we profess, for he who promised is faithful.
Hebrews 10:23 (NIV)

I LOVE GETTING a good deal on new clothes. As a church planter's wife, I am quite resourceful. If any of my friends likes an article of clothing I have on, I have a very difficult time not yelling out the price and the store where it was purchased: "Only $5.99 at Ross Dress for Less!" I am equally proud of the fact that (a) I am wearing something cute and (b) I got it on the cheap. Solomon took it to another level. I don't think he thought much about good deals or yelled out the prices of his clothes. He owned about half the world. If it was beautiful and expensive, he probably had it. I couldn't be less like Solomon.

There have been many times in my life when there were no new clothes on the horizon. Budgets get tight, bills are piling up, and I am not just worried about looking cute. I'm worried if we will have all we need to make it to the end of the month. Sometimes worries can crowd out your joy.

I love the fact that Jesus understands our concerns for clothes, for food, and for shelter. He is interested in our souls, but He is also interested in meeting our physical needs. He wants us to rest in the fact that when we are following Him, every detail of our lives is of interest to Him and He will take care of us. If we trust Him, even when it comes to the basics, we will never be disappointed. —SUSANNA FOTH AUGHTMON

FAITH STEP: *Think of an area of need in your life right now. Ask Jesus to provide for that need. When He provides for you, write it down so you can remember His amazing provision.*

DNE TUESDAY, AUGUST 9

For those whom he foreknew he also predestined to be conformed to
the image of his Son, in order that he might be the firstborn among many brothers.
Romans 8:29 (ESV)

MY FRIEND BERNIE was moving from a large house into a small apartment. As she was downsizing her furniture, I offered to store anything she wanted to keep. There was a particular favorite of hers, a wooden hutch with glass doors that she wasn't ready to sell. She asked if I'd like to use it. "I'm afraid to, because, with small children, I can't guarantee it will look the same if you decide you want it back," I said.

"Just use it as your own," Bernie said. "Whatever wear and tear happens we'll chalk up to *Wabi-sabi.*"

Wabi-sabi is the Japanese concept of imperfect beauty. It's an appreciation of asymmetry, roughness, and/or the natural processes that give things their unique appearance—things like knotholes in wood or variations in rock. Wabi-sabi celebrates things like scars and gray hair.

Sure enough, by the next time Bernie came to my house my dog had chewed a corner of the hutch, and one of my kids had banged a tricycle into the wood, nicking it. "I love it!" Bernie declared. "The marks of a good life."

It occurred to me that Wabi-sabi is closely akin to the way Jesus works in our hearts. Often my vision of how things should be is unrealistically perfect. I tend to stress out when reality falls short of that vision—my house a mess, my family late to church, or worse things—someone loses a job or falls ill. But those things don't stress out Jesus. As Elisabeth Elliot said, "In every event He seeks an entrance to my heart."

Each perceived imperfection is an opportunity to be conformed to His likeness—to become more beautiful in His time.

—GWEN FORD FAULKENBERRY

FAITH STEP: *What are the ugliest things you're dealing with right now? Ask Jesus to give you Wabi-sabi eyes—eyes to see the beauty He can create out of imperfections.*

one WEDNESDAY, AUGUST 10

In him was life, and that life was the light of all mankind. The light shines in the darkness, and the darkness has not overcome it. There was a man sent from God whose name was John. He came as a witness to testify concerning that light, so that through him all might believe. He himself was not the light; he came only as a witness to the light. The true light that gives light to everyone was coming into the world. John 1:4—9 (NIV)

WE PULLED INTO THE DRIVEWAY, arriving home late after visiting a friend's home. The windows of the house were dark. Darkness coated every surface as we opened the door and stepped into our hallway.

I could have grabbed a broom and tried to sweep the darkness out of the entry and into the front yard. Or I could have rolled up my sleeves and pushed against the darkness, trying to force it out of our house.

Instead, I turned on the light. Instantly, the darkness was banished.

Sometimes when I'm especially aware of the darkness that lurks in my soul, I try to fight it as if it were a tangible foe, and as if I had some way to defeat it myself. Darkness is only an absence of light. Darkness in my heart grows when I've turned away from the presence of Jesus.

Jesus offers a better answer than trying to sweep the darkness away. As I spend time with Him—the Light of the world—the darkness disappears under the radiance of His presence. We no longer need to fear darkness, even the dimness of our doubts, the shadows of our selfishness, or the deep corners of our anger. Jesus offers to overcome all of that as He shines into our lives. —SHARON HINCK

FAITH STEP: *Walk into a dark room and turn on the light. Thank Jesus for being the Light that overcomes all darkness.*

THURSDAY, AUGUST 11

When the sun was setting, the people brought to Jesus all who had various kinds of sickness, and laying his hands on each one, he healed them. Luke 4:40 (NIV)

EVERYONE KNOWS WHAT A HYPOCHONDRIAC IS, but I don't think there's a word for my problem. I have a fear that I'll go to a doctor when I don't really need to—a fear of being *thought* to be a hypochondriac. Sounds odd, doesn't it? Twenty years ago, I slipped on the ice. Since it happened around Christmas, I was on my feet more than usual, including the huge purple one. Years later, a doctor noticed the hard bump poking through the side of my foot and X-rayed it. Turns out a bone had been broken and didn't heal properly.

Then there was the time I got wild pushing my grandkids on the merry-go-round. Two days later I noticed that my sore knee was bigger than the other one. By the time I went to a doctor, the cartilage had been damaged. This past summer, I threw both hands behind my head to catch my hat. Somehow the top of my right little finger got pushed backward. Although the discoloration and swelling improved quickly, it still hurts when it bends and looks a little crooked.

Just as I can't get medical help if I don't go to the doctor when I'm sick, I can't get emotional or spiritual healing unless I go to Jesus. I remember to pray for loved ones who need His touch when they're hurting or bruised by life's hard knocks. But I sometimes forget to talk to Him about my own invisible wounds, especially those from the past that still hurt.

Jesus wants me to develop the habit of going to Him immediately when I sense emotional pain. He will heal where no one else can, no appointment required. —DIANNE NEAL MATTHEWS

FAITH STEP: *Examine your heart to see if you have any wounds from recent events or from the past. Take them to Jesus and ask Him for healing.*

one FRIDAY, AUGUST 12

For I will pour out water to quench your thirst. . . . Isaiah 44:3 (NLT)

WHEN WE DESIGNED OUR GARDENS, along with the perennial ones, I potted other annual plants—mostly ferns—around the house. These required watering by hand. So my usual trek around the north, west, and east sides of the house included lugging a plastic container filled with water to quench their thirst. I rarely visited the sunny south side.

Months later when I was walking in the neighborhood in front of my home, I spotted a bit of gold along the south side of my house. I detoured up my neighbor's driveway to take a closer look. There, against the side, nestled between hedges of holly bushes with their sharp, thorny leaves, sat beautiful, golden iris in full bloom—in October. I had first transplanted a bunch of those thirty-year-old irises from my mom's house almost two decades earlier. But in my shady backyard, they had not done well. In order for them to grow and flourish, I had transplanted them in one of the few sunny spots in our yard and then forgotten about them. What a surprise to see those flowers bloom!

Enjoying those plants meant including an important ritual in my normal watering or walking pattern: checking out the sunny side. If I didn't, I'd miss a beautiful part of God's creation. Sure enough, they bloomed again in the spring.

Enjoying the sunny side of life begins with the "Son" Himself—time with Jesus. When we make moments with Him a part of our normal routine, rooted in His Word and with faith in our eyes, we'll see "gold." Jesus will quench our own thirst with His living water, and we'll experience new joys and surprises we previously neglected. —REBECCA BARLOW JORDAN

FAITH STEP: *Set a time to drink from God's Word daily and let Jesus quench your thirst. And don't forget to record the surprises you find along the way.*

SATURDAY, AUGUST 13

But God demonstrates his own love for us in this: While we were still sinners, Christ died for us. Romans 5:8 (NIV)

I WAS TALKING TO MY FRIEND Marie France on the phone today, discussing our kids. It is one of our favorite topics. She was telling me how her kids want approval for different things that they have done. And she said, "I am not going to tell them I am proud of the things that they've done. I tell them, 'I am proud of who you are.' My feelings about them aren't based on what they do. I love them for who they are."

That was a lightbulb moment for me. I am pretty sure how I feel about myself is based on what I have done. I am proud of myself for the good things that I have done. I also am disappointed in myself for some of the dumb things that I have done. I have a yo-yo relationship with myself. I like myself. I don't like myself. I am happy with who I am. I am not happy with who I am. It's not the best way to live. Jesus doesn't have a yo-yo relationship with me. I expect Jesus to be proud of me when I do well and to be disappointed when I mess up. But I keep forgetting that His love for me is not based on what I do or don't do. Sinner or saint? Walking with Him or not walking with Him? He loves me. Period. He doesn't sway in His feelings for me from moment to moment. Because Who He is doesn't change from moment to moment. He is love. When I begin to grasp His unconditional love for me, His love can begin to change who I am and transform my life. —SUSANNA FOTH AUGHTMON

FAITH STEP: *Sing the song "How Great the Father's Love for Us" and realize it is true. Every moment of every day, you are wholly and completely loved.*

SUNDAY, AUGUST 14

"Happy are you when people insult you and harass you and speak all kinds of bad and false things about you, all because of me." Matthew 5:11 (CEB)

THE CARTOON SHOWED an anxious patient sitting on the exam table and a serious-faced doctor reading from the patient's chart. "What is it, Doc?"

"You tested positive."

"I just knew there was something wrong. How long do I have?"

"You tested positive," the doctor said, "for being too negative."

One of the definitions of the word *dour* is "relentlessly gloomy." Know anyone that diagnosis fits?

The skies overhead have been relentlessly gloomy for the last several weeks. What a difference it's made for the people who live under them. What a difference it makes to those who live with or work with the dour.

It was to a people whose lives were anything but easy that Jesus first spoke the "Happy are those who…" sermon we know as the Beatitudes. So many of the second halves of those nine verses in Matthew chapter five describe those whom we would assume would live sour, gloomy lives.

"Happy," Jesus said, "are people who grieve…the humble…the hungry and thirsty…people whose lives are harassed because they are righteous" (Matthew 5:4–6, 10, CEB).

Jesus declared that tough, unfair, miserable, heartbreaking circumstances shouldn't give us a negativity pass, but that instead, with Him and through Him, we can know joy and will eventually be rewarded for our faithfulness *despite the pain*. According to Jesus, none of His followers should test positive for being negative. —CYNTHIA RUCHTI

FAITH STEP: *Take a fresh look at the Beatitudes that Jesus included in His Sermon on the Mount. Mark the verses that particularly express something that is a tender spot in your life right now, and note its hope for reversing the polarity from negative to positive.*

MONDAY, AUGUST 15

"My sheep hear my voice, and I know them, and they follow me." John 10:27 (ESV)

I'M ENDLESSLY AMAZED at the variety of ring tones and alerts people have on their cell phones. Snatches of songs, notes from musical instruments, ocean waves, the click of typewriter keys—any sound imaginable. For a while, I used the Sherwood Forest setting for new voice mails. But it made me want to look around for Robin Hood. I thought that a certain office had a parrot until I noticed how the birdcalls were identical. My old hair stylist knew when her husband was phoning her because a snooty voice said, "Your husband is trying to contact you on your cellular device."

Jesus's voice can come in different forms too. He often speaks to us while we're reading the Bible. A verse or passage suddenly jumps out at us and fills us with comfort, encouragement, or conviction. When we're praying and seeking His will, we may sense Him communicating with our Spirit, nudging us in the direction He would have us go or filling us with peace about a decision. We may hear His voice speaking to us through a pastor's sermon, words on a radio program, or advice from a trusted friend.

The voice of Jesus also comes at times when we least expect it. While standing in the checkout line thinking about our next errand. In our brief exchange with a stranger who looks like he needs a friend. In our conversation with a relative or friend who has a hint of desperation in her tone.

I don't have to set a fancy ring tone to recognize when Jesus speaks to me, but I do need to tune my spirit to listen for Him, moment by moment. After all, I don't want to miss a single word He has to say.
—DIANNE NEAL MATTHEWS

FAITH STEP: *Begin your morning by asking Jesus to help you to be attentive to His voice all day long. In the evening, list the different ways He spoke to you and how you responded to His voice.*

one

TUESDAY, AUGUST 16

---

*"So you are a king?" Jesus responded, "You say I am a king.
Actually, I was born and came into the world to testify to the truth.
All who love the truth recognize that what I say is true." John 18:37 (NLT)*

"IT'S NOT THE WAY YOU DESCRIBED. I do not like it."

The e-mail took me by surprise. I had sold the item on eBay, and it had arrived at the buyer's home. But she was not happy.

My first thought was to defend myself proudly and argue. I double-checked the pictures I had posted for the buyer, then reexamined the words I had used to describe it. They appeared accurate.

On second thought, I could choose another response. I had been studying about Jesus's character and wondered how He would answer. Jesus did get angry occasionally and spoke firmly, like when merchants cheated others and interrupted worship in the Temple (Matthew 21:12). But those times always involved Jesus's righteous anger. *Gentle* is the way Jesus was described on earth. And He always spoke truth.

I appreciate good customer service, and I wanted to mirror Jesus's values, so I asked more questions to see why the buyer was dissatisfied. Her reasons puzzled me. Her tone turned accusatory, even angry, but I kept trying to be kind, knowing a "gentle response" often "defuses anger" (Proverbs 15:1, MSG).

Still dissatisfied, she wanted a discount. But my offer wasn't enough. That's when I replied firmly but gently that people were more important to me than the money. "What would you like me to do?" I finally asked.

I granted her request. We left on good terms. She even apologized.

That day, I thanked Jesus for helping me respond rightly—and asked forgiveness for all the times when I haven't. Regardless of their reactions, people really are more important than our pride. —REBECCA BARLOW JORDAN

FAITH STEP: *The next time someone criticizes or accuses you, take time to listen. Instead of reacting, respond gently.*

WEDNESDAY, AUGUST 17

For godly grief produces a repentance that leads to salvation without regret, whereas worldly grief produces death. 2 Corinthians 7:10 (ESV)

I LIKE TO COLLECT MEMORIES. I have a basket with ticket stubs in my office. I have a shelf with coffee mugs from various vacation locations. I have a jar filled with special rocks, pinecones, and shells to remind me of places I've traveled for research. I've even written a novel called *The Memory Jar* about a young woman who collects things just like I do.

But for many years I also collected things that I had no right holding on to: unforgiveness, anger, and especially regrets. I regretted ways I treated my parents. I regretted becoming sexually active as a teen. I regretted having an abortion in high school. I regretted the hurtful ways I lashed out at my husband in the early years of our marriage, and I carried those regrets as heavy burdens on my heart.

It's easy to go back and relive these regretful memories; in fact the devil wants us to do exactly that. Instead we need to "Give all your worries and cares to God, for he cares about you" (1 Peter 5:7, NLT).

Do you have regrets? Know that if you've repented Jesus has removed those sins from you and has cast them away. We will never forget our wrong choices, but they shouldn't become a heavy, daily burden to carry. Ask Jesus to heal your heart. Ask Jesus to help you be watchful against the enemy's attempt to burden you when Jesus has set you free. Regrets can clog up your memory jar. Instead, make room for the good memories of all Jesus has done for you. —TRICIA GOYER

FAITH STEP: *Start a memory jar. Fill it with notes or small items that remind you of Jesus's goodness. Also, whenever you feel a regret burdening you, pray and turn it over to Jesus.*

ome

THURSDAY, AUGUST 18

One day as Jesus was walking along the shore beside the Sea of Galilee, he saw two brothers—Simon, also called Peter, and Andrew—fishing with a net, for they were commercial fishermen. Jesus called out to them, "Come, be my disciples, and I will show you how to fish for people!" And they left their nets at once and went with him. Matthew 4:18–20 (NLT)

I'VE HEARD PEOPLE SAY that evangelism is best left to the experts—pastors, missionaries, and the like. I disagree. If we're disciples of Jesus, then telling others about Him is our responsibility. In that context, little excites me more than watching Him use men and women from all walks of life.

One of my nieces owns a beauty salon in southern Alberta. This farming community attracts foreign immigrants like a magnet. Many women from other cultures visit her salon, and she's establishing trusted relationships with them. God's using her hairstyling skills as the tool to introduce women to Jesus.

Several Christian friends work as nurses in the local hospital. They're not allowed to speak openly about Jesus, but they can answer questions of a spiritual nature and pray with patients who ask for it.

My husband plays soccer weekly with a group of men his age. He's gained their trust over time, and now they're asking questions about the ministry he directs. What a perfect opportunity to tell them about Jesus!

God has hardwired you uniquely to build His kingdom. What work skills do you possess? What hobbies do you enjoy? What topics are you passionate about? How can you use these abilities and interests to reach the lost for Jesus Christ? —GRACE FOX

FAITH STEP: *Which one activity brings you great joy when you do it? Which one activity makes time fly by unnoticed when you're doing it? The answer reveals your passion. Ask Jesus how to use this passion to share His love with others.*

FRIDAY, AUGUST 19

Everyone who competes in the games goes into strict training. They do it to get a crown that will not last, but we do it to get a crown that will last forever. Therefore I do not run like someone running aimlessly; I do not fight like a boxer beating the air. 1 Corinthians 9:25–26 (NIV)

MY HUSBAND TRAINED for a ten-mile run to celebrate a milestone birthday. He hadn't done much running in the past year, so in the months before the race he mapped out a training schedule. Each morning that he got up early to train or stayed after work to run with friends, I admired his dedication and commitment. Now his medal hangs in our office, a reminder of hard work and accomplishment.

There have been times in my life when Jesus has asked me to follow Him in ways that feel as daunting and impossible as a ten-mile run. Yet when I look back, I can see that He first led me through smaller tasks that helped prepare my spirit to endure the new challenge. His guidance and presence make the race of life possible.

There's one other thing that keeps us going when our limbs quiver from exhaustion: knowing that we're not running aimlessly. There is a purpose to the long sleepless nights of caring for babies, the challenge of devotion time with restless children, the years of teaching a youth group while wondering if anyone is listening, the effort to share Jesus with a coworker.

Today as I wrestle words together, my brain feels like a marathon runner on mile twenty-six. If I were running for a laurel wreath, I'd stop and sit on the curb instead. But our race is worth every drop of sweat, every pulled muscle, every blister, because we are running with Jesus as He brings His grace and love to each person in need. —SHARON HINCK

FAITH STEP: *Spend a few moments looking toward the finish line. Ask Jesus to reassure you that the race is worth the effort.*

SATURDAY, AUGUST 20

We can say with confidence, "The Lord is my helper, so I will have no fear.
What can mere people do to me?" Hebrews 13:6 (NLT)

My LITTLE GIRL WAS UPSET recently by a TV commercial for a scary movie when I wasn't in the room. For the past several weeks, Calianne hasn't wanted to go upstairs by herself, and she wants either her dad or me to stay with her at night until she falls asleep. She has never been scared this much or for this long, and it's tough to see.

But as she works through those fears, she's learning more about the power of prayer. During our family Bible story time before bed, each of us takes a turn praying. As the youngest, Cali goes first, and, without fail, she asks Jesus to help her get over her scared thoughts from the commercial.

Jesus knows the real horrors that happen on earth. He warns us against sin that destroys and makes this world unsafe, but He also has sovereign power over all of it. My daughter can say with confidence that her Savior is her helper, so she can reject fear. She is perfectly loved by Jesus, and perfect love destroys fear (1 John 4:18). Little by little we are praying with her for truth and love to win over fear.

Her childlike faith is power-packed and inspires me to trust my Savior with my own fears. Jesus sometimes allows pain to touch His own, a fact I want to run from. But the Ruler of the universe encourages us to be confident of His care. And knowing He is always guarding us makes all the difference in handling this life.

He is present and available and in control. Trust Him to carry you through the brokenness of this life. —ERIN KEELEY MARSHALL

FAITH STEP: *What scares you? Create a memorial of stones somewhere in your yard or in a decorative bowl in your home to remind you of the ways Jesus has been faithful and promises to be faithful to help you.*

SUNDAY, AUGUST 21

"Who of you by worrying can add a single hour to your life?" Luke 12:25 (NIV)

I'VE OFTEN WONDERED if people who have the biggest, most vivid imaginations struggle with worry more than others. Personally speaking, I can always come up with a load of worst-case scenarios and "what-ifs" concerning the future. So I'm grateful that Jesus speaks directly to me in His teaching on worry. He points out the foolishness of worrying about tomorrow since that accomplishes nothing. He also advises me that each day brings enough concerns to take care of on its own without also trying to take care of tomorrow before it happens.

Jesus doesn't tell us not to think about tomorrow or plan for it. Scripture endorses the wisdom of saving for the future and setting goals. But there's a fine line between planning for the future and obsessing over what troubles it might bring into our lives. We may have a hard time telling the difference if worry has become an ingrained habit in our thought lives.

An honest examination of my attitude toward the future will tell me much about my level of trust in the Lord's sovereignty, provision, and care. Do I believe that He controls all future events? Can I have faith that He will see me through any troubles that come my way and work everything out for His good purposes?

Worrying about what may or may not happen tomorrow is a waste of my time and energy. It blinds me from seeing what Jesus wants me to do for Him today. It steals my joy and peace and stunts my spiritual growth. I don't want to miss the blessings God has for me each day by obsessing over what tomorrow might bring. I want to fully enjoy the gift of today before it slips away. —DIANNE NEAL MATTHEWS

FAITH STEP: *List any worries you have about the future. Talk them over with Jesus one by one; then destroy the list.*

MONDAY, AUGUST 22

"When I fall, I will rise; if I sit in darkness, the Lord is my light." Micah 7:8 (CEB)

NOT LONG AFTER knee replacement surgery, I slipped on a piece of ice on my dining room floor, landing first on my surgery knee, then slamming to my back with my surgical leg bent so far that the sole of my foot pressed against the part of me I normally use for sitting. My head clunked the hardwood with enough force to create a concussion.

I lay on my back, imagining the surgery wasted, the recovery to that point pointless, the progress I'd made reversed, and like a turtle on its back, I was helpless to right myself. I fully expected that when my husband got home from work that night, he'd find me still writhing in pain, still calling out, "O Lord Jesus!"—the only words I could form.

The fall threw a suffocating shroud over my recovery hopes. As humans are so adept at doing, while still lying on the floor, I calculated how many things the fall had destroyed or set me back. Eventually the pain abated enough for me to roll over, then sit, then stand. Even though the concussion sent me to the couch in a dark fog, the bent knee actually forced more mobility than I'd had previously. Only God could bring good out of what looked like a setback.

In that and every other black moment—no matter its source or its severity—we can cling to the simple but profound truth that Jesus declared Himself the Light of the world (John 8:12). Light when questions seem to have no answers. Light when a job loss threatens to literally douse the lights. Light when the darkness isn't outside but within. —CYNTHIA RUCHTI

FAITH STEP: *What darkness enshrouds you? You may need a visual reminder that Jesus is the Light of the world. Purchase a small flashlight to keep where you feel most vulnerable to that darkness—your bedroom, your chair in the living room, the spot where you "fell."*

TUESDAY, AUGUST 23

I am my beloved's and my beloved is mine....
Song of Songs 6:3 (NIV)

"YOU WANT US TO DO that for an hour?" I asked, hoping the answer was no.

My husband and I both looked at the instructors, then at each other. As part of our marriage enrichment leadership training over twenty years ago, we were required to talk together for an hour. Sixty minutes—facing each other in the center of the circle—while a dozen other participants eavesdropped on our private conversation. Our leaders encouraged us to share honest feelings, especially about any pending "issues."

We started at the "hall closet"—the symbol of one of our hot-button subjects: organization versus creativity. At first, our conversation stuttered. But the more we applied the principles we'd learned, like focusing on really listening and understanding each other, a strange thing happened. Little by little we shut out everyone else and concentrated solely on each other.

Our sharing flowed more like a river than a rocky road. At one point, I was so caught up in the moment, I felt transported into my husband's heart. For the first time in a very long time, we each felt totally understood. Those same habits have carried us through other rocky issues in our marriage, increasing our love daily as we've focused on learning, loving, and listening. And we've learned to appreciate our differences, accepting each other's faults.

Those same principles apply to my relationship with Jesus. If I insist on defending or doing all of the talking, my relationship with Him becomes stagnant. But when I learn to listen to His sweet voice, focusing on Him, our love flows like a peaceful river, always forging ahead.

—REBECCA BARLOW JORDAN

FAITH STEP: *Would you describe your relationship with Jesus as a smooth river or a rocky road? Today, listen to Jesus's voice for understanding as you meditate on His Word.*

WEDNESDAY, AUGUST 24

But for you who fear my name, the Sun of Righteousness will rise with healing in his wings. And you will go free, leaping with joy like calves let out to pasture.
Malachi 4:2 (NLT)

I'VE BECOME FRIENDS with a woman named Esther. Recently, she told me about losing her father tragically when she was only twelve.

The incident took place on a Sunday evening in a small wooden hall bordering Northern Ireland and the Republic of Ireland. Approximately eighty believers had gathered there to worship. Esther's dad and two other men were greeting latecomers in the foyer when a number of gun-toting members of a warring faction burst into the church and opened fire. Multiple bullets hit Esther's father. He spent his last breaths running up the aisle warning the congregation to protect themselves by lying on the floor.

I listened to Esther's testimony and asked how this event has affected her life. She said that losing her dad, especially in such traumatic circumstances, was deeply painful. "Eventually—in my midtwenties—I found a blessing in the midst of my pain," she said. "I've discovered much about God's faithfulness, and I've grown spiritually in a way that wouldn't have been possible otherwise." Esther knows Jesus, and it shows. True to His word, He's healed her heart.

Do you carry pain from a past experience? Ask Jesus to take it from you and to heal your hurting heart. He loves you deeply, so He will answer your prayer. It might take time, so don't despair. Eventually you, too, will go free and leap with joy. —GRACE FOX

FAITH STEP: *From what hurtful event would you like inner healing? Write your answer on a piece of paper and then ask Jesus to fulfill His promise to heal. Either shred the paper or burn it as a representation of His removing your pain and setting you free.*

THURSDAY, AUGUST 25

For I do not do the good I want to do, but the evil I do not want to do—
this I keep on doing. . . . Thanks be to God, who delivers me through Jesus Christ
our Lord! . . . Romans 7:19, 25 (NIV)

THE STORY GOES THAT when the edges of known geography were reached, ancient maps read, "Here there be dragons." Over the years I've come to learn where dragons live in my life.

Sometimes the trigger is a happy, active photo on a social media site. My heart veers toward the border of envy because my circumstances are different, and soon I've drifted into the waters of self-pity, a truly lethal dragon.

Other times I hear about a mistake or bad choice that a friend has made. Instead of humbly acknowledging how broken we all are apart from Christ, I feel relieved or even a bit smug that I'm not in her shoes. I subtly sail toward an ugly monster of pride.

Then there are days where the weight of illness, physical pain, and isolation blows me toward shoals of despair. Bible verses about joy and hope seem to mock me, and all I hear are the howls of the dragon telling me to abandon faith.

I don't want these wrong attitudes. I want to be happy for the joys of others, compassionate for the failings of others, and strong in faith no matter the circumstances. Yet again and again, despite my best efforts, I get blown off course.

I'm so grateful for these verses in Romans. Here on earth, still hampered by our sinful nature, we all face this struggle. But there is an answer. Jesus has delivered us from sin. Forgiveness is available. And He can rescue us from dragons and guide the ship of our life back to the waters He has created for us. —SHARON HINCK

FAITH STEP: *Draw a map of your life and identify the dragons that lurk on the borders. Ask Jesus to defeat those dragons.*

DONE

FRIDAY, AUGUST 26

Your word is a lamp for my feet, a light on my path. Psalm 119:105 (NIV)

WE JUST GOT A NEW BLENDER. It is one of those blenders that can chop, dice, process, and blend in 2.7 seconds. Scott decided to make a smoothie and started throwing in all kinds of fruit. Apple, orange, banana, kiwi, and one leaf of kale. We are reticent about vegetables in smoothies. It is hard to drink something green for breakfast. When he finished blending, we tried it and the taste was great. But the consistency reminded us of marshmallow fluff. A lot of air. We tossed in more ice cubes. We added more juice. Still fluffy. The one thing we didn't do is read the manual. Because that would be too easy. We wanted to work this one out on our own. So we ended up drinking a pretty fluffy smoothie...because we couldn't figure out how to get it right. It was okay but it wasn't great.

Sometimes we forget that this life has a manual. We think, *We are Jesus followers; we know what we are doing,* and we try our best to live a good life. But the thing is, Jesus gave us instructions for the best life possible in His Word. Why are we trying to live by memory when we have access to his illuminating words? Jesus's words, His thoughts, His actions, His perspectives on life are something we need to partake of daily. His instruction brings light into our darkness and guidance when we begin to falter or stray from His commands. His Word renews our hearts and minds. It is a good thing to start your morning with a healthy, nonfluffy smoothie. It is even better to start it with the life-giving words of the One Who loves us most of all. —SUSANNA FOTH AUGHTMON

FAITH STEP: *Take twenty minutes at the beginning of your morning and read your favorite passage in Scripture. Soak up the words of light and life that Jesus has for you.*

DONE SATURDAY, AUGUST 27

"He calls his own sheep by name and leads them out. After he has gathered his own flock, he walks ahead of them, and they follow him because they know his voice. They won't follow a stranger; they will run from him because they don't know his voice." John 10:3–5 (NLT)

MY HUSBAND CARRIED GOOD NEWS with the manure he hauled home for the garden. He brought pictures of sheep, excited to find shepherds raising the same rare breed we loved so much. When he told them how much I missed our sheep since we laid down our staffs, they invited us to shearing day.

We came dressed to help. We were familiar with their handling equipment so they assigned us the operation of confining the group until they had to enter the chute. Here three or four single-file sheep waited for their turn to be shorn. The problem was that entering the chute sent them in our direction. We coaxed them, called them, and used every trick that worked for our sheep in the past to get them to cooperate. But these weren't our sheep. And they wouldn't come toward us.

We walked into the barn to give the sheep time to settle down. Before we went back out, I suggested working silently. Mike and I tried again, using hand signals. This time, they walked right through. When we were down to the last few sheep, just to test the theory, we broke our silence. The remaining sheep developed a marked reluctance to head our way. I'd known that sheep know their shepherd's voice since before I was a shepherd, but I must've skipped the verse about their not knowing a stranger's.

Our world has never been so full of voices, and we are wise to be wary. Not all voices speak to our best interests. Listen always for the voice of the One Who loves you most. The One Who laid down His life for the sheep. —SUZANNE DAVENPORT TIETJEN

FAITH STEP: *Jesus speaks to us, even if not with an audible voice. Today spend some time in silence, listening.*

SUNDAY, AUGUST 28

And the Lord's servant must not be quarrelsome but kind to everyone . . . correcting his opponents with gentleness. God may perhaps grant them repentance leading to a knowledge of the truth, and they may come to their senses and escape from the snare of the devil. . . . 2 Timothy 2:24–26 (ESV)

SOME PEOPLE SEEM BENT ON BEING quarrelsome, cantankerous, and controlling. Some people don't fight fair, to the point of being irrational in the heat of a disagreement. All of us can be those people at times, but most of us don't stay in that mode after we have a chance to regain our better judgment. How do we deal with someone who won't engage in a healthy way to work through differences or who refuses to look at a situation from someone else's viewpoint?

Jesus speaks about turning the other cheek (Matthew 5:39) and offering forgiveness (Matthew 18:21–22). But He also says not to "throw your pearls to pigs" (Matthew 7:6, NIV) and to "have nothing to do with foolish, ignorant controversies."

I love the rest of today's passage too, because it states that our actions that show Jesus's character may be tools that help a difficult person come to his senses. Jesus did not gloss over sin. But His truth is marked by gentleness and grace that fly in the face of being controlling and unkind. I also love that Jesus doesn't leave us without an action plan; that would feel debilitating. Jesus wants us to be influential in others' lives, but we can only do that by sticking with His methods instead of succumbing to our own.

Rage behind our words only promotes more wrong anger. For sure, there is a time to speak truth strongly about someone's behavior. But Jesus still must be given room to shine through us. —ERIN KEELEY MARSHALL

FAITH STEP: *Pray for a difficult person in your life and that you will seek to understand how Jesus would have you respond.*

MONDAY, AUGUST 29

Unless a grain of wheat falls into the ground and dies, it remains alone; but if it dies, it produces much grain. . . . If anyone serves Me, let him follow Me. . . . John 12:24, 26 (NKJV)

HAVE YOU EVER BEEN in a situation in which you had to make a life-and-death decision? Most of us don't face that choice—at least physically—very often, but as followers of Jesus we face it daily in ways big and small. On the surface the choice seems easy. Of course we want life. But for me at least, choosing life sometimes is next to impossible. The thing that makes it difficult is that life can look a lot like death when we're staring the choice in the face.

A few years ago I went through a troubled time in my marriage. Like the grain of wheat in the verse, my dreams fell to the ground. Choosing life in that situation meant that I had to let my own vision of the perfect marriage die. I had to wait and I had to work, trusting Jesus to produce something good. Even when all I could see was darkness. It has not been an easy process—dying never is—but day by day I am choosing life. And something beautiful is growing.

There are a lot of choices we can make in life, but the choice to follow Jesus is a choice to die in order to live. You can't have one without the other. In Him, our inner lives are places of constant death. We must die to ourselves, our desires, our pride, our feelings. Daily. But it is precisely through those deaths that life springs up, producing more beauty than we ever imagined possible. —GWEN FORD FAULKENBERRY

FAITH STEP: *What needs to die in you today so that the character of Jesus may spring up? Take it to the Cross and leave it there; then wait for the Resurrection He promises.*

TUESDAY, AUGUST 30

Then Agrippa said to Paul, "You almost persuade me to become a Christian."
Acts 26:28 (NKJV)

THERE'S AN OLD SAYING: *"Almost* doesn't count." That's true for so many people. Look at the faces of the Olympians who medal. Gold medalists beam and bronze medalists flash relieved smiles. But sometimes the silver medalists frown or even cry when they receive their medals—they failed to win first place.

The apostle Paul tells us about someone who looked like a winner to everyone around him but missed out on the prize of eternal life. Agrippa was Herod the Great's grandson. The Roman Emperor, Caligula, gave him rule over more and greater territories until he was finally given the title of king. Agrippa ruled over all of Palestine. He, like Paul, had persecuted Christians and he listened with interest when Paul told the story of his conversion and presented his defense. Agrippa was convinced by the facts that Paul had done nothing wrong, but he fell short of believing he, himself, needed salvation. His heart was not changed. Agrippa, wearing a crown and looking like a winner, left not knowing he was lost.

In 1871, a Reverend Brundage closed a sermon about Agrippa's sad loss, saying, "He who is almost persuaded is almost saved, and to be almost saved is to be entirely lost." Philip Paul Bliss, who wrote many of my favorite hymns, heard that sermon and responded by writing the hymn "Almost Persuaded," which closes this way:

> *"Almost" cannot avail;*
> *"Almost" is but to fail!*
> *Sad, sad, that bitter wail—*
> *"Almost," but lost!*

—SUZANNE DAVENPORT TIETJEN

FAITH STEP: *Thank Jesus today for winning our salvation. Ask Him to stir up your concern for the lost and to help you be ready to speak up at the Holy Spirit's leading.*

WEDNESDAY, AUGUST 31

She opens her mouth with wisdom, and the teaching of kindness is on her tongue.
Proverbs 31:26 (ESV)

I LEAD A TEEN MOM SUPPORT GROUP in inner-city Little Rock, and I wouldn't be able to do what I do without help from the other amazing volunteers. Some volunteers speak with a thick Southern drawl. And many of them talk the local slang. I clearly remember one meeting when one of the young moms shared about verbally sparring with one of her teachers. "Girl, tell me you didn't just say that," one of the volunteers called out from the other side of the table. "If you talked to me like that you know I woulda kicked you out of class. You better go back tomorrow and apologize."

The volunteer then shared how she used to have the same lofty, self-righteous attitude and it didn't get her far in life. The volunteer "called out" the young woman in a way she understood, and I was amazed by how well the young mom responded!

Romans 1:14 (NLT) says, "For I have a great sense of obligation to people in both the civilized world and the rest of the world, to the educated and uneducated alike." There are some who are educated in the world's eyes—with degrees and accomplishments under their belt. Then there are those who are educated through their life experiences.

I'm so thankful for the godly women whom Jesus has brought into our group—those who can speak truth in a way young moms understand and accept. It goes to show me that sometimes kindness and truth are shared with a bob of one's head and a little attitude. And it's just what the young moms need. —TRICIA GOYER

FAITH STEP: *Make a point this week of having a conversation with someone who is different from you: a store clerk, a cashier, or the woman standing in the checkout line with you. Find ways to offer encouragement in a way he or she will understand.*

one

THURSDAY, SEPTEMBER 1

I rise early, before the sun is up; I cry out for help and put my hope in your words.
Psalm 119:147 (NLT)

EARLY MORNING IS my favorite time of day. I rise between five thirty and six o'clock, pour myself a cup of coffee, and snuggle into my love seat for quiet time with Jesus.

Several years ago I began the discipline of reading through the Bible in a year using the New Living Translation edition written expressly for this purpose. Each day, Old Testament and New Testament passages merge with Psalms and Proverbs to challenge and encourage me. And each day, the assigned Scriptures satisfy a need. When I need wisdom for making big decisions, Jesus promises to guide me on the best pathway. When I worry about my kids' future, Jesus reminds me that He's their shepherd and takes responsibility for their well-being.

When I struggle with my attitude toward someone who hurt me, Jesus convicts me to forgive so my relationship with Him and others can thrive.

Time spent with Jesus, reading His words, sets the tone for my entire day. It's my lifeline, and I guard it emphatically. That's not to say I never miss a day or two. A demanding travel schedule challenges my efforts to remain consistent, but I do my best because it's important to me.

I pray that the same is true for you. May your love for Jesus and your passion for His words grow deeper and stronger than you ever dreamed possible, and may your times with Jesus bring sheer delight. —GRACE FOX

FAITH STEP: *Imagine time with Jesus as a date with your best friend. Talk to Him as if you're face-to-face, and express your appreciation for His words of comfort, encouragement, conviction, and hope.*

FRIDAY, SEPTEMBER 2

"Be especially careful when you are trying to be good so that you don't make a performance out of it. It might be good theater, but the God who made you won't be applauding." Matthew 6:1 (MSG)

WHEN I WAS YOUNGER, football season (on TV) drew more yawns from me than cheers. However, as I've grown older, I enjoy sports more, especially when it's our Texas teams playing.

One thing still bothers me about football games. I compared the reactions of players last week after they scored touchdowns. Some spiked the ball, chest bumped other players, or wagged an index finger in a winning number one gesture. It was pure joy of accomplishment, although "excessive celebration" always draws a penalty.

But a few other players couldn't resist the temptation to pound their chests like Tarzan or point to themselves as in "Look what I did!" when they caught a winning pass or leaped over the goal line—making it seem more like a personal performance than a team effort. We all enjoy seeing our team score touchdowns. And others are always involved in making that score possible, not just one player.

In the same game, I noticed the response of another running back who'd just crossed the goal line. Immediately, he knelt and bowed his head, then arose, embracing his teammates. The gesture reminded me of Jesus's words in Matthew chapter 6.

No matter what we do, whether it's on a football field, in an office, inside a church, or in our own neighborhood, our gratitude should point heavenward. Everything Jesus did, He did for His Father.

We can appreciate each accomplishment without flaunting it. And His is the only applause we'll ever need. —REBECCA BARLOW JORDAN

FAITH STEP: *How do you usually respond to praise? The next time you achieve something special, take time to stop, drop, and thank Jesus for the accomplishment.*

SATURDAY, SEPTEMBER 3

The Word became flesh and made his dwelling among us. We have seen his glory, the glory of the one and only Son, who came from the Father, full of grace and truth. John 1:14 (NIV)

I LOVE TO GET MAIL that begins with, "You are invited…" or "Come join us…" As a young family, we received a lot of children's birthday party invitations and home business parties. These transitioned to more graduation celebrations, weddings, and "over the hill" parties for friends—occasionally, a going-away party or welcome-home celebration. Now that my husband and I live so far away from family and old friends, the invitations are fewer.

During the time Jesus ministered on earth, He invited the disciples to follow Him and become fishers of men. Jesus invited the thirsty to come to Him and drink. He invited the weary to come and find rest for their souls by being yoked together with Him. And Jesus invited everyone He met to lay aside the burden of sin and be born again to new life through Him.

The Bible itself is a sort of invitation, beckoning us to meet our Savior and learn how to live in relationship with Him and those around us. In Revelation we see Christ asking for an invitation from those who believe in Him. Jesus pictures Himself knocking on the door of our heart, waiting to be invited in. If we open the door, He promises to enter and have fellowship with us.

Think about it: Jesus invites us to invite Him in because He wants to enjoy our company. He desires more than our acquaintance; He wants an intimate relationship with us. Imagine the blessings we miss when we shut Him out of any part of our lives. The best response is found in some of the Bible's closing words: "Come, Lord Jesus!" (Revelation 22:20).
—DIANNE NEAL MATTHEWS

FAITH STEP: *Do you desire deeper fellowship with Jesus? Visualize yourself throwing open a door with Him on the other side. Now think about what you will say or do when He steps inside.*

SUNDAY, SEPTEMBER 4

"You trust God, don't you? Trust me." John 14:1 (MSG)

MY DAUGHTER, BETHANY, and I drove down the lane on our way home from church. We were a little nervous about leaving the farm during lambing season. Molly, a young ewe, was penned with her lamb, but otherwise everything looked all right, so we went. As I pulled in, Bethany pointed at our century-old barn. "What's that?" she said. "It looks like steam coming out the window."

It wasn't. The barn was on fire! A few sheep milled around in the yard. Bethany ran for a bucket, slipping in the snow. A deicer in the trough kept the water open.

I went through the open door and found the sheep. They charged around in the smoke, wide-eyed and terrified. Flames blackened the hay around a shattered heat lamp and licked at the wooden wall and the lambing pen. I shooed out the flock, then unplugged the lamp and doused the fire.

Molly was still in her pen, trying and failing to escape. The old wooden barn and pen were ripe for an inferno. Molly had serious burns on her hindquarters. The vet recommended steroids, so she wouldn't die from fright, along with scrupulous cleanliness and pure aloe on the burns, "If she'll let you get near them."

She did. That once-frightened sheep stood still for every painful treatment. My daughter and I still remember her face—she looked at us with such trust. We renamed her Molly the Brave. Able to be brave because of her trust.

Jesus, help me trust like that. —SUZANNE DAVENPORT TIETJEN

FAITH STEP: *You may be overwhelmed by your circumstances. Jesus is with you in them. He promised to be with you always. Look to Him. No matter what the circumstances, thank Him today for His presence.*

MONDAY, SEPTEMBER 5

Being confident of this, that he who began a good work in you will carry it on to completion until the day of Christ Jesus. Philippians 1:6 (NIV)

DURING A PARTICULARLY STRESSFUL deadline recently, I determined to read the book of Philippians every day until the project was finished. The discipline kept me focused on the joy and power of Jesus rather than on my own inadequacies. One verse in particular spurred me to the task: "I'm sure about this: the one who started a good work in you will stay with you to complete the job" (Philippians 1:6, CEB).

I could have stopped reading there. What wonderful encouragement. Jesus would not just be faithful to help me. He would *stay with me* until the job was done. But I kept reading. Verse after verse spoke to my heart and reminded me for whom I was writing and why. I underlined especially meaningful words in pale blue.

The next day, I read all four chapters again, clinging to the truths and fortifying my soul for the daunting task ahead of me. I found more words to circle, more verses to underline, this time in purple.

Day three, I read the chapters again, this time underlining in orange, to show myself there was still more in those heartening pages.

Day four, pencil. Day five, black pen. Day six, red pen. Day seven, pink highlighter...Notes in the margins. Exclamation marks. Asterisks.

I'd milked everything possible from those sacred pages. Hadn't I? No. I reread the passages and discovered still more. Green pen, this time.

Jesus, the Living Word. The Logos. God's Word alive, punctuated by its inexhaustible nature and its ability to constantly amaze and change a day. Or an attitude. Or a heart. —CYNTHIA RUCHTI

FAITH STEP: *Read Philippians each day for a week. Keep a pen or highlighter handy to mark verses or words that resonate with what your soul needs.*

TUESDAY, SEPTEMBER 6

In Him you have been made complete; and He is the head over all rule and authority. Colossians 2:10 (NAS)

EVERYWHERE WE TURN we are bombarded with the message "You are not enough." A student of mine told me about taking an IQ test in high school. Coming out with a low number, she believed from there on that she was not smart enough for college. My daughter sits on the bench during all of her basketball games, even though she practices several hours a day. The message she has received from her coach is she is not good enough to play. Perhaps the place we get this message the most is from the media. Open any glossy magazine for women, watch almost any commercial, look at a billboard, and study the models used. With their flawless skin, shiny hair, white teeth, and perfect bodies, they all tell us, "You are not pretty enough as you are. But if you buy this product…"

In this environment it is important to remember the truth of who we are in Jesus. Because He is God, what He says about us matters more than what any other voice tells us. His feelings for us trump even the feelings we may have about ourselves. So what does the Bible say? In Song of Solomon 4:7, He speaks to us as a lover when He says, "You are altogether beautiful, my darling; there is no flaw in you." In 2 Corinthians 12:9 He promises, "My grace is sufficient for you." Psalm 139:14 declares we are fearfully and wonderfully made. And in Isaiah 43:4, He says, "You are precious and honored in my sight, and…I love you." I could go on and on, because He goes to great lengths to let us know how loved we are—and that in Him, we are more than enough. We lack nothing.
—GWEN FORD FAULKENBERRY

FAITH STEP: *Stand in front of the mirror and repeat after me: "I am fearfully and wonderfully made. I am complete in Jesus. There is no flaw in me." Now, go live like you believe it!*

one

WEDNESDAY, SEPTEMBER 7

Therefore, if anyone is in Christ, the new creation has come: The old has gone, the new is here! 2 Corinthians 5:17 (NIV)

SOMETIMES I THINK WHEN PAUL was telling the Corinthians that they were new creations (the old has gone and the new is here), some of them didn't feel very new. Like me. Sometimes when my kids disobey me, I get upset and yell and my voice raises an octave or so. It's not pleasant. For me or anyone else.

When we are in Jesus, we can't hide from who we are or what we have done. It all hangs out there. It's ugly. But He can't work on that area in our hearts if we keep it to ourselves. And for some reason, He keeps on loving us. Even when we yell. Slipping into that old skin of anger and selfishness and self-righteousness is so much easier than asking Jesus to make us new.

But in order to be a new creation, we have to be willing to invite Him into the heat of the moment and say, "Okay, what does being 'new' look like in this moment?" Instead of giving in to the rush of emotion that overwhelms us, what would it be like to feel the rush of His presence, holding us steady, leveling us out with His peace and self-control? Being a new creation is a daily business. Sitting with Jesus, letting Him see us for who we are, is an ongoing process. Letting Him work out His grace in our lives is like oxygen. We have to have it, every moment of every day, to live the new life that He has for us. So... let the grace flow and the good, new work begin. —SUSANNA FOTH AUGHTMON

FAITH STEP: *Sit and breathe deeply, thinking of Jesus's grace as His oxygen in your life. Meditate on 2 Corinthians 5:17, reflecting on each section of the verse.*

252 | MORNINGS WITH JESUS 2016

THURSDAY, SEPTEMBER 8

The Lord said, "Go out and stand on the mountain in the presence of the Lord, for the Lord is about to pass by." Then a great and powerful wind tore the mountains apart and shattered the rocks before the Lord, but the Lord was not in the wind. After the wind there was an earthquake, but the Lord was not in the earthquake. 1 Kings 19:11 (NIV)

WHEN JOHN AND I FIRST CHOSE to start the adoption process, two family members approached us with their concerns. "If you adopt you'll take away attention from your other children," one family member said. "I had a friend who adopted and her daughter brought pain to the family," said another family member.

I understood where they were coming from. There are many concerns that come with adoption. Yet John and I also knew what Jesus told us in the Spirit's whisper that spoke to our hearts—that He wanted us to care for orphans.

Like Elisha in the Bible, we discovered that God doesn't come in the way we expect Him. Elisha faced the winds and the earthquake, but more was to come. First Kings 19:12 says, "After the earthquake came a fire, but the Lord was not in the fire. And after the fire came a gentle whisper."

I've learned not to let the doubts of others ring louder than Jesus's whispers to my spirit. Sometimes Jesus's whispers are harder to hear, but they're to be trusted the most. John and I went ahead with the adoptions, and we've added three children to our family. It hasn't been easy. There have been days when I felt as if I were being hit by winds, earthquakes, and fires, but Jesus has proven to be faithful. When I hear our small children praying and thanking Jesus for their forever homes, I'm thankful that I listened to those whispers above all else. —TRICIA GOYER

FAITH STEP: *Is there something that you need to do that Jesus has been whispering to your heart? Write out a prayer confessing your worries. Then write out a prayer asking Jesus to help you take steps of obedience.*

FRIDAY, SEPTEMBER 9

"If you give even a cup of cold water to one of the least of my followers, you will surely be rewarded." Matthew 10:42 (NLT)

MY HUSBAND, STEVE, and I entered the restaurant to unwind. It was ten thirty on a Friday night, and we had just come from volunteering at a foster children's home.

It had been a great night until bedtime, a very unsettling part of the day for many foster children. By the time we left, Steve and I felt spent from the effort to stay patient and offer comfort while remaining in authority.

Those kids had so many hurts we didn't know the source of and fears that still haunted and surfaced when the lights went out. It is heavy to enter into someone else's pain, particularly that of a child.

To be honest, I've been tempted to quit our monthly evenings as respite parents. But then I remember that all of their painful memories need the touch of Jesus, which I can offer. Heaven's power is big enough for any pain. In fact, heaven's power is exactly what is needed. I have the Source of healing within me because He saved me. They need Him first and most.

I have the option to leave the reality that is their lives, but they cannot escape it, however horrible things have been for them. Still, whenever I feel like excusing myself from what Jesus asks of me on their behalf, I understand that this verse is the truth that *I* cannot escape.

Today's verse talks about a reward for helping those who need it. Although giving can be inconvenient and heartbreaking, I'm discovering that the greatest reward is being on the healing side, doing something to combat brokenness as Jesus's hands and feet this side of heaven.
—ERIN KEELEY MARSHALL

FAITH STEP: *Do something this week that requires you to help someone who needs Jesus's healing.*

SATURDAY, SEPTEMBER 10

"No one sews a patch of unshrunk cloth on an old garment. Otherwise, the new piece will pull away from the old, making the tear worse. And no one pours new wine into old wineskins. Otherwise, the wine will burst the skins, and both the wine and the wineskins will be ruined. No, they pour new wine into new wineskins."
Mark 2:21–22 (NIV)

I LOVE THRIFT-STORE BARGAINS. One day I found a terrific dress by a famous designer for only a few dollars; but there were a few problems. The dress was way too big and an ugly gray color.

No problem, I decided. Since it was cotton it would probably shrink when washed in hot water. And a package of dye would transform the color into a soft rose shade.

When the dress refused to shrink, I tried making some alterations. Because of the design, with elastic gathering the waist, I struggled with where to cut and seam. Eventually I decided I'd cut the garment in half and use it as a skirt and top—which looked completely ridiculous. Meanwhile my attempts to dye the dress resulted in odd blotches. In the end, my great deal gave me nothing but wasted time, frustration, and a mess of mottled fabric.

Sometimes I have the same sort of frustration in my spiritual life. I think I can cut and paste, take a little tuck here or there, try a new color, and somehow make it work. But Jesus calls for a brand-new garment. My old nature will split at the seams if I try to add "a bit of Jesus" to my old pattern of trying to earn God's favor.

What Jesus offers us is so much better. A new way, inside and out. Yes, my life choices begin to change, but from the inside out. Legalism and focus on my own efforts don't fit with the new wine of grace. —SHARON HINCK

FAITH STEP: *Next time you clean your closet and get rid of a tattered old piece of clothing, thank Jesus for giving you the perfect garment of righteousness.*

SUNDAY, SEPTEMBER 11

---

*For the Lord gives wisdom; from his mouth come knowledge and understanding.
He holds success in store for the upright, he is a shield to those whose walk is
blameless, for he guards the course of the just and protects the way of
his faithful ones. Proverbs 2:6–8 (NIV)*

IS THERE AN ISSUE THAT RUBS you the wrong way? Is there someone's need you can't stop thinking about? Perhaps you can relate to a specific cause that tugs at your heart. I'm passionate about helping teen moms because I used to be one. My friend Kayleigh is dedicated to reaching out to women caught up in human trafficking. Why? Because she was victimized as a young girl. She knows what it's like to be in their shoes. She also knows the freedom that can be found when one surrenders to Jesus.

Every life-changing ministry or outreach started with one first step. And the work can't be continued without dedicated, passionate volunteers…people just like you. Have you considered aligning yourself with a professional organization that cares about the things you care about? The hardest step is usually the first one, but as you take it, next steps become clear. As Proverbs 8:14 (NIV) says, "Counsel and sound judgment are mine; I have insight, I have power." The more you know, the more you are able to act.

The best thing is that the results of your efforts aren't up to you, they're up to Jesus. He didn't give you this passion and then say, "There you go…have fun trying to make it work." Jesus puts the passion for a cause within you, and then He seeks to give you the wisdom and strength to make a difference. —TRICIA GOYER

FAITH STEP: *What's one cause that you're passionate about? Research the cause and find a ministry or outreach that is having an impact. Then pray about how you can contribute resources or support that ministry.*

~~onik~~ MONDAY, SEPTEMBER 12

He will hide me in his shelter in the day of trouble; he will conceal me under the cover of his tent; he will lift me high upon a rock. Psalm 27:5 (ESV)

MY SON IS HOME FROM SCHOOL with a fever, two ear infections, and aches that go along with a bug that has taken him down. It's a bummer of a day to miss school because there's a party this afternoon. I'm typing on my laptop on the couch while Paxton sleeps next to me. He's in his pj's, and I'm snuggled under a cozy blanket. Not a bad way to share what could be an otherwise icky day.

I'm thinking that Jesus's protective cover over us feels something like this, but on a much grander scale. Even more than we care for our children, the Lord blankets us in the cold realities of life; He doesn't always keep us from hurting because earth is a place of pain, but He covers us through the aches.

And He goes beyond that. More than just covering us, He restores us and lifts us high on a stable rock, a place of security. His care is a balm, a comfort that overcomes whatever threatens to take us down, even our own sin.

Jesus's care is lavish.

I love this. The biggest work Jesus did was to save us from our sins. But he keeps helping us every day, as our greatest comfort in a world of brokenness that tries us, such as the bug that flattened my young son on the couch today.

I'm trusting that with a little care, Paxton will be up and running soon. Will I trust Jesus on a broader scale to cover us through the big things?

—ERIN KEELEY MARSHALL

FAITH STEP: *Name three signs of God's comfort in your week.*

TUESDAY, SEPTEMBER 13

So now there is no condemnation for those who belong to Christ Jesus.
Romans 8:1 (NLT)

A FEW YEARS AGO, my older son was the victim of a false accusation. One evening a deputy knocked on Eric's door and accused him of harassment. Someone had been bothering the residents of the Midwestern town while trying to sell satellite TV services. Eric told the officer he had the wrong person. But the deputy had "proof." Someone had given a description of the culprit: a man with shaggy brown hair, wearing jeans and a white T-shirt. The victim had seen Eric jogging that evening and called the police.

The officer returned later that night, talking tough and making threats. He dismissed Eric's idea of going to the victims' homes and asking for identification. He had Eric sign a paper about a court date. Then the deputy came by a third time, at 2:00 AM, and sheepishly took back the paper. He had remembered that solicitors were required to fill out an application and have their driver's license copied. The satellite-television service rep only resembled Eric.

I felt angry at my son's ordeal but relieved it had been resolved so quickly. Unfortunately, these situations don't always play out the way they should. False accusations can be hurtful, sometimes devastating. So it makes no sense that I would ever do that to myself. But sometimes I wrestle with guilt over a mistake I've already confessed. Or I agonize over imaginary offenses. That's when I need to remember that Jesus has already freed me from condemnation. Jesus promises to forgive me when I confess a sin and repent. Whether I'm the victim of false accusations from others or from myself, He has already cleared my name. —DIANNE NEAL MATTHEWS

FAITH STEP: *Do you make false accusations against yourself? Write down 1 John 1:9 and keep it within reach. The next time you struggle with guilty feelings, read the verse and thank Jesus for His forgiveness.*

WEDNESDAY, SEPTEMBER 14

For you know that when your faith is tested, your endurance has a chance to grow.
James 1:3 (NLT)

I DON'T KNOW ABOUT YOU, but I was a messy child and teen. Growing up, my room could have been considered a danger zone. Clothes, books, and shoes were strewn everywhere. My mom would ask me to clean my room over and over again, and then—when she couldn't take it anymore—she'd clean it for me. She'd also repeat the same thing each time, "I hate to see what your house is going to be like when you grow up!"

When I grew up I took over my mother's neat tendencies. I like my house clean and orderly. I enjoy organized drawers, and I arrange my books on my shelves in alphabetical order (also sorted by fiction and non-fiction). I also inherited my mother's frustration. My kids are messy, and this has tested my faith. I can be perfectly calm when I get cut off by a car on the highway but then grumble and whine when my four-year-old empties out her drawer onto the floor to find her favorite pajamas.

The messiness of parenthood has shown me how much I need Jesus. I turn to Him for peace and for patience...often.

Right now my kids are messy, but it's my hope they'll come around, just as I did. In the meantime, Jesus is using this messy season of life to do His work in me. Jesus is teaching me to focus my mind on things that will matter for the long haul. He's also reminding me to turn to Him when life becomes overwhelming. —TRICIA GOYER

FAITH STEP: *List three things in the dailiness of life that leave you frustrated. Next time you need peace or patience, turn to Jesus. Ask Jesus to use this messy season of your life to draw closer to Him.*

THURSDAY, SEPTEMBER 15

For I have stayed in God's paths; I have followed his ways and not turned aside . . . Whatever he wants to do, he does. So he will do for me all he has planned. He controls my destiny. Job 23:11, 13–14 (NLT)

MY SON MATTHEW was a high school senior with big dreams. He wanted to attend a Christian university, but the cost was prohibitive for our family budget. Not to be deterred, he applied for multiple scholarships. Imagine his disappointment when, one after the other, his applications were rejected despite meeting every qualification. One day Matthew said, "I think God doesn't want me to attend that university." He turned his sights toward volunteering for two years with a well-established nonprofit ministry. Doing so meant raising money to pay his expenses.

At that time, our family had lived on faith support for over five years. I wondered who Matthew could ask to donate toward his ministry, and I worried about his facing another disappointment. And so I asked him, "Do you have a backup plan if these plans don't work?"

Matthew looked into my eyes and said, "Mom—I don't need a backup plan if I'm doing what Jesus wants me to do." My son's confidence in Christ's sovereignty and power did not disappoint. He received more donations than necessary even when his two years stretched into three.

What are you trusting Jesus for? Follow His path for your life, and know without a doubt that He will accomplish everything that concerns you. He will provide, open doors, and make a way when it seems there is no way. He alone controls your destiny. No backup plans needed. —GRACE FOX

FAITH STEP: *"In Christ Alone," a popular contemporary worship song, talks about how from our first cry to our final breath, Jesus directs our future paths. Recall a situation in which Jesus clearly steered your path and thank Him.*

FRIDAY, SEPTEMBER 16

By the Holy Spirit who dwells within us, guard the good deposit entrusted to you.
2 *Timothy 1:14 (ESV)*

IT'S FRIDAY NIGHT, and my husband's favorite TV show is on. Ever seen *Gold Rush*? When it's on, our kids are told to hush or play in the next room!

The quest for gold is timeless. Yesterday's gold rushes in Alaska and San Francisco helped build America's wealth, and they whet the appetites of today's treasure hunters we can watch on TV shows like *Gold Rush*, *Bering Sea Gold*, *Alaska Gold Diggers*, and *Jungle Gold*, to name a few.

The shows are fascinating but often painful to watch. Most times the treasure hunters have put everything on the line for their adventure, and, as some have said, "The earth does not give up its gold easily." Many are broken time and again in the hunt.

But the greatest wealth we could search for is living inside every believer in Jesus. We have all the treasures of eternity inside of us, and they're guarded by the Holy Spirit. And it isn't just hard to make Him give up His place in our lives; it is impossible. He never lets go of His own.

Jesus puts His greatest treasure, His own Spirit, into those who belong to Him to show His power through us. That's gold!

Our role in guarding the good deposit entrusted to us is to make sure we're giving Him free reign in us. —ERIN KEELEY MARSHALL

FAITH STEP: *List several of your greatest treasures. Thank Jesus for each one, and then ask Him to help you live daily through the power of His Spirit, His treasure, within you.*

one SATURDAY, SEPTEMBER 17

Look to the Lord and his strength; seek his face always. Psalm 105:4 (NIV)

I READ A STORY about a woman who was trying to find herself. Literally. The woman was a passenger on a tour bus in Iceland. When the bus stopped near a volcanic canyon, she went to change clothes and freshen up. When she returned, she looked different enough that no one recognized her. Shortly after she returned to the bus, the tour leader alerted everyone there was a missing passenger. The woman, not realizing they were describing *her*, joined a group of fifty people on foot and in vehicles, looking for the lost woman. Hours later, the search finally ended when the woman was "found" among the group, searching for herself.

We laugh at the irony, because we all search for ourselves. Our teen years were one extended identity search. Even when our youth is far behind us, we still do it. When we see the group picture of an event or, these days more likely, when someone hands us the smartphone to be sure everyone's eyes are open, whose eyes do we check? My eyes are too often on myself, physically, mentally, and emotionally. When I forget myself, it's because I'm loving someone else more. When I fell in love, when each of my children was born and placed in my arms, it was only then I looked on the face of another with no thought of myself.

I want to love Jesus, to see Jesus, like that. Like Stephen, face aglow, who looked at Jesus standing at the right hand of God before the first stone flew. I pray His Holy Spirit will help me love like that.

—SUZANNE DAVENPORT TIETJEN

FAITH STEP: *Look at people's faces today. Imagine it's Jesus Himself having a conversation with you. Would you interrupt? Or frame a response while He is still speaking? How would you treat that person if he took on the appearance of Jesus?*

SUNDAY, SEPTEMBER 18

Who shall separate us from the love of Christ? Shall trouble or hardship or persecution or famine or nakedness or danger or sword?
Romans 8:35 (NIV)

OVER THE COURSE OF SEVERAL YEARS, my son, who was a church music director, felt more and more called to become a pastor. So he and my daughter-in-law made a bold decision. They left secure jobs, a home they'd lovingly remodeled, a rich community of friends, and a church home that had embraced them. They packed up and moved so my son could go back to school.

Within the first few months they suffered extreme hardships. Their old home wouldn't sell or even rent. We prayed daily for a breakthrough as they faced financial stress. Their new apartment was broken into, ransacked, and precious items stolen. We prayed as they battled the sense of violation. Next, tragic deaths rocked them. We prayed as wave after wave of grief and loss battered them.

In my prayer time, I sometimes echoed St. Teresa of Avila, "Dear God, if this is how you treat your friends, no wonder you have so few of them!"

But soon I realized I'd slipped into the faulty theology of thinking that when we follow Jesus, He will make the way easy—and that we especially deserve extra blessings if we make sacrifices for His sake.

Instead, Jesus is honest in reminding us that we will have trouble in this world. Yes, He pours out blessings on His followers, but not always the blessing of removing every trial and heartache. Instead, He grants the greatest gift: the blessing of His presence in the midst of the hard roads of life. —SHARON HINCK

FAITH STEP: *What trouble are you facing today? Ask Jesus to grant you His overcoming peace.*

one MONDAY, SEPTEMBER 19

Those who control their tongue will have a long life;
opening your mouth can ruin everything. Proverbs 13:3 (NLT)

WE'VE ALL SAID THINGS we wished we could take back as soon as the words left our mouths. I know I struggle with the problem of speaking before thinking. Sadly, my mouth works much faster than my brain. For a while, my e-mail password was taken from Psalm 141:3: "setaguard-overmymouth." I have a feeling I need more than a password reminder to help me improve in this area.

The books of Proverbs and James offer plenty of sound advice about our speech, plus we have the role model of Jesus. We can learn a lot from His conversations recorded in the Bible. Although His righteous anger flared at times against those who made a mockery of worship, He spoke to people with great gentleness, patience, and respect. His answers to questions were always well thought out and intended to correct and enlighten.

Jesus always spoke the truth, even when it was hard to hear. He told the young man who claimed to diligently obey the Ten Commandments, "One thing you lack…" (Mark 10:21). He complimented without flattery. Jesus referred to Nathanael as "a true Israelite, in whom there is nothing false" (John 1:47, NIV). Just before His arrest, Jesus pushed aside His own concerns for what lay ahead and focused on comforting His disciples: "Let not your heart be troubled" (John 14:1, NKJV).

No matter whom Jesus spoke with, His words were designed to encourage, to teach, to strengthen, to heal. His conversations always glorified God and benefited the other person. His example sets high standards for me to follow; I need all the divine help I can get to know when to speak, what to say, and how to express it. —DIANNE NEAL MATTHEWS

FAITH STEP: *Each time you have a conversation today, ask Jesus for wisdom to know what the other person needs to hear. Speak those words with compassion, patience, and respect.*

TUESDAY, SEPTEMBER 20

*Surely your goodness and love will follow me all the days of my life,
and I will dwell in the house of the Lord forever. Psalm 23:6 (NIV)*

THIS MORNING I GOT TO SIT next to my niece, Chloe, on the couch. She had a giant bowl of sugar cereal in her lap. Crunchy sugary bits of oats with rainbow-colored marshmallow treats. She was cuddled into me and that in itself was a treat. She looked at me and, without saying a word, held out a hot-pink marshmallow. I shook my head and said, "That's okay, Chloe, you don't have to share with me."

She looked at me and popped the marshmallow in her mouth. A few minutes later she nudged me again. This time she was holding out a purple marshmallow. I was about to tell her I didn't need the marshmallow when she grinned at me and said, "Come on, Aunt Sue! They are *soooooo* good!"

I took it from her hand and popped it in my mouth. And she was right. It was *soooooo* good. I grinned back at her and said, "I love these things." She snuggled closer, munching away and said, "Me too." Chloe was not content to let me have a marshmallow-free morning. She likes me. She likes marshmallows. She thought we could get along. That is the thing about goodness. We can't keep it to ourselves. We want everyone that we love to get in on it.

Jesus wants us to get in on the good stuff too. He wants us to snuggle into Him, spend time in His presence and take the gifts He has for us. His mercy. His grace. His love. His joy. His hope. His deliverance. His healing. His wisdom. He won't force it on us but is waiting, palms out, for us to take what He is offering. A life of goodness. I don't know about you...but I want in. —SUSANNA FOTH AUGHTMON

FAITH STEP: *Memorize the verse, "Taste and see that the Lord is good; blessed is the one who takes refuge in him" (Psalm 34:8, NIV).*

One

WEDNESDAY, SEPTEMBER 21

*Then I heard what seemed to be the voice of a great multitude,
like the roar of many waters and like the sound of mighty peals of thunder,
crying out, "Hallelujah! For the Lord our God the Almighty reigns."*
Revelation 19:6 (ESV)

"Now this is what I call *puhsketti*!"

I love my girl, Calianne, and I am not quite ready to correct the few remaining words she hasn't learned to pronounce correctly. She is my youngest, and she's been talking proficiently for years. But I haven't let go of a few final gems like *puhsketti* and *cob on the corn* and *callapitter*. She is six now, and soon enough she will say *napkin* instead of *nackin* and *pistachio* instead of *spudashio*.

I had to turn and hide my smile when, earlier this week, she proclaimed with gusto how excited she was about the puhsketti for supper. She was all in—heart, soul, and taste buds—and we all heard about it. She doesn't hold back. She's a "This is the BEST. DAY. EVER!" kind of gal.

That's how our *Hallelujah!* should be to Jesus. Body, mind, soul, thoughts, words, deeds—no matter that our praise is offered from imperfect humans like us who still have a lot to learn.

Jesus knows we haven't reached full maturity, but He delights with the praise we offer Him now. This is the best day ever to praise Him.

Calianne loves Jesus. I can just picture her someday bowing in worship and proclaiming, "Now that's who I call Savior! This is the BEST. ETERNITY. EVER!"

I'd like to be nearby to smile and say it along with her.

—Erin Keeley Marshall

Faith Step: *Read Psalm 150:1–6. How do these verses inspire you to worship Jesus with "Hallelujah!" today?*

THURSDAY, SEPTEMBER 22

Be kind and compassionate to one another, forgiving each other,
just as in Christ God forgave you. Ephesians 4:32 (NIV)

A LETTER FROM A READER told me the sad story of a family member's betrayal and the reader's desire to forgive. "I know Jesus expects more of me," she wrote. "I know how toxic resentment can be, so I want to forgive in my heart. But here is my problem. Everyone talks about the importance of forgiveness but no one says how to accomplish it if the other person refuses to participate in repairing things.... Can I forgive but not be in the relationship anymore? Is that okay in God's eyes?"

I believe this is a common problem. We hear all kinds of advice about seventy times seven, turning the other cheek, and so forth, but I think much of our teaching fails to address the difference between forgiveness and reconciliation. What does it mean to forgive "as in Christ God forgave" us?

A good illustration of this can be found in the Old Testament story of David and Saul. David loved Saul and wanted a relationship with him. But Saul became jealous of David and tried to kill him numerous times. David forgave Saul and went on loving him. But when it became apparent David could do nothing to mend the relationship, David fled.

In Jesus, God forgives all of our sin. But because of free will, He does not force us to be reconciled to Him. That's a choice we have to make. It's the same in our relationships with others. We can—and should—forgive the wrongs of others. But reconciliation takes both sides. When one continues in dysfunctional behavior, the other cannot mend the relationship alone. We must get away in order to survive. —GWEN FORD FAULKENBERRY

FAITH STEP: *Is there a broken relationship you've tried to mend on your own? If the other person hasn't apologized and changed the harmful behavior, make sure you've forgiven, but then move on. Not everyone chooses a relationship with Jesus, and not everyone will choose to reconcile with you. It's okay. Trust Him and let it go.*

FRIDAY, SEPTEMBER 23

"Whoever doesn't honor the Son doesn't honor the Father who sent Him."
John 5:23 *(CEB)*

I'M CONVINCED I'D HAVE BEEN a much better new mother now that I'm a grandmother. I learned so much during those thirty-four years of having a child living at home (oldest and youngest were thirteen years apart). And I've learned even more watching my children as parents. They're parenting magnificently, even though it isn't always easy.

When asked, most parents would say, "If I had it to do over again, I would be more/less _____" and they'd have an immediate answer to fill in the blank. More patient. Less strict. More strict. Less concerned about messy rooms and more concerned about teaching good communication skills.

Among the house rules that worked for us was this one: "Kids, you can tell us anything, as long as you say it in a respectful manner."

In many homes, respect has disappeared from the list of nonnegotiables. Sadly, the same can be said for the way some people treat Jesus and their relationship with Him. There's no demanding, no entitlement, no disrespectful language in the hearing of the King of kings. No culturally acceptable taking His Name in vain. No rude behavior. He invites us to pour our longings and concerns before Him. And He'll listen, no matter what it is, as long as it comes from the mouth and heart of a person who honors Him, and the words are said respectfully. "Jesus, I don't see any good coming out of this diagnosis. But I trust You." "Jesus, I can't bear one more disappointment. But I trust You." "Jesus, this seems so grossly unfair. But I trust You."

Our trust in Him no matter the circumstance demonstrates our respect.
—CYNTHIA RUCHTI

FAITH STEP: *Do you keep a prayer journal? Does it have a page or pages reserved for unburdening your heart? Consider putting this message across the top of the page as a reminder of His willingness to hear: Anything. Respectfully.*

ᴅᴍ SATURDAY, SEPTEMBER 24

"Be strong and courageous! Do not be afraid of them! The Lord your God will go ahead of you. He will neither fail you nor forsake you." Deuteronomy 31:6 (NLT)

MY HUSBAND AND I HAD WORKED in Christian camping ministry for eleven years when someone approached us with a new opportunity—launch a Canadian office for an American ministry that focuses on Eastern Europe. Our role would include recruiting, training, and leading two-week mission trips to the post-Communist bloc.

We'd never dreamed of doing something like this. Neither had we envisioned the work it would entail—leaving the camp where housing was provided, moving to a new location, and having to raise additional financial support to cover the increased living expenses.

We prayed for guidance and sensed God's go-ahead. Step-by-step we moved forward while facing giant-size unknowns: Where would we find suitable office space? Could we raise sufficient funds to pay monthly bills? Where would we find affordable housing? How would we fit into our new role?

Focusing on Christ's presence bolstered our confidence. Every day we praised Him for His sovereignty over the details. We envisioned Him going before us and clearing our path, toppling one uncertainty after another. And He did exactly that: He provided an office space, affordable housing, sufficient funds to pay our bills, and He gave us wisdom to do our job.

What uncertainty faces you today? Is it illness? Financial stress? A troubled marriage? Be encouraged—Christ is with you. He walks before you and will deal with the details concerning your unknown. There's no need to fear. The Faithful One will never fail you. —GRACE FOX

FAITH STEP: *Place three small objects in a row on a flat surface. Imagine the first as the unknown you face. The last represents you. The middle represents Christ. Note how, because He goes before you, He faces the unknown on your behalf. Thank Him for doing so.*

one SUNDAY, SEPTEMBER 25

Now this is what the Lord says . . . "Do not fear, for I have redeemed you; I have called you by your name; you are Mine. Isaiah 43:1 (HSC)

WHEN MY MOM FELL at work a few years ago, I was a basket case. I found out from my brother that Mom had suffered a brain injury and skull fracture and was being transported to a larger city for emergency surgery. That night I was relieved to hear that doctors deemed the surgery unnecessary. But the next day, while driving several hundred miles to the hospital, I got the news that Mom seemed worse; doctors were preparing to perform a procedure. By the time I arrived at the hospital, I learned that medication alone had taken care of the brain swelling. What a roller coaster!

Walking through the doors of Intensive Care, I had no idea what to expect. Then I saw through the glass partition that Mom was conscious. I teared up, relieved to see her better than I'd expected. Her eyes lit on me. She smiled and waved. I read her lips as she told the doctor, "That's my daughter." I thought my heart would burst with joy.

I'm proud to be acknowledged as my parents' daughter, my husband's wife, my children's mom, my grandchildren's nana. But the idea that Jesus knows me and acknowledges me as His own blows me away. To think that I have a personal relationship with the Creator of the universe! That He's never ashamed of me, in spite of my flaws and mistakes. The best part is, I never have to worry about His turning away from me no matter how I mess up.

Knowing Jesus and being known by Him gives my life meaning and strengthens me to face tough times. And I find joy and comfort in knowing that when this earthly journey ends, I will hear the King of kings say, "That's My daughter." —DIANNE NEAL MATTHEWS

FAITH STEP: *Do you ever struggle with loneliness, poor self-esteem, or feelings of rejection? Spend a few moments focusing on what it means to be known by Jesus. Write Him a prayer of thanks.*

MONDAY, SEPTEMBER 26

If any of you lacks wisdom, you should ask God, who gives generously to all without finding fault, and it will be given to you. James 1:5 (NIV)

I'M A PERSON WHO LIKES to give advice. If I have a brand or a favorite product that I love, I talk about it. If a parenting tactic or skill has worked with my children, I blog about it. If a friend calls me up with a question, I share my personal advice.

The problem comes when I don't have an answer. I've had younger women ask me for advice on how to forgive a spouse's unfaithfulness or how to face a child's disability. Those are issues I haven't dealt with. When it comes to answering questions on topics that I'm not knowledgeable about, my thoughts are anything but stable. They waver and change.

Thankfully, Jesus's thoughts are solid. They never change. Jesus is wisdom, and, when we turn to Him, He can be wisdom for us! First Corinthians 1:30 (NIV) says, "It is because of him that you are in Christ Jesus, who has become for us wisdom from—God—that is, our righteousness, holiness and redemption." When I seek wisdom from Jesus, He reminds me that it's not my job to share tips for specific problems, instead I need to point others to where they can go for peace, for strength, and for guidance—to Him!

Jesus has all the answers to the world's problems, and He freely gives His wisdom to anyone. There have been numerous times when I had no answers of my own, yet one whispered prayer later and the answer came.

Prayer gives us access to Jesus's wisdom. He gives us wisdom for others and for ourselves. All we have to do is ask. —TRICIA GOYER

FAITH STEP: *Need wisdom? Make a list of things you need advice about. Then pray over each of those things. Keep your list and return to it later, writing down the answer and how it came to you.*

TUESDAY, SEPTEMBER 27

And we know that all things work together for good to them that love God, to them who are the called according to his purpose. For whom he did foreknow, He also did predestinate to be conformed to the image of his Son.
Romans 8:28, 29 (KJV)

AFTER TWO MISCARRIAGES, my brother and sister-in-law were expecting a baby boy. Each appointment that ended in a good report excited the family more and more. We began to let ourselves believe everything was going to be okay. Then came the call from the doctor's office. "Your test results were abnormal. We need to do further testing to see whether the baby may have [some major problems]." The "further testing" involved considerable expense and weeks of waiting for conclusive results. During those weeks I was touched by the peace and calm Jim and Rene exhibited. It could only be described as supernatural.

My brother told me that when he talked to our pastor after receiving the call, our pastor shared the above verse with him. He said, essentially, we either believe that "all" or we don't. If "all" things work together for good, that includes even ordeals like this. My brother was challenged by that. He and Rene chose to believe that "all," willing themselves to accept whatever results came as part of God's plan for their baby's and their good. As part of that process their faith deepened, their peace became more unshakable, their purpose more defined. In short, they became a little more like Jesus. When the results showed that the baby was completely normal, of course we were all relieved. But, in a way, the results were just a footnote to the spiritual gains my brother and sister-in-law made by trusting Jesus with their all. —GWEN FORD FAULKENBERRY

FAITH STEP: *Is there something you have a hard time believing God could work for your good? Write this on a scrap of paper and stick it somewhere you'll see it often: I know God is working in _____ for my good, and through this I will become more like Jesus.*

WEDNESDAY, SEPTEMBER 28

"I will sprinkle clean water on you, and you will be clean; I will cleanse you from all your impurities and from all your idols. I will give you a new heart and put a new spirit in you; I will remove from you your heart of stone and give you a heart of flesh. And I will put my Spirit in you and move you to follow my decrees and be careful to keep my laws." Ezekiel 36:25–27 (NIV)

MY MOM ALWAYS TOLD ME to spend my birthday doing things I would like to do the whole coming year. That encouraged a day full of fun and favorite activities. However, as an earnest little girl, I gradually shifted my focus. One year I decided I would be extravirtuous on my birthday (and thus all year): make my bed perfectly, practice my piano scales without complaint, read my Bible an extralong time, share toys with the neighbor kids, and do all my chores without being reminded.

Less than an hour into the day, I'd already skimped on some chores, lost my temper when a favorite toy broke, and talked back to my mom. The entire enterprise only showed me the futility of creating the best version of me in my own strength.

I wanted to change my heart, but good intentions weren't cutting it. Can you imagine a woman on an operating table trying to perform heart surgery on herself? Our efforts to conquer our sinful natures in our own power are just as silly. We need a total heart replacement, and that's not a do-it-yourself activity. It requires a skilled surgeon.

Only Jesus can change our heart to be more like His. He can bring fruit from our lives in ways that our straining and self-absorption can't accomplish. —SHARON HINCK

FAITH STEP: *Draw a picture of a heart. Stop trying to do surgery on yourself and ask Jesus to transform your heart to be like His.*

THURSDAY, SEPTEMBER 29

"But when he, the Spirit of truth, comes, he will guide you into all the truth. He will not speak on his own; he will speak only what he hears, and he will tell you what is yet to come." John 16:13 (NIV)

IN HIS LOVE of all things Alaska, my husband is devoted to the flood of shows about families surviving in the Alaskan wilderness. Am I nervous about an upcoming announcement of the "Let's homestead in Alaska!" variety? Slightly. My hesitation is only partially related to the cold. Right now, our kids and grandkids live only fifteen minutes away.

On a recent episode of one of the shows, a homesteading family navigated an awkward barge-type transport vessel through a narrow waterway in the fog. The tide wasn't ideal for the trip. Dangerous as it was, the experienced man who served as boat captain wove the clunky vessel safely past the visible obstacles. Impressive. Even more impressive was his ability to direct the boat around the hidden, underwater obstacles—sandbars, rock formations, half-sunken logs.

On high-traffic waterways, underwater obstructions can be problematic. In a wilderness situation, they can be catastrophic. Navigating through a wilderness experience right now? Jesus is a River Guide Who not only knows the tides but was there when they were created. He sees beneath the water, around the water, and knows everything about you—the vessel—including your limits. Who else could we trust to steer us safely through?

Is the fog making it impossible to see the obstacles or know where they're hiding? Fog is no threat to Jesus. Uncertain where you are on the map? He knows. He's traveled this way often enough to have memorized the terrain. —CYNTHIA RUCHTI

FAITH STEP: *Take time this week to sit on the shore—or watch a video—and focus on the wonder that Jesus knows every obstacle beneath the surface, every rock, every bump, every previous shipwreck. Praise Him for His flawless guidance.*

FRIDAY, SEPTEMBER 30

Cleanse me with hyssop, and I will be clean; wash me,
and I will be whiter than snow. Psalm 51:7 (NIV)

"MOM, IT'S SO FUNNY...you keep doing laundry but the pile never goes down," my son Jack said as he walked by the laundry in our hallway. He was grinning. I was not. Because it is never funny when you do something endlessly and see little or no improvement. Yesterday I walked by the laundry to see a three-foot pile of dirty towels. I yelled out, "Who just brought all those dirty towels?"

Jack said, "Me. I found them under my bed."

It appears that the children are conspiring against me. They have decided, "No matter what, let's never let the laundry basket get all the way empty." They are winning. I am losing. Over these long years, they have watched me crack under the never-ending mounds of laundry. I say things like, "Didn't I just wash this?" and "Wasn't this clean yesterday?"

Sometimes I feel like I experience the same thing in my journey of faith. I come up against the same dirty laundry in my life over and over again: anxiety, selfishness, pride, coveting...the list goes on. I call out things like, "Didn't I just deal with this?" and "Am I ever going to be done with these issues?" The thing that I need to remember is that my life isn't like a never-ending laundry basket of problems. I have a promise from Jesus that He has cleansed me from all unrighteousness because of His holiness. Because of His gift of pardon and grace. And daily, He is working out His salvation in me. Changing me. Redeeming me. And the most beautiful thing of all? He has promised to wash me whiter than snow. —SUSANNA FOTH AUGHTMON

FAITH STEP: *As you put in your next load of laundry, use it as a physical reminder that Jesus has cleansed you from all unrighteousness and that He is working out His salvation in you daily.*

ome

SATURDAY, OCTOBER 1

[Jesus said . . .] "The seed scattered on good soil are those who hear the word and embrace it. . . . " Mark 4:20 (CEB)

IN AUTUMN, WHEN THE SUN is warm and everything growing takes on a new look—trees, gardens, lawns—our grandchildren love to skirt the edge of our pond looking for mature cattail pods and milkweed pods.

Say what you will about how both milkweeds and cattails have the potential for becoming a nuisance, they do serve a purpose and provide entertainment for adventurous children.

Our grandkids live near enough that they can observe the entire life cycle of cattails and milkweeds. They appreciate when the cattails' velvety dark brown seedpod matures and when the milkweed seedpods grow plump and start to dry out. In the fall, the children pop open the cattail pods to reveal thousands of white fluff-seeds that silently explode out of the pod. The same for the milkweeds. Breaking open a mature milkweed seedpod sends hundreds or thousands of downy, almost weightless, wispy seeds into the air.

When small hands on our property break open the seedpods, the fluff inside is carried on a breath of a breeze farther than the children imagined possible.

Sometimes we imagine that sharing the truth about Jesus—the Gospel—is far more complicated than it really is. Rather than a dissertation, it's more like breaking open a pod and setting the seeds loose with a puff of our breath.

We open God's Word, expose the hope Jesus brings, and breathe on it with our own story of His impact on our life and future. The seeds are carried on that breeze . . . farther than we ever dreamed. —CYNTHIA RUCHTI

FAITH STEP: *Take note today of the small things you can do to help spread the good news of Jesus to contribute to a soul's rest. Consider keeping a record of milkweed moments.*

SUNDAY, OCTOBER 2

Do not be anxious about anything, but in every situation, by prayer and petition, with thanksgiving, present your requests to God. Philippians 4:6 (NIV)

I AM NOT THE BEST PRAY-ER. I have prayer amnesia. I will hear about someone or something I want to pray for, and two seconds later the thought slips from my mind and is replaced by the thought, *We need light bulbs* or *Wow, my pants feel tight.*

But I am keeping at it. Because I believe prayer links me to the heart of the Creator of the universe. And I want in on what He wants for me and for those around me. I have a chalkboard in my kitchen that I used to write the boys' chores on. Now I use it as a physical reminder of all the people I am praying for. I have started standing in front of the chalkboard after the boys leave for school. Then I mention the names I have written there to Jesus. I let Him know who is hurting, who is hoping, who needs healing, and who could use a divine reminder of His presence. I know that He knows this already. But I want Him to know that I am on His team. I am standing in the gap for the people that I love. I want what He wants for those He has placed in my life. I am saying the words that sometimes they are too sad or tired or flattened to say. I am hoping the hopes they are afraid to speak out. I am telling Him of their dreams that only He can bring to pass.

I don't really know what He should do in these situations but He always does it better than I can, and so I tell Him that too. And the best part is? I know He will. —SUSANNA FOTH AUGHTMON

FAITH STEP: *Write out the names of those you love and are praying for, and tape the list to the wall. Each time you pass it, pray for them.*

~~one~~ MONDAY, OCTOBER 3

When the disciples saw him, they screamed in terror, thinking he was a ghost. But Jesus spoke to them at once. "It's all right," he said. "I am here! Don't be afraid." Matthew 14:26–27 (NLT)

I HAVE A COPY of the book *Alexander and the Terrible, Horrible, No Good, Very Bad Day*. It features a little boy whose day is filled with one calamity after another. Frustrated, he says he wants to move to Australia.

Maybe you experience days when nothing seems to go well. I do. So did Jesus's disciples. One such day dawned with news about John the Baptist's beheading. The disciples had no time to mentally process this tragedy before Jesus-seeking crowds mobbed them. After ministering to the masses for many hours, they experienced a heart-stopping moment when Jesus told them to feed the thousands gathered there.

Shortly afterward, Jesus told them to board a boat and cross the lake without Him. A massive storm descended during the night, and wind and waves tossed their boat like a plastic toy. Circumstances exhausted them, and fear overwhelmed them. It seems as if the culmination of the day's events blinded their eyes to recognizing Jesus when He approached them in the storm.

Maybe you can relate. You've experienced one calamity or stressor after another, and you feel like running away. Rest assured, my friend— as surely as Jesus met His disciples in the midst of the storm, so He will meet you. Focus on the reality of Christ's presence in your life. Doing so will renew your strength and restore your courage. Trust Him, and do not be afraid. —GRACE FOX

FAITH STEP: *Draw a vertical line down the center of a piece of paper. On the left side, briefly name the circumstances that make your days challenging. On the right side, write a prayer thanking Jesus for being present amid those circumstances.*

TUESDAY, OCTOBER 4

Don't hold back. Throw yourselves into the work of the Master, confident that nothing you do for him is a waste of time or effort. 1 Corinthians 15:58 (MSG)

I CAN'T COUNT THE TIMES in my nursing career that my efforts have failed. One awful season, we took care of three newborns on extra-corporeal membranous oxygenation. ECMO involves routing the infant's blood outside the body with a pump through a man-made lung to remove carbon dioxide and put oxygen back in the bloodstream before it returns to the baby. It sounds (and looks) like science fiction.

Two nurses care for each patient—one handles the pump while the other tends to the baby, who looks pink, healthy, and interactive during the ECMO run. Specially trained teams on constant alert even eat at the infants' bedsides in an exception to Joint Commission rules. The nurses and specialists work days on end to give these critically ill babies time to rest and heal. To have a chance to live. That year, all three of those precious babies died. It crushed us and devastated the families. The medical team went over each case looking for lessons, but the runs had been textbook. Had we wasted our time?

God says nothing we do in His name is done in vain.

The mothers gave us the answer. No, none of us got what we wanted, but every mother looked into her baby's eyes. And every baby looked back. Each baby grasped a father's finger. These little ones knew their families, and their families knew them. They died comfortably in their parents' arms listening to lullabies rather than the chaos taking place pre-ECMO.

Much of what Jesus did looked like a failure at first, but there's always a purpose. We gave the babies time with their earthly families. And heaven awaits. —SUZANNE DAVENPORT TIETJEN

FAITH STEP: *We all get discouraged when things turn out wrong. Today, give Jesus your hopes, then work with all your heart. Let Him handle the outcomes.*

WEDNESDAY, OCTOBER 5

For I am convinced that neither death nor life, neither angels nor demons, neither the present nor the future, nor any powers, neither height nor depth, nor anything else in all creation, will be able to separate us from the love of God that is in Christ Jesus our Lord. Romans 8:38–39 (NIV)

A BIBLE STUDY LEADER WRAPPED duct tape around a class member's hands and had others try to pull it off. When they failed, he explained that in a similar way, we are bonded with Christ and can't be pulled apart. Later, the leader learned that a simple arm movement allows a person to break free of duct tape binding the hands. I once saw a speaker hold a tube of superglue to represent our relationship with Jesus, but I thought about how many times my own repaired items had not held together.

In reality, is there any way to adequately illustrate these verses? A single phrase or statement wasn't enough to express such a huge promise; Paul lists ten things that will never be able to separate us from Christ, and then throws in "anything else in all creation" for good measure.

It's hard for my brain to soak up the certainty of these reassuring words. I live in a world where people break their promises. Friendships dissolve over minor issues. Spouses who once seemed so devoted to each other separate or divorce. Children are sometimes abandoned. God knew we needed more than just a few words to take in the message.

Absolutely nothing can destroy the bond of my relationship with Jesus. Nobody, including me, can do anything that will weaken His love for me. Maybe the best visual illustration of that promise is not a product but Christ's life, death, and Resurrection. —DIANNE NEAL MATTHEWS

FAITH STEP: *Ask Jesus to fill you with a renewed sense of His love and the truth found in Romans 8:38–39.*

THURSDAY, OCTOBER 6

Everyone should be quick to listen, slow to speak. . . . James 1:19 (CEB)

I HAD MY LAPTOP OPEN on the table in what I thought was the quiet corner booth in a restaurant. As I ate, I took care of several business e-mails, then began to work on a complicated assignment.

A man from the next booth stood to pay his bill. He stepped to my table and started a one-sided conversation. His demeanor, ragged work clothes, and facial expression told me I didn't have anything to fear, but I did need patience. I listened a long time.

He stepped back to leave a tip, then returned. "You can't count on people, you know? I could have had that apartment six months ago but the paperwork got all messed up and I'm not all that great with numbers anymore and I still don't know how I'm going to rent a vehicle to move all my stuff, but on the other hand my brother-in-law said he'd help so I should just take him up on that. Well, I should let you get back to your work. Have a nice... But with this pain I have in my knee, I don't know about my brother-in-law's truck..."

Twenty minutes later, he did pay his bill and exit the restaurant. I picked up my fork to finish my meal.

Within a minute, another man stood at my table. A younger man, neatly dressed. "Excuse me, ma'am. I consider myself a nice person, but you just took 'nice' to a whole new level."

"Everybody has a story to tell," I said, startled that anyone had been watching the scene and convinced it was Jesus who'd given me that much patience. "Sometimes all they want is for someone to listen." —CYNTHIA RUCHTI

FAITH STEP: *Whom can you bless in Jesus's name today by listening to his or her not-always-succinct stories? Are there people you try to avoid because they never seem to get to the end? Who else within earshot might see Jesus in work clothes through your uncommon patience in obedience to Him?*

one FRIDAY, OCTOBER 7

Love must be sincere. Hate what is evil; cling to what is good. Be devoted to one another in love. Honor one another above yourselves. Romans 12:9–10 (NIV)

FRIDAY AFTERNOONS, FRIENDS GATHER in my living room for Bible study. We've been a small group for over a decade, working our way through various topics, sharing all the joys and heartaches of life, and praying together. Each woman shares her love for Jesus in different and remarkable kinds of service: family life, careers, mission trips, serving the church through teaching, singing, or administrating.

I treasure our times together. After a week apart, everyone is eager to catch up. We go around the circle, and each person gives updates on her work, family, needs, and answers to prayer.

Recently, I've noticed a problem in my heart. As others share, I begin to grow restless. Instead of listening intently, I silently prioritize the many things about my life that I want to talk about when it's my turn. My selfish heart is so prone to think that my struggles are worse than others' or my updates more exciting. I'd give my life for any of the women in our small group, yet I struggle to be quiet and listen. Laughable, but also pathetic. When Jesus nudged me to look at my attitudes, it was as if He shined a laser pointer onto my heart. What I saw sent me to my knees, grateful for His forgiveness.

I've always thought that honoring others above myself meant giving up a place in line, or a seat on the bus, or the biggest piece of dessert. I've begun to realize that giving up my selfish mental chatter and truly listening—not jumping in with advice, not interrupting, not impatiently waiting for my turn—is an important way to show love. —SHARON HINCK

FAITH STEP: *In your next conversation, honor the other person above yourself and reflect Jesus's love by fully listening.*

SATURDAY, OCTOBER 8

Let everyone see that you are gentle and kind. The Lord is coming soon.
Philippians 4:5 (NCV)

"BE EASY TO APPROACH and hard to make angry." I stumbled across this quote on someone's Facebook status, and I had to share it. I think I tweeted it too. Though I am not sure who said it, its truth is timeless, even based in Scripture from James 1:19. It struck a nerve in me.

How I would love to be always gracious and approachable and hard to make angry! But alas, my character fails me more often than I'd like. Jesus and I are working on me, though, and little by little I trust that I'll look a bit more like Him despite my mistakes.

The tone of today's verse is gentle and warm. It doesn't tell me I better be kind or else. It doesn't condemn me for failing each day. Jesus's Spirit was moving alive and well in Paul, the man who penned those words. Paul didn't start out gentle or kind. But Jesus's Spirit within him changed him into a man who dealt with people as a caring parent, a guiding shepherd, much as Jesus described Himself as the Good Shepherd (John 10:11).

Our job as Christ-followers is simply to let everyone see the Holy Spirit in us, gentling our rough edges, showing itself in kindness that doesn't anger easily. We cannot maintain such goodness without Him.

He is coming back soon to us, a promise of hope that sustains us if we know Him as Savior. If we live as He did, embodying Philippians 4:5, He will work through us to draw others to Himself.

Our aim is not to sell others on our own goodness. We are to be vessels that reveal His. —ERIN KEELEY MARSHALL

FAITH STEP: *Think of someone you struggle to get along with or a person who you sense needs Jesus's gentleness. Pray for that person, and ask the Lord to provide an opportunity to share His life through you.*

SUNDAY, OCTOBER 9

Remain in Me, and I in you. Just as a branch is unable to produce fruit by itself unless it remains on the vine, so neither can you unless you remain in Me.
John 15:4 (HSC)

MY FELLOW TEACHER AND FRIEND Paola Gemme, who is Italian, taught me a phrase, "Il dolce far niente." The sweetness of doing nothing. We like to apply it to long summer days when we are able to sit in the sun watching our children play, sipping on lemonade with no papers to grade, no lesson plans to make, doing nothing except *being*, and doing it together. How sweet it is to do nothing with a friend!

I think John 15:4 relates to this concept. As followers of Jesus, so often we think that the more we do, the more activity we generate, the better Christians we are. Go to church every time the doors are open. Teach Sunday school. Play the piano. Sing in the choir. Tithe. Go on mission trips. Attend a Bible study. The list goes on and on. And while none of these are bad things per se, I believe they are often misdirected.

Jesus tells us to remain in Him. He is the vine, and we are the branches. The metaphor clearly illustrates that we can do nothing without Him. It's really more about being than doing—just *being* in Him. In other words, the vine is the life of the branch. It directs the branch where to go and provides everything it needs to flourish, and ultimately, produce fruit. The branch doesn't do anything but abide in the vine.

I'm not saying we should be lazy. I'm saying we need to be willing to let the vine direct us, whether into activity or out of it. The sweetness of doing nothing is that it's not about generating activity; it's all about being in the vine. —GWEN FORD FAULKENBERRY

FAITH STEP: *Make a list of the things you "do" for Jesus. Prayerfully consider each one. If it's more about you, or other people's expectations, cross it off and get out of it.*

one MONDAY, OCTOBER 10

"Impossible!" they exclaimed. "We have only five loaves of bread and two fish!"
Matthew 14:17 (NLT)

WHEN I FIRST SENSED GOD calling me to write for publication nearly twenty years ago, the fear of inadequacy nearly overwhelmed me. I seriously doubted my ability to write anything worthy of other people's time and attention, but the desire to hone my skills and begin submitting magazine articles was unquenchable.

My daily prayer became, "Father, my abilities are like the disciples' five loaves and two fish. They're small, but I offer them to You. Take them, bless them, and use them for Your glory."

The disciples struggled with the fear of inadequacy, too, when Jesus asked them to feed more than five thousand men, women, and children. "Are You kidding? Feed the masses? We have only five loaves and two fish—what good can they do when the task is so large?"

But Jesus showed no fear. He calmly took the disciples' meager offering, asked His Father to bless it, and broke it into pieces for distribution. The result? The limited supply stretched miraculously. It fed everyone, and the disciples collected twelve baskets of leftovers.

"Little is much when placed in the Father's hands," someone said. We might feel as though we have little to offer Jesus. *What good can we possibly do?* But He thinks differently. He simply wants us to share the talents and resources He's given us and to trust Him with the outcome. He wants to bless our offering, no matter how meager it may seem, and use it to build His kingdom. Let's focus not on our limitations but on His unlimited power to accomplish His purposes through us. —GRACE FOX

FAITH STEP: *Write "My Five Loaves and Two Fish" at the top of a piece of paper. Underneath, make a list of your talents—haircutting, knitting, gardening, car or house maintenance, et cetera. Offer these skills to Jesus and ask Him to bless others through them.*

TUESDAY, OCTOBER 11

"But the Lamb will emerge victorious, for he is Lord of lords and King of kings. . . . "
Revelation 17:14 (CEB)

HE STOLE A COP CAR, rammed it into a building, then set fire to the building in order to smoke out the men inside. He bugged an office without legal permission, held the receptionist against her will, and hacked into the computer system. And he was the hero of the story.

One of the challenges many parents and grandparents face today relates to the trend toward "bad boy" heroes. Where do they find heroes worth their children's attention? Many television, movie, and book heroes aren't merely understandably flawed, as we all are, but show a dark side, an angry streak, or use illegal and sometimes immoral means to win the day. They flout the law or bypass the basic life lessons Jesus taught, in the name of their cause.

Even some of the people we call heroes of the faith in the Bible had moments of moral failure or poor judgment. And all too often, we see supposed leaders of the faith community in anything but heroic light. If we use as our hero standard anyone but Jesus, we risk following an illusion or an inadequate definition of a hero.

He always spoke truth, sacrificed everything for those He loves, remains as protector, has a flawless record as conqueror, and has flawless character. Only Jesus rescues no matter the cost to Himself and yet stays in compliance with the laws established by God the Father. Only Jesus. The rider on the white horse. The rider called Faithful and True. The conquering hero called the Word of God (Revelation 19:11–13). We don't need to look as far as we might think for a hero worth emulating. His name is Jesus.
—CYNTHIA RUCHTI

FAITH STEP: *As you pray today, remember to thank Jesus for being a complete, ever-faithful, integrity-rich, flawless hero.*

WEDNESDAY, OCTOBER 12

In all their distress he too was distressed, and the angel of his presence saved them. In his love and mercy he redeemed them; he lifted them up and carried them all the days of old. Isaiah 63:9 (NIV)

MY FRIEND KAREN ORGANIZED field trips for a large homeschooling co-op and put a lot of effort into that volunteer position. One week she asked us to pray about an upcoming trip that would be a full-day event, a long drive away, with dozens of families involved.

The day before the field trip, Karen and her children were all sick. She fretted about what to do and worried about disappointing or inconveniencing the other co-op members. Other parents reassured her they could manage and encouraged her not to worry. She stayed home and cared for her family, relieved that the field trip was a success even though she was absent.

"I needed this experience to remind me that Jesus can work things out, even when I have to step back," she told me. "I didn't realize I had been wearing the Tiara of Field Trips."

I love that expression. We all carry weights we aren't meant to carry. We crown ourselves the boss of one part of life, and soon find the crown is too heavy. Jesus asks us to stop trying to rule—not because He is mean and wanting to limit us. Instead, He has so much compassion that He sees what our self-appointed tiaras can do to us—and He wants to save us from that pain.

He is distressed by our distress. He delights in lifting us up and carrying us. We don't have to live under the burden of feeling indispensable. Jesus really can run the universe without our help. And when He graciously invites us to serve with Him, the responsibility can be joyful instead of stressful when we allow Him to wear the crown. —SHARON HINCK

FAITH STEP: *Draw a picture of a crown and write any roles or responsibilities that have felt burdensome recently. Ask Jesus to take the crown and carry you today.*

one THURSDAY, OCTOBER 13

Anyone who loves their brother and sister lives in the light,
and there is nothing in them to make them stumble. 1 John 2:10 (NIV)

THE OTHER NIGHT, I walked into my thirteen-year-old Jack's room and found all three of my boys curled up on his double bed, arms flung over each other, feeling safe and close. I wanted to throw myself on top of them because that much love is beautiful, and I wanted in. There is nothing that brings me more joy than seeing my kids treating each other with gentleness and care. Probably because more often than not, they are trying to pound each other or conk each other on the head. But there is something so precious and so pure about seeing them hold each other, it makes me tear up with happiness.

I think Jesus feels the same way and wants in on the action when He sees us loving and caring for each other. He loves it even more when we begin inviting Him into the midst of our lives with our thoughts and our words, when we talk to Him on behalf of our brothers and sisters. I think He wants to squeeze our heads off because hearing that we love each other gets Him all whipped up. I know this because I get all whipped up when I see my kids loving each other, and He made me like Him. I think our prayers for each other keep us feeling safe and close. Knitting our hearts together with love. Bolstering us up on the dark days. Holding us in the palm of the One Who loves us the most. Filling us with hope and peace and strength in the midst of chaos. And that is a beautiful thing.
—SUSANNA FOTH AUGHTMON

FAITH STEP: *Hold someone close that you love today. Tell them you love them. And pray a prayer of blessing over them, reminding them that Jesus loves them most of all.*

FRIDAY, OCTOBER 14

I will lead the blind by ways they have not known, along unfamiliar paths
I will guide them; I will turn the darkness into light before them and
make the rough places smooth. These are the things I will do;
I will not forsake them. Isaiah 42:16 (NIV)

WHEN JOHN AND I ADOPTED two children from the foster care system in 2012 the expression "rough road" was an understatement. We met two preschoolers one day, and the next day they were ours to take home. Both children were considered "special needs" since they were behind physically and emotionally. Even though I'd raised three kids into adult years I was on "unfamiliar paths." I was soon dealing with behavioral, occupational, and speech therapists. I learned new ways to handle discipline and how to create loving bonds with children who were content to push me away.

Many days, when my children's behaviors seemed out of control, I felt as if I was walking through darkness. Turning to Jesus through prayer changed everything. Jesus guided me to the right services and to the right people to offer advice. He gave me strength to follow suggested methods, and I felt His hand guiding me along the way. As Luke 3:5 (NIV) says, "Every valley shall be filled in, every mountain and hill made low. The crooked roads shall become straight, the rough ways smooth."

Jesus brought two children into our lives, and He guided me in getting them the help that they needed. As the months passed, the therapies did their work, and soon my children graduated from those services.

Whatever rough roads we face, Jesus is there. As we seek Him in prayer, He can direct our paths. Even when He calls us to hard places, we can step out in confidence knowing that He is by our side. —TRICIA GOYER

FAITH STEP: *Think of someone who is walking an unfamiliar path and share these verses with them. Write it on your calendar to regularly pray that every mountain she or he faces will be made low and the crooked roads will become straight.*

SATURDAY, OCTOBER 15

Greater love has no one than this, that he lay down his life for his friends.
John 15:13 *(NIV)*

IN 2014 *TIME* MAGAZINE'S person of the year was actually a group of people: the Ebola Fighters. It is worth noting that the accompanying article, "The Ebola Fighters: The Ones Who Answered the Call," lists many Christian individuals and organizations as the main responders to a crisis that world governments and health officials weren't prepared—or, in some cases, willing—to confront.

One of my friends, a retired doctor who now volunteers with Doctors Without Borders, told me how much he admired those on the front lines of the fight with Ebola. "I couldn't do it," he said. "There's just too much at stake. People are dying every day—there's no way to guarantee you won't get it. I admire them, but I just couldn't leave my kids and grand-baby like that."

I understand where my friend is coming from. Even though I feel compassion for the suffering, I could not knowingly go into a situation that posed a serious risk to my life either, out of the responsibility I feel to my family. And yet, what if no one answered the call?

Jesus understood what was at stake when He chose to go to the Cross. What if He had not been willing to put His life on the line? We would have been lost, without hope, without a Savior. But in His great love, He determined that our lives were more valuable than His, and He made the ultimate sacrifice. We're not all called to literally die, but we can follow His example by laying down anything He asks of us for the good of others.
—GWEN FORD FAULKENBERRY

FAITH STEP: *What does it mean to you to lay down your life? Make a list of ways you can lay down your life for others today.*

~~Dn~~ SUNDAY, OCTOBER 16

"Stretch out your hand. . . . " Luke 6:10 (CEB)

SOME OF THE MIRACLES JESUS PERFORMED created a spectacle. Blind men given sight. Lame men walking. A dead daughter raised to life. Lazarus called from the grave. Thousands fed with a boy's lunch.

Others might have seemed less spectacular to the crowds but no less meaningful to the person healed. We read one example in Luke 6—the story of the man with the withered hand. Most people might not have even recognized he had a problem. He could have hidden his hand in a pocket. But Jesus called him out. "Get up and stand in front of everyone" (Luke 6:8). He obeyed. (Great decision, buddy.)

Jesus used the opportunity to teach the legal experts and Pharisees an important lesson. Jesus didn't make eye contact with the man with the withered hand, but instead looked around at the doubters and nitpickers when he said to the man, "Stretch out your hand." The man obeyed. (Another great decision.) And his hand was made healthy and whole. Instantly.

I'm picturing the electricity in that room as Jesus healed the man's hand while locking gazes with those who had no idea what to do with this One Who spoke with such authority and healed when it wasn't convenient but because it was necessary. "Stretch out your hand." A simple instruction, simple obedience, simple healing. An unforgettable moment created by Jesus, Who always knows the right thing to do.

When a storm's on its way, and my hands stiffen, I will remember the moment when Jesus silenced the unbelievers and restored the believer's hand. —CYNTHIA RUCHTI

FAITH STEP: *Have you sensed Jesus asking you to stretch out your hand to Him, to reach out for what He's offering you? Imagine the story it will create when you do.*

MONDAY, OCTOBER 17

And the special gift of ministry you received when I laid hands on you and prayed—keep that ablaze! . . . 2 Timothy 1:6 (MSG)

LIKE MANY OF OUR NEIGHBORS in the North Woods, we heat with an outdoor wood boiler. Firewood is abundant, and you can get a permit to haul all the "dead and down" wood you want out of the National Forest for a small fee. Our heating system meets strict environmental standards, but it requires forethought, physical labor, and daily human presence to keep us cozy and warm during the cold months.

This winter I've found it is far easier to keep the boiler burning than to restart it. It *could* burn twenty-four to thirty-six hours, but instead of sitting inside, hoping for that, I go outside several times a day to clear the air paths and scrape the edge of the door to help it seal. I stir up the coals before they have a chance to turn to ash.

This fire-tending reminds me of my writing. When I sit down daily to write, the words flow. When I skip a day or two, I start to struggle. When chaos enters my life and writing takes a backseat, I falter. It takes determination, prayer, and the grace of God for me to get back on track.

Paul knew the importance of diligence. He told young Timothy not to neglect his gift (2 Timothy 1:6) and implored him to stir it up. *The Amplified Bible* reads, "(rekindle the embers of, fan the flame of, and keep burning) the [gracious] gift of God, [the inner fire] that is in you…"

We may not all have a fire to tend, but we all have spiritual gifts given by Jesus. Discover yours. Exercise it. Fan the flame.

—SUZANNE DAVENPORT TIETJEN

FAITH STEP: *When Jesus ascended, He gave gifts to His people. You're included. If you don't know your gift, pray. Ask Him to show you. Don't neglect it any longer. Stir it up.*

Anne TUESDAY, OCTOBER 18

A fool gives full vent to his spirit, but a wise man quietly holds it back.
Proverbs 29:11 (ESV)

"I HAVE TO LET THIS GO and let her be her."

"Yes, you do. So do I."

"Even if that means her room will be messier than I'd like."

"Yep."

That's the short version of the parenting growth my husband and I underwent yesterday.

Our daughter, Calianne, prefers her room messy. "It's cozier this way!"

Thinking myself wiser, I told her she was wrong; a messy room is hard to function in. "And, Cal, your room is so pretty underneath all this stuff."

She doesn't like to get rid of anything. Not a scrap of paper, not an old drawing, and, as I found out, definitely not her alphabet puppets she made last year. She hadn't mentioned them for months, but two days ago she wanted those old cardstock puppets...if only I hadn't thrown them away.

She was crushed. Big tears and anger. And so it went...my apologies, then telling her she needed to get rid of some things every now and then...her telling me I should have asked her first.

I think Jesus got through to me about what's more important. My daughter's messes are tools Jesus is using to help me let go and grow. You see, Calianne is a delightful spirit. She bounces through the house, scattering cheer and dreams everywhere she goes.

I need to hush my directives more often to delight in who she is. Sure, she has to learn to straighten up more often and toss something occasionally. But I need to minimize my "wisdom" and focus on the endless smiles she brings to the world. I'd be a fool to stifle her with my own imperfections. —ERIN KEELEY MARSHALL

FAITH STEP: *Ask Jesus to open your heart to something you need to let go of so you can grow. Memorize Proverbs 29:11.*

one

WEDNESDAY, OCTOBER 19

But, as it is written, "What no eye has seen, nor ear heard, nor the heart of man imagined, what God has prepared for those who love him." 1 Corinthians 2:9 (ESV)

IN THE WEEKS BEFORE my husband's autumn birthday, he mentioned that fall would be a good time to find a grill on sale at one of the local hardware stores. Thinking it would be a great birthday surprise, my daughter headed to the store and texted me pictures of various options. Together we decided on a big shiny model, which the store put in the back of the van for her.

Once she got it home, the two of us looked like a Laurel and Hardy movie as we muscled the heavy box onto a dolly, wobbled it down a hill at the side of the house, and squeezed it through the back door. Next we pulled bins and furniture out of the back basement room we use for storage, and worked to hide a box the size of a small house.

In the following weeks, we hoped my husband wouldn't start a project that necessitated digging for something in the storage room. There would be no way to hide the surprise if he looked too closely.

The night before his birthday, I signaled my daughter once my husband was asleep, and she hauled the box out and assembled the grill. The next morning I led him downstairs, and all of our efforts were rewarded when we heard his laughter at the sight of the huge grill assembled in the family room. Surprising him was a delight.

I hear a similar delight in Jesus's words throughout the Gospels. He is preparing something wonderful for each of us in the next life. We get hints in Scripture, but much is a surprise. But we can trust that the surprises are prepared with love and will bring us great joy. —SHARON HINCK

FAITH STEP: *Plan a small surprise for someone you love. Think about how Jesus is planning good things for you, as well.*

THURSDAY, OCTOBER 20

Let us be glad and rejoice, and let us give honor to him. For the time has come for the wedding feast of the Lamb, and his bride has prepared herself. Revelation 19:7 (NLT)

I LOVE WEDDINGS. The climax for me is that moment when everyone in the wedding party is in place except for the bride. There's this pause before the music swells and everyone turns toward the back, where double doors open for the bride to make her entrance.

Except for me.

I used to turn with everyone else, until one time I didn't—and saw instead the look on the bridegroom's face as he caught sight of his Love walking toward him. Now, I always look at the groom, and every time, I'm sure I've never seen anything more beautiful.

Photographers catch the bride from an abundance of angles, but many miss this fleeting moment. I tell my young marrying coworkers to request this shot. Whether or not it makes the album, the bride will never forget that expression on her groom's face.

Here's even more good news: those of us saved by grace will see Jesus look at each of us like that. With His perfect love.

You see, Jesus is crazy about us. Believe it.

I admit I have a hard time imagining this. I can somehow believe Jesus loves me enough to die for me. But to believe that He treasures me, loves me, and some days even likes me? That's hard.

I heard singer Andrew Peterson once say, "Your job is discovering more and more every day—maybe for eternity—how precious you are." I scribbled it down because it rings with truth.

Yes, Jesus loves us. Each of us. More than we can imagine.

We *are* precious in His sight. —SUZANNE DAVENPORT TIETJEN

FAITH STEP: *We can't understand God, but the Bible says we have the mind of Christ. Imagine Jesus looking at you with nothing but love in His eyes. Think of it as a rehearsal.*

FRIDAY, OCTOBER 21

"But many who are first will be last, and the last first." Mark 10:31 (ESV)

ONE DAY, I STOPPED AT my favorite fast-but-fairly-healthy-food place. As usual it was packed. Two women chatting on cell phones walked in ahead of me. I stood in the throng of people waiting to order until the young man behind the register looked at me and called, "I can help the next person." I turned around to look for the woman who had come in before me. She was still on the phone, with her back turned toward me. I gently touched her shoulder and pointed toward the counter.

She stepped forward but then told me to go ahead since her friend had walked away. After I ordered my chicken sandwich, the cashier said, "I'll be glad to take care of that for you today." The employees at this place normally say polite things like that, so it took me a couple of minutes to figure out that he planned to pay for my lunch. When I protested, he said quietly, "I just saw a good deed; now I can do one of my own."

I have to admit that I'm not always so scrupulous about letting other people go ahead of me. I've been known to quicken my step to get to a door or checkout counter first. But Jesus calls me to embrace a way of living that requires me to flip my thinking. To willingly take a backseat rather than seek the limelight.

We tend to focus on earthly status, popularity, and rank, but Jesus has a different perspective. In heaven some who are considered lowly on earth will be honored; some whom we consider great won't be there. What matters is putting myself last before God and other people—whether or not a free chicken sandwich is involved. —DIANNE NEAL MATTHEWS

FAITH STEP: *Today look for opportunities to put yourself last instead of first. Each time you do, thank Jesus for putting Himself last when He went to the Cross on your behalf.*

SATURDAY, OCTOBER 22

Life itself was in him [Jesus], and this life gives light to everyone. The light shines through the darkness, and the darkness can never extinguish it. John 1:4–5 (NLT)

LIGHT IS EASY TO TAKE for granted because it shows up every morning without our help and without our consciously thinking about it. Truth is, we need it desperately:

Light enables us to see. Without it, we're cast into pitch-black darkness.

Light sustains plant life. Without it, plants die. That means oxygen disappears. And if oxygen disappears, then other life dies too.

Light sustains earth's temperatures. Remove it, and our planet turns into a celestial ice sphere.

Physical light sustains physical life. The same principle holds true in the spiritual realm, so it's no wonder Jesus made this declaration: "I am the light of the world. If you follow me, you won't be stumbling through the darkness, because you will have the light that leads to life" (John 8:12).

By calling Himself "the light of the world," Jesus implied that He alone is the source and sustainer of spiritual life. Apart from Him, it cannot exist. In Him we find salvation, and in Him we are fulfilled.

Our society encourages us to look elsewhere for spiritual fulfillment, but everything it suggests is worthless. Even regular church attendance alone isn't enough to give spiritual life and health.

Knowing Jesus and pursuing a vital relationship with Him—the Light of the world—is what gives abundant life now and eternal life tomorrow. We dare not take Him for granted for we need Him desperately.
—GRACE FOX

FAITH STEP: *Buy a small plant and place it in a sealed paper bag or darkened place in your home for two weeks. Note the condition of its leaves when you retrieve it. Compare this to your spiritual life apart from regular time in the Light's presence.*

SUNDAY, OCTOBER 23

Wait and listen, everyone who is thirsty! Come to the waters; and he who has no money, come, buy and eat! Yes, come, buy [priceless, spiritual] wine and milk without money and without price [simply for the self-surrender that accepts the blessing]. Isaiah 55:1 (AMP)

I LIVE FIFTEEN MILES FROM the largest freshwater lake in the world. Lake Superior is breathtaking—in more ways than one, if you take into account its average temperature of forty degrees. It also may be the cleanest lake in the world.

A Copper Harbor captain told me a story about a young man who fell adrift on the lake when his personal watercraft malfunctioned. When rescuers pulled him out, severely dehydrated, days later, they asked why he didn't just drink the water. Surprised, he answered, "You never do that." He thought it was saltwater. He never tasted it.

Jesus invited everyone to drink from the waters of salvation, but they made a bigger mistake than that incurious fellow. Now a wanted man, Jesus showed up at the Temple in Jerusalem on the last day of the Feast of Tabernacles, when Israel celebrated God's giving water from the rock. The priests paraded seven times around the altar singing Psalm 118:25: "Save now, save now." Next, Isaiah 12:3 (MSG): "Joyfully you'll pull up buckets of water from the wells of salvation," while they carried water from the river under the Temple Mount to the altar, where they poured it out. Probably at that very moment, Jesus stood and cried, "If anyone thirsts, let him come to me and drink."

Some recognized Him as a prophet, some as the Messiah, and many as a threat. They took His meaning, but they didn't take Him up on His offer of salvation.

Will we? Will you? —SUZANNE DAVENPORT TIETJEN

FAITH STEP: *"If it sounds too good to be true, it probably is" doesn't apply to salvation. Jesus gave Himself freely. Tell Him you accept. He's so good. It's true.*

MONDAY, OCTOBER 24

I will remember the deeds of the Lord; yes, I will remember your wonders of old.
I will ponder all your work, and meditate on your mighty deeds.
Psalm 77:11–12 (ESV)

I MADE MY WAY DOWN the stairs to empty the dryer in the laundry room. When I reached the bottom of the stairs, I looked around, confused. Why had I come downstairs? My mind was blank.

It happens to all of us. We search for our glasses, forgetting they are on our head. We write a check and forget what year it is. We forget to return a phone call or pay a bill or send a birthday card.

I've found a way to prevent the problem of walking into a room and forgetting why I was heading that way. I recite to myself as I go. "Going downstairs to get the laundry. Getting the laundry. I'm here to get the laundry." That way the task doesn't have a chance to slip away from memory.

Jesus knows we are also prone to forgetting important things. We can slip away from the secure awareness of how much He loves us, that He died for us, that He continues to guide our steps, that He can meet our needs. The most important knowledge in the universe can get lost in the muddle of our brains as they are flooded with tidbits of information throughout the day.

The Psalms point us to a solution. When we deliberately remember, ponder, and meditate on the powerful and loving acts of Jesus, He stays at the forefront of our thoughts. —SHARON HINCK

FAITH STEP: *To help you remember, write a list of ways that Jesus has shown His love to you in the past year. Carry it in your pocket and look at it frequently today.*

one

TUESDAY, OCTOBER 25

Therefore if any person is [ingrafted] in Christ (the Messiah) he is a new creation (a new creature altogether); the old [previous moral and spiritual condition] has passed away. Behold, the fresh and new has come! 2 Corinthians 5:17 (AMP)

I HAD BEEN MARRIED almost twenty years when a particularly painful thing happened, causing me to question a lot of my ideals about marriage and family. Stone and I had to work hard to get through it, rebuilding trust, and reimagining our love story.

One day during this challenging time I came across a song by Gungor called "Beautiful Things." It's a song that expresses the work God does as He transforms us to be more like Jesus. It describes the process of new creation, that we—and sometimes the circumstances of our lives—may be dust, but He makes beautiful things from dust.

As I let those simple words soak down into my soul, something shifted for me. I realized that sometimes I hang on tightly to old things, wanting to hold them long after they are dust. I saw that when I do this I could be missing any beauty that might be found in the new thing God is doing. As I finally let go of the old, I began to look for new beauty and found hope in Jesus for the life and love that are to come as He makes me new. —GWEN FORD FAULKENBERRY

FAITH STEP: *What old thing do you need to let go of today? Write it down on a piece of paper and then shred it or burn it to symbolize your release of the past. Now set your eyes on the new thing God is doing through Jesus!*

WEDNESDAY, OCTOBER 26

Your attitude should be the same that Christ Jesus had. Though he was God, he did not demand and cling to his rights as God. Philippians 2:5–6 (NLT)

MY HUSBAND AND I TRAIN and lead short-term mission teams to Eastern Europe and Asia. During training, we address the topic of personal rights. This helps identify the things to which many folks subconsciously feel they're entitled: A comfortable mattress. Hot showers. Food that satisfies both tummy and taste buds. Private space. Good coffee.

We encourage our volunteers to ask Jesus to align their attitudes about personal rights with His before heading overseas to serve others. "Doing so will help you adapt to the new culture and promote positive team relationships," we say. They nod in agreement. And then reality hits.

The right to a comfy mattress isn't fulfilled. A morning shower runs cold. Food doesn't taste as delectable, private space becomes shared, and coffee isn't like it's brewed at home.

Some of the volunteers get frustrated. Thankfully, most realize that learning to yield personal rights is an important part of spiritual growth. It's also critical to effective service. Jesus modeled this beautifully.

Jesus, being fully God, could have demanded that others treat Him like royalty. He could have required leaders to address Him with respect. He could have owned a mansion filled with fine furnishings. And He could have expected others to worship Him everywhere He went.

But He did not. Rather, He opened His hands and released them. He placed our need for salvation above His personal rights, and it cost Him dearly. Do we love others enough to do the same? —GRACE FOX

FAITH STEP: *What three rights do you feel you deserve? How might these interfere with your serving others? Ask Jesus to align your attitude about rights with His so He can use your life for His highest purpose.*

THURSDAY, OCTOBER 27

For all the promises of God find their Yes in him. That is why it is through him that we utter our Amen to God for his glory. 2 Corinthians 1:20 (ESV)

I'VE WORKED IN NEONATAL INTENSIVE CARE at every level for almost three decades. The babies ask no questions, but the families all ask the very same one: "Is my baby going to be all right?"

We tell them the odds are in their favor (if they are) and what challenges the baby faces. We explain the disease process in language they can understand. We answer lots of specific questions, but not the biggest one. We can't say *yes* because we just don't know.

As you can guess, they don't like the lack of a promise. Many parents spend the first days in the NICU "taking a survey"—asking that question of every doctor, specialist, and each new nurse, trying to find someone who'll say what they want to hear. The team passes this along in its report to help us respond consistently and to gauge where the family is emotionally during this crisis.

Oh, how we love to hear *yes*. We've hated *no* since we were toddlers but as we mature we come to fear the awful uncertainty of the missing, hoped-for affirmative.

Would you like to hear *yes*? You have.

In Jesus, all the promises of God are certain.

Unlike the medical team, God doesn't hesitate to promise a positive outcome for anyone who trusts His beloved Son. He gave us our *yes*. His Spirit is our guarantee.

Our part is to shout a resounding "Amen—so be it!" for His glory.

Yes! —SUZANNE DAVENPORT TIETJEN

FAITH STEP: *Do you have unanswered questions? Write down the first two that come to mind, maybe on index cards. Take them to Jesus in prayer. Let Him keep them for you.*

FRIDAY, OCTOBER 28

I remind you to fan into flame the gift of God. . . . 2 Timothy 1:6 (ESV)

THERE IS NOTHING BETTER in late fall than a crackling fire in the woodstove. I love to curl up in a chair near it with a good book or snuggle my family close while we gaze at the dancing flames. Its light mesmerizes me.

Midway through this morning I hear the woodstove's fan kicking in every couple of minutes as it tries to make the most of the fading heat. I take a break from my work to stoke the embers and add wood. Within minutes new flames lick at the bark, and, soon after that, the fire climbs and curls inside the firebox.

I head back to my office, and when the fan is satisfied I hear it shut off. The house settles back into the warmth, and I think about 2 Timothy 1:6: how we are to approach our faith in Jesus with similar care.

Faith in God is a gift from Him, possible through Jesus's life and death. But we play a role in its growth. If we don't nurture our relationship with Jesus, its intensity eventually peters out.

However, when we feed it, it not only warms us from the inside; it spreads that warmth to everyone we are near. When we spend time each day feeding the fire of faith by reading God's Word and talking with Jesus, He does the supernatural work of stoking the flames.

When we ask Him to light the fire in us, Jesus can take the smallest spark of faith and set it ablaze. When we continue going to Him daily, we do our part to keep that fire burning in our hearts to warm the lives of a world in need of His light. —ERIN KEELEY MARSHALL

FAITH STEP: *Read 2 Timothy 1 and ask Jesus to put it on your heart each day to care for the gift of faith He gives you.*

one SATURDAY, OCTOBER 29

The Lord is not slow in keeping his promise, as some understand slowness.
Instead he is patient with you, not wanting anyone to perish,
but everyone to come to repentance. 2 Peter 3:9 (NIV)

MY DAUGHTER IS A MISSIONARY in the Czech Republic. She's been there two years, and she lives in a city where less than 1 percent of all people consider themselves Christian. People depend on their own efforts and hard work instead of turning their trust to an unseen Jesus.

I've been to the Czech Republic numerous times on short-term mission trips. As I walk the streets, I can't help but look around and realize it's possible everyone within my view needs to know about Jesus: the older woman with the scarves and cane, the business professional in his suit, the teenagers with their skinny jeans and dyed hair.

I also consider my own prayer at times: "Come back soon, Lord Jesus." Seeing the pain, heartache, and evil in this world makes the idea of Jesus ushering in a new heaven and a new earth that much more appealing. But I must wait patiently for the kingdom to come. It's in the waiting that more men, women, and children will be drawn to repentance.

Isaiah 30:18 (NIV) says, "Yet the Lord longs to be gracious to you; therefore he will rise up to show you compassion. For the Lord is a God of justice. Blessed are all who wait for him!"

Jesus shows us compassion as we wait for His return, and because of our waiting, others have time to hear about the salvation that comes through Jesus alone. And as God directs, it's our job to minister to those still needing to hear that good news. Waiting is never easy, but in the case of lost souls, it is gracious indeed. —TRICIA GOYER

FAITH STEP: *Choose an atheistic country and begin to pray for the hearts of the people there. Also pray for the missionaries who serve in that country. Finally, pray for yourself and peace as you wait for the Lord's return.*

SUNDAY, OCTOBER 30

It was there at Antioch that the believers were first called Christians.
Acts 11:26 (NLT)

WHEN A WOMAN MARRIES and adopts her husband's last name, it can make for interesting combinations. Like my friend who became Annette Almen Fudge. When I recently met one of my new neighbors, she told me her name sounded like an Italian dessert: Renella DeLoney.

Believers in Jesus were given a new name in Antioch of Syria. This is significant because it demonstrates that believers were now recognized as a distinct group. They were developing their own identity apart from other Jews. Scholars theorize that pagan citizens came up with the label out of scorn and derision, combining the Latin suffix that means "belonging to the party of" and "Christ." Beginning in the second century, believers accepted the term as a badge of honor.

In our culture, "Christian" is sometimes used as a contemptuous label; other times it's tossed around in meaningless ways, applied to someone simply because they believe in some vague idea of "a higher power." When we choose to follow Jesus, we take on His name, signifying that we identify with Him. We trust Him to guide, protect, and sustain us. Jesus is the foundation of our life and shapes our thoughts, decisions, and behavior.

Being a Christian doesn't mean we belong "to the party of" Jesus; we actually belong to *Him*. He has forgiven all our sins—past, present, and future. He daily lavishes us with His grace, mercy, and unconditional love. Regardless of how others use the term, being called a Christian is a privilege and a badge of honor, and something that should set us apart from the rest of our society. —DIANNE NEAL MATTHEWS

FAITH STEP: *Examine your way of living to see how it demonstrates that you have taken on the identity of Jesus. Think of a way you can wear that badge of honor more proudly.*

Ame MONDAY, OCTOBER 31

_"Take care that your hearts aren't dulled by . . . the anxieties of
day-to-day life. . . . " Luke 21:34 (CEB)_

"TAKE CARE NOW." It's a phrase often concluding a phone conversation or
personal interaction in the region where I live. A good parting thought.
Positive. Caring. Even if it is almost automatic.

I hadn't known until recently that the concept appears in the Bible in at
least one of the conversations Jesus had with the people He taught.

In the Luke 21 passage, He expressly pointed out that even though
heaven and earth will eventually pass away, His Word would certainly not
pass away. Immediately following that prediction, He cautioned those
listening to take care: "Take care that your hearts aren't dulled by [among
other things] . . . the anxieties of day-to-day life." Later in that passage He
couples the teaching with, "Stay alert at all times" (Luke 21:36).

Had you considered how anxieties of day-to-day living can _dull_ us?

When my sister and her husband moved in with us for a short time,
we shared kitchen duties. My sister pulled out a knife and attempted to
cut carrots for the stew. Three days later, she walked into the house with
a brand-new set of knives. "How have you been working with those old
ones? They're not only dull, they're beyond sharpening anymore," she said.

I had to be extracareful the first few times I used the higher quality
knives. I wasn't used to sharp. I'd been using the duller knives, unaware
how bad they'd gotten compared to what they should have been.

Are you taking care to stay sharp spiritually? Or have the worries of life
dulled that edge? —CYNTHIA RUCHTI

FAITH STEP: _Which activities work best to keep you spiritually sharp when the cares of
life threaten to dull your edge? Bible reading? A retreat? A walk in which you talk with
Jesus? Determine not to neglect the activities that keep your heart from becoming dulled._

TUESDAY, NOVEMBER 1

"Who among you by worrying can add a single moment to your life?"
Matthew 6:27 (CEB)

I LIVE TWENTY MILES FROM the nearest fitness center. I work fourteen feet from the nearest soup can. Unrelated? Not at all.

Fitness experts tell me I don't need a gym or fancy weights for strength training. I can sculpt my arm muscles by lifting soup cans, holding them extended out to the sides.

Easy for the first few seconds. A soup can doesn't weigh much. After a minute, shoulders, muscles, biceps, triceps start to ache. Same weight, held longer. After ten minutes of holding the soup cans out at arms' length, I'll need to set down the cans. The weight of the cans hasn't increased. An interesting principle of physics. It's not the weight, as others have observed. It's how long we carry the weight that has the greatest effect.

Like worry. It taxes the body and mind little in the initial seconds of carrying it. When we try to manage worry for a longer stretch of time, it causes pain and can eventually cripple us. Jesus spent time instructing people about the negative effects of worry and the absolute lack of need for it. He not only said "don't worry" twice (Matthew 6:25, 31), "stop worrying" (Matthew 6:34), and "why do you worry?" (Matthew 6:28), He also said that memorable but often forgotten line: "Who among you by worrying can add a single moment to your life?" (Matthew 6:27).

Later today, when I exercise with two unopened cans of butternut squash soup, I'm going to take special note of their relationship to worry. And set them down —CYNTHIA RUCHTI

FAITH STEP: *If you're prone to worry, read the encouraging words Jesus spoke, recorded in Matthew 6:25–34. Wrap a soup can in paper printed with the word* **worry.** *Carry it in your nondominant hand all morning. Feel any different about the need to set aside worry?*

one WEDNESDAY, NOVEMBER 2

There is more than enough room in my Father's home. If this were not so, would I have told you that I am going to prepare a place for you. John 14:2 (NLT)

THE WORDS *HOME SWEET HOME* assumed new meaning for me after my husband and I began traveling internationally for ministry purposes. Don't get me wrong—we love God's call on our lives and feel fulfilled, but weeks of eating unfamiliar foods, striving to understand other languages, driving in sometimes dangerous conditions, and sleeping in different beds leaves us longing for the familiar.

That desire is met the moment we set foot in our own house again. The sense of sanctuary and belonging is tangible. We're *home*. Within these walls is our personalized place to retreat, rest, and be refreshed.

A popular contemporary worship song encourages us to imagine what heaven will be like. Our finite minds can never comprehend its beauty, but one thing we know for sure: Because Jesus is preparing it, it's going to be very, very good. And someday, when our journey in this foreign land is complete, we'll take up residence in our heavenly home.

Within those divinely constructed walls we'll find rest. The stress of living in a culture that encourages us to live life contrary to Jesus's teachings will be forever over. The physical challenges we face as sojourners on earth will be forgotten. The emotional pain we endure will be a thing of the past. A sense of sanctuary and belonging will flood us. We'll be *home*. This promised certainty ought to fill us with hope no matter what life brings our way in the temporary here and now. —GRACE FOX

FAITH STEP: *Write the words* Home Sweet Home *on a piece of paper. Now list five ways in which you can make your earthly home feel like a piece of heaven on earth for those who live or visit there.*

THURSDAY, NOVEMBER 3

"At that time the kingdom of heaven will be like ten virgins who took their lamps and went out to meet the bridegroom. Five of them were foolish and five were wise. The foolish ones took their lamps but did not take any oil with them. The wise ones, however, took oil in jars along with their lamps." Matthew 25:1–4 (NIV)

WHEN MY CHILDREN WERE YOUNG, their wardrobe choices baffled me. On a bitter cold fall day, they'd head for the door sans jacket, hat, or scarf—wearing shorts and flip-flops.

"Wait just a minute. You need real shoes. What if the bus breaks down and you have to walk somewhere? And you're just getting over an ear infection. Wear a hat."

As a mom, I'd developed the instinct to think ahead. From the first days of packing a diaper bag with everything we might possibly need on an outing, to the school days of checking if their homework was in their backpack, to the settling in to a college dorm, I tried to think of every eventuality.

Yet each morning as I venture into a new day of serving Jesus's kingdom, I'm often like my children on a cold morning, dashing out the door unprepared, or like the unwise virgins who set out without oil in their lamps.

How can we better prepare? We can recommit our lives to Jesus before our feet hit the floor. We can ask His protection over our hearts because we know the enemy of our souls will send temptations. We can seek His guidance as we plan our schedule. We can let Him fuel our spirits with praise. —SHARON HINCK

FAITH STEP: *Do you remember this old song? Sing it with me: "Give me oil in my lamp, keep me burning. Give me oil in my lamp I pray. Give me oil in my lamp, keep me burning, burning, burning. Keep me burning 'til the break of day."*

FRIDAY, NOVEMBER 4

"Arise, shine, for your light has come, and the glory of the Lord rises upon you."
Isaiah 60:1 (NIV)

WE JUST HAD A FREEZE this past weekend, which is a rarity in California. The impatiens I planted last year were not appreciative. They dropped all their leaves and flowers in protest. They are looking very sad and very skinny at the moment. The rosebush in the backyard that normally boasts full apricot and yellow blooms is merely twigs and thorns. The Japanese maples stand in stark relief against the gray sky. The lawn is a mottled series of brown patches. This is winter. I wonder if people say the phrase "in the dead of winter" because everything actually looks dead.

But the thing is, even though I can't tell it is happening, the sun is at work. Even though the sky is dark and dreary, its rays are penetrating the earth, getting ready for what is just around the corner. Even though the ground looks barren, new growth is coming. In a matter of weeks, everything in my yard will be green and blooming. Sometimes life feels like winter. Cold. Brown. Dead. It is hard to imagine anything new or beautiful coming out of something that seems so desolate.

But the Light of the World is still at work.

Even when we can't see Jesus or feel Him. I love the thought that up from the dreariness of winter springs new life. And up from the dead places in our hearts can spring something new and beautiful when we invite Jesus into them. He is the Life-Giver. He is the One Who conquered death both physically and spiritually. Death is not death to Him. And everything He touches is restored to what it should be. And that is the beginning of hope. —SUSANNA FOTH AUGHTMON

FAITH STEP: *Take a walk outside. Notice the plants, trees, and flowers, whether they are dying or flourishing. Remind yourself that Jesus brings light and life to all that He touches, including you.*

SATURDAY, NOVEMBER 5

Love from the center of who you are; don't fake it. Run for dear life from evil;
hold on for dear life to good. Be good friends who love deeply;
practice playing second fiddle. Romans 12:9–10 (MSG)

ON WINTER SATURDAY NIGHTS in the frozen Upper Peninsula of Michigan, people gather at The Falling Rock Cafe for an eclectic schedule of concerts. The staff lines up a bunch of mismatched dining, easy, and rocking chairs in rows facing a spotlighted area that serves as a stage.

We who live year-round in this small northern town hold on to each other for support. It's cold here, and there's lots of snow. Many live alone in isolated cabins with no one to talk to. We look forward to Saturdays when the owners give out hugs and shake hands before we all settle down to hear something beautiful together.

Tonight it was a string quartet, four lovely women making equally lovely music. Since I was in the first row, I enjoyed watching their fingers and the way their bodies danced as they played. Their eyes flitted to the first violin player at crucial moments, when they took their cues and timed their rests in the absence of a conductor. During the last piece, I watched the second violinist. She sat back from the other three and slightly behind the first violinist, who, except for when her eyes closed briefly, was her constant focus.

The community, the quartet, and particularly the second violinist tonight were a beautiful metaphor for the church. These humble people love from the center of who they are. They, for the most part, hold on to what is good. This is what the body of Christ looks like. May none of us be afraid to play second fiddle. —SUZANNE DAVENPORT TIETJEN

FAITH STEP: *Our culture says to strive to be noticed. Jesus said not to let our left hand know what our right hand's doing when we perform a kindness. Support someone quietly today. Let someone else shine.*

SUNDAY, NOVEMBER 6

Draw near to God, and he will draw near to you.... James 4:8 (ESV)

MANY PEOPLE CRITICIZE GOD for seeming distant and aloof. But He proved He is anything but those things when He sent His Son to earth with His hope of salvation.

I was reminded of this fact several weeks ago in church, when the teaching pastor quoted James 4:8. The verse is one I've heard countless times and could repeat verbatim. But that evening Jesus revealed something fresh and new about it.

Our Savior promises to draw near to us when we draw near to Him.

What other religion offers that kind of intimacy? The Savior of humankind, the eternal and Holy One, invites us to draw near to Him because He longs for us to experience all that it means to know Him well, to be in His care. *And He will draw near to us.*

Have you ever tried to give someone a hug, but the person pulled away? Maybe it was a child exercising his independence or impatience to get back to play. Maybe it was a friend who couldn't handle feeling vulnerable and wanted to put up a strong front even though you knew he or she really felt like crumbling. Or possibly it was someone who never had known the security of being loved, and withdrew to guard herself.

What a relief that we can trust God to come close to us—and what an equally great reassurance that He never pulls back when we approach Him. God is a mystery, but He wants to reveal Himself to us. That's why He sent Jesus to show us how real He is and how much we need Him.

The lingering mystery is why so many people keep fighting against drawing near to Him. —ERIN KEELEY MARSHALL

FAITH STEP: *Draw near to Jesus today, and thank Him for not being aloof toward you. Ask Him to reveal His mysteries to you.*

MONDAY, NOVEMBER 7

"You are My friends if you do what I command you." John 15:14 (HSC)

MY SON IS TWELVE. I can't believe I just wrote that sentence. He should be a baby in my arms, or a toddler, or even just starting school. But not twelve. Twelve is entirely too old. With twelve comes things like girls. Puberty. Sleepovers with friends. Increased independence in just about every area of life.

Harper, like my girls, is the apple of my eye. I am constantly trying to connect with him, keep him close, teach him, give him the space he needs. It's a tricky balance sometimes! The other day I picked him up from a school activity, and it was just him and me in the car. I asked him all sorts of questions to which he replied, "Yes." "No." "Good." "Fine." One-word answers—that's all I was getting. Later, however, when it was time for bed, it seemed he wanted to talk. So even though the timing wasn't the best, I lay down on his bed and listened. No way was I missing my chance to hear his stories.

One of the things he told me was about an experience he'd had with a group of friends during a recent sleepover. They'd gone out in the woods and found a raccoon in a trap. While some of the boys poked at it with a stick, one of the friends told them to stop. He said he wanted to leave before it made him cry. "I was so impressed by that, Mom," Harper said. "He didn't care what anybody else thought. He knew it was wrong and he spoke up. It helped me to do the right thing."

I told him, "There are times you will have to stand alone, and I want you to be able to do that. Jesus is always with you." He nodded. "But it is a wonderful thing to find another person who will stand with you. That kind of friend gives us strength and helps us do what's right no matter what everyone else is doing." —GWEN FORD FAULKENBERRY

FAITH STEP: *Who needs your encouragement today? Let someone see you are a friend of Jesus because you do what He says, no matter what others are doing.*

TUESDAY, NOVEMBER 8

"Whoever is not with me is against me. Whoever does not work with me is working against me." Matthew 12:30 (NCV)

I RECENTLY VOTED FOR the first time since moving to a new state—and had a major embarrassing moment. Before I admit the stupid thing I did, let me make excuses. I'm used to electronic machines that require a mere punch of a stylus. At the church my current voting precinct uses, people use paper ballots and ink pens. Let me add that, at the time, I was writing devotions for this book, hoping to get ten done each week before leaving town for a month.

Sitting down, I began to color in boxes. Then I started thinking about how I'd only finished nine devotions the week before. And since I'd gone to Bible study that morning, I'd only written one. That put me two behind already…Suddenly, I noticed that I had colored in the boxes for both the Republican and the Democratic candidates for governor. I sheepishly asked for help. When someone came over to see how I had "spoiled" my ballot, I nervously joked, "I guess I was undecided."

If we're going to vote in an election, we can't be neutral. We have to choose which candidate we want to support. In life, we can't be neutral about Jesus. We have to make the choice whether or not we will believe Him, follow Him, trust Him with our life. Some people try to cop out and acknowledge Jesus only as a good man or a wise teacher. But that is not really an option.

Jesus said that if we haven't chosen to follow Him, then we've made the choice to oppose Him. If we haven't accepted the gift of salvation He made possible, then we've rejected Him. When it comes to Jesus, there is no middle ground. —DIANNE NEAL MATTHEWS

FAITH STEP: *Have you made the choice to follow Jesus? List a few ways your life demonstrates that you are on His side.*

WEDNESDAY, NOVEMBER 9

Again, the devil took him to a very high mountain and showed him all the kingdoms of the world and their glory. And he said to him, "All these I will give you, if you will fall down and worship me." Then Jesus said to him, "Be gone, Satan! For it is written, "'You shall worship the Lord your God and him only shall you serve.'"
Matthew 4:8–10 (ESV)

ON AN ICY WINTER NIGHT, I made my way up the imposing stairs of a college's library. Writing students and professors had gathered to share their work and hear from a local author—me. A beautiful young woman with dreadlocks and a hip style read her edgy, profound poetry.

I sank lower in my chair, feeling irrelevant. What could I possibly offer this savvy and talented group? When it was my turn, I shared about the adventure of following Jesus and working in the arts; then I invited questions. A young man asked, "What do you do on a day when you feel discouraged about the work?"

"You mean every day?" We laughed together while I formed an answer. "I try to focus on writing for the audience of One. When we find joy in creating for Jesus, then the process is worth the struggle, regardless of the human measures of success." The words spoke to my own insecurities. I wasn't here to impress but to serve—imperfectly, uncomfortably, while full of doubts, but all in a desire to be available for Jesus.

Artist, executive, parent, nurse, whatever our day-to-day work, we can all fall prey to focusing on "the kingdoms of this world." We ache under the weight of goals unachieved. But when we follow Jesus's example and serve only the Lord our God, He enables that service to encourage others.
—SHARON HINCK

FAITH STEP: *Prepare your own answer to the question, "What do you do on a day when you feel discouraged about your work?"*

THURSDAY, NOVEMBER 10

Remember, your Father knows exactly what you need even before you ask Him!
Matthew 6:8 (TLB)

WHEN HARPER WAS LITTLE, he had some bad bouts with asthma. We were referred to a pediatric pulmonologist who figured out what Harper needed and helped us immensely. With regular visits, we developed a sweet relationship with the doctor, learning from him about his homeland of Syria, and sharing our wild-wilderness-living stories with him.

On our most recent visit, we were assigned to the room nearest his office. I saw him at his desk as we passed the door. When he came in, he asked, "Which one of you is coughing?"

I raised my hand and smiled.

"You need a Z-pack," he said. "I hear bronchitis." He proceeded to write me a prescription, though I am not his patient.

After that appointment, he released Harper, joking that we wouldn't need to come back for at least forty years. We were happy, but sad to realize we probably wouldn't see our dear doctor again, as he's close to retirement. We hugged him good-bye, and I thanked him for the prescription.

On the way home, Harper and I talked about how you can find kindred spirits in all sorts of places. We were both touched by how the doctor reached out and took care of me, even though I never asked him for anything. He was just listening when I coughed.

In the above verse, Jesus reveals the Father's character to be like that. Before He gives instructions on what we call the Lord's Prayer, He lets us know that it's not what we say that really counts. It's more about Who's listening. He knows what we need, and stands ready to give it.

—GWEN FORD FAULKENBERRY

FAITH STEP: *Look up the Lord's Prayer in Matthew 6. What else does Jesus reveal to you about the Father's character in this teaching on prayer?*

FRIDAY, NOVEMBER 11

He said to me, "My grace is sufficient for you, for my power is made perfect in weakness." Therefore I will boast all the more gladly about my weaknesses, so that Christ's power may rest on me. 2 Corinthians 12:9 (NIV)

AFTER I DROPPED OFF the kids at school and straightened the kitchen, I took a deep breath and sat down to write. Normally I love the blank 8:00 AM screen, all glowy and rich with potential, but this time I just stared at it. That particular writing assignment was proving to be elusive.

The cursor blinked at me, waiting. I tried a few lines, crossed out half of them. My writing voice felt wrong; emotion wrapped the words like vines, flowery and sappy.

I couldn't work the words, so I stared at the cursor for another second before checking Facebook and Twitter. How about the day's headlines? Yep, the world was moving along. The clock said I had three hours until lunch.

Jesus, help me. Make something of this because I can't. It's up to You.

I'm glad the Lord already knows where I lack and need Him. But do you know what? I'm realizing that this perspective is too narrow, misguided even. There's so much more to His strength than just filling in for our weaknesses.

Jesus often places us where He knows we'll fail without completely surrendering to His lordship. I will fail to convey anything Kingdom-worthy without acknowledging to God that I'm empty but for Him. He isn't showing up to fill in my gaps. His presence and power are everything.

He doesn't join my work; I join His. His strength sees it to completion, not my flagging confidence and scrambled attempts to write from my own resources.

When I realized this, I was ready to write. —ERIN KEELEY MARSHALL

FAITH STEP: *Consider a challenge you're facing. Ask Jesus to show you that He holds the power to work through you.*

SATURDAY, NOVEMBER 12

No one has ever seen God; but if we love one another, God lives in us and his love is made complete in us. 1 John 4:12 (NIV)

I WAS THANKFUL I'd worn rubber boots as I walked down the muddy path in the Kibera slums in Nairobi, Kenya. The sludge was human waste mixed with garbage. I was in Kibera with AWANA International—a child discipleship organization—to learn about how they share the good news of Jesus in some of the most poverty-stricken places on earth. We walked for ten minutes, and then we approached a building made of sticks and mud. As we approached, the voices of children greeted our group. The songs filled me with joy, and I forgot the filth around me.

We stepped inside the mud building and saw two hundred children inside a crowded room. They stood in front of handmade benches, the younger children in front and the older children in back. They sang praise songs to Jesus, and then they quoted Scripture. In that moment I realized there was no place on earth I'd rather be.

The Kibera Fruitful Orphanage sat in the middle of filth and garbage, but the love of Christ was as strong as I'd ever felt. I felt the love of the volunteers who care for the children. I felt the love of the children themselves. These children weren't focused on what they didn't have, but instead they lifted their faces in thankfulness for what they did have: the love of Jesus.

Seeing the children's faces radiating joy showed me firsthand how Jesus's love is made complete in us—no matter who we are or where we are. It's not what we have that matters most, but Who we have in us. —TRICIA GOYER

FAITH STEP: *Find a local organization that serves orphans or children and then find a way to help. Your time, money, and talents can go a long way toward showing the love of Jesus to a child.*

SUNDAY, NOVEMBER 13

Restore to me the joy of your salvation, and make me willing to obey you.
Psalm 51:12 (*NLT*)

MY SPIRITUAL LIFE FELT AS cold and barren as the weather outside. As the numbers on the thermometer plunged into the negatives, so did my attitude. *Pray? Sorry, I don't have time. Read the Word? It's too dry.*

As I gazed out the living room window and watched the blowing snow bury my flower bed, I heard the Holy Spirit whisper for the umpteenth time, *Talk to Karen.* I wanted to resist, but I knew obedience was not optional.

I regarded Karen as a good friend, but a misunderstanding had driven a wedge between us several weeks earlier. Pride stopped me from taking the first step toward reconciliation, and that stubborn pride had chilled my relationship with Jesus. The warmth of my friendship with Him could not be rekindled until I did what I knew to be right.

Even as I picked up the phone to call Karen, part of me wished she'd call me first and admit her fault. Again, the Holy Spirit convicted me, this time with only one word: *humility.* Again, I knew obedience was not optional.

"Jesus, forgive me for my attitude," I prayed. "Thank You for Your example of obedience even though it was difficult. Change my heart and make me willing to obey You in this matter."

And He answered.

My relationship with Karen was restored and, thanks to Jesus helping me to obey, my relationship with Him revived and flourished again.

I now pray this prayer routinely, especially when faced with situations that call for obedience in the midst of pride: "Jesus, make me willing to obey Your commands to humble myself, trust, and not be afraid."

—GRACE FOX

FAITH STEP: *What in your life requires obedience to Jesus? Ask Him to make you willing to obey and thank Him in advance for what He's about to do.*

MONDAY, NOVEMBER 14

To them God has chosen to make known among the Gentiles the glorious riches of this mystery, which is Christ in you, the hope of glory. Colossians 1:27 (NIV)

WE WERE SITTING AT the breakfast table this morning when my middle son, Will, said, "Mom, I can't tell if my basketball coach is a Christian or not."

"What makes you think he might be a Christian?" I asked.

"He told us everyone makes mistakes, even God, and this is His world."

"Well, that's not quite right. God doesn't make mistakes but does give us free choice so that we can make mistakes. This is the thing, Will. You are going to meet all different kinds of people in life who believe all different kinds of things. It isn't your job to judge them..."

At this my oldest son, Jack, jumped in with his two cents' worth: "Ya! Will, it is your job to tell them how wrong they are!"

"No." The boys were laughing. "It is your job to let Jesus's love shine through you. That is when people will start asking you, 'Why are you different?' People will be attracted to Jesus because of what is inside of you."

To which Will said, "Because I am full of cookies!" Which sent the boys into another round of laughter.

Sometimes my teachable moments turn into comic free-for-alls around the table. But even though my children may not have been listening to me, what I said was true. It is Jesus in us that is attractive to those around us. Why are we loving? Why are we kind? Why are we forgiving and compassionate? It is not because we are good. It is simply because we have invited Jesus to shine His glory through us. When we do that, we give hope to everyone we come in contact with. —SUSANNA FOTH AUGHTMON

FAITH STEP: *Remind yourself as you meet people throughout your day that Jesus residing in you offers them hope.*

TUESDAY, NOVEMBER 15

Don't be concerned only about your own interests, but also be concerned about the interests of others. Have the same attitude that Christ Jesus had.
Philippians 2:4–5 (GW)

LAST WEEK I WATCHED a man unloading groceries. Even though he was parked right next to a shopping-cart corral, he rolled his empty cart to the *other* side of his truck and left it on the edge of his parking space. By midday, many stores have carts scattered all over the parking lot, some of them only a few steps away from the designated corral. It bugs me to no end.

Failing to put carts away creates extra work for the store's employees and makes it hard for other customers to park. Once, on a windy day, I saw a cart roll several feet and bump a parked car. I've joked that this unwillingness to walk a few steps to put away a cart is tied to our nation's obesity epidemic. But I think it's actually a symptom of something else.

Although we're capable of altruistic behavior, sin has marred our human nature. Selfishness comes naturally to us; we're wired to think of ourselves first. But as believers, we're called to have just as much concern for the needs of others as we have for our own personal interests. To look out for others and guard their welfare instead of "looking out for number one."

I may be smug about something so minor as taking a few extra steps to put my cart away, but I can come up with a list of ways that I fall short in the Loving-Your-Neighbor-as-Yourself category. That's why I need to continually remind myself how Jesus put my interests ahead of His own, all the way to the Cross. —DIANNE NEAL MATTHEWS

FAITH STEP: *Think ahead to your day's activities and decide how you will deliberately seek to put others before yourself. If it involves a difficult sacrifice, ask Jesus to help you to have the right attitude.*

WEDNESDAY, NOVEMBER 16

While he was still confined to the prison quarters,
the Lord's word came. . . . Jeremiah 33:1 (CEB)

OVER THE PAST SEVERAL YEARS, I've learned more than I ever wanted to know about prison, some of it research for writing projects, some of it because of people who have come across my path who have spent time or are now spending time behind bars. I've listened to the stories of prisoners' families—some whose relationships have fallen apart because of the incarceration, they say, and others whose relationships are growing, deepening, despite the distance.

How is it possible that men and women could have more than a "come to Jesus" moment in prison but a true spiritual awakening, developing a genuine faith in Jesus?

It happened with Joseph in Potiphar's prison, with Jeremiah, Paul, Silas...

This supposedly simple introduction to one of my favorite verses of Scripture moved me: "While he was still confined to the prison quarters, the Lord's word came...." What word? Jeremiah 33:3 explains what it was: "Call to me and I will answer and reveal to you wondrous secrets that you haven't known." While still in prison.

Those who assume we can only "hear" from Jesus when conditions are perfect, perhaps in church or at a weekend retreat, can take courage from that soul-satisfying introduction. While we still feel imprisoned by our circumstances, our work situation, health concerns...Jesus speaks.

In the New Testament, He made it very clear that the imprisoned are not to be abandoned (Matthew 25:36–45). Maybe one of the reasons is that, for some, it's a place where they can powerfully connect with Him despite their surroundings. Bars and razor wire are not barriers to Him.
—CYNTHIA RUCHTI

FAITH STEP: *How do you reach out to the imprisoned or their families? Is there another layer of ministry in which you can get involved? Sending books for prison libraries? Supporting children of the incarcerated? Ask Jesus to lay an idea on your heart. It matters.*

THURSDAY, NOVEMBER 17

*All of us! Nothing between us and God, our faces shining with the
brightness of his face. And so we are transfigured much like the Messiah,
our lives gradually becoming brighter and more beautiful as God enters our lives
and we become like him.* 2 Corinthians 3:18 (MSG)

THIS MORNING I SPENT more time than usual watching the fire in my little
woodstove. I love to watch fires. I didn't have enough kindling so it took a little longer to get it started. Burning paper helped the cold chimney draw, and
fat-lighter wood eased the transition to the smallest available pieces of wood.

The fire caught with, first, a hiss and a wisp of smoke, and then finally
a flicker of flame. It took more tending than usual so I spent some of that
time on my belly, feet up behind me, my head on my hands like a kid.

Finally hot, the logs at the bottom maintained their form but gradually
changed color. They abandoned their browns and began to glow, undu-
lating orange. The color rippled like northern lights, occasionally allowing a glimpse of red or yellow.

Fine gray ash coated the logs, but the light shone through. Each finally
reached a point where it wasn't what it had been before. The log-shapes
had become nearly weightless containers for heat and light. When I put
dry, cold wood near them, the heat set the new pieces ablaze.

When I was finally forced to make room for more wood, I hated to
reach for the poker. The oldest of the coals dissolved into ash with the
slightest touch, while newer ones broke into pieces, still carrying their
treasure, ready to pass it on.

We transition too. Because Christ is in us, we can't stay the same. Daily,
with our assent, we are changed into His likeness.

—SUZANNE DAVENPORT TIETJEN

FAITH STEP: *Old paintings of Jesus sometimes show His burning heart. See your heart
aflame like His. Let Him change you.*

FRIDAY, NOVEMBER 18

Whatever you do, do it from the heart for the Lord and not for people.
Colossians 3:23 (CEB)

MY DAUGHTER GRACE is in the eighth grade. A great student, excellent musician, and all-around wonderful kid, she experiences a lot of success in her life. But her greatest challenge right now is basketball.

Grace matured early. So when she played little-kid basketball, she was the tallest one on the team. The main strategy was to dribble down and throw the ball to Grace, who, towering over everyone else, would usually shoot and make points. This was a good gig, and she had lots of fun. Then along came school basketball, about the same time the rest of the girls caught up with her in height, and it became less fun. Suddenly, she started competing with people taller and bigger for a position and spending quite a bit of time on the bench. This is her second year of that.

After implementing her own practice schedule at home, in addition to daily practice at school, she still comes home many days in tears. "Does the coach notice how hard I'm working?" "Why won't he give me a chance?" The questions I have no answers for go on and on, leading us both to near despair.

Finally Grace and I had an epiphany with the above verse. When we do what we do, be it work, practice, cooking, cleaning, writing, whatever, for the approval of other people, we put ourselves at their mercy. If they are happy with us we are happy, but if they seem unappreciative, it can break our hearts. Not so with Jesus. We can offer whatever we do, giving our best for Him, and He receives it as something special. We can trust He loves us, values our efforts, and is always pleased with us. This is freedom!
—GWEN FORD FAULKENBERRY

FAITH STEP: *Pray this prayer with me: Jesus, whatever I do today, (FILL IN THE BLANK), I do in Your name, with all of my heart, not for another's approval. Receive it as a love offering to use (or not use) as You will.*

SATURDAY, NOVEMBER 19

Endurance produces character, and character produces hope.
Romans 5:4 (ESV)

IT WAS STILL EARLY when I pulled on my snow pants, boots, hat, gloves, and coat and headed to the side yard to help my husband wrangle three huge piles of logs through the splitter that he had rented for the weekend. We faced an enormous job with a one-below windchill.

One by one Steve lugged sections of tree trunk under the splitter's blade while I ran the lever. Up and down the blade went, slicing and splitting and breaking the fibers into pieces to fit inside the woodstove. With each section cut, the pile behind Steve grew.

My thoughts wandered in the drone of the motor and exhaust fumes. One idea they landed on was the truth of Romans 5:4, how endurance builds our character, which in turn produces hope.

While we battled the cold, our efforts grew into a mountain of split wood. We felt weary, our muscles ached, and my head pounded from the motor's noise. We finished up for Saturday and then got up and did the same thing Sunday. But I noticed a strange thing that day. As we worked, I felt more accustomed to the exertion. Steve's muscles didn't ache as much either, and we both felt a little lighter, more hopeful.

I experienced what Jesus's Word teaches about the connections among endurance, character, and hope. Little by little we did our best, and as we pushed through, we experienced growth and abundance.

Commit your work to Him, and trust Him to produce character and hope in you. —ERIN KEELEY MARSHALL

FAITH STEP: *Ask Jesus to reveal where you need to keep enduring. Ask Him to do what He wants to with your character, and claim His hope.*

SUNDAY, NOVEMBER 20

Enter his gates with thanksgiving, and his courts with praise!
Give thanks to him; bless his name! Psalm 100:4 (ESV)

I'VE READ SEVERAL ARTICLES about the benefits of thankfulness. Studies show that cultivating feelings of gratitude leads to improved mental and physical health. Increased optimism helps us handle stress better, which in turn boosts our immune system. These studies always remind me that the Bible urges us to make a deliberate choice to have a grateful spirit.

Jesus exposed our human tendency toward a lack of gratitude in Luke 17. Ten lepers begged Him to heal them. Jesus told them to go to the priests; as they walked, they were healed. Only one man returned to thank Jesus. When I read Jesus's question, "Where are the nine?" I can't help wondering: Do I only remember to thank Him for my blessings one time out of ten?

I decided to be more intentional about developing the right attitude. I bought a journal to write down things for which I'm thankful. At first, I wondered if it might be hard to think of something to record every evening. But God helped me kick-start this habit the very first day. That morning I had prayed that I would hear from my children over the weekend. It had been a while since I'd talked with my sons; they hadn't returned my latest phone calls. Early in the evening, both of them phoned while I was talking with my daughter. I was able to merge the calls and talk to all three of my children at the same time.

Whenever I hesitate to write in my journal at bedtime, all I have to do is read that first entry. Then I think of all kinds of reasons to be grateful.
—DIANNE NEAL MATTHEWS

FAITH STEP: *Why not develop the habit of beginning or ending your day with gratitude for your blessings? List as many specific reasons to thank Jesus as you can think of.*

ono MONDAY, NOVEMBER 21

Hope deferred makes the heart sick, but a longing fulfilled is a tree of life.
Proverbs 13:12 (NIV)

YESTERDAY, I HAD A THOUGHT pop into my head that caught me completely off guard. *I wish Scott and I could own a house.* This is one of those dreams I don't ever talk about since it is an impossibility. The cute 1,400-square-foot home we rent on the San Francisco peninsula would sell for a little under a million dollars. Talking about owning a home here is crazy talk.

For those of you who have hoped for something for a really long time and have not seen that hope come to pass, you know it can make you heartsick. So I have decided not to hope for a house. So I won't be disappointed. When that thought flitted across my mind, I just started talking out loud in the car. "Jesus, You have blessed us so much. We have all we need and more. Forgive me for not being content with what I have."

And in that moment, I had the thought, which I think was Jesus because I don't usually think that clearly. And the thought was this: *Jesus made me to want more.* He is the One Who gives us hopes and dreams. Not to be mean. Not in a "*Na-na-na-na-na!* You can't have this!" kind of way. But because hopes and dreams are the currency He deals in. Just ask Abraham and Joseph and Hannah. Jesus births dreams in us because He loves us and He wants us to see that only He can bring them to pass. He loves impossible odds. It is in those circumstances that His glory shines brightest. So with that thought in mind...I think it might be time to start dreaming again. —SUSANNA FOTH AUGHTMON

FAITH STEP: *Write out your dream on a slip of paper and put it in the back of your Bible. Remind Jesus that this is the dream He gave you and that you are entrusting Him with it.*

Join us for our Thanksgiving Day of Prayer.
Find out more at guideposts.org/ourprayer.

One TUESDAY, NOVEMBER 22

"Come, follow me," he [Jesus] said. . . . Mark 1:17 (CEB)

EVEN THOUGH I WAS FAMILIAR with the store and its layout, I was stymied about where I could find a seldom-used product. I'd checked all the spots I thought logical and a few that didn't seem logical at all. I couldn't complete my shopping list without that much-needed item. So I asked an employee.

"Follow me. I'll show you," she said, setting aside what she was doing and inviting me to follow her across the store to the shelf where I'd find it.

Only by following would I find what I was looking for.

Can you imagine *not* following when someone offers to show you what you need? Yet we do it all the time.

Or we misunderstand the way Jesus offers us His guidance. He doesn't point, disinterested, "Uh, yeah. Over…um…over there somewhere. I think. Pretty sure. Yeah. Try that."

He's not a slacker store employee. And we do Him a gross disservice when we assume that's how He gives guidance.

Rather, He leads. "Here. I'll show you." He doesn't tell. He leads. We'll still be lost unless we follow.

"Just tell me, Lord. Just tell me how this is going to turn out. Tell me what You want me to do about this job shake-up. Tell me how to handle this relationship crisis. It's unnerving me. Tell me where I'll find the answer to reducing this family drama."

He responds in the way that most benefits us: "Come. Follow Me. Here, I'll show you." We'll find the answers to all of those questions, to every question that troubles our souls, in one way only: by following when He says, "Here, I'll show you." —CYNTHIA RUCHTI

FAITH STEP: *If you're like most people, you're well aware of an area in your life where you're resistant to following where Jesus is leading. Make that a matter of targeted prayer today. Answers are waiting for you.*

WEDNESDAY, NOVEMBER 23

Let your conversation be always full of grace, seasoned with salt, so that you may know how to answer everyone. Colossians 4:6 (NIV)

IT'S JUST DAYS BEFORE THANKSGIVING, and the country is aflutter with reminders to be grateful. From social-media updates to morning-show news features to devotions like these, we are reminded to give thanks.

These are great words to recall as we cook and clean and prepare. I've got my shopping list ready and my spice rack at attention as I consider the dishes I'm adding to the menu.

And I'm also reminded that being watchful with our words of gratitude should be part of everyday life. It isn't just the holidays when we can be stretched to find the right response to a stressful family member or when our patience is taxed by words that grate on us. And it isn't only a handful of special days when responsibilities, disappointments, difficult memories, and battles with character growth wear on us.

During this season of Thanksgiving, it's worthwhile to start and stop our conversations with the words of Colossians 4:6. Grace filled Jesus's talk no matter if He was affirming someone's faith or calling a person out on sin. Grace doesn't brush over the truth when it needs to shine in the darkness. Neither does it withhold forgiveness or mercy when those are called for.

Offering grace is like seasoning just the right amount, which is always appropriate to make the recipe delectable. Grace is appetizing; everyone's got a taste for it, and we all hunger for it. Let's follow Jesus into the day and season our conversation with His grace, trusting that His Spirit will guide us to the right response at the right time. —ERIN KEELEY MARSHALL

FAITH STEP: *Think of a time when you did not offer a response Jesus would have offered. Now think of a time when you did. Ask Him to flavor your conversation.*

THURSDAY, NOVEMBER 24

Return to your home, and recount [the story] of how many and great things God has done for you. And [the man] departed, proclaiming throughout the whole city how much Jesus had done for him. Luke 8:39 (AMP)

I REMEMBER GOING TO my grandparents' mobile home for Thanksgiving dinner as a child. I'd sit at the kids' table with my brother and two cousins. I was the oldest, and it was work trying to keep my younger cousins out of trouble. I'd eat until my belly was full, and while my brother and cousins played outside I'd listen to the grown-ups talk. I was interested in their world, their stories.

Now I'm the grown-up. I'm the one in the kitchen cooking. I'm also the one sitting with the other adults sharing stories. Each family has important stories that need to be passed on and shared. We often talk about how my grandfather grew up in Kansas and moved to California during the Dust Bowl. Or about how my grandmother was born to Mexican immigrants and grew up in a boxcar. John and I even share funny stories like how our first VCR had a remote control that was connected to the box by a long cord. Or the first time I saw someone with a car phone (before cell phones). But most of all we love sharing stories about our faith—about answered prayers and the ways Jesus has shown up. It's these stories that pass down a heritage of faith.

It's important to go out and to share the good news of Jesus with others, but it's also important to start at home. Thanksgiving is a time for family, and it's a time for sharing stories. Family members know our strengths and weaknesses, high and lows. They can also see Jesus's transformation in our lives, and then desire it for their own. —TRICIA GOYER

FAITH STEP: *Think of one personal faith story to share at your Thanksgiving celebration, and pray for the perfect moment to share it.*

FRIDAY, NOVEMBER 25

"The one who offers thanksgiving as his sacrifice glorifies me; to one who orders his way rightly I will show the salvation of God!" Psalm 50:23 (NIV)

IT HAPPENS EVERY THANKSGIVING without fail. No matter who sits at our table, we all participate. As soon as the last bite of turkey has been consumed, but before pumpkin cheesecake enters our mouths, we each take three pieces of food in our hands. But not to eat. Three pinto beans per person, one bean at a time, plop into an already half-filled jar that's passed around the table. And one at a time, each person shares a blessing from the past year: something for which to be thankful. Tears flow from adults, and giggles may follow freely from younger members.

Our Thanksgiving ritual began over thirty years ago when our family chose to spend our American holiday giving blessings—instead of receiving them. We took our girls to Mexico on mission trips where we ate beans and tortillas instead of turkey and dressing. As the time passed during our stays there, we noticed something strange: no one missed the food or the football games. And instead of early Christmas shopping, we placed our own gifts into the hands of eager children.

Our group showed Christian movies, and we visited homes where hungry hearts waited to hear our message. We sang, we played games, and we cuddled the little ones in the cardboard huts. But most of all, we shared the most important blessing we had to give: the love of Jesus.

The memories of those trips have lingered longer than any other Thanksgiving celebrations. I'm not sure why we chose three beans to pass around our table. Maybe because if we had no time limitations, we'd go on forever. Because when it comes to counting blessings that Jesus gives us, the numbering never stops. —REBECCA BARLOW JORDAN

FAITH STEP: *How do you celebrate Thanksgiving? If you don't already have a creative tradition, begin one as a family to express your thanks to Jesus in a new way.*

SATURDAY, NOVEMBER 26

"But giving thanks is a sacrifice that truly honors me. If you keep to my path, I will reveal to you the salvation of God." Psalm 50:23 (NLT)

I FIND AN ATTITUDE OF GRATITUDE easy to maintain when all's well. Not so much when the unexpected complicates my life. Like when a storm knocks out the power before the Thanksgiving turkey's cooked. Or when the flu hits my home the day before vacation starts. Or when winter weather leaves me stranded in airports, struggling to reschedule flights.

On one mid-January night, a canceled flight in Chicago meant catching a bus to my destination in a major blizzard. The flight would have taken forty-five minutes; the bus ride took five hours. And I'd forgotten my coat in a friend's car when she dropped me at the airport.

That night I practiced what I preach. I thanked Jesus for the bus, its warmth, and safety on icy roads. When we arrived at our intended airport, the only car rental company closed for the night was the one holding my reservation. Cold and stranded again, I thanked Jesus in advance for providing me with a ride to my hotel (with a retired taxi driver).

Giving thanks in difficulty is a sacrifice. It demonstrates our willingness to surrender control and trust Jesus's wisdom and sovereignty. It proves that we believe He is Who He says He is—the faithful One. And it demonstrates our love and respect for Him in return. But there's more.

Offering the sacrifice of thanksgiving helps us evolve as Christians. It shifts our focus from our circumstances to Jesus. His presence becomes more real, and His peace calms our anxious thoughts. —GRACE FOX

FAITH STEP: *Many folks find refreshment by taking a midday tea or coffee break. Why not start a new habit? Take a gratitude break once a day. Keep a journal for this purpose, writing down one thing per day for which you're thankful.*

SUNDAY, NOVEMBER 27

Wait for the Lord; Be strong and let your heart take courage;
Yes, wait for the Lord. Psalm 27:14 (NAS)

THE LAST YEAR HAS BEEN a year of waiting. John and I have been waiting to adopt from the foster care system again. We've waited for home studies. We've waited for paperwork. We've waited to be matched with a child. We are still waiting, and it breaks my heart to think there is a child waiting and wondering if he or she will ever have a forever home. Not having a family is hard for a child. Waiting to open our home is hard too. It's not like waiting for an event, or a special gift. We're waiting to share good news: "We want you to be ours" and "Come and see your new home."

You'd think the waiting would be discouraging. Instead it's given us fearless trust. Some of the themes from Psalm 27 have echoed in my heart this year: "Be gracious to me and answer me" (Psalm 27:7). "Your face, O Lord, I shall seek" (Psalm 27:8), and "I would have despaired unless I had believed that I would see the goodness of the Lord in the land of the living" (Psalm 27:13).

Fearless trust only comes when our prayers aren't answered right away. It's then we must remember Who Jesus is and what He has done for us. In the case of foster children who need forever homes, it's remembering that Jesus loves them even more than we do, and He's already picked the perfect child for our home.

Waiting is hard. Waiting on the Lord takes strength and courage. But someday the wait will be over, and at the end of the wait we'll receive Jesus's perfect answer...whatever that answer may be. *Whoever* that answer may be. —TRICIA GOYER

FAITH STEP: *Create a "waiting" journal. Record the things you're waiting for, and then record Jesus's answers. Keeping track of the many ways that Jesus answers your prayers will give you the strength and the courage for the next time you wait!*

MONDAY, NOVEMBER 28

"So you want first place? Then take the last place. Be the servant of all."
Mark 9:35 (MSG)

"ME FIRST!" we often hear children say. Even as adults, those words unconsciously pour out of our mouths easier than oil from a bottle. "Black Friday," the day after Thanksgiving, finds streams of early-bird shoppers lined up in front of closed department store doors, all vying for first position. Whether it's a grocery store or post office line, a promotion or a special honor, we like to station ourselves at the front.

But that's not the desire of Jesus.

One day Jesus confronted the disciples for their discussion of who would be the greatest in God's kingdom. Mark 9:34 says, "The silence was deafening." Immediately, Jesus sat the twelve down, found a child nearby, and cradled that young person in His arms. Then, using the child for a stronger object lesson, He corrected the disciples' me-first tendency: their childish behavior—and their obvious lack of humility.

If you want to be first, He said to choose the low road—the road to humility. Society considered children among the least important citizens. In fact, the same word for *child* was often used for the word *servant*. The road to true greatness is to become a servant. Jesus could have added, "like me." Because He exemplified the epitome of servanthood more than anyone. Humble, gentle, unselfish—these describe God's Son. "Whoever embraces one of these children as I do embraces me" (Mark 9:37).

Grasping the concept of greatness begins with replacing our "me-first" thinking, by treating others as more important than ourselves.

I'm grateful Jesus showed us how. —REBECCA BARLOW JORDAN

FAITH STEP: *Make a deliberate effort to put others first in both small and big ways. Pay it forward in a fast-food lane; offer your place in line at the store; or leave a close parking spot for someone else. Be creative, and ask Jesus to show you how.*

DMK

TUESDAY, NOVEMBER 29

The Lord directs the steps of the godly. He delights in every detail of their lives.
Psalm 37:23 (NLT)

IT WAS LATE NOVEMBER, and I was flying from British Columbia to Saskatchewan to speak at two church events the next day. The first leg of my trip ended with a two-hour layover in Alberta. Unfortunately, a sudden blizzard canceled seven flights during that time—mine included. My first thought was *This can't be happening. What if the storm continues through the night? I'll miss my 9:00 AM event.*

The choice was mine. I could let the "what if" stress me, or I could believe that Jesus directs my steps and delights in every detail of my life—blizzards included. I chose the latter.

I will trust and not be afraid. Work out the details as You wish, I prayed silently as I joined the mile-long line at the ticket counter.

Jesus answered in an unexpected way. He immediately planted me beside a chatty young woman who spoke about her recent divorce, her new beau, and her desire for a loving, permanent marriage. Our conversation led to the importance of honoring one's spouse and what that looks like in day-to-day life. "This is all new to me," she said. "I'm really glad we met. I'm sure this was no accident."

My new friend and I parted ways two hours later. The blizzard lifted, and I caught a flight that enabled me to speak at my early morning event.

Does Jesus orchestrate the details of our lives? Absolutely. And because He's loving and wise—and sees a bigger picture than we see—we don't need to fear or worry when He's in control. —GRACE FOX

FAITH STEP: *Ask a friend to tell you about a time when Jesus clearly directed her circumstances. How did this grow her faith? Ask Jesus to give you opportunities to see Him obviously work on your behalf.*

WEDNESDAY, NOVEMBER 30

"Look! I stand at the door and knock. If you hear my voice and open the door, I will come in, and we will share a meal together as friends." Revelation 3:20 (NLT)

PERHAPS YOU'RE FAMILIAR with the painting *Christ at Heart's Door* by Warner Sallman. It features a white-robed Jesus standing before a closed door, His hand raised to knock. The door contains a square grid at eye level, implying that the home's occupant can see the visitor and recognize that He's trustworthy. However, the door lacks an outside knob, indicating that the occupant chooses whether or not Jesus gains entry.

I opened the door of my heart to Jesus when I was eight years old, but many years passed before I understood the depth of the relationship He desires. Jesus wants more than access; He wants a willing and welcome invitation into the hub of my heart's home.

In my physical home, visiting friends and family gather around the table for food, fun, and fellowship. We share hopes and dreams, struggles and secrets. We encourage one another, and we pray for the other's concerns.

I love it that Jesus desires this type of relationship with His followers. Imagine—He wants to come in and share a meal with us. Picture yourself sitting at your table, enjoying meaningful conversation with Him. You trust Him implicitly, and you know He always has your best interest in mind, so you're free to share anything with Him. He listens and gives wise counsel. His presence fills you with peace, courage, and hope.

Jesus wants our friendship. He won't force His way into our lives, but He waits for our invitation: "Come in! Make Yourself at home."

Have you opened your heart's door to Jesus? —GRACE FOX

FAITH STEP: *Prepare your favorite snack. Set two places at your table—for you and for Jesus. Talk to Him as your best friend. Savor this time in His presence.*

THURSDAY, DECEMBER 1

And so it was, that, while they were there, the days were accomplished that she should be delivered. Luke 2:6 (KJV)

WE HAVE NO INDICATION that Jesus was born prematurely or overdue. He came on time, when the days were accomplished. Like other promises of God, Christ's arrival was "not overdue a single day" (Habakkuk 2:3, TLB).

Knowing the inexpressible heartache a failed pregnancy can cause, I'm overwhelmed with the thought that Jesus wasn't merely conceived miraculously, but He also was held safely until "the days were accomplished." Mary's pregnancy didn't end in miscarriage or stillbirth. All the days were accomplished according to divine decree from eternity past. Jesus was born healthy, whole. The unusual circumstances of the trip from Nazareth to Bethlehem and the stable's atmosphere didn't threaten His safe delivery. He grew to toddler, child, young man, adult—protected by loving earthly parents and by His Heavenly Father until the days were accomplished that He should be delivered into the hands of people who insisted on His Crucifixion and death.

Then the days were accomplished that He should be delivered from the grave to Resurrection life. Soon after, the days were accomplished that He should be delivered back to sit at the side of His Father in heaven.

Rest assured that whatever long-awaited moment you hold in your heart, if it was birthed by the Holy Spirit, eventually—not too soon and not too late—the days will be accomplished. As you reflect on the perfect timing of Christ's birth, reflect too on the perfect timing of His life, death, Resurrection, and every promise still in wait for you. —CYNTHIA RUCHTI

FAITH STEP: *Ten minutes before the angel appeared to them, the shepherds tended their sheep, unaware that all heaven was about to break open, changing them and us. Make a list of the ways hope shows up while you wait for the days to be accomplished for your answers' due dates.*

FRIDAY, DECEMBER 2

"I am the light of the world. Whoever follows me will never walk in darkness, but will have the light of life." John 8:12 (NIV)

EVERY DECEMBER I START REMINDING my husband that there are only three weeks left until the days start to get longer again. And every time I do, he jokes that he knew there was a reason he married me! Steve isn't fond of darkness descending early, so he loves to hear that, when daylight diminishes to its briefest, it's on the brink of getting longer again.

The saying "It is always darkest just before dawn" usually refers to the twenty-four-hour day-and-night cycle, but it also applies to the seasonal changes of the sun's setting and rising. That saying can also apply to the dark times we face in life. When we're in the middle of a painful season and we feel our hope falter, we can trust that Jesus—the Light of the world—will arrive to help us just in time.

It is significant that the Bible tells of the kings who followed a star through the darkness to find the young Savior. He came to be with us amid the darkness of Israel's captivity, and He shined His light everywhere He went as He drew people to salvation. More than once Jesus called Himself the light of the world (John 9:5), but during the Sermon on the Mount, He also told His disciples, "You are the light of the world. A town built on a hill cannot be hidden" (Matthew 5:14, NIV).

Can you picture it, the Light of the world up there on the mountain, inviting His own to identify with Him, to join the kingdom that shines and cannot be hidden? It's a majestic image, a holy one that we're part of as believers in Him. Where does His light shine out from you in this world? —ERIN KEELEY MARSHALL

FAITH STEP: *Ask Jesus to help you live full of His light among the world where He placed you. Thank Him for inviting you to be part of His light.*

SATURDAY, DECEMBER 3

The Lord will work out his plans for my life—for your faithful love,
O Lord, endures forever. . . . Psalm 138:8 (NLT)

I'VE ALWAYS HAD A VIVID IMAGINATION but, looking back, my expectations for what Jesus could do with my life were far too low. At seventeen, I prayed for Jesus to "do something with my life." I imagined a good husband, a few kids, and teaching Sunday school. That happened, and so much more. My life today is filled with writing books, mentoring teenage mothers, and mothering six children…more than I could have hoped for or imagined!

As I've sought Jesus, He's opened doors—all of which have taken faith to walk through. As I've grown to trust Him, I've learned it's not about me. Each opportunity has allowed me to spread His good news. Yes, I get to be part of this journey, but I'm simply a small part of His overall plan.

A line from an old gospel hymn says, "For the love of God is broader than the measure of man's mind; and the heart of the Eternal is most wonderfully kind." Jesus gave me the free gift of eternal life through His sacrifice, but I'd formerly believed that a "good life with Jesus" was adequate. Instead, Jesus has shown me that His plans for me—for my life—are far more than adequate. As I've dared to follow where He leads, Jesus has opened amazing doors. More than that, He walks through them with me.

My expectations of what Jesus can accomplish in the life of a very ordinary person have grown, and I can't wait to see what He has in store for the years to come! —TRICIA GOYER

FAITH STEP: *Write down three expectations you had for Jesus when you first became a believer. Then write down three discoveries you've made as you've walked with Him. In what ways has your walk with Jesus exceeded your expectations?*

SUNDAY, DECEMBER 4

When the Lord returns, he will bring our darkest secrets to light and will reveal our private motives. Then God will give to each one whatever praise is due.
1 Corinthians 4:5 (NLT)

KNOWING THAT JESUS WILL someday shine His light on our deepest secrets and motives should prompt us to ask this question: "What's my intention?" The answer reveals a lot about our heart's condition and whether or not it needs to undergo change. Let's look at a few hypothetical situations:

We give generous offerings to our church. Why? To gain a pat on the back? To manipulate those in leadership to do things our way? Or to worship Jesus, build His kingdom with our resources, and be wise stewards of what belongs to Him anyway?

We habitually seek ways to earn more money. Why? Because we struggle with the fear of financial insecurity? To gain a reputation as a successful businessperson within our community? Or to earn more so we can give more to those in need?

We say yes to yet another request for our services at church or our kids' school. Why? So we can fill our need to feel wanted? To avoid disappointing someone by saying no? Or to use our gifts to bless others in this way because we've asked God for direction and truly believe He wants us to say yes?

Sometimes we deceive ourselves into believing our motives are pure. Asking the why question, and answering honestly so we can respond appropriately, helps us sort out things and ensures that our motives measure up to Christ's standard. When He returns and we meet Him face-to-face, nothing will matter more than seeing Him smile and hearing Him say, "Well done, good and faithful servant." —GRACE FOX

FAITH STEP: *Write "What's my intent?" on two blank recipe cards. Post one card on your fridge, and put the other in your purse or wallet. Use these as reminders to ask Jesus for clarity and wisdom when you're making decisions.*

MONDAY, DECEMBER 5

"For I was hungry and you gave me something to eat, I was thirsty and you gave me something to drink, I was a stranger and you invited me in, I needed clothes and you clothed me, I was sick and you looked after me, I was in prison and you came to visit me." Matthew 25:35–36 (NIV)

IN MY COMPOSITION CLASSES I assign a research paper at the end of the semester. Students must choose a controversial issue, research it, and write a "Take a Stand" paper in which they argue their beliefs about the issue. We were working on this the other day in the library when a student came up to me. She had chosen immigration as her issue. "I keep finding articles about churches helping immigrants. I've never heard of that. I had no idea they were so involved in this issue!"

This was so sad to me that she was surprised—but it opened the door for us to discuss the history of social change in our country. I was able to tell her how Christians were behind virtually every social advancement we've made, from abolishing slavery to fighting for women's rights to the Civil Rights Movement. Clearly, our reputation is not as good in the twentieth century.

Sometimes the loudest "Christian" voices aren't using Jesus's words at all, but instead spout the ideology of political parties. His voice—and His mission—can be found in these verses in Matthew 25. Wherever we stand on "issues," we can carry out His mission for people by being His hands and feet in our communities, and seeing and serving Him when we encounter the least of these. —GWEN FORD FAULKENBERRY

FAITH STEP: *Who is hungry or thirsty in your town? Who needs clothes? Who is sick, a stranger, or in prison? Imagine that person as Jesus, because He said they are Him. Make a plan for how you can reach out and help in His name.*

TUESDAY, DECEMBER 6

"To give light to those who sit in darkness and in the shadow of death, and to guide us to the path of peace." Luke 1:79 (NLT)

As NOVEMBER TURNED TO DECEMBER, I created a playlist of favorite Christmas songs that accompanied any car travel, housework, and sometimes computer work as I prepared my heart for a Jesus-centered holiday.

A handful of songs rose above the rest. More than atmosphere-setters, they became part of the illumination of the season for me. I hit Replay over and over and let the Holy Spirit use the music to pry my heart open wider for the celebration of Christ's birth. One of those songs has a title not instantly connected with Christmas classics: "All Is Well." But in some ways, it defines the message of Christmas.

The year I most appreciated the song, everything seemed anything but "well" in our household. Personal messages from friends told of family crises, rough diagnoses, breath-stealing challenges. And in our own home, we were approaching the date predetermined for my husband's company's downsizing, which meant the end of his job.

Against that backdrop came the song "All Is Well." As soon as the last note ended, I hit "replay." I needed to hear it again. It turned into a prayer of gratitude that Jesus came to our messy world to let us know it would get even messier, but we could still know deeply embedded peace. The poetry of the lyrics found their footing in the truth foretold in ancient times in anticipation of the arrival of Jesus on the scene: "For tonight darkness fell/Into the dawn of love's light."

Circumstances have no power against the relentless "dawn of Love's light," against the unstoppable presence of Jesus, the Light of the world.
—CYNTHIA RUCHTI

FAITH STEP: *This Advent season, inscribe your "darkness" concerns into the wax of a pillar candle. As you burn that candle each evening, watch those concerns melt as the light—the Light—takes over.*

WEDNESDAY, DECEMBER 7

The steps of a man are established by the Lord, when he delights in his way.
Psalm 37:23 *(NIV)*

THIS PAST WEEK I have been wrestling with life. I have had the thought over and over again, *Your prayers are too small.* I think it is Jesus trying to get my attention. I am asking the One Who can make molten lava spew and shift tectonic plates with a snap of His fingers for good deals on groceries. And it is not that He doesn't care about groceries or that He can't move on the hearts of those who print coupons...He does. He delights in the details of our lives. But He wants to give us our daily bread and more. It's almost as if He is challenging me: *Give Me a prayer that I can sink My teeth into.*

When my prayers are small, I limit Him with what I am believing. Why am I not upping the ante? When did I stop believing that He wanted to do the miraculous in my life? Why am I not giving Him the opportunity to do more than I could ever possibly hope for or imagine? The truth is this: when I am in charge of my life, my life is small. When I let Jesus have my life, the possibilities are endless.

So I have a new plan: I don't have a plan. I am asking Jesus to let me in on His plan. I am asking Him to give me His dreams, His thoughts, His hopes and to do whatever He wants with my life.

I have no idea what is going to happen, but I have a hunch it's about to get good. —SUSANNA FOTH AUGHTMON

FAITH STEP: *Take out your journal and say this simple prayer, "Jesus, I want Your dreams, Your thoughts, and Your hopes for me." Write down the ideas that come to mind as you spend time with Him.*

THURSDAY, DECEMBER 8

He embraced his chosen child, Israel; he remembered and piled on the mercies, piled them high. It's exactly what he promised, beginning with Abraham and right up to now. Luke 1:54–55 (MSG)

SOON AFTER MARY RECEIVED a visit from the angel telling her she would give birth to Jesus, the Son of God, she left to visit her cousin Elizabeth, who was also miraculously pregnant in her older age, carrying the forerunner of Jesus: John the Baptist.

Following Elizabeth's joyful greeting, Mary broke into a spontaneous song of her own. In the well-known "Magnificat," Mary's praise-filled words acknowledged the wonder of what had happened to her and how it would affect future generations. But her declaration of praise centered on the One Who had made all things possible—for her and for Elizabeth.

I love this *Message* translation that shows so clearly heaven's track record. Mary told how God had "embraced" the nation of Israel like a chosen child. And beginning with Abraham, where God first revealed His covenant of blessing, Mary said God "remembered and piled on the mercies, piled them high...right up to now." Not only was Mary talking about herself as a recipient of those mercies, but she also was carrying the Promise fulfilled inside her: Jesus.

We, as God's children, are also the beneficiaries of that covenant blessing. At Christmas, and all year long, Jesus continues to pile on the mercies. Romans 5:5 (MSG) says, "We can't round up enough containers to hold everything God generously pours into our lives." For us, like Mary, His grace, mercy, and love are overwhelming benefits to those who will believe—and receive. That would make anyone want to break out in song.
—REBECCA BARLOW JORDAN

FAITH STEP: *How has Jesus piled on mercies in your life this year? Take time to remember today, and thank Him for remembering His promise—and that you are a recipient of those mercies.*

FRIDAY, DECEMBER 9

For God Who said, Let light shine out of darkness, has shown in our hearts so as [to beam forth] the Light for the illumination of the knowledge of the majesty and glory of God [as it is manifest in the Person and is revealed] in the face of Jesus Christ (the Messiah). 2 Corinthians 4:6 (AMP)

I HANG CRYSTAL SUN CATCHERS in my windows. A heart, a cross, a shell— their shapes suggest the meanings they hold for me: God's love, Jesus's death and Resurrection, my baptism. The one hanging in the tiny octagonal sauna window has no particular significance. I bought it for the many-hued beads that hold up a lone colorless teardrop. Today, between bands of lake-effect snow, the sun used it to put on quite a show.

The brightly colored beads are prettiest when you look directly at them, but, of course, that's not what sun catchers are for. The colorful crystals didn't let enough light through to have any effect, but the plain pendant caught the sun's intermittent gleam as it broke through the clouds again and again. It projected blinking colors all over the cedar walls. Rainbow streaks shimmered behind the stove as shattered light passed through the rising heat waves. I stayed, fascinated.

Jesus called Himself the Light of the world and said those who follow Him wouldn't walk in darkness but in light. Then He told His followers that *they* were the light of the world. How? They didn't look like much. They couldn't do anything on their own. Like us, if we're honest.

When He lived on earth, Jesus said He also could do nothing on His own, yet the power of God shone brightly through His life. He expects it to shine through ours as well, just like a bit of glass turned just so, in a sauna in Northern Michigan. —SUZANNE DAVENPORT TIETJEN

FAITH STEP: *Offer up your ordinary self. Make something—draw, tell a story, bake a cake. Let Jesus shine through you.*

SATURDAY, DECEMBER 10

So here's what I want you to do, God helping you: Take your everyday, ordinary life—your sleeping, eating, going-to-work, and walking-around life— and place it before God as an offering. Embracing what God does for you is the best thing you can do for him. Romans 12:1 (MSG)

WE ALL NEED A PURPOSE, an unselfish one. We weren't made to be whole by living for ourselves. Our Creator created us first of all to bring glory to Himself and then to share His glory with us.

Loving Him is our primary purpose, and we accomplish that purpose in our daily life, however unglorious that may feel while driving to work or changing a diaper or taking out the trash.

Laundry and cleaning don't seem like much to offer. Neither does a patient attitude on a commute to work. And we may be tempted to think we're merely being good parents when we respond with gracious discipline instead of harshness when a child shows us disrespect.

But when we belong to Jesus, all of these actions reveal godliness that glorifies Him. So let's not underestimate the power of the humdrum.

Just as He is not impressed by our large efforts to do great things for Him, He is not unimpressed by a follower of His who gives her best to share His grace in the mundane. It's in the daily events that life and faith are worked out.

One day we will bask in His glory; eternal life will not hold the drudgery that makes us doubtful of our earthly purpose.

For now, take your everyday life and commit it to Him and watch Him make something glorious out of it for eternity. —ERIN KEELEY MARSHALL

FAITH STEP: *What is your least-exciting task of the day? Pray over it and determine to be joyful, knowing that you are bringing glory to Jesus when you do it for Him.*

SUNDAY, DECEMBER 11

That night there were shepherds staying in the fields nearby, guarding their flocks of sheep. Suddenly, an angel of the Lord appeared among them, and the radiance of the Lord's glory surrounded them.... —Luke 2:8–9 (NLT)

ONE OF MY FAVORITE CHRISTMAS MEMORIES happened when my kids were elementary-school age. We lived in Lacey, Washington, about eight hundred miles from my parents' home in Brooks, Alberta, Canada.

Driving to Brooks took nearly thirteen hours in the summer. That time increased dramatically in the winter. Consequently, my folks never expected us to visit for Christmas.

One year, we decided to make the journey but kept our plans a secret. We arrived at lunchtime on Christmas Eve and parked in the back alley, out of sight. Then we sent our kids to ring the doorbell. "Surprise!" the kids shouted when my mother opened the door.

"What on earth?" she exclaimed, then burst into happy tears.

If our appearance impacted them to that degree, imagine how the shepherds felt when a host of angels showed up as told in Luke 2:10–11 (NLT): "I bring you good news that will bring great joy to all people! The Savior—yes, the Messiah, the Lord—has been born today in Bethlehem, the city of David!"

Initial terror turned to wonder and delight when the shepherds saw the Savior incarnate, and they spread the good news to everyone they met before returning to their flocks, singing praise to God as they went.

This season we celebrate Jesus's coming to earth. Imagine: because of His arrival, we can experience joy—not just for one night or a season but for eternity. —GRACE FOX

FAITH STEP: *Luke 2:19 says that Mary pondered the events surrounding Jesus's birth in her heart. Pause today to ponder how His birth impacts your life and give Him thanks.*

MONDAY, DECEMBER 12

Many, O Lord my God, are the wonders which You have done, and Your thoughts toward us; there is none to compare with You. If I would declare and speak of them, they would be too numerous to count. Psalm 40:5 (NAS)

As I was growing up, my dad was a police officer. When I was a kid, I always wanted to stick to the rules. I love it when I get kudos for a job well done. I hate it when I feel as if I've disappointed someone.

Too often I find myself treating Jesus as if He too were a police officer—hanging around, waiting to catch me crossing the line. And sometimes this is the message we get from other Christians. All around us there are people telling us we need to be good, to do the right thing, to follow the right path, and to care for others more than ourselves.

Jesus does hang around us, but He doesn't do it with the intention of catching us doing wrong. He has the best intentions. As Jeremiah 29:11 (NLT) says, "For I know the plans I have for you," says the Lord. "They are plans for good and not for disaster, to give you a future and a hope."

There are many things we need to understand better, but one of the most important things is that the knowledge of Jesus's goodness sinks into the depths of our beings. We need to realize more and more that Jesus thinks of us often, and His thoughts center around good plans.

Yes, it's important to know right and wrong. It's even important to try to live with godly intentions, but more important than the rules is the relationship, on this earth and in eternity. —TRICIA GOYER

FAITH STEP: *Which rules are hardest for you to follow? Make a list. Instead of focusing on all the ways you've fallen short, see the things on your list in view of your relationship with Jesus. How do they appear to you through Jesus's eyes?*

TUESDAY, DECEMBER 13

"Sky and earth will wear out; my words won't wear out." Mark 13:31 (MSG)

MOMS KNOW THE FRUSTRATION of trying to stuff their children's feet into outgrown shoes or dress their kids in holey jeans that are two inches too short. Every year can bring moans when they try to squeeze more from an already-shrinking clothing budget. And with children, the timing is cyclical, whether clothes are needed for school, church, or growth spurts. They're either growing, or the clothes are wearing out.

But growing out of things is not always the problem—and not only with kids. Clothes don't last forever. Every time I try to match up my husband's socks, I find the same results: multiple washings and wearings leave the heels almost threadbare.

Clothes are not the only thing in our world that won't last forever. Jesus was talking to His disciples one day, warning them of fake Messiahs who would come to them with false teachings. He described events that would happen, warning them to stay alert, watching for His Second Coming.

In describing those events, like the sun fading, the stars falling, and the heavens trembling, He said that even the sky and earth would wear out. Nothing would remain the same (Mark 13:24–25).

Except His words. Jesus, the one true Messiah and Son of God, would always be the same (Hebrews 13:8). His truthful words to His disciples and to us will never wear out. They promote holiness, not "holey-ness." And they will guide us to wholeness in Jesus—at His return, when He comes to take us to our forever home (John 14:3). —REBECCA BARLOW JORDAN

FAITH STEP: *The next time you open your drawers or closets (or your kids'), thank Jesus that He and His words will never wear out (and that He will provide what we need in the meantime).*

WEDNESDAY, DECEMBER 14

Now to him who is able to do immeasurably more than all we ask or imagine, according to his power that is at work within us, to him be glory in the church and in Christ Jesus throughout all generations, for ever and ever! Amen.
Ephesians 3:20–21 (NIV)

RECENTLY WE WATCHED AN OLD VIDEO of a Christmas that took place nine years ago. Our boys were so small and sweet. Our oldest son, Jack, will be fourteen this year. He couldn't take his eyes off his five-year-old self. In the video, he was so excited about each present he opened he could barely contain himself. He was especially thrilled with an art kit he had received. He looked straight into the camera and said, "Hey! I think I wished for that!" I heard myself, off camera, laugh and say, "You did wish for that, Jack! How fun that you got it!" More often than not, we don't expect the things we wish for. We are not sure they will come to pass. We are incredibly surprised when the things we wish for come true, just like Jack was when he got the art kit he wanted so much.

But what is even better than getting what we wish for is when our hopes and dreams are surpassed and we receive more than we ever thought possible. As Christ followers, we get far more than we ever asked or hoped or wished or dreamed for. When we asked Jesus to save us from our sins, He didn't stop there. He is an over-the-top gift-giver. He didn't just save us, He offered us forgiveness, mercy, restoration, grace, healing, freedom, hope, joy, peace, a new way of thinking, a new way of living, a clean heart, and the list goes on…and on…and on. He does more in us and for us than we could ever begin to wish for. —SUSANNA FOTH AUGHTMON

FAITH STEP: *Thank Jesus for five different ways that He has exceeded your expectations in your life.*

THURSDAY, DECEMBER 15

"As long as the earth remains, there will be planting and harvest, cold and heat, summer and winter, day and night." Genesis 8:22 (NLT)

I'VE BEEN BLESSED TO LIVE in three unique places around the United States. I've lived through the blazing hot summers of Northern California, where temperatures can reach 116 degrees. And long Montana winters where I've been snowed in because of twelve-foot drifts and learned to drive on a sheet of ice. Now, living in Arkansas, I've survived humidity. Lots of humidity. And while each place has had challenging seasons, I never feared that we'd get stuck in a season. Hot summers slip into crisp falls. Frigid winters last only so long, and as the snow melts, colorful flowers peek out their happy heads in bloom.

In Psalm 74:17 (NIV) we read, "It was you who set all the boundaries of the earth; you made both summer and winter." The heat, the cold, and the humidity are oppressive at times, but with them comes the joy found in cool creeks, glittering snowflakes, and fireflies—all by our Creator's design.

Seasons change in my life too. When the sin I struggled with blazed in my soul, a dear friend prayed with me and our friendship grew. When I found myself out in the cold after the door had been shut on a dream, another dream was planted, one that later bloomed. And when sticky family situations put me at odds with a harsh family member, Jesus protected my heart and reminded me of His love.

What do the challenging seasons teach us about everyday life? No harsh season lasts forever, and good can be found in even the hardest times. Rainbows come after the rain, and fireflies after hot, humid days.
—TRICIA GOYER

FAITH STEP: *Spend two minutes outside contemplating the season. What hardships does it bring? What joys? Consider the current season of your life. What good things have come out of your challenging season? Thank Jesus for the small gifts each season brings.*

FRIDAY, DECEMBER 16

So we have stopped evaluating others. At one time we thought of Christ merely from a human point of view. How differently we know him now!
2 *Corinthians* 5:16 (NLT)

A YEAR AGO, I MET A WOMAN I initially perceived as shy and lacking in self-confidence. My opinion changed as our friendship grew. I soon realized that she's a woman of depth and wisdom. She listens before she speaks, and her insights are always considerate and thought-provoking.

Haste in forming opinions about others easily leads to incorrect assumptions. It's also easy to develop false impressions if we allow other people's sometimes-skewed perspectives to influence us.

For instance, a woman once told me that she felt a mutual acquaintance was a busybody. Rather than automatically adopting her opinion, I spent time getting to know this acquaintance better. I discovered that she genuinely cares about others' well-being.

Just as we ought to be careful in our evaluation of others, so we ought to be cautious about our evaluation of Jesus. Let's not base conclusions on our emotions, which fluctuate with circumstances. Neither let us settle solely for what other people say about Him. Their opinions might be rooted in truth, but then again, they might not.

Biblical preaching can reveal Who Jesus is, but ultimately we develop a more complete understanding through personal Bible study and asking the Holy Spirit to teach us.

Let's ensure that our evaluation of Christ is accurate, for how we regard Him plays a huge role in the direction our lives will take. —GRACE FOX

FAITH STEP: *Jesus is the Light of the world. Celebrate Him by lighting a candle today. Ask Him to shine His light of truth, hope, and life through you to those within your sphere of influence who don't yet know Him.*

SATURDAY, DECEMBER 17

Then God opened her eyes and she saw a well of water. So she went and filled the skin with water and gave the boy a drink. Genesis 21:19 (NIV)

A HEARTBREAKING SCENE is recorded in Genesis. Hagar had become the focus of Sarah's jealous anger and was sent away with her young son, Ishmael. While she was lost in the desert, her supplies ran out. Hagar placed her little boy under a bush and moved a distance away because she couldn't bear to watch him die. As she sobbed, an angel came to reassure her of God's love. Then God opened her eyes to see a well.

Had the well been there all along, and Hagar's weary, tear-filled eyes missed it? Or did God suddenly create what they needed in order to survive?

Whatever the case, He helped Hagar find the answer before her.

My recent prayers weren't as dire as Hagar's, but they were heartfelt. I longed to spend time with my children and grandchild, yet travel is difficult for me and our budget is tight. We were facing another holiday time, knowing half our children wouldn't be able to visit.

One day my daughter handed me the mail and said, "There's an envelope from your agent." Inside was a surprise—unexpected royalties for a Dutch translation of two of my books dating back several years. We squealed with delight, even before I realized I was holding an answer to my prayers. That weekend we called our out-of-town children and offered to get them plane tickets for a small after-Christmas reunion. Now I'm excitedly preparing for their visit. The answer had been there long before the need, but Jesus uncovered it at the perfect time.

Have you recently found yourself, like Hagar, sobbing to Jesus in a desert place? He may have already prepared the answer, and is waiting to open your eyes to a solution. —SHARON HINCK

FAITH STEP: *Today as you pray over your needs, ask Jesus to reveal any potential answers that might already be in place.*

SUNDAY, DECEMBER 18

"They will call him Immanuel" (which means, "God with us").
Matthew 1:23 (NIV)

OUR CHOIR MUSICAL AT CHURCH this Christmas season was called "He Is Here." In my daily life I found myself humming all of the songs from it, meditating on the words. More than any other words in the program, these kept coming back to me: *God is in us, God is for us, God is with us, Immanuel.*

Those truths are transformative. "God is in us" means I am more than just flesh and blood. My biology is real—but just as real, and more powerful, is the Spirit that lives in me. Because of Jesus I can overcome unhealthy choices, bad habits, even genetic predispositions. And because He is for us, I have an advocate Who leads me, instructs me, fights for me, helps me. The Bible asks in Romans 8:31 if God is for us, who can be against us?

Most transformative of all, however, at least for me, is that God is with us. I need power and strength. I need a champion. But more than anything, I need Him to be there all of the time. In the good times and the difficult, in the busy as well as the quiet, lonely places. In my times of triumph as well as my times of tragedy—how good it feels to hold the hand of Jesus and to know that nothing can ever separate me from His love. —GWEN FORD FAULKENBERRY

FAITH STEP: *Every time you come across the word* Immanuel *this season, take a moment to meditate on its meaning. He is with you! Every moment, right where you are.*

MONDAY, DECEMBER 19

"Why do I have this honor, that the mother of my Lord should come to me?"
Luke 1:43 *(CEB)*

WHAT TO EXPECT WHEN YOU'RE EXPECTING JESUS. I haven't seen that book on the shelves anywhere. And it might be a very *looong* book, since the world was expecting or waiting for Jesus the Messiah for a very long time.

The people had needed a redeemer since Eve's and Adam's sins. They'd expected a messiah because he was promised to the people in the Old Testament. Historical records tell us that many women in that ancient culture wondered if they themselves would be the one through whom the Christ Child would be born. For long centuries, the answer was "no."

Then the day came when a young woman named Mary heard the divine, "Yes. Yes, you are the one through whom the Savior will come to earth."

She had no reference book, no *What to Expect When You're Expecting the Savior of the World.* Mary didn't even have a Bible on her bookshelf. She had God's Word in her heart and the Living Word growing arms and legs and ears and a heartbeat in her womb.

Expecting, but unsure what to expect.

Who taught her the basics? Her aunt Elizabeth, with whom she lived for the three months immediately following the night the Holy Spirit came upon her and Jesus was uniquely conceived. Why Elizabeth?

We're not told. But it may be this. Her reaction showed that she was a woman who revered God, a woman who would not doubt but who grew almost irrepressibly excited that Jesus was on the way.

That's how I want my Advent attitude to resonate this year. Uncontainable excitement. It is, in fact, the news that changes everything. —CYNTHIA RUCHTI

FAITH STEP: *What ornament on your tree this year will reflect the life-changing excitement about the Baby on the way? Consider purchasing or making an ornament that mindfully and unmistakably expresses the kind of joy that Mary and Elizabeth shared.*

TUESDAY, DECEMBER 20

"My grace is all you need. My power works best in weakness." So now I am glad to boast about my weaknesses, so that the power of Christ can work through me.
2 Corinthians 12:9 (NLT)

TODAY STARTED BADLY. After four hours of sleep, I had to be on call for neonatal transports anywhere in the Upper Peninsula of Michigan. I charged up my cell phone, turned on the ringer, and got ready.

In the car, I patted my purse to be sure the phone was there. It wasn't. I checked the pockets of everything I'd worn. Took my purse apart. Then my tote. Prayed. Looked in the snow between the house and garage. Called my number. I didn't find it. I told Jesus I trusted Him, but I was frustrated and crying, which made that statement untrue.

I drove through a lake-effect whiteout blizzard and arrived safely at Starbucks, where I camped out so the unit could reach me. I calmed down. When I overstayed my welcome, I moved to the hospital lobby.

My online friends advised trying an app that would locate the smartphone and make it *ding* so I could follow the sound to my phone. I expected to find it easily when I got home. I didn't. It was there, but silent.

I spent my evening searching in and around my house. The snow was knee-deep and now I couldn't use my snowblower until I found the phone for fear of harming it.

Finally, I gave up and said so, singing, "Jesus, Take the Wheel..." for effect. That's when I kicked something in the snow at the edge of the porch—my phone in its waterproof case, too cold to *ding*.

Helpless, I needed grace, not science. There's no app for that.
—SUZANNE DAVENPORT TIETJEN

FAITH STEP: *Jesus understands our frustrations. Include Him in your difficult moments. Ask Him to help you trust Him when nothing goes right. He will.*

WEDNESDAY, DECEMBER 21

So they hurried off and found Mary and Joseph, and the baby, who was lying in the manger. When they had seen him, they spread the word concerning what had been told them about this child, and all who heard it were amazed at what the shepherds said to them. Luke 2:16–18 (NIV)

YOU LOOK AMAZING in that sweater! The steaks at that place are phenomenal! My new smartphone is awesome! Does anybody else think that we've started to overuse superlatives? Apparently one is not always enough; now we have combinations (fantastic + fabulous = fantabulous; giant + enormous = ginormous). The problem is that when we use superlatives so frequently on trivial things, the words lose some of their meaning. What do we say about something that deserves our highest praise? Or someone?

A theme of "amazement" or "astonishment" runs throughout Luke's account of Jesus's birth, life, and death. And rightly so. The people who heard the shepherds repeat the angel's message about baby Jesus expressed amazement. As a twelve-year-old, Jesus astounded the rabbis in the temple with His deep understanding and wisdom. Years later, He astonished the religious leaders with the way He answered their questions. His disciples were amazed that the winds and waves obeyed Him. The crowds were astonished by the way He performed miracles and taught with an authority they'd never heard before. After Jesus rose from the dead, His followers could hardly believe it was Him because of their joy and amazement.

When I meditate on Who Jesus is, how He lived His life, and why He died, I know there is no fitting superlative (or combination) to describe Him. When I think about what Jesus has done in my life, it no longer seems necessary to have a *merry* Christmas. Because His presence alone is enough to make it an *amazing* Christmas. —DIANNE NEAL MATTHEWS

FAITH STEP: *Go through the alphabet thinking of an apt adjective for Jesus using each letter. If you come up with twenty-six, tell Him why that's not enough to describe Him.*

THURSDAY, DECEMBER 22

*You have made known to me the paths of life; you will fill me
with joy in your presence. Acts 2:28 (NIV)*

LAST YEAR I STARTED USING ESSENTIAL OILS. I've been to several classes, and my family's hooked as well. In one class I heard that if an oil's scent is appealing, our bodies need it physically. If we don't like the scent, we need it emotionally.

I like most of the scents, but I did not enjoy Joy. If there's anything to the theory, I need more joy in my life.

It's been said that expectations kill relationships. But expectations can also kill joy . . . that is, unless you're living Jesus-filled and expecting Him to fill you with joy.

Joy is Jesus's guarantee, but only if we're in His presence. The Bible says a lot about staying close to Him. Galatians 5:22 lists the fruit of the Spirit, of which joy is a part. Even though the Spirit lives inside each believer, we often quench His power, and His joy.

In 2 Corinthians 7:4, Paul wrote that in the midst of affliction he overflowed with joy. Circumstances didn't determine his potential for it.

Jesus is the determiner of our joy, as long as we seek Him first and consistently. Luke, the author of Acts, expected Jesus's gift of joy. Look at the wording: "You will fill me." A confident "You will."

Jesus will do it. He will fill you with joy when you live in Him, because He is joy.

We need to take seriously the promise in Acts 2:28. Settling for anything less than being filled with joy is not Jesus's will for you or for me.

Seek Him, love Him first, and expect the fruit of joy.

—ERIN KEELEY MARSHALL

FAITH STEP: *If repetition is the mother of learning, try some old-fashioned sentence writing to impress truth on our hearts. Spend fifteen minutes writing out Acts 2:28 over and over, letting its truth sink in.*

FRIDAY, DECEMBER 23

So if the Son sets you free, you will be free indeed. John 8:36 (NIV)

SOMETIMES CHRISTMAS DOES NOT FEEL like the season of joy and light that it should. Sometimes Christmas feels like a giant snowball of expectations and activities that roars in the Friday after Thanksgiving and doesn't roll out until the new year has been rung in. If we aren't careful, it can squash us flat. I have ordered Christmas cards, purchased Christmas presents for my family, organized the advent calendar, decorated the house, bought the tree, decorated the tree, marched in a Christmas parade, and gotten Christmas packages together for our kiddos we sponsor in Africa. And I am exhausted. If you need me, I will be in bed until January.

Maybe you have also been squashed by the Christmas snowball. (I may have picked you up when I was rolling down the mountain of bills I was paying yesterday...sorry about that.) But here is the thing. Almost none of these activities that are flattening me or you are really Christmas. They are all the trappings we have added to Christmas.

We don't need more parties, or decorations, or gifts, or worries, or expectations to be added to Christmas. What we really need is some grace. For ourselves and others. And we need to love people. My husband just told me that all of us need at least eight hugs a day. He read it somewhere. It sounds about right. And mostly, we need to remember Jesus. Jesus. The Savior. Emmanuel. Breath of Heaven. Redeemer. Bright and Morning Star. Friend. He loves us. There is nothing snowballish about Him. He came so that we could be free...not flattened. So breathe.

Grab some grace and spread it around. Hug somebody. And remember that the Light of the World loves you. Completely. Wholly. Without reservation. And that is the real Christmas. —SUSANNA FOTH AUGHTMON

FAITH STEP: *Repeat the names of Jesus out loud, slowly, pondering their meaning and letting the knowledge that He loves you completely penetrate your heart.*

DNE

SATURDAY, DECEMBER 24

But the angel said to them, "Do not be afraid. I bring you good news that will cause great joy for all the people. Today in the town of David a Savior has been born to you; he is the Messiah, the Lord. This will be a sign to you: You will find a baby wrapped in cloths and lying in a manger." Luke 2:10–12 (NIV)

YEARS AGO, OUR CHURCH WAS in the midst of a major remodeling project. Vaulted overhead windows were leaking, structural damage needed repair, and the old pews had to be refinished. Fund-raising commenced. Work began with a goal to finish before Christmas. The chaos of construction was a challenge for everyone. As often happens, the project took longer than expected. The staff decided to go ahead with the planned Christmas Eve worship service, even though the sanctuary was a mess.

We arrived for the candlelight service to find orange cones and tape blocking off dangerous areas, along with scaffolding everywhere. I sighed with disappointment. I always loved the sparkling decorations and special beauty of Christmas worship. As we slid into a pew and looked around, my heart caught in my throat. The beams around the church looked like the frame for a barn. The wooden scaffolds each held a small votive candle. Tiny lights flickered among the disarray.

Suddenly, our broken-down building became the perfect setting to celebrate Jesus, Emmanuel, Who was born in a humble stable. He is not a Savior of polished elegance. He is the Light of the world, but came like the gently flickering candles around us, into our splintered and rough-edged world.

Do you ever feel your heart has more in common with a half-finished construction project than a royal palace? Take comfort. Your life is exactly the sort of place Jesus wants to abide in. —SHARON HINCK

FAITH STEP: *Sing "Away in a Manger" and ponder the wonder of our Savior Who still is present in humble places.*

SUNDAY, DECEMBER 25

But Mary treasured up all these things and pondered them in her heart.
Luke 2:19 *(NIV)*

ONE OF MY FAVORITE CHRISTMASES was the last one our extended family shared before my father died. We usually exchanged gifts only with our parents and our own immediate families. But this time I wanted to do something different. I gave each person a special ornament.

One of my daughters started the idea several years earlier in our own family. She handpicked a unique ornament for each of us that represented a special character quality she admired, such as wisdom or generosity. I love the resin lamb she bought for me that represented "gentleness" to her. It was a small gift, but a huge blessing I will always treasure.

As I thought about the character traits of each family member, I searched for special ornaments, such as bells for cheerfulness or helping hands for encouragement. The hunt was as much fun as giving the actual gift.

Mary, too, received a small gift one Christmas—at least in size. Much thought went into the gift—and extensive planning as to the character of the recipient. She would give birth to the Son of God, the Savior of the world! When the time finally came, this tiny, special gift arrived: born in a simple manger, proclaimed by a host of angels, worshipped by humble shepherds, and later visited by distant kings. The Bible says Mary "treasured" all that had happened. Her heart must have swelled with joy as she pondered the significance of that tiny baby and all that she had experienced.

That small gift, baby Jesus, became a huge blessing we now treasure forever. —REBECCA BARLOW JORDAN

FAITH STEP: *What was one of your most significant Christmas gifts? How has the gift of Jesus become a huge blessing to you?*

MONDAY, DECEMBER 26

The Lord gives his people strength. The Lord blesses them with peace.
Psalm 29:11 (NLT)

I PLACED MY FAITH IN Jesus Christ for salvation when I was eight years old. His presence in my life has blessed me with a gift many people only dream about—inner peace.

This reality struck home while I was on a flight from Seattle to Minneapolis. During the trip, the young woman seated next to me asked what I did for a living. "I'm an inspirational speaker and author," I said.

"Really?" she responded. "I've always wanted to write a book."

"What would you write?" I asked. "What's on your heart?"

The woman paused. Then she answered, "Perhaps I could write about a personal quest. I'm looking for peace. Have you found it?" My jaw nearly dropped. I shot an arrow prayer heavenward asking for the right words. Then I told this young professional about Jesus, the Prince of Peace, and how He desires a relationship with us. I also told her a couple of stories about challenges I've faced and how peace replaced fear in their midst because Jesus gave me wisdom, courage, and perseverance. Our conversation continued with the woman asking several probing questions, ending only when the plane landed.

That encounter helped me understand that peace is not to be taken for granted. Jesus said, "I am leaving you with a gift—peace of mind and heart. And the peace I give is a gift the world cannot give. So don't be troubled or afraid" (John 14:27).

The world is filled with hurting people longing for inner peace and looking in all the wrong places. Let's point them toward Jesus, the Prince of Peace, so their longing can be satisfied. —GRACE FOX

FAITH STEP: *People longing for inner peace surround us. They're our neighbors, coworkers, grocery-store clerks, kids' teachers, and so many more. Ask the Lord to give you the opportunity to tell someone about the Prince of Peace this week.*

TUESDAY, DECEMBER 27

"I will set out and go back to my father and say to him: Father,
I have sinned against heaven and against you." Luke 15:18 (NIV)

WE LIVE IN A BROKEN WORLD. Pain, loss, and evil litter our lives. As a young Christian I couldn't understand why Jesus allowed children to die, mothers to suffer, and the helpless to be abused. Wouldn't a loving Jesus be quick to ease the pain of those who turn to Him in prayer?

Yet if it wasn't for the pain of this world, we wouldn't need Jesus. I need Jesus because I can't face the pain alone. I turn to Him when I don't have anywhere else to go, and He is always there waiting.

In Hosea 2:6–7, the nation of Israel turned from God. God described their misdeeds through the example of a harlot: "Therefore, behold, I will hedge up her way with thorns, and I will build a wall against her so that she cannot find her paths. She will pursue her lovers, but she will not overtake them; and she will seek them, but will not find them. Then she will say, 'I will go back to my first husband, for it was better for me then than now!'" As was true for this woman, the pain of wrong paths and the pain of the world—through no fault of our own—often lead us to the feet of Jesus.

While we are on this earth, evil and pain will overwhelm us, and in our own brokenness we'll turn back to the only place where we can find hope and peace: to Him. And when we find Jesus we'll discover all we need for today and for eternity. —TRICIA GOYER

FAITH STEP: *Consider a hard time in your life. How did that difficult situation draw you back to Jesus? Share that story with someone who is currently going through a painful situation. Offer to pray with him or her too.*

WEDNESDAY, DECEMBER 28

Don't become so well-adjusted to your culture that you fit into it without even thinking. Instead, fix your attention on God. You'll be changed from the inside out. Readily recognize what he wants from you, and quickly respond to it. Unlike the culture around you, always dragging you down to its level of immaturity, God brings the best out of you, develops well-formed maturity in you.

Romans 12:2 (MSG)

"IF YOUR FRIENDS JUMPED OFF A CLIFF, *would you? Don't blindly follow what the crowd does.*" Remember hearing that as a kid? Both of mine are in school now, and we've begun speaking similar mantras as they deal with peer influences. I pray they grow strong in character and confident in faith. I pray they always pursue Jesus first, with the Holy Spirit's power to discern black and white in a gray world.

It isn't hard to look around at grown-up society and be disappointed by so many who still live led by the crowd. We can teach our kids one thing, but do we live our own lives blindly following, or do we stick to the path Jesus Himself walked, separate from the crowd, even going against the crowd when it doesn't align with Him?

When society's standards are assumed to be right because the masses feel good about them, biblical truth often is ignored or seen as an antagonist.

Jesus knew it would be difficult to live by His ways. The book of Acts offers many grim details about the rough life of early believers who bucked the worldly system to follow Him. Living for Him is a guaranteed invitation to persecution by a humanity that wants its way. But when that crowd is headed for the cliff because it doesn't want Jesus above all, which way will you go? We could face that choice even today. —ERIN KEELEY MARSHALL

FAITH STEP: *Ask Jesus to plant His truth in your heart and give you the confidence to stand up for His ways.*

THURSDAY, DECEMBER 29

I will praise You, O Lord, with my whole heart. . . . Psalm 9:1 (NKJV)

FOR THE MAJORITY of the last four decades, I've worked from home as a writer, minister's wife, and stay-at-home mom. My morning ritual rarely varied when I woke up: greet Jesus, get dressed, apply makeup, comb hair, and fix breakfast. Sometimes I'd even fit in an early morning walk. Later, when the house emptied, I'd spend more time alone with Jesus. The ritual helped me greet my family with a more cheerful attitude.

I'm not sure how that pattern began. Maybe it stemmed from an old romantic song about not sending off your husband with your hair in curlers. Or maybe I was still trying to make over my schoolgirl image of that string-bean, freckle-faced girl in the mirror.

Kids and writing—and maybe the fresh realization that my husband loved me "just as I am"—changed that routine a bit. Now, years later, if I'm on a writing deadline, I may still be dressed in my pajamas at ten o'clock. But I greet my husband with an early morning kiss. I also enjoy stopping midmorning, "putting on my face," and getting dressed for the rest of the day. I feel better and want my husband to know he is worth the effort.

That process is the same when I approach Jesus, only it involves attitude more than clothes or cosmetics. He is still my first stop—before breakfast and before dressing. Maybe because I know He invites me to come to Him "just as I am." But even then, I come into His presence with an attitude that wants to honor Him. The King deserves no less than my best.

Jesus is not impressed with our outer shell, but He does want our wholehearted attitude. He is definitely worth the effort.

—REBECCA BARLOW JORDAN

FAITH STEP: *How do you approach each day? Make a special effort this week to come to Jesus with your best attitude.*

FRIDAY, DECEMBER 30

Trust in the Lord with all your heart and lean not on your own understanding;
in all your ways submit to him, and he will make your paths straight.
Proverbs 3:5–6 *(NIV)*

MY HUSBAND FREQUENTLY SUFFERS from buyer's remorse. He'll study all the information he can find about brands and ratings, but once he purchases the appliance or tool, he begins to second-guess. I tease him about the tendency, but in many ways I struggle with a worse type of second-guessing.

I've taken career paths, made relationship choices, or even made small daily decisions believing Jesus was guiding me. Yet the path doesn't always seem very straight. I agreed to go on a lengthy trip even though I was sick. I didn't want to miss out on the fun. However, the exertion caused a major health setback. "Lord, was I wrong to think You'd called me to go on that trip?" I sent a letter to someone who was angry with me, but the response only caused turmoil. "Was I barreling ahead of where You wanted me, Lord?"

Part of my challenge is that my own understanding is so limited. Human measures of a successful outcome are fickle. My emotional responses to situations can change in an instant. The advice of friends often contradicts.

I think it's great to keep questioning the path we're on. The important issue is where we bring our questions. Our own understanding, apart from Jesus, will only sow more confusion. Instead, we can heed Jesus's call to trust Him. We can ask Him to reassure us that we're where He wants us, or show us if we've veered off course. Even when we get it wrong, He loves, forgives, and guides—and that's something we don't ever have to second-guess. —SHARON HINCK

FAITH STEP: *Have you had questions or been confused about a choice? Take your questions to Jesus today.*

SATURDAY, DECEMBER 31

"These are the words of the Amen. . . ." Revelation 3:14 (NIV)

NOTHING IS MORE SATISFYING than the ending of a good novel, especially when it turns out like we'd hoped. The protagonist (hero or heroine) reaches his or her goals; the couple falls in love; or the underdog team wins the championship.

And even in nonfiction, especially autobiographies, we like to know that the character overcame great obstacles or made a lasting difference. We all enjoy a good story, and we all need hope and encouragement.

We often analyze the past year like the plot of a story. Was it satisfying? Did we reach our goals? Did we overcome obstacles? Did our lives make a difference? Sometimes the answers are not positive. Our memory shelves may hold more disappointment than encouragement. Regardless of our conclusions, when we look back over the last year, we can find encouragement and hope in God's Word.

I especially enjoy studying the names of Jesus. Three of those names are particularly meaningful as I think about the ending of one year and the beginning of another. He is *"the Alpha and the Omega, the Beginning and the End"* (Revelation 21:6, NIV). He is the One Who started it all, and He is the One Who will bring it to a conclusion. He is what life is all about.

As we close this year's chapter and look to Him as the Beginning and the End, the One Who brings good out of anything, the only One Who can take our ordinary lives and help us make an extraordinary difference in spite of our weaknesses, we can only respond one way: Amen.
—REBECCA BARLOW JORDAN

FAITH STEP: *Take time to evaluate your own past year. Then give Jesus a shout-out for His faithfulness to you all year long.*

ABOUT THE AUTHORS

SUSANNA FOTH AUGHTMON is the mother of thirteen-year-old Jack, eleven-year-old Will, eight-year-old Addison, and is the wife of Scott, the lead pastor of Pathway Church in Redwood City, California. She loves connecting with fellow Christ followers through her books and speaking engagements, using humor and a focus on how God's grace intersects in our daily lives. Susanna has written *All I Need Is Jesus and a Good Pair of Jeans, My Bangs Look Good and Other Lies I Tell Myself,* and *I Blame Eve.* She has coauthored four other books in addition to writing for Guideposts' *Mornings with Jesus* devotional. She blogs regularly about her life at tiredsupergirl.blogspot.com.

GWEN FORD FAULKENBERRY spends her mornings with Jesus, coffee, and her family of six in the Ozark Mountains of Arkansas. During the day she teaches writing and literature at her local university. Evenings are reserved for cooking, eating dinner, watching ballgames, studying, and playing. She does her best thinking when she is "wogging" (walking + jogging) and her best writing in the wee hours of the morning. Gwen is the author of five novels and three devotional books. She enjoys hearing from readers, so drop her an e-mail at gfaulkenberry@hotmail.com or connect with her on Facebook at Gwendolann Adell Ford Faulkenberry.

GRACE FOX lives in Abbotsford, British Columbia, where she and her husband codirect International Messengers Canada, a mission organization that has taken her to Nepal, China, Thailand, Romania, and Egypt. Her favorite things are using her writing and speaking skills to help people connect the dots between faith and real life, spending time with her family (especially babysitting her six grandkids), motorbiking with her husband, and prayer walking. Grace has written more than a thousand magazine articles and eight books, including *Morning Moments with God*, and is a regular columnist for Just 18 Summers. She'd love to have you visit her at gracefox.com and fb.com/gracefox.author.

TRICIA GOYER is a homeschooling mom of ten, grandmother of two, and wife to John. A best-selling author, she has published fifty books and more than five hundred articles! She is a two-time Carol Award winner as well as a Christy and ECPA Award nominee. Tricia blogs at TheBetterMom.com, FortheFamily.com, and NotQuiteAmishLiving.com, and mentors teen moms. She is the founder of Hope Pregnancy Ministries in northwestern Montana and currently leads a Teen MOPS (Mothers of Preschoolers) group in Little Rock, Arkansas.

SHARON HINCK writes "stories for the hero in all of us"—about ordinary people experiencing God's grace in unexpected ways. Her award-winning novels include inspirational women's fiction and fantasy. This is her fifth year writing for *Mornings with Jesus*, and she loves spending mornings—and all day—with Jesus. This year Sharon has also been hard at work on a new novel, *The Deliverer*, and she's excited to share another story about both the challenges and joys of following God's call. Sharon and her husband enjoy spending time with their grown children and their energetic granddaughter, and she loves interacting with readers at her Web site: sharonhinck.com.

REBECCA BARLOW JORDAN is a best-selling, inspirational author who has penned eleven books—including the *Day-votions®* three-book series for women—and more than two thousand greeting cards, articles, and devotions. She is a day-voted follower of Jesus who is passionate about home, family, and helping others see God bigger. She and her minister-husband have two children and four grandchildren and live in East Texas, where she also loves gardening and reading great fiction. Learn more about Rebecca and read her encouraging, weekly blogs at rebeccabarlowjordan.com.

ERIN KEELEY MARSHALL has enjoyed contributing to *Mornings with Jesus* since its beginning in 2012. She is the author of *Navigating Route 20-Something* and *The Daily God Book,* and is a collaborating writer for *365 Pocket Prayers for Mothers; Hope of Heaven: God's Eight Messages of Assurance to a Grieving Father;* as well as for *Becoming 2* and *Becoming 2008* New Testaments, the *Revolve 2007* New Testament, and the *Revolve Devotional Bible.* Erin lives in Arkansas with her husband, Steve, and their kids, Paxton and Calianne. She calls erinkeeleymarshall.com her home on the Web, and she can also be found on Facebook and Twitter (@EKMarshall).

DIANNE NEAL MATTHEWS is a freelance writer and the author of four daily devotional books, including *The One Year Women of the Bible* and *Designed for Devotion: A 365-Day Journey from Genesis to Revelation.* She and her husband, Richard, have been married for forty-one years and currently live in southeast Texas, too far away from their three children and three adorable grandchildren. To learn more, visit DianneNealMatthews.com or connect with her through Facebook or Twitter @DianneNMatthews.

Award-winning author and speaker CYNTHIA RUCHTI tells stories hemmed with hope. Her novels, novellas, and non-fiction have been recognized by honors such as Christian Retailing's BEST awards, the Selah awards, the Golden Scroll awards, and others. Among her recent releases are the novel *As Waters Gone By* and the nonfiction *Tattered and Mended: The Art of Healing the Wounded Soul.* She and her husband live in the heart of Wisconsin, not far from their three children and five grandchildren. Follow Cynthia at cynthiaruchti.com.

SUZANNE DAVENPORT TIETJEN is the author of *The Sheep of His Hand* and *40 Days to Your Best Life for Nurses* and a contributor to *Mornings with Jesus 2015*. A few years back, she and her husband, Mike, moved to a cabin deep in the forest where they enjoy breathtaking beauty and an outdoor way of living. A former shepherd, she has also cared for tiny and sick newborns in four states for over twenty-five years. You can find out more at suzannetietjen.com or follow her on Twitter @suzishepherd.

SCRIPTURE REFERENCE INDEX

TOPICAL INDEX

A NOTE FROM THE EDITORS

WE HOPE YOU ENJOY *Mornings with Jesus 2016*, created by the Books and Inspirational Media Division of Guideposts, a nonprofit organization that touches millions of lives every day through products and services that inspire, encourage, help you grow in your faith, and celebrate God's love in every aspect of your daily life.

Thank you for making a difference with your purchase of this book, which helps fund our many outreach programs to military personnel, prisons, hospitals, nursing homes, and educational institutions. To learn more, visit GuidepostsFoundation.org.

We also maintain many useful and uplifting online resources. Visit Guideposts.org to read true stories of hope and inspiration, access Our-Prayer network, sign up for free newsletters, download free e-books, join our Facebook community, and follow our stimulating blogs. To delve more deeply into *Mornings with Jesus*, visit Guideposts.org/MorningswithJesus.

You may purchase the 2017 edition of *Mornings with Jesus* anytime after July 2016. To order, visit ShopGuideposts.org, call (800) 932-2145, or write to Guideposts, PO Box 5815, Harlan, Iowa 51593.

Discover resources that help connect faith-filled values to your daily life

Digging Deeper

Enrich your devotional time with additional Scripture readings referenced at the close of each day's devotion.

 DailyGuideposts.org

Free Newsletters

Sign up for newsletters on positive living, faith in daily life, helping others, the power of prayer, and more!

 Guideposts.org/Newsletters

Free eBooks

Visit us to download more inspirational reading on subjects like prayer, personal growth, and positive thinking.

 Guideposts.org/SpiritLifters

Follow Us on Social Media

See what's happening with your favorite authors and more!

 DailyGuideposts

 DailyGuideposts

DAILY GUIDEPOSTS

Celebrating 40 years of spirit-lifting devotions